George Rawlinson

The Five Great Monarchies of the Ancient Eastern World

George Rawlinson

The Five Great Monarchies of the Ancient Eastern World

ISBN/EAN: 9783741173233

Manufactured in Europe, USA, Canada, Australia, Japa

Cover: Foto ©ninafisch / pixelio.de

Manufactured and distributed by brebook publishing software
(www.brebook.com)

George Rawlinson

The Five Great Monarchies of the Ancient Eastern World

THE

FIVE GREAT MONARCHIES

OF THE

ANCIENT EASTERN WORLD;

OR,

THE HISTORY, GEOGRAPHY, AND ANTIQUITIES OF CHALDÆA,
ASSYRIA, BABYLON, MEDIA, AND PERSIA,

COLLECTED AND ILLUSTRATED FROM ANCIENT AND MODERN SOURCES.

By GEORGE RAWLINSON, M.A.,

CAMDEN PROFESSOR OF ANCIENT HISTORY IN THE UNIVERSITY OF OXFORD;
LATE FELLOW AND TUTOR OF EXETER COLLEGE.

IN THREE VOLUMES.—Vol. I.

LONDON:
JOHN MURRAY, ALBEMARLE STREET.
1862.

The right of Translation is reserved.

TO MY BROTHER,

HENRY CRESWICKE RAWLINSON, K.C.B., D.C.L.,

&c.   &c.   &c.,

TO WHOSE GENIUS, LABOURS, AND CONSTANT KINDNESS

I FEEL MYSELF INDEBTED

MORE THAN I CAN EXPRESS,

THIS WORK

IS DEDICATED,

AS A SMALL TOKEN

OF GRATEFUL AND AFFECTIONATE REMEMBRANCE.

PREFACE

THE history of Antiquity requires from time to time to be re-written. Historical knowledge continually extends, in part from the advance of critical science, which teaches us little by little the true value of ancient authors, but also, and more especially, from the new discoveries which the enterprise of travellers and the patient toil of students are continually bringing to light, whereby the stock of our information as to the condition of the ancient world receives constant augmentation. The extremest scepticism cannot deny that recent researches in Mesopotamia and the adjacent countries have recovered a series of "monuments" belonging to very early times, capable of throwing considerable light on the Antiquities of the nations which produced them. The author of these volumes believes, that, together with these remains, the languages of the ancient nations have been to a large extent recovered, and that a vast mass of written historical matter of a very high value is thereby added to the materials at the Historian's disposal. This is, clearly, not the place where so difficult and complicated a subject

can be properly argued. The author is himself
content with the judgment of "experts," and believes
it would be as difficult to impose a fabricated language on Professor Lassen of Bonn and Professor
Max Müller of Oxford, as to palm off a fictitious for
a real animal form on Professor Owen of London.
The best linguists in Europe have accepted the
decipherment of the cuneiform inscriptions as a
thing actually accomplished. Until some good
linguist, having carefully examined into the matter,
declares himself of a contrary opinion, the author
cannot think that any serious doubt rests on the
subject.*

The present volumes aim at accomplishing for the
Five Nations of which they treat what Movers and
Kenrick have accomplished for Phœnicia, or (still
more exactly) what Wilkinson has accomplished for
Ancient Egypt. Assuming the interpretation of
the historical inscriptions as, in general, sufficiently
ascertained, and the various ancient remains as assigned on sufficient grounds to certain peoples and
epochs, they seek to unite with our previous knowledge of the five nations, whether derived from
Biblical or classical sources, the new information
obtained from modern discovery. They address

---

* Some writers allow that the Persian cuneiform inscriptions have been
successfully deciphered and interpreted, but appear to doubt the interpretation of the Assyrian records. (See *Edinburgh Review* for July, 1862,
Art. III., p. 109.) Are they aware that the Persian inscriptions are accompanied in almost every instance by an Assyrian transcript, and that
Assyrian interpretation thus follows upon Persian, without involving any
additional "guess-work"?

themselves in a great measure to the eye; and it is hoped that even those who doubt the certainty of the linguistic discoveries in which the author believes, will admit the advantage of illustrating the life of the ancient peoples by representations of their productions. Unfortunately, the materials of this kind which recent explorations have brought to light are very unequally spread among the several nations of which it is proposed to treat, and, even where they are most copious, fall short of the abundance of Egypt. Still, in every case there is some illustration possible; and in one—Assyria—both the "Arts" and the "Manners" of the people admit of being illustrated very largely from the remains still extant.*

The Author is bound to express his obligations to the following writers, from whose published works he has drawn freely:—MM. Botta and Flandin, Mr. Layard, Mr. James Fergusson, Mr. Loftus, Mr. Cullimore, and Mr. Birch. He is glad to take this occasion of acknowledging himself also greatly beholden to the constant help of his brother, Sir Henry Rawlinson, and to the liberality of Mr. Vaux of the British Museum. The latter gentleman kindly placed at his disposal, for the purposes of the present work, the entire series of unpublished drawings made by the artists who accompanied Mr. Loftus in the last Mesopotamian Expedition, besides securing him undisturbed access to the Museum sculptures, thus enabling him to

---

* See the last chapter of the present, and the first chapter of the forthcoming volume.

enrich the present volume with a large number of
most interesting Illustrations never previously given
to the public. In the subjoined list these illustrations are carefully distinguished from such as, in one
shape or another, have appeared previously.

Oxford, September, 1862.

CONTENTS OF VOL. I.

THE FIRST MONARCHY.

CHALDÆA.

CHAPTER I.

General View of the Country 1

CHAPTER II.

Climate and Productions.. 35

CHAPTER III.

The People 53

CHAPTER IV.

Language and Writing 77

CHAPTER V.

Arts and Sciences 89

CHAPTER VI.

Manners and Customs 133

CHAPTER VII.

Religion 138

CHAPTER VIII.

History and Chronology 189

THE SECOND MONARCHY.

ASSYRIA.

CHAPTER I.

Page

DESCRIPTION OF THE COUNTRY 225

CHAPTER II.

CLIMATE AND PRODUCTIONS 264

CHAPTER III.

THE PEOPLE 295

CHAPTER IV.

THE CAPITAL 310

CHAPTER V.

LANGUAGE AND WRITING 328

CHAPTER VI.

ARCHITECTURE AND OTHER ARTS 347

LIST OF ILLUSTRATIONS.

		Page
Map of Mesopotamia and the adjacent regions	To face title-page.	
1. Plan of Mugheir Ruins (after *Taylor*)		21
2. Ruins of Warka (after *Loftus*)		23
3. Akkerkuf (after *Ker Porter*)		25
4. Hammam (after *Loftus*)		29
5. Tel-Ede (after *Loftus*)		30
6. Palms (after *Oppert*)		43
7. Chaldean Reeds, from a slab of Sennacherib (*Layard*)		47
8. Wild-sow and pigs, from Koyunjik (*Layard*)		50
9. Ethiopians (after *Prichard*)		66
10. Cuneiform Inscriptions (drawn by the *Author* from bricks in the British Museum)		80
11. Chaldean Tablet (*Layard*)		86
12. Signet Cylinder (after *Ker Porter*)		87
13. Bowariyeh (after *Loftus*)		94
14. Mugheir Temple (ditto)		96
15. Ground Plan of Do. (ditto)		98
16. Early Chaldean Temple (by the *Author*)		99
17. Fragment of Agate (after *Taylor*)		103
18. Terra cotta cone (after *Loftus*)		104
19. Plan and wall of building patterned with cones (after *Loftus*)		105
20. Ground Plan of Houses (after *Taylor*)		106
21. Brick vault at Mugheir (ditto)		109
22. Clay Coffin and Skeleton (ditto)		111
23. Chaldean jar-coffin (ditto)		112
24. Section of drain (ditto)		113
25. Chaldean vases of the first period (drawn by the *Author* from vases in the British Museum)		114
26. Chaldean vases, drinking-vessels, and amphora of the second period (ditto)		115
27. Chaldean lamps of the second period (ditto)		116
28. Seal-cylinder on portal axis (drawn and partly restored by the *Author*)		117
29. Signet-cylinder of King Urukh (after *Ker Porter*)		118
30. Flint Knives (drawn by the *Author* from the originals in the British Museum)		119
31. Stone hammer, hatchet, adze, and nail (chiefly after *Taylor*)		120
32. Chaldean spear and arrow heads (drawn by the *Author* from the originals in the British Museum)		121
33. Bronze Implements (ditto)		122
34. Flint Implements (after *Taylor*)		122
35. Earrings (drawn by the *Author* from the originals in the British Museum)		123

Page

36. Leaden pipe and jar (*drawn by the Author* from the originals in the British Museum) 124

37. Bronze langles (ditto) 124

38. Smkareh Table of Squares 129

39, 40. Costumes of Chaldæans from the cylinders (after *Cullimore* and *Rich*) 132

41. Serpent symbol (after *Cullimore*) 154

42. Symbols of the Moon-God (ditto) 157

43. Symbols of the Sun-God (ditto) 161

44. Symbols of the Sun-goddess (ditto) 163

45. Flaming Sword (ditto) 164

46. Figure of Nin, the Fish-God (*Layard*) 167

47. Nin's emblem, the Man-Bull (ditto) 168

48. Fish symbols (after *Cullimore*) 168

49. Bel-Merodach (ditto) 171

50. Nergal's emblem, the Man-Lion (*Layard*) 173

51, 52. Figures of Ishtar (after *Cullimore* and *Layard*) 176

53. Nebo (*drawn by the Author* from a statue in the British Museum) .. 179

54. Signet of a Chaldæan king (*drawn by the Author* from an impression in the possession of Sir H. Rawlinson) 211

55. The Khabour, from near Arban, looking north (after *Layard*) 213

56. Koukab (ditto) 237

57. Lake of Khatouniyeh (ditto) 239

58. Colossal lion, near Seruj (after *Chesney*) 248

59. Plan of the Ruins at Nimrud (reduced by the *Author* from Captain Jones's survey) 251

60. View of the same (*Layard*) 253

61. Hand-swipe (ditto) 271

62. Assyrian Lion, from Nimrud (ditto) 278

63. Ibex, or Wild-Goat, from Nimrud (ditto) 279

64. Wild Ass (after *Ker Porter*) 280

65. Leopard, from Nimrud (after *Layard*) 281

66. Wild Ass, from Koyunjik (from an unpublished drawing by *Mr. Boutcher* in the British Museum) 281

67. Gazelle, from Nimrud (after *Layard*) 282

68. Stag and Hind, from Koyunjik (from an unpublished drawing by *Mr. Boutcher* in the British Museum) 282

69. Fallow Deer, from Koyunjik (after *Layard*) 283

70. Hare and Eagles, from Nimrud (ditto) 283

71. Hare, from Khorsabad (after *Botta*) 284

72. Chase of Wild Ox, from Nimrud (after *Layard*) 284

73. Vulture, from Nimrud (ditto) 285

74. Vulture feeding on Corpse (ditto) 285

75. Ostrich, from a cylinder (after *Cullimore*) 286

76. Ostrich, from a bronze bowl (after *Layard*) 286

77. Partridges, from Khorsabad (after *Botta*) 287

78. Unknown Birds (ditto) 287

79. Assyrian garden and fish-pond (*Layard*) 288

80. Bactrian, or two-humped Camel, from Nimrud (ditto) 290

81. Mesopotamian Sheep (ditto) 290

82. Loading a Camel (ditto) 290

83. Head of an Assyrian Horse (ditto) 291

Page

84. Assyrian Horse, from Nimrud (after *Layard*) 291
85. Mule ridden by two women (ditto) 292
86. Loaded Mule (ditto) 292
87. Cart drawn by Mules (ditto) 292
88. Dog modelled in clay, from the palace of Asshur-bani-pal, Koyunjik (drawn
by the Author from the original in the British Museum) 293
89. Dog in relief, on a clay tablet (after *Layard*) 293
90. Assyrian Duck (ditto) 294
91. Assyrians (ditto) 297
92. Mesopotamian Captives, from an Egyptian monument (*Wilkinson*) .. 298
93. Limbs of Assyrians (after *Layard*) 299
94. Capture of a City (ditto) 303
95. Captives of Sargon (after *Botta*) 304
96. Captive women in a cart (*Layard*) 304
97. Ruins of Nineveh (reduced by the Author from Captain Jones's survey) .. 316
98. Khorsabad and Mound of Nebbi-Yunus (after *Layard*) 318
99. Gate in the North Wall, Nineveh (ditto) 322
100. Outer defences of Nineveh, in their present condition (ditto) 326
101. Assyrian Cylinder (after *Birch*) 330
102. Assyrian Seals (*Layard*) 331
103. Assyrian Clay Tablet (ditto) 332
104. Black obelisk from Nimrud (ditto) 343
105. Terrace-wall at Khorsabad (after *Botta*) 349
106. Pavement-slab, from the Northern Palace, Koyunjik (*Fergusson*) .. 350
107. Mound of Khorsabad (ditto) 351
108. Plan of the Palace of Sargon, Khorsabad (ditto) 352
109. Hall of Esar-haddon's Palace, Nimrud (ditto) 354
110. Plan of the Mound and Palace of Sargon, Khorsabad (ditto) 356
111. Remains of Propylaeum, or water gateway, Khorsabad (*Layard*) .. 361
112. King and attendants, Khorsabad (after *Botta*) 363
113. Plan of Palace Gateway (ditto) 364
114. North-West Court of Sargon's Palace at Khorsabad, restored (after
Fergusson) 365
115. King punishing prisoners, Khorsabad (after *Botta*) 366
116. Sargon in his war-chariot, Khorsabad (ditto) 368
117. Cornice (*Fergusson*) 371
118. Armenian towers (after *Botta*) 382
119. Armenian buildings, from Koyunjik (*Layard*) 383
120. Interior of an Assyrian Palace, restored (ditto) 384
121. Assyrian castle on Nimrud obelisk (drawn by the Author from the original
in the British Museum) 386
122. Assyrian altar, from a bas-relief, Khorsabad (after *Botta*) 386
123. Assyrian temple (ditto) 387
124. Assyrian temple, from Lord Aberdeen's black stone (after *Fergusson*) .. 387
125. Assyrian temple, Nimrud (drawn by the Author from the original in the
British Museum) 388
126. Assyrian temple, North Palace, Koyunjik (ditto) 388
127. Circular pillar-base, Koyunjik (*Layard*) 389
128. Basement portion of an Assyrian temple, North Palace, Koyunjik (drawn
by the Author from the original in the British Museum) 391

	Page
128. Porch of the Cathedral, Trent (from an original sketch made by the Author)	392
129. Tower of a temple, Koyunjik (Fergusson)	393
131. Tower of ditto, restored (by the Author)	393
132. Ziggurat of Nimrud Temple, restored (after Layard)	395
133. Basement of Temple tower, Nimrud (ditto)	396
134. Plan of Gallery (ditto)	397
135. Ground Plan of Temples (ditto)	399
136. Entrance to smaller temple, Nimrud (ditto)	401
137. Assyrian Village (ditto)	403
138. Village near Aleppo (ditto)	404
139. Assyrian battlemented wall (ditto)	405
140. Masonry and section of platform wall, Khorsabad (after Botta)	406
141. Masonry of town-wall, Khorsabad, (ditto)	407
142. Masonry of tower or moat, Khorsabad (ditto)	408
143. Arched drain, North-West Palace, Nimrud (Layard)	409
144. Arched drain, South-East Palace, Nimrud (ditto)	410
145. False arch (Greek)	411
146. Assyrian patterns (Layard)	413
147. Do. (ditto)	414
148. Bases and Capitals of Pillars (chiefly drawn by the Author from bas-reliefs in the British Museum)	416
149. Ornamental Doorway, North Palace, Koyunjik (from an unpublished drawing by Mr. Boutcher in the British Museum)	417
150. Water-transport of stone for building (after Layard)	421
151. Assyrian statue from Kileh-Sherghat (ditto)	423
152. Statue of Sardanapalus I. from Nimrud (ditto)	424
153. Clay statuettes of the god Nebo (after Botta)	425
154. Clay statuette of the Fish-god (drawn by the Author from the original in the British Museum)	426
155. Clay statuette from Khorsabad (after Botta)	426
156. Lion-hunt, from Nimrud (after Layard)	429
157. Assyrian seizing a wild bull (ditto)	431
158. Hawk-headed figure and sphinx (ditto)	431
159, 160. Death of a wild bull, and King killing a lion (ditto)	432
161. Trees from Nimrud (ditto)	433
162. Trees from Koyunjik (ditto)	434
163. Grooms and Horses (ditto)	436
164. Assyrian men (ditto)	436
165. Assyrian oxen (ditto)	437
166. Assyrian goat and sheep (ditto)	437
167. Vine trained on a fir, from the North Palace, Koyunjik (drawn by the Author from a bas-relief in the British Museum)	439
168. Lilies from the North Palace, Koyunjik (ditto)	440
169. Death of two wild sows, from the North Palace, Koyunjik (from an unpublished drawing by Mr. Boutcher in the British Museum)	441
170. Lion about to spring, from the North Palace, Koyunjik (ditto)	442
171. Wounded wild-ass, seized by hounds, from the North Palace, Koyunjik (ditto)	442
172. Wounded Lion, about to fall, from the North Palace, Koyunjik (ditto)	443

Page

173. Wounded Lion, biting a chariot wheel, from the North Palace, Koyunjik
  (from an unpublished drawing by Mr. Boutcher in the British Museum)   444
174. King shooting a lion on the spring, from the North Palace, Koyunjik (ditto)   445
175. Lion Hunt in a river, from the North Palace, Koyunjik (ditto)   447
176. Bronze lion, from Nimrud (after Layard)   454
177. Fragments of bronze ornaments of the throne, from Nimrud (ditto).. ..   454
178. Bronze casing, from the throne, Nimrud (ditto)..   455
179. Feet of tripods in bronze and iron (ditto)   456
180. Bronze bull's head from the throne (ditto)..   456
181. Bronze head, part of throne, showing bitumen inside (ditto)   456
182. End of a sword-sheath, from the N. W. Palace, Nimrud (ditto)   457
183. Stool or chair, Khorsabad (after Botta)   487
184. Engraved Scarab in centre of cap from the N. W. Palace, Nimrud (Layard)   457
185. Egyptian bead-dresses on bronze dishes from Nimrud (ditto)   458
186. Ear-rings from Nimrud and Khorsabad (ditto)   461
187. Bronze cubes inlaid with gold (ditto)..   462
188. Egyptian scarab (Wilkinson)   462
189. Fragment of ivory panel, from Nimrud (after Layard)   463
190. Fragment of a lion in ivory, Nimrud (ditto)   463
191. Figures and cartouche with hieroglyphics, on an ivory panel, from the N. W.
       Palace, Nimrud (ditto)   464
192. Fragment of a stag in ivory, Nimrud (ditto)   465
193. Royal Attendant, Koyunjik (ditto)   466
194. Arcade work, on enamelled brick, Nimrud (ditto)   467
195. Human figure, on enamelled brick, from Nimrud (ditto)   470
196. Ram's head, on enamelled brick, from Nimrud (ditto)   470
197. King and attendants, on enamelled brick, from Nimrud (ditto)   471
198. Impression of ancient Assyrian Cylinder, in Serpentine (ditto)   474
199. Assyrian seals (ditto)..   475
200. Assyrian cylinder, with the Fish-god (ditto)   475
201. Royal cylinder of Sennacherib (ditto)   475
202. Assyrian vases, amphora, &c. (Birch)   479
203. Funeral Urn, from Khorsabad (after Botta)   479
204. Nestorian and Arab workmen, with jar discovered at Nimrud (Layard) ..   480
205. Lustral ewer, from a bas-relief, Khorsabad (after Botta)   480
206. Wine vase, from a bas-relief, Khorsabad (after Botta)   481
207. Assyrian clay-lamps (after Layard and Birch)..   481
208. Amphora, with twisted arms, Nimrud (Birch)   482
209. Assyrian glass bottles and bowl (Layard)   483
210. Glass vase, bearing the name of Sargon, from Nimrud (ditto)   483
211. Fragments of hollow tubes in glass, from Koyunjik (ditto)   484
212. Ordinary Assyrian tables, from the bas-relief (by the Author)..   485
213, 214. Assyrian tables, from bas-reliefs (ditto)   486
215. Table, ornamented with rams' heads, Koyunjik (after Layard)   486
216. Ornamented table, Khorsabad (ditto)   486
217. Three-legged table, Koyunjik (ditto)..   487
218. Sennacherib on his throne, Koyunjik (ditto)   487
219. Arm-chair or throne, Khorsabad (after Botta)   488
220. Assyrian ornamented seat, Khorsabad (ditto)   488
221. Assyrian couch, from a bas-relief, Koyunjik (by the Author)   489

Page

222. Assyrian footstools, Koyunjik (ditto) 489
223. Stand, for jars (Layard) 490
224. Royal embroidered dresses, Nimrud (ditto) 492
225. Embroidery on a royal dress, Nimrud (ditto) 492
226. Circular breast ornament on a royal robe, Nimrud (ditto) 493
227. Assyrians moving a human-headed bull, partly restored from a bas-relief at Koyunjik (ditto).. 497
228. Labourer employed in drawing a colossal bull (ditto) 498
229. Attachment of rope to sledge, on which the bull was placed for transport (ditto) 498
230. Part of a bas-relief, showing a pulley and a warrior cutting a bucket from the rope (ditto) 499

THE FIRST MONARCHY.

CHALDÆA.

CHAPTER I.

GENERAL VIEW OF THE COUNTRY.

"Behold the land of the Chaldæans." — ISAIAH xxiii. 13.

THE broad belt of desert which traverses the
eastern hemisphere, in a general direction from
west to east (or, speaking more exactly, of W.S.W.
to N.E.E.), reaching from the Atlantic on the one
hand nearly to the Yellow Sea on the other, is
interrupted about its centre by a strip of rich vegetation, which at once breaks the continuity of the
arid region, and serves also to mark the point
where the desert changes its character from that
of a plain at a low level to that of an elevated
plateau or table-land. West of the favoured district,
the Arabian and African wastes are seas of sand,
seldom raised much above, often sinking below, the
level of the ocean; while east of the same, in Persia,
Kerman, Seistan, Chinese Tartary, and Mongolia,
the desert consists of a series of plateaus, having
from 3000 to nearly 10,000 feet of elevation. The
green and fertile region, which is thus interposed
between the "highland" and the "lowland" deserts,[1]
participates, curiously enough, in both characters.

---

[1] Humboldt, *Aspects of Nature*, vol. i. pp. 77, 78, E. T.

Where the belt of sand is intersected by the valley of the Nile, no marked change of elevation occurs; and the continuous low desert is merely interrupted by a few miles of green and cultivable surface, the whole of which is just as smooth and as flat as the waste on either side of it. But it is otherwise at the more eastern interruption. There the verdant and productive country divides itself into two tracts, running parallel to each other, of which the western presents features not unlike those that characterise the Nile valley, but on a far larger scale; while the eastern is a lofty mountain-region, consisting for the most part of five or six parallel ranges, and mounting in many places far above the level of perpetual snow.

It is with the western or plain tract that we are here concerned. Between the outer limits of the Syro-Arabian desert and the foot of the great mountain-range of Kurdistan and Luristan intervenes a territory long famous in the world's history, and the chief site of three out of the five empires of whose history, geography, and antiquities it is proposed to treat in the present volumes. Known to the Jews as Aram-Naharaim, or "Syria of the two rivers;" to the Greeks and Romans as Mesopotamia, or "the between-river country;" to the Arabs as Al-Jezireh, or "the island," this district has always[2] taken its name from the streams, which constitute its most striking feature, and to which,

---

[2] Even the title of Shinar, the earliest known name of the region (Gen. xi. 2), may be no exception; for it is perhaps derived from the Hebrew שְׁנֵי, "two," and ar or nahr (Heb. נָהָר), "a river." The form ar belongs to the early Scythic or Cushite Babylonian, and is found in the Ar-malchar of Pliny (H. N. vi. 26), and the Armacales of Abydenus—terms used to designate the Nahr-malcha (Royal River) of other authors. (See the Fragmenta Historicorum Graecorum, vol. iv. pp. 283, 284.)

in fact, it owes its existence. If it were not for
the two great rivers—the Tigris and Euphrates—
with their tributaries, the more northern part of
the Mesopotamian lowland would in no respect
differ from the Syro-Arabian desert on which it
adjoins, and which in latitude, elevation, and
general geological character, it exactly resembles.
Towards the south, the importance of the rivers is
still greater; for of Lower Mesopotamia it may be
said, with more truth than of Egypt,[1] that it is
"an acquired land," the actual "gift" of the two
streams which wash it on either side; being, as it
is, entirely a recent formation—a deposit which the
streams have made in the shallow waters of a gulf
into which they have flowed for many ages.[4]

The division, which has here forced itself upon
our notice, between the Upper and the Lower Mesopotamian country, is one very necessary to engage
our attention in connexion with the ancient Chaldæa.
There is no reason to think that the term Chaldæa
had at any time the extensive signification of Mesopotamia, much less that it applied to the entire flat
country between the desert and the mountains.
Chaldæa was not the whole, but a part, of the great
Mesopotamian plain; which was ample enough to
contain within it three or four considerable monarchies. According to the combined testimony of geographers and historians,[5] Chaldæa lay towards the
south, for it bordered upon the Persian Gulf; and

---

[1] Herodotus, ii. 5. Sir Gardner
Wilkinson observes that Herodotus
is mistaken in this instance. The
Nile never emptied itself into a
gulf, but from the first laid its deposits on ground already raised above
the level of the Mediterranean. (See

the author's *Herodotus*, vol. ii. p. 6,
note [4].)

[4] Loftus's *Chaldæa and Susiana*,
p. 282.

[5] See Strabo, xvi. 1, § 6; Pliny,
H. N. vi. 28; Ptolemy, v. 20; Beros.
ap. Syncell. pp. 29, 30).

towards the west, for it adjoined Arabia. If we
are called upon to fix more accurately its boundaries,
which, like those of most countries without strong
natural frontiers, suffered many fluctuations, we
are perhaps entitled to say, that the Persian Gulf
on the south, the Tigris on the east, the Arabian
desert on the west, and the limit between Upper
and Lower Mesopotamia on the north, formed the
natural bounds, which were never greatly exceeded
and never much infringed upon. These boundaries
are for the most part tolerably clear, though the
northern only is invariable. Natural causes, hereafter to be mentioned more particularly,[*] are perpetually varying the course of the Tigris, the shore
of the Persian Gulf, and the line of demarcation
between the sands of Arabia and the verdure of
the Euphrates valley. But nature has set a permanent mark, half way down the Mesopotamian
lowland, by a difference of geological structure, which
is very conspicuous. Near Hit on the Euphrates,
and a little below Samarah on the Tigris,[t] the traveller
who descends the streams, bids adieu to a somewhat
waving and slightly elevated plain of secondary
formation, and enters on the dead flat and low level
of the mere alluvium. The line thus formed is
marked and invariable; it constitutes the only
natural division between the upper and lower portions of the valley; and both probability and history

---

[*] See below, pp. 16, 19, &c.

[t] Ross came to the end of the
alluvium and the commencement
of the secondary formations in lat.
34°, long. 44°. (*Journal of Geographical Society*, vol. ix. p. 446.)
Similarly Captain Lynch found the
bed of the Tigris change from pebbles to mere alluvium near Khan
Tholiyeh, a little above its confluence with the Adhem. (Ib. p. 472.)
For the point where the Euphrates
enters on the alluvium, see Fraser's
Assyria and Mesopotamia, p. 27.

point to it as the actual boundary between Chaldæa and her northern neighbour.

The extent of ancient Chaldæa is, even after we have fixed its boundaries, a question of some difficulty. From the edge of the alluvium a little below Hit, to the present coast of the Persian Gulf at the mouth of the Shat-el-Arab, is a distance of above 430 miles; while from the western shore of the Bahr-i-Nedjif to the Tigris at Serut is a direct distance of 185 miles. The present area of the alluvium west of the Tigris and the Shat-el-Arab may be estimated at about 30,000 square miles. But the extent of ancient Chaldæa can scarcely have been so great. It is certain that the alluvium at the head of the Persian Gulf now grows with extraordinary rapidity, and not improbable that the growth may in ancient times have been even more rapid than it is at present. Accurate observations have shown that the present rate of increase amounts to as much as a mile each seventy years,[1] while it is the opinion of those best qualified to judge that the *average* progress during the historic period has been as much as a mile in every thirty years![2] Traces of post-tertiary deposits have been found as far up the country as Tel Ede and Hammam,[3] or more than

----

[1] Loftus, *Chaldæa and Susiana*, p. 282.

[2] Sir H. Rawlinson, in the *Journal of the Geographical Society*, vol. xxvii. p. 186. The increase did not escape the notice of the ancients. It is mentioned and exaggerated by Pliny, who says that Charax of Spasinus was originally built by Alexander the Great at the distance of little more than a mile from the shore, but that in the time of Juba

the Mauritanian it was 50 miles from the sea, and in his own day 120 miles (*Hist. Nat.* vi. 27.) This would give for the first period a rate of increase exceeding a mile in seven years, and for the second a rate of about a mile a year; or for the whole period, a rate of a mile in 3½ years.

[3] Loftus, in *Journal of the Geographical Society*, vol. xxvi. p. 146.

200 miles from the embouchure of the Shat-el-Arab ; and there is ample reason for believing that, at the time when the first Chaldæan monarchy was established, the Persian Gulf reached inland, 120 or 130 miles further than at present. We must deduct therefore from the estimate of extent grounded upon the existing state of things, a tract of land 130 miles long and some 60 or 70 broad, which has been gained from the sea in the course of about forty centuries. This deduction will reduce Chaldæa to a kingdom of somewhat narrow limits ; for it will contain no more than about 23,000 square miles. This, it is true, exceeds the area of all ancient Greece, including Thessaly, Acarnania, and the islands ;[1] it nearly equals that of the Low Countries, to which Chaldæa presents some analogy ; it is almost exactly that of the modern kingdom of Denmark ; but it is less than Scotland, or Ireland, or Portugal, or Bavaria ; it is more than doubled by England, more than quadrupled by Prussia, and more than octupled by Spain, France, and European Turkey. Certainly, therefore, it was not in consequence of its size that Chaldæa became so important a country in the early ages, but rather in consequence of certain advantages of soil, climate, and position, which will be considered in the next chapter.

It has been already noticed that in the ancient Chaldæa, the chief—almost the sole—geographical features, were the rivers.[2] Nothing is more remarkable even now than the *featureless* character of the region, although in the course of ages it has

---

[1] See Clinton's *Fasti Hellenici*, vol. ii. p. 473, where the whole area of European Greece, including Thessaly, Acarnania, Ætolia, Eubœa, and the other littoral islands, is shown to be 22,231 miles.

[2] See above, p. 2.

received from man some interruptions of the original
uniformity.   On all sides a dead level extends
itself, broken only by single solitary mounds, the
remains of ancient temples or cities, by long lines
of slightly elevated embankment marking the course
of canals, ancient or recent, and towards the south
by a few sand-hills.   The only further variety is
that of colour; for while the banks of the streams,
the marsh-grounds, and the country for a short
distance on each side of the canals in actual opera-
tion, present to the eye a pleasing, and in some
cases a luxuriant verdure; the rest, except in early
spring, is parched and arid, having little to distinguish it from the most desolate districts of Arabia.
Anciently, except for this difference, the tract must
have possessed all the wearisome uniformity of the
steppe region; the level horizon must have shown
itself on all sides unbroken by a single irregularity;
all places must have appeared alike, and the traveller can scarcely have perceived his progress, or
have known whither or how to direct his steps.
The rivers alone, with their broad sweeps and bold
reaches, their periodical changes of swell and fall,
their strength, motion, and life-giving power, can
have been objects of thought and interest to the
first inhabitants; and it is still to these that the
modern must turn who wishes to represent, to himself or others, the general aspect and chief geographical divisions of the country.

The Tigris and Euphrates rise from opposite sides
of the same mountain-chain.   This is the ancient
range of Niphates (a prolongation of Taurus), the
loftiest of the many parallel ridges which intervene
between the Euxine and the Mesopotamian plain, and

the only one which transcends in many places the limits of perpetual snow. Hence its ancient appellation, and hence its power to sustain unfailingly the two magnificent streams which flow from it. The line of the Niphates is from east to west, with a very slight deflection to the south of west; and the streams thrown off from its opposite flanks, run at first in valleys parallel to the chain itself, but in opposite directions, the Euphrates flowing westward from its source near Ararat to Malatiyeh, while the Tigris from Diarbekr "goes eastward to Assyria."[3] The rivers thus appear as if never about to meet; but at Malatiyeh the course of the Euphrates is changed. Sweeping suddenly to the south-east, this stream passes within a few miles of the source of the Tigris below Lake Göljik, and forces a way through the mountains towards the south, pursuing a tortuous course, but still seeming as if it intended ultimately to mingle its waters with those of the Mediterranean.[4] It is not till about Balis, in lat. 36°, that this intention appears to be finally relinquished, and the convergence of the two streams begins. The Euphrates at first flows nearly due east, but soon takes a course which is, with few and unimportant deflections, about south-east, as far as Suk-es-Sheioukh, after which it runs a little north of east to Kurnah. The Tigris from Til to Mosul pursues also a south-easterly course, and draws but a very little nearer to the Euphrates. From Mosul, however, to Samarah, its course is only a point east of south; and though, after that, for some miles it

---

[3] Gen. ii. 14, marginal reading.
[4] See the remark of Mela:—"Oc- cidentem petit, ni Taurus obstet,

in nostra maria venturus." (*De Sit. Orb.* iii. 8.)

flows off to the east, yet resuming, a little below the
thirty-fourth parallel, its southerly direction, it is
brought about Baghdad within twenty miles of the
sister stream. From this point there is again a
divergence. The course of the Euphrates, which
from Hit to the mounds of Mohammed (long. 44°)
had been E.S.E., becomes much more southerly,
while that of the Tigris—which, as we have seen,
was for a while due south—becomes once more
only slightly south of east,[2] till near Serut, where
the distance between the rivers has increased from
twenty to a hundred miles. After passing respectively Serut and El Khitr, the two streams con-
verge rapidly. The flow of the Euphrates is at first
E.S.E., and then a little north of east to Kurnah,
while that of the Tigris is S.S.E. to the same point.
The lines of the streams in this last portion of their
course, together with that which may be drawn
across from stream to stream, form nearly an equi-
lateral triangle, the distances being respectively 104,
110, and 115 miles.[3] So rapid is the final convergence of the two great rivers.

The Tigris and Euphrates are both streams of
the first order. The estimated length of the former,
including main windings, is 1146 miles; that of the
latter is 1780 miles.[4] Like most rivers that have
their sources in high mountain regions, they are
strong from the first, and, receiving in their early
course a vast number of important tributaries, become broad and deep streams before they issue upon

---

[2] In one part of its course, viz.
from Kut-el-Amarah at the mouth
of the Shat-el-Hie to Hussun Khan's
fort, 50 miles lower down the stream,
the direction of the Tigris is even
north of east.

[3] From El Khitr to Serut the
direct distance is 104 miles, from
Serut to Kurnah 110, and from
Kurnah to El Khitr 115.

[4] Chesney, *Euphrates Expedition*,
vol. i. pp. 38 and 40.

the plains. The Euphrates is navigable from Sumeïsat (the ancient Samosata), 1200 miles above
its embouchure; and even 180 miles higher up, is
a river "of imposing appearance," 120 yards wide
and very deep.[1] The Tigris is often 250 yards
wide at Diarbekr,[2] which is not a hundred miles
from its source, and is navigable in the flood time
from the bridge of Diarbekr to Mosul,[10] from which
place it is descended at all seasons to Baghdad, and
thence to the sea.[1] Its average width below Mosul
is 200 yards, with a depth which allows the ascent
of light steamers, unless when there is an artificial
obstruction.[1] Above Mosul the width rarely exceeds
150 yards, and the depth is not more in places
than three or four feet. The Euphrates is 250
yards wide at Balbi, and averages 350 yards from
its junction with the Khabour to Hit; its depth
is commonly from fifteen to twenty feet.[1] Small
steamers have descended its entire course from Bir
to the sea. The volume of the Euphrates in places
is, however, somewhat less than that of the Tigris,
which is a swifter and in its latter course a deeper
stream. It has been calculated that the quantity
of water discharged every second by the Tigris at
Baghdad is 164,103 cubic feet, while that discharged
by the Euphrates at Hit is 72,804 feet.[1]

---

[1] Chesney, *Euphrates Expedition*, vol. i. p. 44.

[2] Ibid. p. 15. It only attains this width, however, in the season of the floods. Generally it is at Diarbekr about 100 or 120 yards wide.

[10] Loftus, *Chaldæa and Susiana*, p. 3.

[1] Chesney, *Euphrates Expedi-tion*, vol. i. p. 32; compare Layard, *Nineveh and its Remains*, vol. ii. ch. xiii. p. 92.

[1] The 'Euphrates' steamer, under Lieutenant Lynch, ascended the Ti-gris nearly to Nimrud in 1838; but was stopped by an artificial bund or dam thrown across the stream, near that place. (Chesney, vol. i. p. 32.) The 'Nitocris' in 1846 attempted the ascent, but was unable to pro-ceed far above Tekrit, from a want of sufficient power. (*Nineveh and its Remains*, vol. i. ch. v. p. 139.)

[1] Chesney, vol. i. pp. 53-57.

[1] Ibid. p. 62.

The Tigris and Euphrates are very differently circumstanced with respect to tributaries. So long as it runs among the Armenian mountains, the Euphrates has indeed no lack of affluents; but these, except the Kara Su, or northern Euphrates, are streams of no great volume, being chiefly mountain-torrents which collect the drainage of very limited basins. After it leaves the mountains and enters upon the low country at Sumeïsat, the affluents almost entirely cease; one, the river of Sajur, is received from the right, in about lat. 36° 40'; and two of more importance flow in from the left—the Belik (ancient Bilichus), which joins it in long. 39° 9', and the Khabour (ancient Habor or Chaboras), which effects a junction in long. 40° 30', lat. 35° 7'. The Belik and Khabour collect the waters which flow from the southern flank of the mountain range above Orfa, Mardin, and Nisibin, best known as the "Mons Masius" of Strabo.[1] They are not, however, streams of equal importance. The Belik has a course which is nearly straight, and does not much exceed 120 miles. The Khabour, on the contrary, is sufficiently sinuous, and its course may be reckoned at fully 200 miles. It is navigable by rafts from the junction of its two main branches near the volcanic cone of Koukab,[2] and adds a considerable body of water to the Euphrates. Below its confluence with this stream, or during the last 800 miles of its course, the Euphrates does not receive a single tributary. On the contrary, it soon begins to give off its waters right and left, throwing out branches,

---

[1] Strab. xi. 12, § 4; 14, § 2, &c. | ch. xv. p. 328. Compare ch. xi.
[2] Layard, *Nineveh and Babylon*, | pp. 280, 270.

which either terminate in marshes, or else empty
themselves into the Tigris. After a while indeed it
receives compensation, by means of the Shat-el-Hie
and other branch streams, which bring back to it
from the Tigris, between Mugheir and Kurnah, the
greater portion of the borrowed fluid. The Tigris,
on the contrary, is largely enriched throughout the
whole of its course by the waters of tributary streams.
It is formed originally of three main branches: the
Diarbekr stream, or true Tigris, the Myafarekin
River, and the Bitlis Chai, or Centrites of Xenophon,[1] which carries a greater body than either of
the other two.[2] From its entry on the low country
near Jezireh to the termination of its course at
Kurnah, it is continually receiving from the left a
series of most important additions. The chain of
Zagros, which, running parallel to the two main
streams, shuts in the Mesopotamian plain upon the
east, abounds with springs, which are well supplied
during the whole summer from its snows,[3] and these
when collected form rivers of large size and most
refreshing coolness. The principal are, the eastern
Khabour, which joins the Tigris, in lat. 37° 12′; the
Upper Zab, which falls in by the ruins of Nimrud;
the Lower Zab, which joins some way below Kileh
Sherghat; the Adhem, which unites its waters half
way between Samarah and Baghdad; and the Diyaleh
(ancient Gyndes), which is received between Baghdad
and the ruins of Ctesiphon.

By the influx of these streams the Tigris continues

[1] Xenophon, *Anabasis*, iv. 3, §1.
[2] Layard, *Nineveh and Babylon*, ch. iii. p. 40. The Bitlis Chai at Til, just above the point of conflu-ence, was found by Mr. Layard to be "about equal in size" to the united Myafarekin and Diarbekr rivers.
[3] Loftus, *Chaldæa and Susiana*, p.308; *Journal of Geograph. Society*, vol. ix. p. 95.

to grow in depth and strength as it nears the sea, and becomes at last (as we have seen) a greater river than the Euphrates, which shrinks during the latter part of its course, and is reduced to a volume very inferior to that which it once boasted. The Euphrates at its junction with the Khabour, 700 miles above Kurnah, is 400 yards wide and 18 feet deep; at Irzah or Werli, 75 miles lower down, it is 350 yards wide and of the same depth; at Hadiseh, 140 miles below Werli, it is 300 yards wide, and still of the same depth; at Hit, 50 miles below Hadiseh, its width has increased to 350 yards, but its depth has diminished to 16 feet; at Felujiah, 75 miles from Hit, the depth is 20 feet, but the width has diminished to 250 yards. From this point the contraction is very rapid and striking. The Saklawiyeh canal is given out upon the left, and some way further down, the Hindiyeh branches off upon the right, each carrying, when the Euphrates is full, a large body of water. The consequence is, that at Hillah, 90 miles below Felujiah, the stream is no more than 200 yards wide and 15 feet deep; at Diwaniyeh, 65 miles further down, it is only 160 yards wide; and at Lamlun, 20 miles below Diwaniyeh, it is reduced to 120 yards wide, with a depth of no more than 12 feet! Soon after, however, it begins to recover itself. The water, which left it by the Hindiyeh, returns to it upon the one side, while the Shat-el-Hie and numerous other branch streams from the Tigris flow in upon the other; but still the Euphrates never recovers itself entirely, nor even approaches in its later course to the standard of its earlier greatness. The channel from Kurnah to El Khitr was found by Colonel Chesney to have

an average width of only 200 yards, and a depth of
about 18 or 19 feet,[10] which implies a body of water
far inferior to that carried between the junction
with the Khabour and Hit. More recently, the
decline of the stream in its later course has been
found to be even greater. Neglect of the banks has
allowed the river to spread itself more and more
widely over the land; and it is said that, except in
the flood time, very little of the Euphrates water
reaches the sea.[1] Nor is this an unprecedented or
very unusual state of things. From the circumstance (probably) that it has been formed by the deposits of streams flowing from the east as well as from
the north, the lower Mesopotamian plain slopes not
only to the south, but to the west.[2] The Euphrates,
which has low banks, is hence at all times inclined
to leave its bed, and to flow off to the right,[3] where
large tracts are below its ordinary level. Over
these it spreads itself, forming the well-known
"Chaldæan marshes,"[4] which absorb the chief portion of the water that flows into them, and in which
the "great river" seems at various times to have
wholly, or almost wholly, lost itself.[5] No such mis-
fortune can befall the Tigris, which runs in a deep

[10] *Euphrates Expedition*, vol. i.
pp. 49, 50.

[1] Layard, *Nineveh and Babylon*,
ch. xxi. p. 475; Loftus, *Chaldæa
and Susiana*, p. 45.

[2] Heeren's statement, which is
directly the reverse of this (*Asiatic
Nations*, vol. ii. p. 131, E. T.), is at
once false and self-contradictory.
The "deep bed" and "bold shore"
of the Tigris are the consequence of
the *higher* level of the plain in its
vicinity. The fall of the Tigris is
much greater than that of the Eu-

phrates in its lower course, and the
stream cuts deeper into the alluvium,
on the principle of water finding its
own level.

[3] Loftus, p. 44.

[4] Arrian, *Exped. Alex.* vii. 21,
22; Strab. xvi. 1, § 11, 12. The
"lacus Chaldaici" of Pliny (*Hist.
Nat.* vi. 27) refer rather to the
marshes on the lower Tigris. (See
the next page.)

[5] Arrian, *Exped. Alex.* vii. 7;
Plin. *Hist. Nat.* l. s. c.

bed, and seldom varies its channel, offering a strong contrast to the sister stream.[*]

Frequent allusion has been made, in the course of this description of the Tigris and Euphrates, to the fact of their having each a flood season. Herodotus is scarcely correct when he says, that in Babylonia "the river does not, as in Egypt, overflow the corn-lands of its own accord, but is spread over them by the help of engines."[7] Both the Tigris and the Euphrates rise many feet each spring, and overflow their banks in various places. The rise is caused by the melting of the snows in the mountain regions from which the two rivers and their affluents spring. As the Tigris drains the southern, and the Euphrates the northern side of the same mountain range, the flood of the former stream is earlier and briefer than that of the latter. The Tigris commonly begins to rise early in March, and reaches its greatest height in the first or second week of May, after which it rapidly declines, and returns to its natural level by the middle of June. The Euphrates first swells about the middle of March, and is not in full flood till quite the end of May or the beginning of June; it then continues high for above a month, and does not sink much till the middle of July, after which it gradually falls till September. The country inundated by the Tigris is chiefly that on its lower course, between the 32nd and 31st parallels, the territory of the Beni Lam Arabs. The territory which the Euphrates floods is far more extensive. As high up as its junction with the Khabour, that stream is described as, in the month of April, "spreading over the surrounding country like a sea."[4]   From Hit downwards it inun-

---

[*] Arrian, vii. 21.
[7] Herod. i. 193.

[4] Layard, *Nineveh and Babylon*, p. 297.

dates both its banks, more especially the country
above Baghdad (to which it is carried by the Saklawiyeh canal), the tract west of the Birs Nimrud and
extending thence by way of Nedjif to Samava, and
the territory of the Affej Arabs, between the rivers,
above and below the 32nd parallel. Its flood is, however, very irregular, owing to the nature of its banks,
and the general inclination of the plain, whereof
mention was made above.[*] If care is taken, the inundation may be pretty equally distributed on either side
of the stream; but if the river banks are neglected,
it is sure to flow mainly to the west, rendering the
whole country on that side the river a swamp, and
leaving the territory on the left bank almost without
water. This state of things may be traced historically from the age of Alexander to the present day,
and has probably prevailed more or less since the
time when Chaldæa received its first inhabitants.

The floods of the Tigris and Euphrates combine
with the ordinary action of their streams upon their
banks to produce a constant variation in their courses,
which in a long period of time might amount to
something very considerable. It is impossible to
say, with respect to any portion of the alluvial plain,
that it may not at some former period have been the
bed of one or the other river. Still it would seem
that, on the whole, a law of compensation prevails,
with the result that the general position of the
streams in the valley is not very different now from
what it was 4000 years ago. Certainly between the
present condition of things and that in the time of
Alexander, or even of Herodotus, no great difference
can be pointed out, except in the region immediately

[*] See page 14.

adjoining on the gulf, where the alluvium has grown, and the streams, which were formerly separate, have united their waters. The Euphrates still flows by Hit (Is) and through Babylon;[10] the Tigris passes near Opis,[1] and at Baghdad runs at the foot of an embankment made to confine it by Nebuchadnezzar.[2] The changes traceable are less in the main courses than in the branch streams, which perpetually vary, being sometimes left dry within a few years of the time that they have been navigable channels.[3]

The most important variations of this kind are on the side of Arabia. Here the desert is always ready to encroach; and the limits of Chaldæa itself depend upon the distance from the main river, to which some branch stream conveys the Euphrates water. In the most flourishing times of the country, a wide and deep channel, branching off near Hit, at the very commencement of the alluvium, has skirted the Arabian rock and gravel for a distance of several hundred miles, and has entered the Persian Gulf by a mouth of its own.[4] In this way the extent of Chaldæa has been at times largely increased, a vast tract being rendered cultivable, which is otherwise either swamp or desert.

---

[10] Herod. i. 170, 180.

[1] Ibid. i. 189; Xen. Anab. ii. 4, § 25. The site of Opis is probably marked by the ruins at Khafaji. (See the remarks of Sir H. Rawlinson in the author's Herodotus, vol. i. p. 328, note [3].)

[2] Sir H. Rawlinson, Commentary on the Cuneiform Inscriptions of Assyria and Babylonia, p. 77, note.

[3] Loftus, Chaldæa and Susiana, p. 112. Some rather considerable changes in the bed of the Tigris are thought to be traceable a little below Samarah. (See Journal of Geographical Society, vol. ix. p. 472.)

[4] Sapor Dhulactuf, in the fourth century of our era, either cut or re-opened this canal. He is said to have intended it as a defence against the Arabs. In Arabian geography it is known as Khandak Sabur, or "Sapor's ditch." The present name is Kerrah Saideh.

Such are the chief points of interest connected
with the two great Mesopotamian rivers. These
form, as has been already observed, the only marked
and striking characteristics of the country, which,
except for them, and for one further feature, which
now requires notice, would be absolutely unvaried and
uniform.   On the Arabian side of the Euphrates,
50 miles south of the ruins of Babylon, and 25 or
30 miles from the river, is a fresh-water lake of
very considerable dimensions—the Bahr-i-Nedjif, the
" Assyrium stagnum " of Justin.[1] This is a natural
basin, 40 miles long, and from 10 to 20 miles broad,
enclosed on three sides by sandstone cliffs, varying
from 20 to 200 feet in height, and shut in on the
fourth side—the north-east—by a rocky ridge, which
intervenes between the valley of the Euphrates and
this inland sea.   The cliffs are water-worn, presenting distinct indications of more than one level at
which the water has rested in former times.[2] At
the season of the inundation this lake is liable to be
confounded with the extensive floods and marshes,
which extend continuously from the country west of
the Birs Nimrud to Samava. But at other times the
distinction between the Bahr and the marshes is
very evident, the former remaining when the latter
disappear altogether, and not diminishing very
greatly in size even in the driest season.   The
water of the lake is fresh and sweet, so long as it
communicates with the Euphrates ; when the communication is cut off it becomes very unpalatable,
and those who dwell in the vicinity are no longer
able to drink it.   This result is attributed to the

--

[1] Justin, xviii. 3, § 2.   [2] Loftus, p. 50.

connexion of the lake with rocks of the gypsiferous series.[1]

It is obvious that the only natural divisions of Chaldæa proper are those made by the river-courses. The principal tract must always have been that which intervenes between the two streams. This was anciently a district some 300 miles in length, varying from 20 to 100 miles in breadth, and perhaps averaging 50 miles, which must thus have contained an area of about 15,000 square miles. The tract between the Euphrates and Arabia was at all times smaller than this, and in the most flourishing period of Chaldæa must have fallen short of 10,000 square miles.

We have no evidence that the natural division of Chaldæa here indicated was ever employed in ancient times for political purposes. The division which appears to have been so employed was one into northern and southern Chaldæa, the first extending from Hit to a little below Babylon, the second from Niffer to the shores of the Persian Gulf. In each of these districts we have a sort of tetrarchy, or special pre-eminence of four cities, such as appears to be indicated by the words—"The beginning of his kingdom was Babel, and Erech, and Accad, and Calneh, in the land of Shinar."[2] The southern tetrarchy is composed of the four cities, Ur or Hur, Huruk, Nipur, and Larsa or Larancha, which are probably identified with the Scriptural " Ur of the

[1] Loftus, l. s. c.

[2] Gen. x. 10. The sacred historian further represents the Assyrians as adopting the Babylonian number on their emigration to the more northern regions:—" Out of that land went forth Asshur, and builded Nineveh, and the city Rehoboth, and Calah, and Resen." (Gen. x. 11, 12.)

Chaldees," Erech, Calneh, and Ellasar.' The northern consists of Babel or Babylon, Borsippa, Cuthа,
and Sippara, of which all except Borsippa are
mentioned in Scripture." Besides these cities the
country contained many others, as Chilmad, Duraba,
Ihi or Ahava, Rubesi, Duran, Tel-Humba, &c. It is
not possible at present to locate with accuracy all
these places. We may, however, in the more important instances, fix either certainly, or with a very
high degree of probability, their position.

Hur or Ur, the most important of the early capitals, was situated on the Euphrates, probably at no
great distance from its mouth. It was probably
the chief commercial emporium in the early times ;
as in the bilingual vocabularies its ships are mentioned in connexion with those of Ethiopia.' The
name is found to have attached to the extensive
ruins (now about six miles from the river, on its right
bank, and nearly opposite its junction with the Shat-
el-Hie) which are known by the name of Mugheir, or
" the bitumened."' Here, on a dead flat, broken only
by a few sand-hills, are traces of a considerable town,
consisting chiefly of a series of low mounds, disposed
in an oval shape, the largest diameter of which runs
from north to south, and measures somewhat more
than half a mile. The chief building is a temple,

---

* In three out of these four cases,
the similarity of the name forms a
sufficient ground for the identification. In the fourth case the chief
ground of identification is a statement
in the Talmud that Nophar was the
site of the Calneh of Nimrod.

" Sippara is the Scriptural Sepharvaim. The Hebrew term has a
dual ending, because there were two

Sipparas, one on either side of the
river.

¹ Sir H. Rawlinson, in the Journal
of the Geographical Society, vol.
xxvii. p. 185.

² Mr. Taylor, in the Journal of
the Asiatic Society, vol. xv. p. 260.
Sir H. Rawlinson prefers the derivation of Um-qir, "the mother of
bitumen."

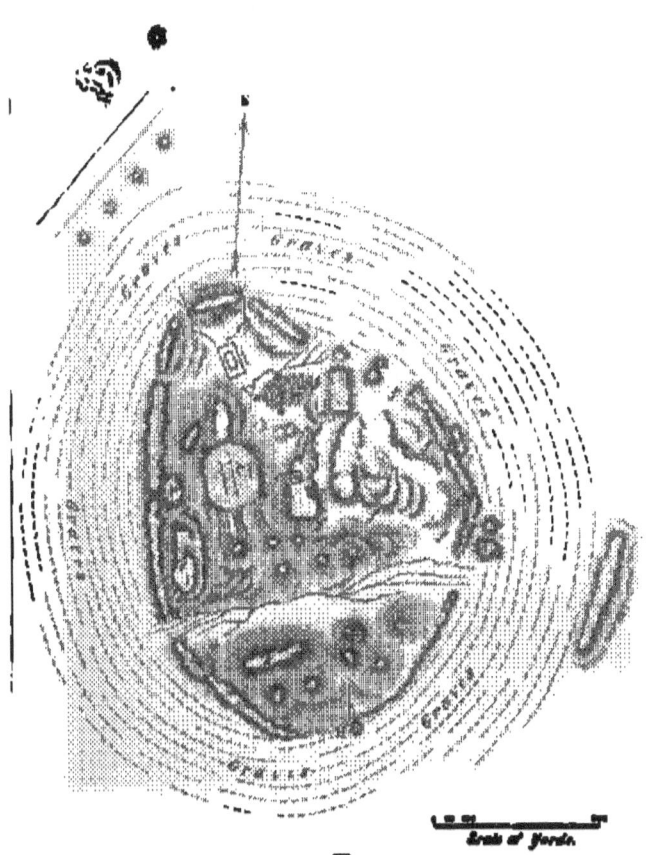

Plan of Mugheir Ruins.

H H H H. 2846 yards round.
a a a. Platform on which the house is built.
z. House cleared.
b. Pavement at edge of platform a, 13 feet below surface.

c. Tomb mound.
d e g h k l m. Points at which excavations were made by Mr. Loftus.
f f f f. Comparatively open space of very low mounds.

hereafter to be more particularly described, which is a very conspicuous object even at a considerable distance, its greatest height above the plain being about seventy feet.[2] It is built in a very rude fashion, of large bricks, cemented with bitumen, whence the name by which the Arabs designate the ruins.

About thirty miles from Hur, in a north-westerly direction, and on the other side of the Euphrates, from which it is distant eight or nine miles, are the ruins of a town, called in the inscriptions Larrak, or Larsa, in which some of the best Orientalists have recognised at once the Biblical Ellasar,[4] the Laranchæ of Berosus,[3] and the Larissa of Apollodorus, where the king held his court who sent Memnon to the siege of Troy.[4] The identification is perhaps doubtful; but, at any rate, we have here the remains of a second Chaldæan capital, dating from the very earliest times. The ruins, which bear now the name of Senkereh or Sinkara, consist of a low circular platform, about four and a half miles in circumference, rising gradually from the level of the plain to a central mound, the highest point of which attains an elevation of seventy feet above the plain itself, and is distinctly visible from a distance of fifteen miles.[7] The material used consists of the ordinary sun-dried and baked bricks; and the basement platforms bear the inscriptions of the same king who appears to have been the original founder of the chief buildings at Ur or Mugheir.

---

[2] Loftus, *Chaldæa and Susiana,* p. 128.
[4] Gen. xiv. 1.
[3] Beros. ap. Syncell., *Chrono-* graphia, p. 39.
[4] Apollod. *Bibliotheca,* ii. 4, § 4.
[7] Loftus, p. 244.

Fifteen miles from Larsa, in a direction a little north of west, and on the same side of the river, are ruins considerably more extensive than those of either Ur or Larsa, to which the natives apply the name of Warka, which is no doubt a corruption of the original

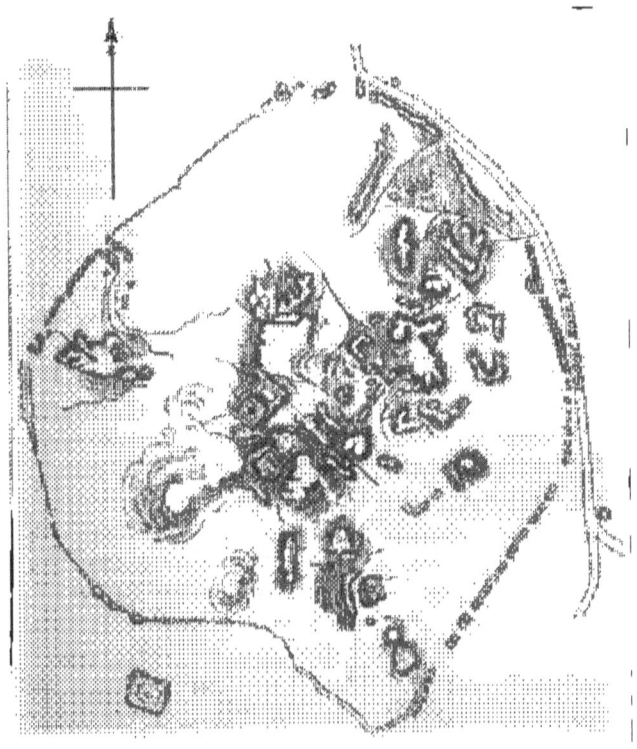

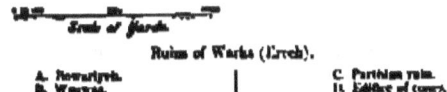

Ruins of Warka (Erech).

A. Bowariyeh.   C. Parthian ruin.
B. Wuswas.   D. Edifice of cones.

appellation. The Erech, or Orech,[7] of the Hebrews,
which appears as Huruk in the cuneiform geographical lists, became known to the Greeks as Orchoë;[8]
and this appellation, probably continuing in use to
the time of the Arab conquest, was then corrupted
into Urka or Warka, in which shape the name given
by Nimrod still attaches to the second of his cities.
The ruins stand in lat. 31° 19', long. 45° 40', about
four miles from the nearest bend of the Euphrates, on
its left or east bank. They form an irregular circle,
nearly six miles in circumference, which is defined
by the traces of an earthen rampart, in some places
forty feet high. A vast mass of undulating mounds,
intersected by innumerable channels and ravines,
extends almost entirely across the circular space, in
a direction, which is nearly north and south, abutting
at either end upon the rampart. East and west of
this mass is a comparatively open space, where the
mounds are scattered and infrequent; while outside
the rampart are not only a number of detached
hillocks marking the site of ancient buildings, but in
one direction—towards the east—the city may be
traced continuously by means of ruined edifices,
mounds, and pottery, fully three miles beyond the
rampart into the desert. The greatest height of the
ruins is about 100 feet; their construction is very
rude and primitive, the date of some buildings being
evidently as early as that of the most ancient structures of either Mugheir or Senkereh.[10]

Sixty miles to the north-west of these ruins, still
on the left or eastern bank of the Euphrates, but at

* The LXX translators express
the Hebrew ר ו א by 'Oρέχ.
* Nimb. xvi. 1, § 6; Ptol. v. 20,
p. 137. See also Pliny, Hist. Nat.
vi. 27.
[10] Loftus, pp. 162-170.

the distance of thirty miles from its present course, are the remains of another city, the only Chaldæan ruins which can dispute, with those already described, the palm of antiquity. They consist of a number of separate and distinct heaps, which seem to be the remains of different buildings, and are divided into two nearly equal groups by a deep ravine or channel 120 feet wide, apparently the dry bed of a river which once ran through the town.[1] Conspicuous among the other hillocks is a conical heap, occupying a central position on the eastern side of the river-bed, and rising to the height of about seventy feet above the general level of the plain.[2] Further on in this direction is a low continuous mound, which seems to be a portion of the outer wall of the city. The ruins are of considerable extent, but scarcely so large as those at either Senkereh or Warka. The name which now attaches to them is Niffer; and it appears, from the inscriptions at the place, that the ancient Semitic appellation was but slightly different.[3] This name, as read on the bilingual tablets, was Nipur; and as there can be little doubt that it is this word which appears in the Talmud as Nopher,[4] we are perhaps entitled, on the authority of that treasure-house of

---

[1] Layard, *Nineveh and Babylon,* ch. xxiv. p. 551. Boats smeared with bitumen, and similar to those still in use in Lower Mesopotamia, are said to be occasionally found, beneath the soil, in this ravine.

[2] Loftus, p. 101.

[3] In the early Scythic or Cushite Babylonian the name of this city is represented by the same characters as are used for the god Belus, though of course with a different determinative; and it thus seems highly probable that we have the vernacular pronunciation of the name in the Βιλλᾶς of Ptolemy, which he joins with Βάρσιτα and Αγγάα, precisely as in the inscriptions are joined Borsip, Nipur, and Cutha or Tiggaba. *Nipur* is given in the bilingual tablets as the Semitic translation of the Scythic *Bilu.*

[4] See above, page 20, note [3].

Hebrew traditions, to identify these ruins with the Calneh of Moses,[1] and the Calno of Isaiah.[2]

About sixty-five miles from Niffer, on the opposite side of the Euphrates, and in a direction only slightly north of west, are the remains of the ancient Borsippa. These consist of little more than the ruins of a single building—the great temple of Merodach—which was entirely rebuilt by Nebuchadnezzar. They have been sometimes regarded as really a portion of the ancient Babylon;[3] but this view is wholly incompatible with the cuneiform records, which distinctly assign to the ruins in question the name of Borsip or Borsippa, a place known with certainty to have been distinct from, though in the neighbourhood of, the capital.[4] A remnant of the ancient name appears to be contained in the modern appellation, Birs-Nimrud or Birs-i-Nimrud, which does not admit of any explanation from the existing language of the country.[5]

Fifteen miles from hence, to the north-east, chiefly but not entirely on the left or east bank of the Euphrates, are the remains of "Babylon the Great," which have been so frequently described by travellers, that little need be said of them in this place. The chief ruins cover a space about three miles long, and from one to two broad, and consist mainly of three great masses: the first a square mound, called "Babil" by the Arabs, lying towards

[1] Gen. x. 10.
[2] Isaiah x. 9.
[3] Rich, Second Memoir on Babylon, p. 32; Heeren, Asiatic Nations, vol. ii. p. 172; Ker Porter, Travels, vol. ii. p. 379. See also Oppert's map, entitled "Babylon. Antiqua,"

in his Expédition Scientifique en Mésopotamie, Paris, Gide, 1858.
[4] Berosus, Fr. 14; Strab. xvi. 1 § 7; Justin. xii. 13; Steph. Byz. ad voc.
[5] Rich, First Memoir, p. 34, note.

the north at some distance from the other remains; the second or central mound, a pile called the "Kasr" or Palace; and the third, a great irregular heap lying towards the south, known as the "mound of Amram," from a tomb which crowns its summit. The "Kasr" and "Amram" mounds are enclosed within two lines of rampart, lying at right angles to each other, and forming, with the river, a sort of triangle, within which all the principal ruins are comprised, except the mound called "Babil." Beyond the rampart, towards the north, south, and east, and also across the river to the west, are various smaller detached ruins, while the whole ground, in every direction, is covered with fragments of brick and with nitre, the sure marks of former habitations.

The other cities of ancient Chaldæa which may be located with an approach to certainty, are Cutha, now Ibrahim, fifteen miles north-east by north of Hymar; Sippara or Sepharvaim, which was at Sura near Mosaib on the Euphrates, about twenty miles above Babylon by the direct route; and Duraba, now Akkerkuf, on the Saklawiyeh canal, six miles from Baghdad, and thirty from Mosaib, in a direction a little west of north. Ihi or Ahava, is probably Hit, ninety miles above Mosaib, on the right bank of the river; Chilmad may be Kalwadha, near Baghdad; and Rubesi is perhaps Zerghul, near the left bank of the Shat-el-Hie, a little above its confluence with the Euphrates. Chaldæan cities appear likewise to have existed at Hymar, ten miles from Babylon towards the east; at Sherifeh and Im Khithr, south and south-east of Hymar; at Zibbliyeh,[18] on the

---

[18] Layard, *Nineveh and Babylon,* p. 509. Mr. Loftus suggests that | the remains here are of a later date. (*Chaldæa and Susiana,* p. 85.) Sir

line of the Nil canal, fifteen miles north-west of
Niffer; at Delayhim and Bismiya, in the Affej
marshes, beyond Niffer, to the south-east; at Phara
and Jidr, in the same region, to the south-west and

Akkerkuf.

south-east of Bismiya; at Hammam,[u] sixteen miles
south-east of Phara, between the Affej and the Shatra
marshes; at Tel-Ede, six miles from Hammam, to
the south-south-west; at Tel-Medineh and Tel-Sifr,
in the Shatra marshes, to the south-east of Tel-Ede
and the north-east of Senkereh; at Yokha, east of

H. Rawlinson regards the existing
buildings at Akkerkuf and Hammam
as also of the Parthian age, though
occupying the sites of earlier Chaldæan cities.

[u] Hammam is thought to be the
Gulaba of the Cuneiform Inscriptions (Loftus, p. 113); but this
identification is uncertain.

Hamman, and Nuffdyji, north of Warka; at Le-
thami, near Niffer; at Iskhuriyeh, north of Zibbliyeh,
near the Tigris; at Tel Kheir and Tel Dhalab, in the
upper part of the alluvium, to the north of Akkerkuf;
at Dunir, on the right bank of the Euphrates, south
of Hilleh and south-east of the Birs Nimrud; at
Jeb Mehari, south of the Bahr-i-Nedjif; at Mal Bat-
tush, near Swaje; at Tel-el-Lahm, nine or ten miles
south of Suk-es-Sheioukh, and at Abu Shahrein, in

Hammam.

the same neighbourhood, on the very border of the
Arabian desert.[1] Further investigation will probably add largely to this catalogue, for many parts
of Babylonia are still to some extent unexplored.

[1] See Fraser's *Mesopotamia and Assyria*, pp. 150-155; Ainsworth's *Researches in Mesopotamia*, p. 127 and
p. 177; Ross and Lynch, in *Journal
of Geographical Society*, vol. ix. pp.
443 et seq.; Loftus *Chaldæa and Susiana*, passim, and *Journal of Geographical Society*, vol. xxvi. pp. 133-144.

This is especially true of the tract between the Shat-el-Hie and the lower Tigris,[2] a district which, according to the geographers, abounds with ruins. No

Tel-Ede.

doubt the most extensive and most striking of the old cities have been visited; for of these Europeans are sure to hear through the reports of natives. But it is more than probable that a number of the most interesting sites remain unexplored, and even un-visited; for these are not always either very exten-sive or very conspicuous. The process of gradual disintegration is continually lowering the height of the Chaldæan ruins; and depressed mounds are com-monly the sign of an ancient and long-deserted city.[3] Such remains give us an insight into the character of the early people, which it is impossible to obtain

[2] This district has been visited by Mr. Taylor, but its marshy charac-ter makes it very difficult to explore at all completely.

[3] Loftus, *Chaldæa and Susiana*, p. 251.

from ruins where various populations have raised their fabrics in succession upon the same spot.

The cities here enumerated may not perhaps, in all cases, have existed in the Chaldæan period. The evidence hitherto obtained connects distinctly with that period only the following—Babylon, Ur or Hur, Larrak or Larsa, Erech or Huruk, Calneh or Nopher, Sippara, Duraba, Chilmad, and the places now called Abu Shahrein and Tel Sifr.[4]   These sites, it will be observed, were scattered over the whole territory from the extreme south almost to the extreme north, and show the extent of the kingdom to have been that above assigned to it.[5]   They are connected together by a similarity in building arrangements and materials, in language, in form and type of writing, and sometimes in actual names of monarchs.   The most ancient, apparently, are those towards the south, at Warka, Senkereh, Mugheir, and Niffer; and here, in the neighbourhood of the sea, which then probably reached inland as far as Suk-es-Sheioukh, there is sufficient reason to place the primitive seat of Chaldæan power.   The capital of the whole region was at first Ur or Hur, but afterwards became Nipur, and finally Babel or Babylon.

The geography of Chaldæa is scarcely complete without a glance at the countries which adjoin upon it. On the west, approaching generally within twenty or thirty miles of the present course of the Euphrates, is the Arabian desert, consisting in this place of tertiary sands and gravels, having a general elevation of a few feet above the Mesopotamian plain, and occasionally rising into ridges of no great

---

[4] Ibid. p. 435.   [5] See page 4.

height, whose direction is parallel to the course of
the great stream. Such are the Hazem and the
Qassaim, in the country between the Bahr-i-Nedjif
and the Persian Gulf, low pebbly ridges which skirt
the valley from the Bahr to below Suk-es-Sheioukh.
Further west the desert becomes more stony, its
surface being strewn with numerous blocks of black
granite, from which it derives its appellation of He-
jerra.[4] No permanent streams water this region;
occasional "wadys" or torrent-courses, only full
after heavy rains, are found; but the scattered inhabitants depend for water chiefly on their wells,
which are deep and numerous, but yield only a
scanty supply of a brackish and unpalatable fluid.
No settled population can at any time have found
subsistence in this region, which produces only a few
dates, and in places a poor and unsucculent herbage.
Sandstorms are frequent, and at times the baleful
simoom sweeps across the entire tract, destroying
with its pestilential breath both men and animals.[5]

Towards the north Chaldæa adjoined upon
Assyria. From the foot of that moderately lofty
range already described,[6] which the Greeks called
Masius, and the modern Turks know as Jebel Tur
and Karajah Dagh, extends, for above 300 miles, a
plain of low elevation, slightly undulating in places,
and crossed about its centre by an important limestone ridge, known as the Sinjar hills, which have a
direction nearly east and west, beginning about
Mosul, and terminating a little below Rakkah. This
tract differs from the Chaldæan lowland, by being at

---

[4] See the *Journal of the Royal Asiatic Society*, vol. xv. p. 404.
[5] See the elder Niebuhr's *Descrip-tion de l'Arabie*, pp. 7, 8.
[6] See p. 11.

once less flat and more elevated. Geologically it is of secondary formation, while Chaldæa proper is tertiary or post-tertiary. It is fairly watered towards the north, but below the Sinjar is only very scantily supplied. In modern times it is for nine months in the year a desert, but anciently it was well inhabited, means having apparently been found to bring the whole into cultivation. As a complete account of this entire region must be given in another part of the present volume, this outline (it is thought) may suffice for our present purpose.

Eastward of Chaldæa, separated from it by the Tigris, which in its lower course is a stream of more body than the Euphrates, was the country known to the Jews as Elam,[*] to the early Greeks as Cissia,[1] and to the later Greeks as Susis or Susiana.[2] This territory comprised a portion of the mountain country which separates Mesopotamia from Persia; but it was chiefly composed of the broad and rich flats intervening between the mountains and the Tigris, along the courses of the Kerkhah, Kuran, and Jerahi rivers. It was a rich and fertile tract, resembling Chaldæa in its general character, with the exception that the vicinity of the mountains lent it freshness, giving it cooler streams, more frequent rains, and pleasanter breezes. Capable of maintaining with ease a dense population, it was likely, in the early times, to be a powerful rival to the Mesopotamian kingdom, over which we shall find that in fact it sometimes exercised supremacy.

On the south Chaldæa had no neighbour. Here a

---

[*] Dan. viii. 2.
[1] Æschylus, Persæ, 123; Hero- dotus, v. 52.
[2] Strabo, xv. 3, § 12.

spacious sea, with few shoals, land-locked, and therefore protected from the violent storms of the Indian
Ocean, invited to commerce, offering a ready communication with India and Ceylon, as well as with
Arabia Felix, Ethiopia, and Egypt. It is perhaps
to this circumstance of her geographical position, as
much as to any other, that ancient Chaldæa owes ·
her superiority over her neighbours, and her right
to be regarded as one of the five great monarchies
of the ancient world. Commanding at once the sea,
which reaches here deep into the land, and the great
rivers by means of which the commodities of the
land were most conveniently brought down to the
sea, she lay in the highway of trade, and could
scarcely fail to profit by her position. There is
sufficient reason to believe that Ur, the first capital,
was a great maritime emporium; and if so, it can
scarcely be doubted that to commerce and trade, at
the least in part, the early development of Chaldæan
greatness was owing.

CHAPTER II.

CLIMATE AND PRODUCTIONS.

" Ager totius Asiæ fertilissimus."—PLIN. *H. N.* vi. 26.

LOWER MESOPOTAMIA, or Chaldæa, which lies in
the same latitude with Central China, the Punjaub,
Palestine, Morocco, Georgia, Texas, and Central
California, has a climate the warmth of which is at
least equal to that of any of those regions. Even in
the more northern part of the country, the district
about Baghdad, the thermometer often rises during
the summer to 120° of Fahrenheit in the shade;[1] and
the inhabitants are forced to retreat to their *serdaubs*
or cellars,[2] where they remain during the day, in an
atmosphere which, by the entire exclusion of the
sun's rays, is reduced to about 100°. Lower down
the valley, at Zobair, Busrah, and Mohammrah, the
summer temperature is still higher;[3] and, owing to
the moisture of the atmosphere, consequent on the
vicinity of the sea, the heat is of that peculiarly
oppressive character which prevails on the sea-coast
of Hindustan, in Ceylon, in the West Indian islands,
at New Orleans, and in other places whose situation

---

[1] Loftus, *Chaldæa and Susiana,*
p. 9.
[2] Chesney, *Euphrates Expedition,*
vol. i. p. 106.

[3] Loftus, p. 280. This traveller
found the temperature at Mohammrah, in June, 1850, to rise often to
124° of Fahrenheit in the shade.

is similar. The vital powers languish under this
oppression, which produces in the European a lassi-
tude of body and a prostration of mind that wholly
unfit him for active duties. On the Asiatic, however, these influences seem to have little effect. The
Cha'b Arabs, who at present inhabit the region, are
a tall and warlike race, strong limbed, and muscular; [1] they appear to enjoy the climate, and are as
active, as healthy, and as long-lived as any tribe of
their nation. But if man by long residence becomes
thoroughly inured to the intense heat of these
regions, it is otherwise with the animal creation.
Camels sicken, and birds are so distressed by the
high temperature that they sit in the date-trees
about Baghdad, with their mouths open, panting for
fresh air. [2]

The evils proceeding from a burning temperature
are augmented in places under the influence of winds,
which, arising suddenly, fill the air with an impal-
pable sand, sometimes circling about a point, sometimes driving with furious force across a wide extent
of country. The heated particles, by their contact
with the atmosphere, increase its fervid glow, and,
penetrating by the nose and mouth, dry up the moisture of the tongue, parch the throat, and irritate or
even choke the lungs. [3] Earth and sky are alike concealed by the dusty storm, through which no object
can be distinguished that is removed many yards; a
lurid gleam surrounds the traveller, and seems to
accompany him as he moves; every landmark is
hid from view; and to the danger of suffocation is
added that of becoming bewildered and losing all

---

[1] Loftus, p. 285.
[2] Ibid. p. 9, note.

[3] Loftus, p. 241; Layard, Nineveh and Babylon, p. 546.

knowledge of the road. Such are the perils encoun-
tered in the present condition of the country. It
may be doubted, however, if in the times with which
we are here concerned the evils just described had
an existence. The sands of Chaldæa, which are still
progressive and advancing, seem to have reached it
from the Arabian Desert, to which they properly
belong : year by year the drifts gain upon the alluvium, and threaten to spread over the whole country.[1]
If we may calculate the earlier by the present rate
of progress, we must conclude that anciently these
shifting sands had at any rate · not crossed the
Euphrates.

If the heat of summer be thus fierce and trying,
the cold of winter must be pronounced to be very
moderate. Frost, indeed, is not unknown in the
country ;[2] but the frosts are only slight. Keen
winds blow from the north, and in the morning the
ground is often whitened by the congelation of the
dew ; the Arabs, impatient of a low temperature,
droop and flag ; but there is at no time any severity
of cold ; ice rarely forms in the marshes ; snow is
unknown ; and the thermometer, even on the grass,
does not often sink below 30°. The Persian kings
passed their winter in Babylon, on account of the
mildness of the climate ; and Indian princes, expelled
from the Peninsula, are wont, from a similar cause, to
fix their residence at Busrah or Baghdad. The cold of
which travellers speak is relative rather than positive.
The range of the thermometer in Lower Chaldæa is
perhaps 100°, whereas in England it is scarcely 80° ;

[1] Ibid. pp. 81, 82.
[2] Layard, *Nineveh and Babylon,*
l. s. c. ; Loftus, *Chaldæa and Susi-*
ana, p. 73 ; Fraser, *Travels,* vol. ii.
pp. 37 and 47.

there is thus a greater difference between the heat
of summer and the cold of winter there than here;
but the actual greatest cold—that which benumbs
the Arabs and makes them fall from their horses*—
is no more than we often experience in April, or
even in May.

The rainy season of Chaldæa is in the winter time.
Heavy showers fall in November, and still more in
December, which sensibly raise the level of the
rivers.¹ As the spring advances the showers become
lighter and less frequent; but still they recur from
time to time, until the summer sets in, about May.
From May to November rain is very rare indeed. The
sky continues for weeks or even months without a
cloud; and the sun's rays are only tempered for a short
time at morning and at evening by a grey mist or
haze. It is during these months that the pheno-
menon of the mirage is most remarkable. The
strata of air, unequally heated, and therefore differing in rarity, refract the rays of light, fantastically
enlarging and distorting the objects seen through
them, which frequently appear raised from the
ground and hanging in mid-air, or else, by a repe-
tition of their image, which is reflected in a lower
stratum, give the impression that they stand up out
of a lake. Hence the delusion which has so often
driven the traveller to desperation—the " image of a
cool rippling watery mirror,"² which flies before
him as he advances, and at once provokes and mocks
his thirst.

* Mr. Loftus tells us that he has
seen this effect of the cold.
¹ Sir H. Rawlinson, in the author's
Herodotus, vol. i. p. 331, note *;
Rich, *First Memoir*, p. 13; Chesney,
Euphrates Expedition, vol. i. pp. 58,
30, and 61, 62.
² Humboldt, *Aspects of Nature*,
vol. i. p. 18. See, for the fact,
Layard, *Nineveh and Babylon*, p.
549; Loftus, p. 113.

The fertility of Chaldæa in ancient times was proverbial. "Of all countries that we know," says Herodotus, "there is none that is so fruitful in grain. It makes no pretension, indeed, of growing the fig, the olive, the vine, or any other tree of the kind; but in grain it is so fruitful as to yield commonly two hundred-fold, and, when the production is at the greatest, even three hundred-fold. The blade of the wheat-plant and of the barley-plant is often four fingers in breadth. As for the millet and the sesame, I shall not say to what height they grow, though within my own knowledge; for I am not ignorant that what I have already written concerning the fruitfulness of Babylonia must seem incredible to those who have not visited the country."[3] Theophrastus, the disciple of Aristotle, remarks—"In Babylon the wheat fields are regularly mown twice, and then fed off with beasts, to keep down the luxuriance of the leaf; otherwise the plant does not run to ear. When this is done, the return, in lands that are badly cultivated, is fifty-fold; while, in those that are well farmed, it is a hundred-fold."[4] Strabo observes—"The country produces barley on a scale not known elsewhere, for the return is said to be three hundred-fold. All other wants are supplied by the palm, which furnishes not only bread, but wine, vinegar, honey, and meal."[5] Pliny follows Theophrastus, with the exception that he makes the return of the wheat-crop, where the land is well farmed, a hundred and fifty-fold.[6] The wealth of the region was strikingly exhibited by the heavy

---

[3] Herodotus, i. 193. [5] Xen. *Anab.* ii. 3, § 14-16.
[4] Theophrast. *Hist. Plant.* viii. 7. [6] Pliny, *Hist. Nat.* xviii. 17.
[5] Strabo, xvi. 1, § 14. Compare

demands which were made upon it by the Persian
kings, as well as by the riches which, notwithstanding
these demands, were accumulated in the hands of
those who administered its government.   The money-
tribute paid by Babylonia and Assyria to the Persians
was a thousand talents of silver (nearly a quarter of
a million of our money) annually ;[1] while the tribute
in kind was reckoned at one-third part of the contributions of the whole empire.[2]   Yet, despite this
drain on its resources, the government was regarded
as the best that the Persian king had to bestow, and
the wealth accumulated by Babylonian satraps was
extraordinary.   Herodotus tells us of a certain Tri-
tantæchmes, a governor, who, to his own knowledge,
derived from his province nearly two bushels of
silver daily!   This fortunate individual had a stud
of sixteen thousand mares, with a proportionate
number of horses.[3]   Another evidence of the fertility of the region may be traced in the fear of
Artaxerxes Mnemon, after the battle of Cunaxa, lest
the Ten Thousand should determine to settle permanently in the vicinity of Sittace upon the Tigris.[4]
Whatever opinion may be held as to the exact position of this place, and of the district intended by
Xenophon, it is certain that it was in the alluvial
plain,[5] and so contained within the limits of the
ancient Chaldæa.

---

[1] Herodotus, lil. 92. If we set
aside the Indian gold tribute, this
was one-ninth of the whole tribute
of the empire.
[2] Ibid. i. 192. This proportion appears excessive.   Perhaps Babylonia
really supplied one-third of the grain
which the court consumed.
[3] Herodotus, l. s. c.

[4] Xen. Anab. ii. 4, § 22.
[5] Ibid. § 13. Compare Ainsworth,
Retreat of the Ten Thousand, pp.
105-114.   He regards the district
intended as that between the Shat-
Eidha and the bend of the Tigris,
in lat. 34°.   I should place it lower
down, below Baghdad, near the ruins
of Ctesiphon.

Modern travellers, speaking of Chaldæa in its present condition, express themselves less enthusiastically than the ancients; but, on the whole, agree with them as to the natural capabilities of the country. "The soil," says one of the most judicious, "is extremely fertile, producing great quantities of rice, dates, and grain of different kinds, though it is not cultivated to above half the degree of which it is susceptible."[3] "The soil is rich," says another, "not less bountiful than that on the banks of the Egyptian Nile."[4] "Although greatly changed by the neglect of man," observes a third, "those portions of Mesopotamia which are still cultivated, as the country about Hillah, show that the region has all the fertility ascribed to it by Herodotus."[5] There is a general recognition of the productive qualities of the district, combined with a general lamentation over the existing neglect and apathy which allows such gifts of nature to run to waste. Cultivation, we are told, is now the exception, instead of the rule. "Instead of the luxuriant fields, the groves and gardens of former times, nothing now meets the eye but an arid waste."[6] Many parts of Chaldæa, naturally as productive as any others, are at present pictures of desolation. Large tracts are covered by unwholesome marshes, producing nothing but enormous reeds; others lie waste and bare, parched up by the fierce heat of the sun, and utterly destitute of water; in some places, as has been already mentioned, sand-drifts accumulate, and threaten to make the whole region a mere portion of the desert.

---

[3] Rich, *First Memoir*, p. 12.
[4] Loftus, *Chaldæa and Susiana*, p. 14.
[5] Chesney, *Euphrates Expedition*, vol. ii. p. 602.
[6] Loftus, l. s. c.

The great cause of this difference between ancient and modern Chaldæa is the neglect of the water-courses. Left to themselves, the rivers tend to desert some portions of the alluvium wholly, which then become utterly unproductive; while they spread themselves out over others, which are converted thereby into pestilential swamps. A well-arranged system of embankments and irrigating canals is necessary in order to develop the natural capabilities of the country, and to derive from the rich soil of this vast alluvium the valuable and varied products which it can be made to furnish.

Among the natural products of the region two stand out as pre-eminently important—the wheat-plant and the date-palm. According to the native tradition,[1] wheat was indigenous in Chaldæa; and the first comers thus found themselves provided by the bountiful hand of Nature with the chief necessary of life. The luxuriance of the plant was excessive. Its leaves were as broad as the palm of a man's hand, and its tendency to grow leaves was so great that (as we have seen[2]) the Babylonians used to mow it twice and then pasture their cattle on it for a while, to keep down the blade and induce the plant to run to ear. The ultimate return was enormous: on the most moderate computation[3] it amounted to fifty-fold at the least, and often to a hundred-fold. The modern Oriental is content, even in the case of a rich soil, with a ten-fold return.[4]

The date-palm was at once one of the most valu-

---

[1] Berosus, Fr. 1.

[2] See p. 39.

[3] That of Theophrastus, the pro-fessed naturalist. See above, p. 30, note [4].

[4] Geograph. Journ. vol. ix. p. 27. Compare Niebuhr, Description de l'Arabie, p. 134.

Palms.

able and one of the most ornamental products of the
country. "Of all vegetable forms," says the greatest of
modern naturalists, "the palm is that to which the
prize of beauty has been assigned by the concurrent
voice of nations in all ages."[1] And though the date-
palm is in form perhaps less graceful and lovely than
some of its sister species, it possesses in the dates themselves a beauty which they lack. These charming
yellow clusters, semi-transparent, which the Greeks
likened to amber,[2] and moderns compare to gold,[3]
contrast, both in shape and tint, with the green

[1] Humboldt, *Aspects of Nature*,
vol. ii. p. 20, E. T.
[2] Xen. *Anab.* ii. 3, § 15; Philo-

strat. *Vit. Apollon. Tyan.* I. 21.
[3] Loftus, *Chaldæa and Susiana*,
p. 25.

feathery branches beneath whose shade they hang,
and give a richness to the landscape they adorn
which adds greatly to its attractions. And the
utility of the palm has been at all times proverbial.
A Persian poem celebrated its three hundred and
sixty uses.[1] The Greeks, with more moderation,
spoke of it as furnishing the Babylonians with bread,
wine, vinegar, honey, groats, string and ropes of all
kinds, firing, and a mash for fattening cattle.[2] The
fruit was excellent, and has formed at all times an
important article of nourishment in the country. It
was eaten both fresh and dried, forming in the latter
case a delicious sweetment.[3] The wine, "sweet but
headachy,"[4] was probably not the spirit which it is
at present customary to distil from the dates, but the
slightly intoxicating drink called *lagby* in North
Africa, which may be drawn from the tree itself by
decapitating it, and suffering the juice to flow.[5] The
vinegar was perhaps the same fluid corrupted, or it
may have been obtained from the dates. The honey
was palm-sugar, likewise procurable from the sap.
How the groats were obtained we do not know; but
it appears that the pith of the palm was eaten
formerly in Babylonia, and was thought to have a
very agreeable flavour.[6] Ropes were made from the
fibres of the bark; and the wood was employed for
building and furniture.[7] It was soft, light, and
easily worked, but tough, strong, and fibrous.[8]

[1] Strabo, xvi. 1, § 14.
[2] Ibid.
[3] Xen. *Anab.* l. s. c. "The peasantry in Babylonia now principally subsist on dates pressed into cakes." Rich, *First Memoir*, p. 59, note.
[4] 'Ἡδὺ μὲν, κεφαλαλγὲς δέ. Xen. *Anab.* l. s. c.
[5] Hamilton's *Wanderings in North Africa*, ch. xiv. pp. 189, 190.
[6] Xen. *Anab.* ii. 3, § 16.
[7] Theophrast. *Hist. Plant.* ii. 7; p. 68.
[8] Ibid. v. 4 and 6.

The cultivation of the date-palm was widely extended in Chaldæa, probably from very early times. The combination of sand, moisture, and a moderately saline soil, in which it delights,[a] was there found in perfection, more especially in the lower country, which had but recently been reclaimed from the sea. Even now, when cultivation is almost wholly laid aside, a thick forest of luxuriant date-trees clothes the banks of the Euphrates on either side, from the vicinity of Mugheir to its embouchure at the head of the Persian Gulf.[b] Anciently the tract was much more generally wooded with them. "Palm-trees grow in numbers over the whole of the flat country," says one of the most observant and truthful of travellers—Herodotus.[c] According to the historians of Julian, a forest of verdure extended from the upper edge of the alluvium, which he crossed, to Mesene and the shores of the sea.[d] When the Arabian conquerors settled themselves in the lower country, they were so charmed with the luxuriant vegetation and the abundant date-groves, that they compared the region with the country about Damascus, and reckoned it among their four earthly paradises.[e] The propagation of the date-palm was chiefly from seed. In Chaldæa, however, it was increased sometimes from suckers or offshoots thrown up from the stem of the old tree;[f] at other times by a species of cutting, the entire head being struck off with about three feet of stem, notched, and then planted in moist ground.[g] Several

[a] Theophrast. *Hist. Plant.* ii. 7; p. 64.

[b] Loftus, *Chaldæa and Susiana*, p. 127 and p. 277; Ainsworth, *Travels in the Track of the Ten Thousand*, p. 105.

[c] Herod. i. 193.

[d] Amm. Marc. xxiv. 3; Zosim. iii. pp. 173-9.

[e] Sir H. Rawlinson, in the *Journal of the Geographical Society*, vol. xxvii. p. 180.

[f] Theophrast. *Hist. Plant.* ii. 2; p. 53.   [g] Ibid. ii. 7; p. 64.

varieties of the tree were cultivated; but one was
esteemed above all the rest, both for the size and
flavour of the fruit. It bore the name of " Royal,"
and grew only in one place near Babylon.[10]

Besides these two precious products, Chaldæa produced excellent barley, millet, sesame, vetches, and
fruits of all kinds.[1] It was, however, deficient in
variety of trees, possessing scarcely any but the palm
and the cypress. Pomegranates, tamarisks, poplars,
and acacias are even now almost the only trees besides the two above mentioned, to be found between
Samarah and the Persian Gulf. The tamarisk grows
chiefly as a shrub along the rivers, but sometimes
attains the dimensions of a tree, as in the case of the
" solitary tree " still growing upon the ruins of Babylon.[2] The pomegranates with their scarlet flowers,
and the acacias with their light and graceful foliage,
ornament the banks of the streams, generally inter-
mingled with the far more frequent palm, while
oranges, apples, pears, and vines are successfully cultivated in the gardens and orchards.

Among the vegetable products of Chaldæa must
be noticed, as almost peculiar to the region, its enormous reeds. These, which are represented with
much spirit in the sculptures of Sennacherib, cover
the marshes in the summer-time, rising often to the
height of fourteen or fifteen feet.[3] The Arabs of the
marsh region form their houses of this material,
binding the stems of the reeds together, and bending

[10] Theophrast. Hist. Plant. ii. 7;
p. 67.

[1] Berosus, Fr. 1, § 2: Herod. i.
193.

[2] Rich, First Memoir, p. 26;
Heeren, Asiatic Nations, vol. ii. p.
158; Ainsworth, Researches in As-

syria, Babylonia, and Chaldæa, p.
125.

[3] Ainsworth, Researches, p. 120;
Layard, Nineveh and Babylon, p.
553. Mr. Loftus says " 12 or 14
feet." (Chaldæa and Susiana, p.
106.)

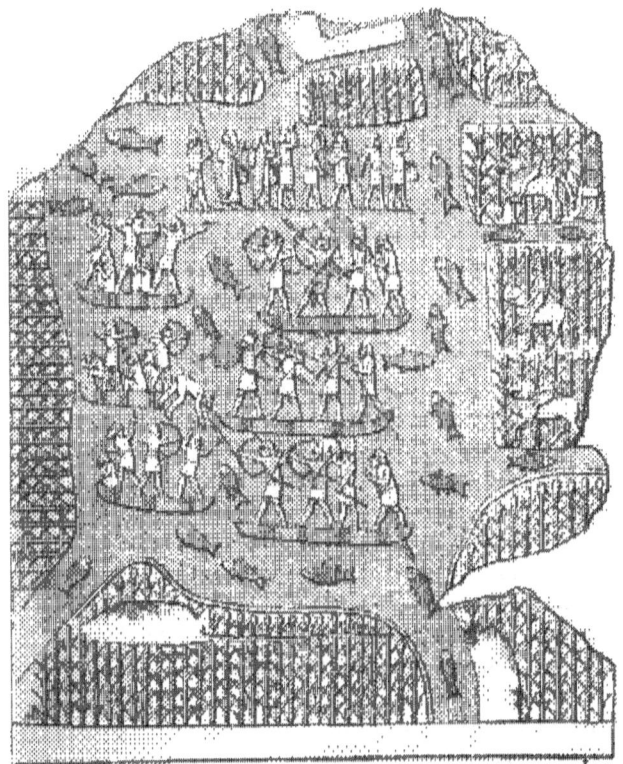

Chaldæan Reeds (from a slab of Sennacherib).

them into arches, to make the skeleton of their
buildings; while, to form the walls, they stretch
across from arch to arch mats made of the leaves.
From the same fragile substance they construct their
terradas or light boats, which, when rendered water-
proof by means of bitumen, will support the weight
of three or four men.[a]

[a] Layard, pp. 522-524.

In mineral products Chaldæa was very deficient indeed. The alluvium is wholly destitute of metals, and even of stone, which must be obtained, if wanted, from the adjacent countries. The neighbouring parts of Arabia could furnish sandstone and the more distant basalt; which appears to have been in fact transported occasionally to the Chaldæan cities.[4] Probably, however, the chief importation of stone was by the rivers, whose waters would readily convey it to almost any part of Chaldæa from the regions above the alluvium. This we know to have been done in some cases;[5] but the evidence of the ruins makes it clear that such importation was very limited. The Chaldæans found, in default of stone, a very tolerable material in their own country; which produced an inexhaustible supply of excellent clay, easily moulded into bricks, and not even requiring to be baked in order to fit it for the builder. Exposure to the heat of the summer sun hardened the clay sufficiently for most purposes, while a few hours in a kiln made it as firm and durable as freestone, or even granite. Chaldæa, again, yielded various substances suitable for mortar. Calcareous earths abound on the western side of the Euphrates towards the Arabian frontier;[6] while everywhere a tenacious slime or mud is easily procurable, which, though imperfect as a cement, can serve the purpose, and has the advantage of being always at hand. Bitumen is also produced largely in some parts, particularly at Hit, where are the inexhaustible springs which have made that spot

---

[4] Layard, *Nineveh and Babylon*, p. 524.

[5] Xenophon states that millstones were supplied to Babylon from a place which he calls Pylæ (Feluiah?), on the middle Euphrates, (*Anab.* i. 5, § 5.)

[6] Rich, *First Memoir*, p. 65.

famous in all ages.' Naphtha and bitumen are here
given forth separately in equal abundance; and these
two substances, boiled together in certain proportions,
form a third kind of cement, superior to the slime or
mud, but inferior to lime-mortar. Petroleum, called
by the Orientals *mumia*, is another product of the
bitumen-pits.'

The wild animals indigenous in Babylonia appear
to be chiefly the following :—The lion, the leopard,
the hyæna, the lynx, the wild-cat, the wolf, the jackal,
the wild-boar, the buffalo, the stag, the gazelle, the
jerboa, the fox, the hare, the badger, and the porcupine. The Mesopotamian lion is a noble animal. Taller
and larger than a Mount St. Bernard dog, he wanders
over the plains, their undisputed lord unless when
an European ventures to question his pre-eminence.
The Arabs tremble at his approach, and willingly
surrender to him the choicest of their flocks and
herds. Unless urged by hunger, he seldom attacks
man, but contents himself with the destruction of
buffaloes, camels, dogs, and sheep. When taken
young he is easily tamed, and then manifests considerable attachment to his master.' In his wild
state he haunts the marshes and the banks of the

---

* Thothmes III. brought bitumen
from Hit to Egypt about B.C. 1400,
(See Sir G. Wilkinson's *Historical
Notice of Egypt* in the author's *Herodotus*, vol. ii. p. 300.) Herodotus
mentions Hit as the great place for
bitumen, about B.C. 450 (Herod. I.
179). Isidore of Charax takes notice
of its bitumen-springs, about B.C.
150 (*Mans. Parth.* p. 5). Shortly
afterwards its name was made to include a notice of the bitumen; and
thus it is called Id-da-kira in the
Talmud, Idi-cara in Ptolemy, and

Dacira by the historians of Julian—
kier or *ghier* (رب) being the Arabic
term for bitumen.

* Rich, *First Memoir*, pp. 63-4.
' Mr. Layard gives an amusing
account of a tame lion which was
given him by Osman Pasha, com-
mandant of Hillah (*Nin. and Bab.*
p. 487). Sir H. Rawlinson had a tame
lion for some years at Baghdad,
which was much attached to him,
and finally died at his feet, not suffering the attendants to remove him.

various streams and canals, concealing himself during
the day, and at night wandering abroad in search of
his prey, to obtain which he will approach with boldness to the very skirts of an Arab encampment. His
roar is not deep or terrible, but like the cry of a child
in pain, or the first wail of the jackal after sunset,
only louder, clearer, and more prolonged.   Two
varieties of the lion appear to exist : the one is maneless, while the other has a long mane, which is black
and shaggy.   The former is now the more common
in the country; but the latter, which is the fiercer of
the two,[2] is the one ordinarily represented upon the
sculptures.   The lioness is nearly as much feared as
the lion ; when her young are attacked, or when she
has lost them, she is perhaps even more terrible.
Her roar is said to be deeper and far more imposing
than that of the male.[3]

The other animals require but few remarks.   Ga-

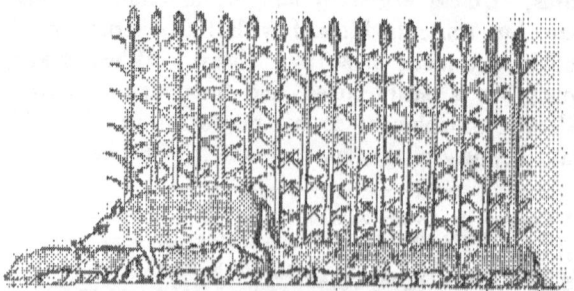

Wild-sow and pigs, from Koyunjik.

---

[2] The inhabitants call the maneless lions " true believers," those
with manes ghaours or " infidels."
The former, they say, will spare a
Mussulman if he prays, the latter
never. (Layard, Nin. and Bab. p.

487, note.)   A similar distinction,
I learn from Sir Gardner Wilkinson,
is made at Cairo between the green
and the black crocodile.
[3] Loftus, Chaldæa and Susiana,
p. 258.

zelles are plentiful in the more sandy regions; buffaloes abound in the marshes of the south, where they are domesticated, and form the chief wealth of the inhabitants;[1] troops of jackals are common, while the hyæna and wolf are comparatively rare; the wildboar frequents the river-banks and marshes, as depicted in the Assyrian sculptures; hares abound in the country about Baghdad; porcupines and badgers are found in most places; leopards, lynxes, wild-cats, and deer, are somewhat uncommon.

Chaldæa possesses a great variety of birds. Falcons, vultures, kites, owls, hawks and crows of various kinds, francolins or black partridges, pelicans, wild-geese, ducks, teal, cranes, herons, kingfishers, and pigeons, are among the most common. The sand-grouse (*Pterocles arenarius*) is occasionally found, as also are the eagle and the bee-eater. Fish are abundant in the rivers and marshes, principally barbel and carp, which latter grow to a great size in the Euphrates. Barbel form an important element in the food of the Arabs inhabiting the Affej marshes, who take them commonly by means of a fish-spear.[2] In the Shat-el-Arab, which is wholly within the influence of the tides, there is a species of goby, which is amphibious. This fish lies in myriads on the mud-banks left uncovered by the ebb of the tide, and moves with great agility on the approach of birds. Nature seems to have made the goby in one of her most freakish moods. It is equally at home in the earth, the air, and the water; and at different times in the day may be observed

---

[1] Layard, *Nineveh and Babylon*, p. 566.   [2] Ibid. p. 567.

swimming in the stream, basking upon the surface
of the tidal banks, and burrowing deep in the mud.[a]

The domestic animals are camels, horses, buffaloes,
cows and oxen, goats, sheep, and dogs. The most
valuable of the last-mentioned are greyhounds, which
are employed to course the gazelle and the hare.
The camels, horses, and buffaloes, are of superior
quality; but the cows and oxen seem to be a very
inferior breed.[b] The goats and the sheep are small,
and yield a scanty supply of a somewhat coarse
wool.[c] Still their flocks and herds constitute the
chief wealth of the people, who have nearly forsaken
the agriculture which anciently gave Chaldæa its
pre-eminence, and have relapsed very generally into
a nomadic or semi-nomadic condition. The inse-
curity of property consequent upon bad government
has in a great measure caused this change, which
renders the bounty of Nature useless, and allows immense capabilities to run to waste. The present
condition of Babylonia gives a most imperfect idea
of its former state, which must be estimated not from
modern statistics, but from the accounts of ancient
writers and the evidences which the country itself
presents. From them we conclude that this region
was among the most productive upon the face of the
earth, spontaneously producing some of the best gifts
of God to man, and capable, under careful manage-
ment, of being made one continuous garden.

---

[a] Ainsworth, *Researches*, pp. 135,
136; Fraser, *Mesopotamia and Assyria*, p. 373.
[c] Chesney, *Euphrates Expedition*,
vol. i. p. 108.
[b] Layard, *Nineveh and Babylon*,
p. 566.

CHAPTER III.

THE PEOPLE.

"A mighty nation, an ancient nation."—JEREM. v. 15.

THAT the great alluvial plain at the mouth of the
Euphrates and Tigris was among the countries first
occupied by man after the Deluge, is affirmed by
Scripture,[1] and generally allowed by writers upon
ancient history.[2] Scripture places the original occupation at a time when language had not yet broken
up into its different forms, and when, consequently,
races, as we now understand the term, can scarcely
have existed. It is not, however, into the character
of these primeval inhabitants that we have here to
inquire, but into the ethnic affinities and characteristics of that race, whatever it was, which first established an important kingdom in the lower part of
the plain—a kingdom which eventually became an
empire. According to the ordinary theory, this
race was Aramaic or Semitic. "The name of Aramæans, Syrians, or Assyrians," says Niebuhr, "comprises the nations extending from the mouth of the
Euphrates and Tigris to the Euxine, the river Halys,

---

[1] Gen. xi. 1-9.
[2] Heeren, *Asiatic Nations*, vol. ii.
p. 130; Sir H. Rawlinson, in the
Journal of the Asiatic Society, vol.

[*] xv. p. 232; Vaux, *Nineveh and Persepolis*, p. 6; Chesney, *Euphrates
Expedition*, vol. ii. p. 18; &c.

and Palestine. They applied to themselves the name
Aram, and the Greeks called them Assyrians, which
is the same as Syrians (?). Within that great extent
of country there existed, of course, various dialectic
differences of language; and there can be little doubt
but that in some places the nation was mixed with
other races."[3] The early inhabitants of Lower Mesopotamia, however, he considers to have been pure
Aramaeans, closely akin to the Assyrians, from whom,
indeed, he regards them as only separate politically.[4]

Similar views are entertained by most modern
writers.[5] Baron Bunsen, in one of his latest works,[6]
regards the fact as completely established by the results of recent researches in Babylonia. Professor M.
Müller, though expressing himself with more caution,
inclines to the same conclusion.[7] Popular works, in the
shape of Cyclopædias and short general histories, dif-
fuse the impression. Hence a difficulty is felt with regard to the Scriptural statement concerning the first
kingdom in these parts, which is expressly said to have
been Cushite or Ethiopian. "And *Cush begat Nimrod:*
(he began to be a mighty one in the earth; he was a
mighty hunter before the Lord; wherefore it is said,
Even as Nimrod, the mighty hunter before the Lord;)
and the beginning of his kingdom was Babel, and
Erech, and Accad, and Calneh, in the land of Shinar."[8] According to this passage the early Chaldæans
should be Hamites, not Semites—Ethiopians, not

---

[3] Niebuhr, *Lectures on Ancient kind,* vol. iv. p. 568; Kitto, *Biblical History,* vol. i. p. 12, E. T. *Cyclopædia,* vol. i. p. 275.

[4] Ibid. p. 11: "We shall begin [6] *Philosophy of Universal History,* with the Assyrians; but with those vol. i. p. 193. of Babylon; not, like Justin, with [7] *Languages of the Seat of War,* those of Nineveh." pp. 24, 25 (first edition).

[5] Heeren, *As. Nat.* vol. ii. p. 145; [8] Gen. x. 8-10. Prichard, *Physical History of Man-*

Aramæans; they should present analogies and points of connexion with the inhabitants of Egypt and Abyssinia, of Southern Arabia and Mekran, not with those of Upper Mesopotamia, Syria, Phœnicia, and Palestine. It will be one of the objects of this chapter to show that the Mosaical narrative conveys the exact truth—a truth alike in accordance with the earliest classical traditions, and with the latest results of modern comparative philology.

It will be desirable, however, before proceeding to establish the correctness of these assertions, to examine the grounds on which the opposite belief has been held so long and so confidently. Heeren draws his chief argument from the supposed character of the language. Assuming the form of speech called Chaldee to be the original tongue of the people, he remarks that it is " an Aramæan dialect, differing but slightly from the proper Syriac."[*] Chaldee is known partly from the Jewish Scriptures, in which it is used occasionally,[1] partly from the Targums (or Chaldæan paraphrases of different portions of the Sacred Volume), some of which belong to about the time of the Apostles, and partly from the two Talmuds, or collections of Jewish traditions, made in the third and fifth centuries of our era. It has been commonly regarded as the language of Babylon at the time of the Captivity, which the Jews, as captives, were forced to learn, and which thenceforth took the place of their own tongue. But it is extremely doubtful whether this is a true account

---

[*] As. Nat. l. s. c.

[1] The portions of the Old Testament written in the so-called Chaldee are Ezra, iv. 8 to vi. 18, and vii. 12- 26; Daniel, ii. 4 to vii. 28; and Jeremiah, x. 10. There is also a Chaldee gloss in Genesis, xxxi. 47.

of the matter. The Babylonian language of the age
of Nebuchadnezzar is found to be far nearer to
Hebrew than to Chaldee, which appears therefore to
be misnamed, and to represent the western rather
than the eastern Aramaic. The Chaldee argument
thus falls to the ground; but in refuting it an admission has been made which may be thought to furnish fully as good proof of early Babylonian Semitism
as the rejected theory.

It has been said that the Babylonian language in
the time of Nebuchadnezzar is found to be far nearer
to Hebrew than to Chaldee. It is, in fact, very close
indeed to the Hebrew. The Babylonians of that
period, although they did not speak the tongue
known to modern linguists as Chaldee, did certainly
employ a Semitic or Aramæan dialect, and so far
may be set down as Semites. And this is the
ground upon which such modern philologists as still
maintain the Semitic character of the primitive Chaldæans principally rely.[2] But it can be proved, from
the inscriptions of the country, that between the date
of the first establishment of a Chaldæan kingdom
and the reign of Nebuchadnezzar, the language of
Lower Mesopotamia underwent an entire change.
To whatever causes this may have been owing—a
subject which will be hereafter investigated—the
fact is certain;[3] and it entirely destroys the force
of the argument from the language of the Babylonians at the later period.

Another ground, and that which seems to have
had the chief weight with Niebuhr, is the supposed

[2] Hansen, *Philosophy of Universal History*, pp. 193 and 201; Muller, *Languages*, &c. l. &c.
[3] See below, ch. iv. pp. 77-87.

identity or intimate connexion of the Babylonians
with the Assyrians. That the latter people were
Semites has never been denied; and, indeed, it is a
point supported by such an amount of evidence as
renders it quite unassailable. If, therefore, the primitive Babylonians were once proved to be a mere portion of the far greater Assyrian nation, locally and politically but not ethnically separate from them, their
Semitic character would thereupon be fully established.
Now that this was the belief of Herodotus must be
at once allowed. Not only does that writer regard
the later Babylonians as Assyrians—" Assyrians of
Babylon," as he expresses it[1]—and look on Babylonia as a mere "district of Assyria,"[2] but, by adopting the mythic genealogy, which made Ninus the
son of Belus,[3] he throws back the connexion to the
very origin of the two nations, and distinctly pro-
nounces it a connexion of race. But Herodotus is a
very weak authority on the *antiquities* of any nation,
even his own ; and it is not surprising that he should
have carried back to a remote period a state of things
which he saw existing in his own age. If the later
Babylonians were, in manners and customs, in religion and in language, a close counterpart of the
Assyrians, he would naturally suppose them descended from the same stock. It is his habit to
transfer back to former times the condition of things
in his own day. Thus he calls the inhabitants of the
Peloponnese before the Dorian invasion "Dorians,"[4]
regards Athens as the second city in Greece when
Crœsus sent his embassies,[5] and describes as the au-

---

[1] Herod. i. 177.   [2] Ibid. ch. 106.   [3] Ibid. vi. 53.   [4] Ibid. i. 56.
[5] Ibid. ch. 7.

cient Persian religion that corrupted form which existed under Artaxerxes Longimanus.[1] He is an excellent authority for what he had himself seen, or for what he had laboriously collected by inquiry from eye-witnesses; but he had neither the critical acumen nor the linguistic knowledge necessary for the formation of a trustworthy opinion on a matter belonging to the remote history of a distant nation. And the opinion of Herodotus as to the ethnic identity of the two nations is certainly not confirmed by other ancient writers. Berosus seems to have very carefully distinguished between the Assyrians and the Babylonians or Chaldæans, as may be seen even through the doubly-distorting medium of Polyhistor and the Armenian Eusebius.[1] Diodorus Siculus made the two nations separate and hostile in very early times.[2] Pliny draws a clear line between the "Chaldæan races," of which Babylon was the head, and the Assyrians of the region above them.[3] Even Herodotus in one place admits a certain amount of ethnic difference; for, in his list of the nations forming the army of Xerxes, he mentions the Chaldæans as serving with, but not included among, the Assyrians.[4]

The grounds, then, upon which the supposed Semitic character of the ancient Chaldæans has been based, fail, one and all; and it remains to consider whether we have data sufficient to justify us in determinately assigning them to any other stock.

Now a large amount of tradition—classical and other—brings Ethiopians into these parts, and con-

[1] Ibid. iii. 16.
[1] Euseb. Chron. Can. i. 4 and 5; pp. 17-21; ed. Mai.
[2] Diod. Sic. ii. 1, § 7.
[3] Plin. H. N. vi. 26.
[4] Herod. vii. 63.

nects, more or less distinctly, the early dwellers upon
the Persian Gulf with the inhabitants of the Nile
valley, especially with those upon its upper course.
Homer, speaking of the Ethiopians, says that they
were "*divided*," and dwelt "at the ends of earth,
towards the setting and the *rising sun*."[4] This passage has been variously apprehended. It has been
supposed to mean the mere division of the Ethiopians
south of Egypt by the river Nile, whereby some inhabited its eastern and some its western bank.[5] Again,
it has been explained as referring to the east and
west coasts of Africa, both found by voyagers to be
in the possession of Ethiopians, who were "divided"
by the vast extent of continent that lay between them.[6]
But the most satisfactory explanation is that which
Strabo gives from Ephorus,[7] that the Ethiopians
were considered as occupying all the south coast
both of Asia and Africa, and as "divided" by the
Arabian Gulf (which separated the two continents)
into eastern and western—Asiatic and African. This
was an "old opinion" of the Greeks, we are told;
and, though Strabo thinks it indicated their ignorance, we may perhaps be excused for holding that
it might not improbably have arisen from real,
though imperfect, knowledge.

The traditions with respect to Memnon serve very
closely to connect Egypt and Ethiopia with the
country at the head of the Persian Gulf. Memnon,
King of Ethiopia, according to Hesiod[8] and Pindar,[9]
is regarded by Æschylus as the son of a Cissian

---

[4] Hom. *Od.* i. 23, 24—
Αἰθίοπας, τοὶ δι χθὰ δεδαίαται, ἔσχατοι ἀνδρῶν,
Οἱ μὲν δυσομένου Ὑπερίονος, οἱ δ' ἀνιόντος.
[5] Strab. i. 2, § 25.
[7] Ibid. § 26.

[6] Ibid. § 26–31.
[8] Hesiod. *Theogon.* 984: "Μέμ-
νονα χαλκοκορυστήν, Αἰθιόπων βα-
σιλῆα."
[9] Pind. *Nem.* iii. 62, 63.

woman,[2] and by Herodotus and others as the founder of Susa.[3] He leads an army of combined Susianians and Ethiopians to the assistance of Priam, his father's brother, and, after greatly distinguishing himself, perishes in one of the battles before Troy.[4] At the same time he is claimed as one of their monarchs by the Ethiopians upon the Nile,[5] and identified by the Egyptians with their king, Amunoph III.,[6] whose statue became known as "the vocal Memnon." Sometimes his expedition is supposed to have started from the African Ethiopia, and to have proceeded by way of Egypt to its destination.[7] There were palaces, called "Memnonia," and supposed to have been built by him, both in Egypt and at Susa;[8] and there was a tribe, called Memnones, near Meroë.[9] Memnon thus unites the Eastern with the Western Ethiopians; and the less we regard him as an historical personage, the more must we view him as personifying the ethnic identity of the two races.

The ordinary genealogies containing the name of Belus point in the same direction, and serve more definitely to connect the Babylonians with the Cushites of the Nile. Pherecydes, who is an earlier writer than Herodotus, makes Agenor, the son of Neptune, marry Damno, the daughter of Belus, and have issue Phœnix, Isæa, and Melia, of whom Melia marries Danaus, and Isæa Ægyptus.[1] Apollodorus,

[2] Ap. Strab. xv. 3, § 2.
[3] Herod. v. 54. Compare Strab. l. s. c.; Diod. Sic. ii. 22, § 3.
[4] Diod. Sic. l. s. c.; Pausan. x. 31, § 2; Cephalion ap. Euseb. Chron. Can. i. 15, § 5.
[5] Diod. Sic. ii. 22, § 4.
[6] Euseb. Chron. Can. ii. p. 278; Syncellus, Chronograph. p. 151, C. Compare Strab. xvii. 1, § 42, and

Plin. H. N. v. 9.
[7] Demetrius ap. Athen. Deipnosoph. xv. p. 680, A.
[8] Herod. v. 53; Strab. xv. 3, § 2, xvii. 1, § 12; Diod. Sic. l. s. c.; Plin. H. N. l. s. c.
[9] Alex. Polyhist. Fr. 111; Plin. H. N. vi. 30.
[1] Pherecyd. Fr. 40.

the disciple of Eratosthenes, expresses the connexion thus :—" Neptune took to wife Libya (or Africa), and had issue Belus and Agenor.   Belus married Anchinoë, daughter of Nile, who gave birth to Ægyptus, Danaus, Cepheus, and Phineus.   Agenor married Telephassa, and had issue Europa, Cadmus, Phœnix, and Cilix." [1]   Eupolemus, who professes to record the Babylonian tradition on the subject, tells us that the first Belus, whom he identifies with Saturn, had two sons, Belus and Canaan.   Canaan begat the progenitor of the Phœnicians (Phœnix ?), who had two sons, Chum and Mestraïm, the ancestors respectively of the Ethiopians and the Egyptians. [2]   Charax of Pergamus spoke of Ægyptus as the son of Belus. [3]   John of Antioch agrees with Apollodorus, but makes certain additions.   According to him, Neptune and Libya had three children, Agenor, Belus, and Enyalius or Mars.   Belus married Sida, and had issue Ægyptus and Danaus ; while Agenor married Tyro, and became the father of five children—Cadmus, Phœnix, Syrus, Cilix, and Europa. [4]

Many further proofs might be adduced, were they needed, of the Greek belief in an Asiatic Ethiopia, situated somewhere between Arabia and India, on the shores of the Erythræan Sea.   Herodotus twice speaks of the Ethiopians of Asia, [5] whom he very carefully distinguishes from those of Africa, and who can only be sought in this position.   Ephorus, as we have already seen, extended the Ethiopians along

---

[1] Apollodor. *Bibliothec.* ii. 1, § 4.
[2] See the Fragments of Polyhistor in Müller's *Fr. Hist. Græc.* vol. iii. p. 212; Fr. 3.
[3] Charax ap. Steph. Byz. s. v. Αἴγυπτος.
[4] Johann. Antiochen. Fr. 6, § 15.
[5] Herod. iii. 94 ; vii. 70.

the whole of the coast washed by the Southern Ocean.
Eusebius has preserved a tradition that, in the reign
of Amenophis III., a body of Ethiopians migrated
from the country about the Indus, and settled in the
valley of the Nile.[1] Hesiod and Apollodorus, by
making Memnon, the Ethiopian king, son of the
Dawn ('Hώs),[2] imply their belief in an Ethiopia situated to the east rather than to the south of Greece.
These are a few out of the many similar notices
which it would be easy to produce from classical
writers, establishing, if not the fact itself, yet at any
rate a full belief in the fact on the part of the best
informed among the ancient Greeks.

The traditions of the Armenians are in accordance
with those of the Greeks. The Armenian Geography applies the name of Cush or Ethiopia to the
four great regions, Media, Persia, Susiana or Elymais,
and Aria, or to the whole territory between the
Indus and the Tigris.[3] Moses of Chorene, the great
Armenian historian, identifies Belus, King of Babylon, with Nimrod;[4] while at the same time he adopts
a genealogy for him only slightly different from that
in our present copies of Genesis, making Nimrod the
grandson of Cush, and the son of Mizraim.[5] He thus
connects, in the closest way, Babylonia, Egypt, and
Ethiopia Proper, uniting moreover, by his identification of Nimrod with Belus, the Babylonians of
later times, who worshipped Belus as their hero-
founder, with the primitive population introduced
into the country by Nimrod.

---

[1] Euseb. Chron. Can. ii. p. 278.   363-5.
[2] Hesiod, l. s. c.; Apollod. iii. 12,   [4] Mos. Choren. Hist. Armen. i. 6;
§ 4.   pp. 19, 20.
[3] Mos. Choren. Geograph. pp.   [5] Ibid. i. 4; p. 12.

The names of Belus and Cush, thus brought into
juxtaposition, have remained attached to some portion or other of the region in question from ancient
times to the present day.   The tract immediately
east of the Tigris was known to the Greeks as
Cissia (Κισσία) or Cossæa (Κοσσαία), no less than as
Elymaïs or Elam.   The country east of Kerman was
named Kusan throughout the Sassanian period.[2] The
same region is now Beloochistan, the country of the
Belooches or Belús, while adjoining it on the east is
Cutch or Kooch, a term standing to Cush as Belooch
stands to Belus.   Again, Cissia or Cossæa is now
Khuzistan, or the land of Khuz (خوز), a name not
very remote from Cush; but perhaps this is only a
coincidence.[3]

To the traditions and traces here enumerated must
be added, as of primary importance, the Biblical tradition, which is delivered to us very simply and
plainly in that precious document, the 'Toldoth
Beni Noah,' or 'Book of the Generations of the
Sons of Noah,' which well deserves to be called
"the most authentic record that we possess for
the affiliation of nations."[4]   "The sons of Ham,"
we are told, "were Cush, and Mizraim, and Phut,
and Canaan. . . . . And Cush begat Nimrod. . . . .
And the beginning of his kingdom was Babel, and
Erech, and Accad, and Calneh, in the land of
Shinar."   Here a primitive Babylonian kingdom is
assigned to a people distinctly said to have been
Cushite by blood,[5] and to have stood in close con-

---

[2] Journal of Asiatic Society, vol.
xv. p. 233.
[3] Ibid. p. 230.
[4] " And Cush begat Nimrod," Gen.
x. 8.   Baron Bunsen says in one
work, "Nimrod is called a Cushite,
which means a man of the land of
Cush" (Philos. of Univ. Hist. vol. i.

nexion with Mizraim, or the people of Egypt, Phut,
or those of Central Africa, and Canaan, or those of
Palestine.   It is the simplest and the best interpretation of this passage to understand it as asserting that
the four races—the Egyptians, Ethiopians, Libyans,
and Canaanites—were ethnically connected, being
all descended from Ham ; and further, that the
primitive people of Babylon were a subdivision of
one of these races, namely of the Cushites or Ethiopians, connected in some degree with the Canaanites,
Egyptians, and Libyans, but still more closely with
the people which dwelt upon the Upper Nile.

The conclusions thus recommended to us by the
consentient primitive traditions of so many races,
have lately received most important and unexpected
confirmation from the results of linguistic research.
After the most remarkable of the Mesopotamian
mounds had yielded their treasures, and supplied the
historical student with numerous and copious documents bearing upon the history of the great Assyrian
and Babylonian empires, it was determined to explore
Chaldæa Proper, where mounds of less pretension,
but still of considerable height, marked the sites of
a number of ancient cities.   The excavations conducted at these places, especially at Niffer, Senkereh,

---

p. 101), and proceeds to argue that
he was only a Cushite "geographically," because he, or the people
represented by him, sojourned for
some time in Ethiopia.   In another,
(*Egypt's Place*, &c., vol. iv. p. 412)
he admits that this view contradicts
Gen. x. 8, and allows that "the
compiler of our present Book of
Genesis" must have meant to derive Nimrod by descent from Ham ;
but this "compiler" was, he thinks,
deceived by the resemblance of

בּרֹ to בֻּשׁ.   Nimrod was not an
Ethiopian, but a Casdan or Cossæan ;
i.e. (he says) a Turanian who conquered Babylon from the mountain
country east of Mesopotamia.   Of
course, if we are at liberty to regard
the "compiler" of Genesis as "mistaken" whenever his statements
conflict with our theories, while at
the same time we ignore linguistic
facts, we may speculate upon ancient
history and ethnography much at
our pleasure.

Warka, and Mugheir, were eminently successful. Among their other unexpected results was the discovery, in the most ancient remains, of a new form of speech, differing greatly from the later Babylonian language, and presenting analogies with the early language of Susiana, as well as with that of the second column of the Achæmenian inscriptions. In grammatical structure this ancient tongue resembles dialects of the Turanian family, but its vocabulary is pronounced to be " decidedly Cushite or Ethiopian ;" [*] and the modern languages to which it approaches the nearest are the Mahra of Southern Arabia and the Galla of Abyssinia. Thus comparative philology is found to confirm the old traditions. An Eastern Ethiopia, instead of being the invention of bewildered ignorance,[1] is proved to be a reality which henceforth it will be the extreme of scepticism to question ; and the primitive race which bore sway in Chaldæa Proper is demonstrated to have belonged to this ethnic type. +

The most striking physical characteristics of the African Ethiopians were their swart complexions, and their crisp or frizzled hair. According to Herodotus the Asiatic Ethiopians were equally dark, but their hair was straight and not frizzled.[*] Probably in neither case was the complexion what we understand by black, but rather a dark red brown or copper-colour, which is the tint of the modern Gallas and Abyssinians, as well as of the Cha'b and Montefik

---

[*] Sir H. Rawlinson, in the author's *Herodotus*, vol. i. p. 442.

[1] "The Bible mentions but one Kush, Æthiopia ; an Asiatic Kush exists only in the imagination of the interpreters, and is the child of their despair." Bunsen, *Philosophy of*

Univ. Hist. vol. i. p. 191. See on the other hand Sir H. Rawlinson's article in the *Journal of the Asiatic Society*, vol. xv. art. ii.; and compare especially Ezek. xxxviii. 5.

[*] Herod. vii. 70.

Arabs and the Belooches. The hair was no doubt
abundant; but it was certainly not woolly like that of
the negroes.   There is a marked distinction between
the negro hair and that of the Ethiopian race, which is
sometimes straight, sometimes crisp, but never woolly.
This distinction is carefully marked in the Egyptian
monuments, as is also the distinction between the
Ethiopian and negro complexions; whence we may
conclude that there was as much difference between
the two races in ancient as in modern times.   The
African races descended from the Ethiopians are on
the whole a handsome rather than an ugly people.
Their figure is slender and well shaped; their features
are regular, and have some delicacy; the forehead is
straight and fairly high; the nose long, straight, and
fine, but scarcely so prominent as that of Europeans;
the chin is pointed and good.   The principal defect
is in the mouth, which has lips too thick and full for
beauty, though they are not turned out like a negro's.[2]

We do not possess any representations of the ancient
people which can be distinctly assigned to the early
Cushite period. Abundant hair has been noticed in

_____

[2] See Prichard's *Physical Hist. of Mankind,* vol. ii. p. 44.

an early tomb;[1] and this in the later Babylonians,
who must have been descended in great part from
the earlier, was very conspicuous;[2] but otherwise we
have as yet no direct evidence with respect to the
physical characteristics of the primitive race.[3] That
they were brave and warlike, ingenious, energetic,
and persevering, we have ample evidence, which will
appear in later chapters of this work; but we can do
little more than conjecture their physical appearance,
which, however, we may fairly suppose to have resembled that of other Ethiopian nations.

When the early inhabitants of Chaldæa are pronounced to have belonged to the same race with the
dwellers upon the Upper Nile, the question naturally
arises, which were the primitive people, and which
the colonists? Is the country at the head of the
Persian Gulf to be regarded as the original abode of
the Cushite race, whence it spread eastward and westward, on the one hand to Susiana, Persia Proper,
Carmania, Gedrosia, and India itself; on the other to
Arabia and the east coast of Africa? Or are we to
suppose that the migration proceeded in one direction only—that the Cushites, having occupied the
country immediately to the south of Egypt, sent
their colonies along the south coast of Arabia, whence
they crept on into the Persian Gulf, occupying Chaldæa and Susiana, and thence spreading into Mekran,
Kerman, and the regions bordering upon the Indus?
Plausible reasons may be adduced in support of either
hypothesis. The situation of Babylonia, and its
proximity to that mountain region where man must

[1] Loftus, *Chaldæa and Susiana,* p. 202.
[2] See the Cylinders, *passim*; and compare Herod. i. 195.
[3] Skeletons have been found in abundance, but they have undergone no scientific examination.

F 2

have first "increased and multiplied" after the
Flood, are in favour of its being the original centre
from which the other Cushite races were derived.
The Biblical genealogy of the sons of Ham points,
however, the other way; for it derives Nimrod from
Cush, not Cush from Nimrod. Indeed this document seems to follow the Hamites from Africa—
emphatically "the land of Ham"[1]—in one line along
Southern Arabia to Shinar or Babylonia, in another
from Egypt through Canaan into Syria. The antiquity of civilization in the valley of the Nile, which
preceded by many centuries that even of primitive
Chaldæa, is another argument in favour of the migration having been from west to east; and the monuments and traditions of the Chaldæans themselves
are thought to present some curious indications of
an East African origin.[2] On the whole, therefore, it
is most probable that the race designated in Scripture by the hero-founder Nimrod, and among the
Greeks by the eponym of Belus, passed from East
Africa, by way of Arabia, to the valley of the
Euphrates, shortly before the opening of the historical period.

Upon the ethnic basis here indicated, there was
grafted, it would seem, at a very early period, a
second, probably Turanian, element, which very im-
portantly affected the character and composition of
the people. The *Burbur* or *Akkad*, who are found
to have been the principal tribe under the early
kings, are connected by name, religion, and in some
degree by language, with an important people of

---

[1] Ps. lxxviii. 51; cv. 23, 27; cvi. 22. Egypt is called *Chemi* in the native inscriptions.

[2] See the Essay of Sir H. Rawlinson, in the author's *Herodotus*, vol. i. p. 442, note (1st edition).

Armenia, called *Burbur* and *Urarda*, the Alarodians (apparently) of Herodotus.[*] It has been conjectured that this race is represented by the Zoroastrian Medes of Berosus, and that at a very remote date—B.C. 2458 probably—they descended upon the plain country, conquering the original Cushite inhabitants, and by degrees blending with them, though the fusion remained incomplete to the time of Abraham. The language of the early inscriptions, though Cushite in its vocabulary, is Turanian in many points of its grammatical structure, as in its use of postpositions, particles, and pronominal suffixes; and it would seem therefore scarcely to admit of a doubt that the Cushites of Lower Babylon must in some way or other have become mixed with a Turanian people. The mode and time of the commixture are matters altogether beyond our knowledge. We can only note the fact as certain, and (if we please) form hypotheses as to its accompanying circumstances.

Besides these two main constituents of the Chaldæan race, there is reason to believe that both a Semitic and an Arian element existed in the early population of the country, which ultimately blended with the others. The subjects of the early kings are continually designated in the inscriptions by the title of *Kiprat-arbat*, which is interpreted to mean "the four nations," or "*tongues*." In Abraham's time, again, the league of four kings seems correspondent to a fourfold ethnic division, Cushite, Turanian, Semitic, and Arian, the chief authority and ethnic preponderance being with the Cushites.[′] The lan-

---

[*] See an Essay by the same writer in the fourth volume of the same | work, pp. 250-254 (1st edition). [′] Chedor-laomer, both by his name

guage also of the early inscriptions is found to contain a considerable Semitic, and a small Arian element ; so that it is at least probable that the " four tongues" intended were not mere local dialects, but distinct languages, the representatives respectively of the four great families of human speech.

It would result from this review of the linguistic facts and other ethnic indications, that the Chaldæans were not a pure, but a very mixed people. Like the Romans in ancient, and the English in modern Europe, they were a " colluvio gentium omnium," a union of various races between which there was marked and violent contrast. It is now generally admitted that such races are among those which play the most distinguished part in the world's history, and most vitally affect its progress.

With respect to the name of Chaldæan, under which it has been customary to designate this mixed people, it is curious to find that in the native documents of the early period it does not occur at all. Indeed it first appears in the Assyrian inscriptions of the ninth century before our era, being then used as the name of the dominant race in the country about Babylon.   Still, as Berosus, who cannot easily have been ignorant of the ancient appellation of his race, applies the term Chaldæan to the primitive people,' and, as Scripture assigns Ur to the Chaldees as early as the time of Abraham, we are entitled to assume that the term, whenever it came historically

---

and by his leadership of the Elamites or Susianians, would be a Cushite ; Tidal, king of nations, i.e., of the wandering tribes, would be a Scyth, or Turanian ; Arioch and Amraphel would respectively lead the Arian and Semitic races.   See a note by Sir H. Rawlinson in the first volume of the author's *Herodotus*, vol. i. Essay vi. § 21, note ¹ (second edition).

' Berosus, Fr. i. § 5, 9, 11, &c.

into use, is in fact no unfit designation for the early
inhabitants of the country. Perhaps the most probable account of the origin of the word is, that it
designates properly the inhabitants of the ancient
capital, Ur or Hur—*Khaldi* being in the Burbur
dialect the exact equivalent of *Hur*, which was the
proper name of the Moon God, and Chaldæans being
thus either " Moon-worshippers," or simply "inhabitants of the town dedicated to, and called after, the
Moon."   Like the term " Babylonian," it would at
first have designated simply the dwellers in the
capital, and would subsequently have been extended
to the people generally.

A different theory has of late years been usually maintained with respect to the Chaldæans.   It
has been supposed that they were a race entirely distinct from the early Babylonians—Armenians, Arabs,
Kurds, or Sclaves—who came down from the north
long after the historical period, and settled as the
dominant race in the lower Mesopotamian valley.[a]
Philological arguments of the weakest and most unsatisfactory character were confidently adduced in
support of these views;[1] but they obtained acceptance chiefly on account of certain passages of
Scripture, which were thought to imply that the

---

[a] Gesenius, *Comment. in Esaiam* xxiii. 18, and *Geschichte der Hebr. Sprache*, pp. 63, 64 ; Heeren, *Asiatic Nations*, vol. ii. p. 147 ; Niebuhr, *Lectures on Ancient History*, vol. I. p. 20, note; Winer, *Realwörterbuch*, vol. l. p. 218 ; Kitto, *Biblical Cyclopædia*, vol. i. p. 406, &c. Mr. Vaux (*Dict. of Antiquities*, vol. i. p. 601) with good reason questions the common opinion.

[1] As that Nebuchadnezzar might be the Sclavonic sentence *Neboe and* senur taur, or " I'e orlo minus dominus,"—that Merodach might be the Persian *mardak*, " homunculus," &c. (See Prichard's *Phys. Hist. of Mankind*, vol. iv. pp. 563-564.) A more refined argument was that of Gesenius, " that the construction of the names was according, not to Semitic, but to Medo-Persian principles ;" but, being based upon mere conjectures as to the possible etymology of the words, it was really worthless.

Chaldæans first colonised Babylonia in the seventh
or eighth century before Christ. The most important of these passages is in Isaiah. That prophet,
in his denunciation of woe upon Tyre, says, according to our translation,—" Behold the land of
the Chaldæans; *this people was not,* till the Assyrian
founded it for them that dwell in the wilderness;
they set-up the towers thereof, they raised up the
palaces thereof; and he brought it to ruin;"[5] or,
according to Bishop Lowth, " Behold the land of the
Chaldæans. This people was of no account. (The
Assyrians founded it for the inhabitants of the
desert, they raised the watch-towers, they set up the
palaces thereof.) This people hath reduced her and
shall reduce her to ruin." It was argued that we
had here a plain declaration that, till a little before
Isaiah's time, the Chaldæans had never existed as a
nation. Then, it was said, they obtained for the
first time fixed habitations from one of the Assyrian
kings, who settled them in a city, probably Babylon.
Shortly afterwards, following the analogy of so many
Eastern races, they suddenly sprang up to power.
Here another passage of Scripture was thought to
have an important bearing on their history. "Lo!
I *raise up* the Chaldæans," says Habakkuk, "that
bitter and hasty nation, which shall march through
the breadth of the land to possess the dwelling places
that are not theirs. They are terrible and dreadful;
their judgment and their dignity shall proceed of
themselves: their horses also are swifter than the
leopards, and are more fierce than the evening
wolves: and their horsemen shall spread themselves,
and their horsemen shall come from far; they shall

---

[5] Isaiah xxiii. 13.

fly as an eagle that hasteth to eat; they shall come
all for violence; their faces shall nip as the east
wind, and they shall gather the captivity as the
sand. And they shall scoff at the kings, and the
princes shall be a scorn unto them; they shall
deride every stronghold; they shall heap dust and
take it."[1]   The Chaldæans, recent occupants of
Lower Mesopotamia, and there only a dominant
race, like the Normans in England or the Lombards
in North Italy, were, on a sudden, "raised up"—
elevated from their low estate of Assyrian colonists
to the conquering people which they became under
Nebuchadnezzar.

Such was the theory, originally advanced by
Gesenius, which, variously modified by other writers,
held its ground on the whole as the established view,
until the recent cuneiform discoveries. It was, from
the first, a theory full of difficulty. The mention of
the Chaldæans in Job,[1] and even in Genesis,[2] as a
well-known people, was in contradiction to the supposed recent origin of the race. The explanation of
the obscure passage in the 23rd chapter of Isaiah,
on which the theory was mainly based, was at
variance with other clearer passages of the same
prophet. Babylon is called by Isaiah the "daughter
of the Chaldæans,"[3] and is spoken of as an ancient
city, long "the glory of kingdoms,"[4] the oppressor
of nations, the power that "smote the people in
wrath with a continual stroke."[5] She is "the lady
of kingdoms,"[6] and "the beauty of the Chaldees'
excellency."[7]   The Chaldæans are thus in Isaiah, as

[1] Habakkuk i. 6-10.
[1] Job l. 17.
[2] Gen. xi. 28 and 31.
[3] Isaiah xlvii. 1 and 5.
[4] Ibid. xiii. 19.
[5] Ibid. xiv. 6.
[6] Ibid. xlvii. 5.
[7] Ibid. xiii. 19.

elsewhere generally in Scripture, the people of Babylonia, the term " Babylonians" not being used by
him ; Babylon is their chief city, not one which they
have conquered and occupied, but their " daughter "
—" the beauty of their excellency ; " and so all the
antiquity and glory which is assigned to Babylon
belong necessarily in Isaiah's mind to the Chaldæans. The verse, therefore, in the 23rd chapter,
on which so much has been built, can at most refer
to some temporary depression of the Chaldæans,
which made it a greater disgrace to Tyre that she
should be conquered by them. Again, the theory of
Gesenius took no account of the native historian,
who is (next to Scripture) the best literary authority
for the facts of Babylonian history. Berosus not
only said nothing of any influx of an alien race into
Babylonia shortly before the time of Nebuchadnezzar, but pointedly identified the Chaldæans of
that period with the primitive people of the country.
Nor can it be said that he would do this from
national vanity, to avoid the confession of a conquest,
for he admits no fewer than three conquests of
Babylon, a Median, an Arabian, and an Assyrian.[1]
Thus, even apart from the monuments, the theory in
question would be untenable. It really originated
in linguistic speculations,[2] which turn out to have
been altogether mistaken.

The joint authority of Scripture and of Berosus will
probably be accepted as sufficient to justify the adoption of a term which, if not strictly correct, is yet
familiar to us, and which will conveniently serve to

---

[1] Berosus, Fr. 11 and 12.
[2] See Niebuhr, *Lectures on Ancient History*, vol. i. p. 20, note ; and

Prichard, *Physical History of Mankind*, vol. iv. pp. 563, 564.

distinguish the primitive monarchy, whose chief seats
were in Chaldæa Proper (or the tract immediately
bordering upon the Persian Gulf), from the later
Babylonian Empire, which had its head-quarters
further to the north. The people of this first kingdom will therefore be called Chaldæans, although
there is no evidence that they applied the name to
themselves, or that it was even known to them in
primitive times. +

The general character of this remarkable people
will best appear from the account, presently to be
given, of their manners, their mode of life, their
arts, their science, their religion, and their history.
It is not convenient to forestall in this place the
results of almost all our coming inquiries. Suffice
it to observe that, though possessed of not many
natural advantages, the Chaldæan people exhibited
a fertility of invention, a genius, and an energy,
which place them high in the scale of nations, and
more especially in the list of those descended from a
Hamitic stock. For the last 3000 years the world
has been mainly indebted for its advancement to
the Semitic and Indo-European races; but it was
otherwise in the first ages. Egypt and Babylon—
Mizraim and Nimrod--both descendants of Ham
—led the way, and acted as the pioneers of mankind in the various untrodden fields of art, literature, and science. Alphabetic writing, astronomy,
history, chronology, architecture, plastic art, sculpture, navigation, agriculture, textile industry, seem,
all of them, to have had their origin in one or
other of these two countries. The beginnings may
have been often humble enough. We may laugh at
the rude picture-writing, the uncouth brick pyramid,

the coarse fabric, the homely and ill-shapen instruments, as they present themselves to our notice in the remains of these ancient nations; but they are really worthier of our admiration than of our ridicule. The first inventors of any art are among the greatest benefactors of their race; and the bold step which they take from the unknown to the known, from blank ignorance to discovery, is equal to many steps of subsequent progress. "The commencement," says Aristotle, "is more than half of the whole." [*] This is a sound judgment; and it will be well that we should bear it in mind during the review, on which we are about to enter, of the language, writing, useful and ornamental art, science, and literature of the Chaldæans. "The child is father of the man," both in the individual and the species; and the human race at the present day lies under infinite obligations to the genius and industry of early ages.

* Arist. *Eth. Nic.* l. 7, ad fin.

Chapter IV.

LANGUAGE AND WRITING.

"Γράμματα καὶ γλῶσσα Χαλδαίων."—Dan. i. 4. (Sept. vers.)

It was noted in the preceding chapter that Chaldæa, in the earliest times to which we can go back, seems to have been inhabited by four principal tribes. The early kings are continually represented on the monuments as sovereigns over the *Kiprat-arbat*, or " Four Races." These " Four Races " are called sometimes the *Arba Lisun* or " Four Tongues," whence we may conclude that they were distinguished from one another, among other differences, by a variety in their forms of speech. The extent and nature of the variety could not, of course, be determined merely from this expression ; but an examination of the written remains has furnished reasons for believing that the differences were great and marked—the languages in fact belonging to the four great varieties of human speech—the Hamitic, Semitic, Arian, and Turanian.

It is with the mixed form of speech, composed of these various elements, such as we find by the monuments to have prevailed in this country more than 2000 years before our era, that we are here concerned. The vocabulary of this tongue—as might be expected —is far from homogeneous. While its analogies seem to be principally with Hamitic dialects, such as the *Mahra* of Arabia, the *Galla* and *Wolaitsa* of Abys-

sinia, and the ancient language of Egypt, in many
cases it more resembles the Turkish, Tatar, and
Magyar (Turanian) dialects; while in some it presents Semitic and in others Arian affinities. This
will appear sufficiently from the following list:—

Dingir or *Dimir*, "God." Compare Turkish *Tengri.*

Atta, "father." Compare Turkish *atta. Etea* is "father" in the
    Wolaitza (Abyssinian) dialect.

Sia, "brother." Compare Wolaitza and Woratta *isha.*

Tur, "a youth," "a son." Compare the *tur-khan* of the Parthians
    (Turanians), who was the Crown Prince.

Dav or *Dam*, "a lady." Compare Latin *domina*, French *dame*, our
    "dame."

E, "a house." Compare ancient Egyptian *é*, and Turkish *ev.*

Ku, "a gate." Compare Turkish *kapi.*

K'harroa, "a road." Compare Galla *kara.*

Hura, "a town."

Ar, "a river." Compare the root *ar* in *Ara*, *Araxes*, *Armacaha*, &c.

Gubri, "a mountain." Compare Arian *giri*, and Arabic *jabal.*

Ki, "the earth." Compare Greek *γῆ* (?).

Kingi, "a country."

San, "the sun."

K'ha, "a fish" (?).

Kurra, "a horse." Compare Hind. *ghora*, and Arabic *gurra.*

Guski, "gold." Compare Galla *werke. Guski* means also "red" and
    "the evening."

Babar, "silver," "white," "the morning." Compare Agau *ber*, Tigre
    burrar.

Zabar, "copper." Compare Arabic *sifr.*

Harud, "iron." Compare Arabic *hadid.*

Zakad, "the head."

Kat, "the hand."

Si, "the eye."

Pi, "the ear."

Gula, "great." Compare Galla *gudu.*

Turn, "little." Compare Gonga *tu* and Galla *tina.*

Kalgn, "powerful."

Ginn, "first."

Mia, "many." Compare Agau *minch* or *mench.*

Gar, "to do." Compare Sanskrit *kri.*

Egir, "after." Compare Ilhamara (Abyssinian) *igria.*

The grammar of this language is still but very little
known. The conjugations of verbs are said to be
very intricate and difficult, a great variety of verbal

forms being obtained from the same root, as in Hebrew, by means of preformatives. Number and person in the verbs are marked by suffixes—the third person singular (masculine) by *bi* or *ani*, the third person plural by *bi-nini*.

The accusative case in nouns is marked by a postposition, *ku*, as in Hindustani. The plural of pronouns and substantives is formed sometimes by reduplication. Thus *ni* is " him," while *nini* is " them;" and *Chanuan, Yavnan, Libnan*, seem to be plural forms from *Chna, Yavan*, and *Liban*.

A curious anomaly occurs in the declension of pronouns.[1] When accompanied by the preposition *kita*, " with," there is a *tmesis* of the preposition, and the pronouns are placed between its first and second syllable; e.g. *ni*, " him " — *ki-ni-ta*, " with him." This takes place in every number and person, as the following scheme will show :—

	1st person.	2nd person.	3rd person.
Sing.	*ki-mu-ta* (with me)	*ki-su-ta* (with thee)	*ki-ni-ta* (with him)
Plur.	*ki-mi-ta* (with us)	*ki-su-nini-ta* (with you)	*ki-nini-ta* (with them)

N.B. The formation of the second person plural deserves attention. The word *su-nini* is, clearly, composed of the two elements, *su*, " thee," and *nini*, " them "—so that instead of having a word for " you," the Chaldæans employed for it the periphrasis " thee-them " ! There is, I believe, no known language which presents a parallel anomaly.

Such are the chief known features of this interesting but difficult form of speech. A specimen may now be given of the mode in which it was written. Among

---

[1] There is, I believe, a near parallel to this peculiarity in the Ostiak.

the earliest of the monuments hitherto discovered are
a set of bricks bearing the following cuneiform inscription :—

This inscription is explained to mean :—" Beltis,
his lady, has caused Urukh (Orchamus), the pious
chief, King of Hur, and King of the land (?) of the
Akkad, to build a temple to her." In the same locality where it occurs,[2] bricks are also found bearing

evidently the same inscription, but written in a different
manner. Instead of the wedge and arrowhead being

---

[2] The bricks in question were
found at Warka, the ancient *Huruk*
or Erech. (See Loftus, *Chaldæa and
Susiana*, p. 168.)

the elements of the writing, the whole is formed by straight lines of almost uniform thickness, and the impression seems to have been made by a single stamp.

This mode of writing, which has been called without much reason " the hieratic," [1] and of which we have but a small number of instances, has confirmed a conjecture, originally suggested by the early cuneiform writing itself, that the characters were at first the pictures of objects. In some cases the pictorial representation is very plain and palpable. For instance the " determinative " of a god—the sign, that is, which marks that the name of a god is about to follow, in this early rectilinear writing is ⟶✳⟵, an eight-rayed star. The archaic cuneiform keeps closely to this type, merely changing the lines into wedges, thus ➤✳⟵, while the later cuneiform first unites the oblique wedges in one ➤✳, and then omits them as unnecessary, retaining only the perpendicular and the horizontal ones ➤⊥. Again, the character representing the word " hand " is, in the rectilinear writing ☰, in the archaic cuneiform ▤, in the later cuneiform ▤. The five lines (afterwards reduced to four) clearly represent the thumb and the four fingers. So the character ordinarily representing " a house " ▭ is evidently formed from the

[1] See Oppert's *Expédition Scientifique en Mésopotamie*, tom. ii. p. 62.

VOL. I.   G original ☐, the ground-plan of a house; and that denoting "the sun" ◁Y, comes from ◇, through ☲Y, and ✦, the original ◇ being the best representation that straight lines could give of the sun. In the case of *ka*, "a gate," we have not the original design; but we may see post, bars, and hinges in ☰Y, the ordinary character.

Another curious example of the pictorial origin of the letters is furnished by the character ☲◢◣, which is the French *une*, the feminine of "one." This character may be traced up through several known forms to an original picture, which is thus given on a Koyunjik tablet ☲☐☰. It has been conjectured that the object here represented is "a sarcophagus."[1] But the true account seems to be that it is a *double-toothed comb*, a toilet article peculiar to women, and therefore one which might well be taken to express "a woman," or more generally the feminine gender. It is worth notice that the emblem is the very one still in use among the Lurs, in the mountains overhanging Babylonia.[2] And it is further remarkable that the phonetic power of the character here spoken of is *it* (or *yat*)—the ordinary Semitic feminine ending.

The original writing, it would therefore seem, was a picture-writing, as rude as that of the Mexicans.

[1] Oppert, tom. ii. p. 66.

[2] See the *Journal of the Geographical Society*, vol. ix. p. 58, where, in speaking of the devices on the tombs of the Lurs, Sir H. Rawlinson notes "the double-toothed comb" as "the distinctive mark of the female sex."

Objects were themselves represented, but coarsely
and grotesquely—and, which is especially remarkable, without any curved lines. This would seem to
indicate that the system grew up where a hard material, probably stone, was alone used. The cuneiform writing arose when clay took the place of stone
as a material. A small tool, with a square or triangular point,* impressed, by a series of distinct touches,
the outline of the old pictured objects on the soft clay
of tablets and bricks. In course of time simplifica-
tions took place. The less important wedges were
omitted. One stroke took the place of two, or sometimes of three. In this way the old form of objects
became, in all but a few cases, very indistinct; while
generally it was lost altogether.

Originally each character had, it would seem, the
phonetic power of the name borne by the object
which it represented. But, as this name was different
in the languages of the different tribes inhabiting
the country, the same character came often to have
several distinct phonetic values. For instance, the
character ⚊⚊, representing "a house," had the
phonetic values of *e*, *bit*, and *mal*, because those
were the words expressive of "a house" among the
Hamitic, Semitic, and Arian populations respectively.
Again, characters did not always retain their original
phonetic powers, but abbreviated them. Thus the
character which originally stood for *Assur*, "Assyria,"
came to have the sound of *as*, that denoting *bil*, "a
lord," had in addition the sound of *bi*, and so on.

* Tools with a triangular point, made in ivory, apparently for employment in cuneiform writing, have been found at Babylon. (See Oppert,
tom. ii. p. 63.)

Under these circumstances it is almost impossible to
feel any certainty in regard to the phonetic representation of a single line of these old inscriptions.
The meaning of each word may be well known ; but
the articulate sounds which were in the old times
attached to them may be matter almost of conjecture.

The Chaldæan characters are of three kinds—letters proper, monograms, and determinatives. With
regard to the letters proper, there is nothing particular to remark, except that they have almost always
a syllabic force.   The monograms represent in a
brief way, by a wedge or a group of wedges, an
entire word, often of two or three syllables, as Nebo,
Babil, Merodach, &c.   The determinatives mark that
the word which they accompany is a word of a
certain class, as a god, a man, a country, a town, &c.
These last, it is probable, were not sounded at all
when the word was read.   They served, in some
degree, the purpose of our capital letters in the
middle of sentences, but gave more exact notice of
the nature of the coming word.   Curiously enough,
they are retained sometimes, where the word which
they accompany has merely its phonetic power, as
(generally) when the names of gods form a part of
the names of monarchs.

It has been noticed already that the chief material on which the ancient Chaldæans wrote was
moist clay, in the two forms of tablets and bricks.
On bricks are found only royal inscriptions, having
reference to the building in which the bricks were
used, commonly designating its purpose, and giving
the name and titles of the monarch who erected it.[1]

---

[1] See above, page 80, where the translation of an inscription is given. | Other translations of the brick legends belonging to the same king

The inscription does not occupy the whole brick, but a square or rectangular space towards its centre. It is in some cases stamped, in some impressed with a tool. The writing—as in all cuneiform inscriptions, excepting those upon seals—is from left to right, and the lines are carefully separated from one another. Some specimens have been already given.[1]

The tablets of the Chaldæans are among the most remarkable of their remains, and will probably one day throw great additional light on the manners and customs, the religion, and even, perhaps, the science and learning, of the people. They are small pieces of clay,[2] somewhat rudely shaped into a form resembling a pillow, and thickly inscribed with cuneiform characters, which are sometimes accompanied by impressions of the cylindrical seals so common in the museums of Europe. The seals are rolled across the body of the document, as in the accompanying woodcut. Except where these impressions occur, the clay is commonly covered on both sides with minute writing. What is most curious, however, is, that the documents thus duly attested have in general been enveloped, after they were baked, in a cover of

are the following:—

1. On a brick from *Mugheir* (Ur):—"Orchamus, king of Ur, is he who has built the temple of the Moon-God."

2. On a brick from the same:—"The Moon-God, his lord, has caused Orchamus, king of Ur, to build a temple to him, and has caused him to build the enceinte of Ur."

3. On a brick from the same:—"The Moon-God, brother's son (?) of Anu, and eldest son of Belus, his lord, has caused Orchamus, the pious chief, king of Ur, to build the temple of *Tsingatha* (?), his holy place."

4. On a brick from *Senkereh*:—"The Sun-God, his lord, has caused Orchamus, the pious chief, king of Ur, king of the land (?) of the Akkad, to build a temple to him."

5. On a brick from *Niffer*:—"Orchamus, king of Ur, and king of the land (?) of the Akkad, who has built the temple of Belus."

[1] See above, page 80.

[2] The size varies from an inch to four or five inches in length, the width being always less. The envelope is of very thin clay, and does not much add to the bulk.

moist clay, upon which their contents have been
again inscribed, so as to present externally a dupli-
cate of the writing within; and the tablet in its
cover has then been baked afresh. That this was
the process employed is evident from the fact that
the inner side of the envelope bears a cast, in relief,
of the inscription beneath it. Probably the object
in view was greater security—that if the external
cover became illegible, or was tampered with, there
might be a means of proving beyond a doubt what
the document actually contained. The tablets in

question have in very few cases been decyphered ; but there is reason to believe that they are for the most part deeds, contracts, or engagements entered into by private persons and preserved among the archives of families.

Besides their writings on clay, the Chaldæans were in the habit, from very early times, of engraving inscriptions on gems. The signet cylinder of a very ancient king exhibits that archaic formation of letters which has been already noted as appearing upon some of the earliest bricks. That it belongs to the same period is evident, not only from the resemblance of the literal type,[1] but from the fact that the

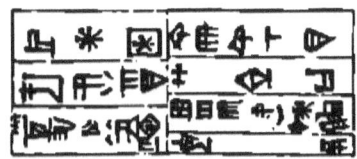

same king's name appears upon both. The signet inscription—so far as it has been hitherto decyphered —is read as follows :—" The signet of Orchamus, the pious chief, king of Ur, ... High-Priest (?) of . . . . Niffer." Another similar relic, belonging to a later monarch in the series, has the inscription : "——sin, the powerful chief, the king of Ur, the king of the Kiprat-arbat (or four races) . . . . his seal." The cylinders, however, of this period are more usually without inscriptions, being often plain,[2] and often engraved with figures, but without a legend.

[1] We have only a representation of this inscription, the cylinder itself being lost. The representation will be found in Sir R. Ker Porter's *Travels*, vol. ii. plate 79, no. 6.

[2] *As. Soc. Journ.* vol. xv. pp. 272, 273.

CHAPTER V.

ARTS AND SCIENCES.

" Chaldæi cognitione astrorum sollertiaque ingeniorum antecellunt."

Cic. de Div. i. 41.

AMONG the arts which the first Ethiopic settlers on
the shores of the Persian Gulf either brought with
them from their former homes, or very early invented
in their new abode, must undoubtedly have been the
two whereby they were especially characterised in
the time of their greatest power—architecture and
agriculture. Chaldæa is not a country disposing men
to nomadic habits. The productive powers of the
soil would at once obtrude themselves on the notice
of the new comers, and would tempt to cultivation
and permanency of residence. If the immigrants
came by sea, and settled first in the tract immediately
bordering upon the gulf, as seems to have been the
notion of Berosus,[1] their earliest abodes may have
been of that simple character which can even now be
witnessed in the Affej and Montefik marshes—that is
to say, reed cabins, supported by the tall stems of
the growing plants bent into arches, and walled with
mats composed of flags or sedge.[2] Houses of this
description last for forty or fifty years,[3] and would

[1] Berosus, Fr. 1, § 3.
[2] Layard, Nineveh and Babylon, pp. 554, 555; Loftus, Chaldæa and Susiana, p. 91; Journal of Geographical Society, vol. xxvi. p. 137.
[3] " We were conducted to the

satisfy the ideas of a primitive race; when greater permanency began to be required, palm-beams might take the place of the reed supports, and wattles plastered with mud that of the rush mats; in this way habitations would soon be produced quite equal to those in which the bulk of mankind reside, even at the present day.

In process of time, however, a fresh want would be felt. Architecture, as has been well observed, has its origin, not in nature only, but in religion.[*] The common worship of God requires temples; and it is soon desired to give to these sacred edifices a grandeur, a dignity, and a permanency corresponding to the nature of the Being worshipped in them. Hence in most countries recourse is had to stone, as the material of greatest strength and durability; and by its means buildings are raised which seem almost to reach the heaven whereof they witness. In Babylonia, as it has been already observed,[*] this material was entirely wanting. Nowhere within the limits of the alluvium was a quarry to be found; and though at no very great distance, on the Arabian border, a coarse sandstone might have been obtained, yet in primitive times, before many canals were made, the difficulty of transporting this weighty substance across the soft and oozy soil of the plain would necessarily have prevented its adoption generally, or, indeed, anywhere, except in the immediate

mudhif or reception-hut of the chief, which resembled the other habitations of the place, but was of gigantic size, forty feet long and eighteen feet high. It boasted the almost fabulous age for a reed building (if the Arabs might be credited) of no less than half a century, and appeared likely to last as long again." (Loftus, *Chaldæa and Susiana*, p. 92.)

[*] Stieglitz, quoted in Smith's *Dictionary of Greek and Roman Antiquities*, ad voc. ARCHITECTURE.

[*] See above, page 40.

vicinity of the rocky region. Accordingly we find that stone was never adopted in Babylonia as a building material, except to an extremely small extent; and that the natives were forced, in its default, to seek for the grand edifices, which they desired to build, a different substance.

The earliest traditions,[6] and the existing remains of the earliest buildings, alike inform us that the material adopted was brick. An excellent clay is readily procurable in all parts of the alluvium; and this, when merely exposed to the intense heat of an Eastern sun for a sufficient period, or still more when kiln-dried, constitutes a very tolerable substitute for the stone employed by most nations. The baked bricks, even of the earliest times, are still sound and hard; while the sun-dried bricks, though they have often crumbled to dust or blended together in one solid earthen mass, yet sometimes retain their shape and original character almost unchanged, and offer a stubborn resistance to the excavator.[7] In the most ancient of the Chaldæan edifices we occasionally find, as in the Bowariyeh ruin at Warka,[8] the entire structure composed of the inferior material; but the more ordinary practice is to construct the mass of the building in this way, and then to cover it throughout with a facing of burnt brick, which sometimes extends to as much as ten feet in thickness. The burnt brick was thus made to protect the unburnt from the influence of the weather, while labour and fuel were greatly economised by the employment to so large an extent of the natural

---

[6] Gen. xi. 3.
[7] Journal of the Asiatic Society, vol. xv. pp. 263 and 405.

[8] This ruin is carefully described by Mr. Loftus in his Chaldæa and Susiana, pp. 167-170.

substance. The size and colour of the bricks vary. The general shape is square, or nearly so, while the thickness is, to modern ideas, disproportionately small; it is not, however, so small as in the bricks of the Romans. The earliest of the baked bricks hitherto discovered in Chaldæa are 11¼ inches square, and 2¼ inches thick,[1] while the Roman are often 15 inches square, and only an inch and a quarter thick.[1] The baked bricks of later date are of larger size than the earlier; they are commonly about 13 inches square, with a thickness of three inches.[2] The best quality of baked brick is of a yellowish-white tint, and very much resembles our Stourbridge or fire brick; another kind, extremely hard, but brittle, is of a blackish blue; a third, the coarsest of all, is slack-dried, and of a pale red. The earliest baked bricks are of this last colour.[3] The sun-dried bricks have even more variety of size than the baked ones. They are sometimes as large as 16 inches square and seven inches thick, sometimes as small as six inches square by two thick.[4] Occasionally, though not very often, bricks are found differing altogether in shape from those above described, being formed for special purposes. Of this kind are the triangular bricks used at the corners of walls, intended to give greater regularity to the angles than would otherwise be attained;[5] and the wedge-shaped bricks, formed to be employed in arches, which were known and used by this primitive people.[6]

[1] *Journal of the Asiatic Society,* vol. xv. p. 261.

[1] Wyttenbach, *Guide to the Roman Antiquities of Trèves,* p. 42.

[2] Rich, *First Memoir,* p. 61.

[3] Loftus, p. 130.

[4] *Journal of Asiatic Society,* vol.

[5] *Ibid.* p. 266.

[6] Loftus, p. 133; *Journal of Asiatic Society, l. s. c.* The "moulded semicircular bricks" found at Warka (Loftus, p. 175) are probably of the Babylonian, not the Chaldæan, period.

The modes of applying these materials to building purposes were various. Sometimes the crude and the burnt brick were used in alternate layers, each layer being several feet in thickness;[1] more commonly the crude brick was used (as already noticed) for the internal parts of the building, and a facing of burnt brick protected the whole from the weather. Occasionally the mass of an edifice was composed entirely of crude brick; but in such cases special precautions had to be taken to secure the stability of this comparatively frail material. In the first place, at intervals of four or five feet, a thick layer of reed matting was interposed along the whole extent of the building, which appears to have been intended to protect the earthy mass from dis-integration, by its projection beyond the rest of the external surface. The readers of Herodotus are familiar with this feature, which (according to him) occurred in the massive walls whereby Babylon was surrounded.[2] If this was really the case, we may conclude that these walls were not composed of burnt brick, as he imagined, but of the sun-dried material. Reeds were never employed in buildings composed of burnt brick, being useless in such cases; where their impression is found, as not unfrequently happens, on bricks of this kind, the brick has been laid upon reed matting when in a soft state, and afterwards submitted to the action of fire. In edifices of crude brick, the reeds were no doubt of great service, and have enabled some buildings of the kind to endure to the present day. They are very strikingly conspicuous where they occur, since

---

Journal of the Asiatic Society, vol. xv. p. 263.   [2] Herod. i. 170.

they stripe the whole building with continuous horizontal lines, having at a distance somewhat the effect of the courses of dark marble in an Italian structure of the Byzantine period.

Another characteristic of the edifices in which crude brick is thus largely employed, is the addition externally of solid and massive buttresses of the burnt material. These buttresses have sometimes a very considerable projection; they are broad, but not high, extending less than half way up the walls against which they are placed.

Two kinds of cement are used in the early structures. One is a coarse clay or mud, which is sometimes mixed with chopped straw; the other is bitumen. This last is of excellent quality, and the bricks which it unites adhere often so firmly together, that they can with difficulty be separated.[*] As a general rule in the early buildings, the crude brick is laid in mud, while the bitumen is used to cement together the burnt bricks.

These general remarks will receive their best illustration from a detailed description of the principal early edifices which recent researches in Lower Mesopotamia have revealed to us. These are for the most part temples; but in one or two cases the edifice explored is thought to have been a residence, so that the domestic architecture of the period may be regarded as known to us, at least in some degree. The temples most carefully examined hitherto are those at Warka, Mugheir, and Abu-Shahrein, the first of which was explored by Mr. Loftus in 1854, the second by Mr. Taylor in the

---

[*] Loftus, *Chaldæa and Susiana*, p. 160.

same year, and the third by the same traveller
in 1855.

Bowariyeh.

The Warka ruin is called by the natives Bown-
riyeh, which signifies "reed mats," in allusion to a
peculiarity, already noticed, in its construction. It
is at once the most central and the loftiest ruin in
the place. At first sight it appears to be a cone or
pyramid ; but further examination proves that it was
in reality a tower, 200 feet square at the base, built
in two stories, the lower story being composed
entirely of sun-dried bricks laid in mud, and protected at intervals of four or five feet by layers of
reeds, while the upper one was composed of the same
material, faced with burnt brick. Of the upper stage
very little remains ; and what remains is of a later
date than the inferior story, which bears marks of a
very high antiquity. The sun-dried bricks, whereof
the lower story is composed, are "rudely moulded
of very incoherent earth, mixed with fragments of
pottery and freshwater shells," and vary in size and
shape, being sometimes square, seven inches each
way ; sometimes oblong, nine inches by seven, and

from three to three and a half inches thick.[1] The
whole present height of the building is estimated at
100 feet above the level of the plain. Its summit,
except where some slight remains of the second
story constitute an interruption, is "perfectly flat,"
and probably continues very much in the condition
in which it was when the lower stage was first built.
This stage, being built of crude brick, was necessarily
weak; it is therefore supported by four massive
buttresses of baked brick, each placed exactly in the
centre of one of the sides, and carried to about one-
third of the height. Each buttress is nineteen feet
high, six feet one inch wide, and seven and a half
feet in depth; and each is divided down the middle
by a receding space, one foot nine inches in width.
All the bricks composing the buttresses are inscribed,
and are very firmly cemented together with bitumen,
in thick layers. The buttresses were entirely hidden
under the mass of rubbish which had fallen from the
building, chiefly from the upper story, and only
became apparent when Mr. Loftus made his excavations.[2]

It is impossible to reconstruct the Bowariyeh ruin
from the facts and measurements hitherto supplied to
us; even the height of the first story is at present
uncertain;[3] and we have no means of so much as
conjecturing the height of the second. The exact
emplacement of the second upon the first is also

[1] Loftus, *Chaldæa and Susiana*, p. 168.
[2] See this traveller's account of his labours (*Chaldæa and Susiana*, pp. 167-170).
[3] The whole building is said to be 100 feet above the surface of the plain; but we are not told what is the height from the plain of the mound or platform upon which the temple stands; nor what height the fragment of the second story attains. All that can be gathered from Mr. Loftus is that the first story was at least 46 feet high.

doubtful, while the original mode of access is un-
discovered; and thus the plan of the building is in
many respects still defective. We only know that
the building was a square; that it had two stories
at the least; and that its height considerably exceeded
100 feet.

Mugheir Temple.

The temple at Mugheir has been more accurately
examined. On a mound or platform of some size,
raised about twenty feet above the level of the plain,
there stands a rectangular edifice, consisting at
present of two stories, both of them ruined in parts,
and buried to a considerable extent in piles of rubbish
composed of their *débris*. The angles of the building
exactly face the four cardinal points.[4] It is not a

---

[4] Loftus, *Chaldæa and Susiana,*
p. 128. According to Mr. Loftus,
this emplacement " is observable in | all edifices (temples?) of true Chal-
dæan origin."

square, but a parallelogram, having two longer and
two shorter sides. The longer sides front to the
north-east and south-west, and measure 198 feet;
while the shorter sides, which face the north-west
and the south-east, measure 133 feet. The present
height of the basement story is 27 feet, but, allowing
for the concealment of the lower part by the rubbish,
and the destruction of the upper part by the hand
of time, we may presume that the original height
was little, if at all, short of 40 feet. The interior
of this story is built of crude or sun-dried bricks of
small size, laid in bitumen; but it is faced throughout with a wall, ten feet in thickness, composed of
red kiln-dried bricks, likewise cemented with bitumen. This external wall is at once strengthened
and diversified to the eye by a number of shallow
buttresses or pilasters in the same material; of these,
there are nine, including the corner ones, on the
longer, and six on the shorter sides. The width of
the buttresses is eight feet, and their projection a
little more than a foot. The walls and buttresses
alike slope inwards at an angle of nine degrees. On
the north-eastern side of the building there is a staircase nine feet wide, with sides or balustrades three
feet wide, which leads up from the platform to the
top of the first story. It has also been conjectured
that there was a second or grand staircase on the
south-east face, equal in width to the second story
of the building, and thus occupying nearly the whole
breadth of the structure on that side.[*] A number
of narrow slits or air-holes are carried through the
building from side to side; they penetrate alike the

[*] Loftus, Chaldæa and Susiana, p. 129.

walls and buttresses, and must have tended to preserve the dryness of the structure.

The second story is, like the first, a parallelogram,
and not of very different proportions.* Its longer
sides measure 119 feet, and its shorter ones 75 feet
at the base. Its emplacement upon the first story is
exact as respects the angles, but not central as
regards the four sides. While it is removed from

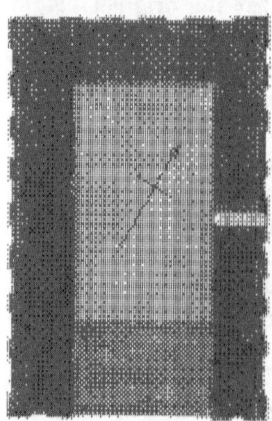

the south-eastern edge a
distance of 47 feet, from the
north-western it is distant
only 30 feet. From the two
remaining sides its distance
is apparently about 28 feet.
The present height of the
second story, including the
rubbish upon its top, is 19
feet; but we may reason-
ably suppose that the original height was much greater.
The material of which its
inner structure is com-
posed, seems to be chiefly
(or wholly) partially-burnt brick, of a light red
colour, laid in a cement composed of lime and ashes.
This central mass is faced with kiln-dried bricks of
large size and excellent quality, also laid, except on
the north-west face,' in lime mortar. No buttresses
and no staircase are traceable on this story; though
it is possible that on the south-east side the grand

* The proportions of the lower
stage are almost exactly as 3 to 2.
Those of the upper are as 3½ to 2.
† On this side the material used is

bitumen. (See Mr. Taylor's article
in the *Journal of the Asiatic Society*,
vol. xv. p. 261.)

staircase may have run the whole height of both
stories.

According to information received by Mr. Taylor
from the Arabs of the vicinity,[1] there existed, less
than half a century ago, some remains of a third
story, on the summit of the rubbish which now crowns
the second. This building is described as a room or
chamber, and was probably the actual shrine of the
god in whose honour the whole structure was erected.
Mr. Taylor discovered a number of bricks or tiles
glazed with a blue enamel, and also a number of
large copper nails, at such a height in the rubbish
which covers up much of the second story, that he
thinks they could only have come from this upper
chamber. The analogy of later Babylonian buildings, as of the Birs-Nimrud and the temple of Belus
at Babylon,[2] confirms this view, and makes it probable that the early Chaldæan temple was a building
in three stages, of which the first and second were
solid masses of brickwork, ascended by steps on the
outside, while the third was a small house or chamber

highly ornamented, containing the image and shrine
of the god.

In conclusion, it must be observed that only the
lower story of the Mugheir temple exhibits the work-

[1] *Journal of the Asiatic Society*, vol. xv. p. 264.   [2] Herod. i. 181.

manship of the old or Chaldæan period. Clay
cylinders found in the upper story inform us that in
its present condition it is the work of Nabonidus,
the last of the Babylonian kings; and most of its
bricks bear his stamp. Some, however, have the
stamp of the same monarch who built the lower
story;[1] and this is sufficient to show that the two
stories are a part of the original design, and therefore that the idea of building in stages belongs to
the first kingdom and to primitive times. There is
no evidence to prove whether the original edifice
had, or had not, a third story; since the chamber
seen by the Arabs was no doubt a late Babylonian
work. The third story of the accompanying sketch
must therefore be regarded as conjectural.

It is not necessary for our present purpose to
detain the reader with a minute description of the
ancient temple at Abu-Shahrein. The general
character of this building seems to have very closely
resembled that of the Mugheir temple. Its angles
fronted the cardinal points; it had two stories, and
an ornamented chamber at the top; it was faced with
burnt brick, and strengthened by buttresses; and in
most other respects followed the type of that building.[2] Its only very notable peculiarities are the
partial use of stone in the construction, and the
occurrence of a species of pillar, very curiously composed. The artificial platform on which the temple
stands is made of beaten clay, cased with a massive
wall of sandstone and limestone, in some places
twenty feet thick. A stone, or rather marble, stair-

---

[1] *Journal of the Asiatic Society,*
vol. xv. p. 264, note.
[2] See Mr. Taylor's description in
the *Journal of the Asiatic Society,*
vol. xv. pp. 405-408.

case also leads up from the platform to the summit
of the first story, composed of small polished blocks,
twenty-two inches long, thirteen broad, and four
and a half thick.   The bed of the staircase is made
of sun-dried brick, and the marble was fastened to
this substratum by copper bolts, some portion of
which was found by Mr. Taylor still adhering to the
blocks.[1]   At the foot of the staircase there appear
to have stood two columns, one on either side of it.
The construction of these columns is very singular.
A circular nucleus composed of sandstone slabs, and
small cylindrical pieces of marble disposed in alternate layers, was coated externally with coarse lime,
mixed with small stones and pebbles, until by means
of many successive layers the pillar had attained the
desired bulk and thickness.   Thus the stone and
marble were entirely concealed under a thick coating
of plaster; and a smoothness was given to the outer
surface, which it would have otherwise been difficult
to obtain.

The date of the Abu-Shahrein temple is thought
to be considerably later than that of the other buildings above described;[2] and the pillars would seem to
be a refinement on the simplicity of the earlier times.
The use of stone is to be accounted for, not so much
by the advance of architectural science, as by the
near vicinity of the Arabian hills, from which that
material could be readily derived.[3]

It is evident, that if the Chaldæan temples were
of the character and construction which we have
gathered from their remains, they could have pos-

---

[1] Journal of Asiatic Society, vol.
xv. p. 406, note.

[2] See below, chapter vii. p. 210.
[3] Supra, ch. i. p. 25 and p. 27.

sessed no great architectural beauty, though they
may not have lacked a certain grandeur. In the
dead level of Babylonia, an elevation even of 100
or 150 feet must have been impressive;[*] and the
plain massiveness of the structures no doubt added
to their grand effect on the beholder. But there
was singularly little in the buildings, architecturally
viewed, to please the eye or gratify the sense of
beauty. No edifices in the world—not even the
Pyramids—are more deficient in external ornament.
The buttresses and the air-holes, which alone break
the flat uniformity of the walls, are intended simply
for utility, and can scarcely be said to be much
embellishment. If any efforts were made to delight
by the ordinary resources of ornamental art, it seems
clear that such efforts did not extend to the whole
edifice, but were confined to the shrine itself—the
actual abode of the god—the chamber which crowned
the whole, and was alone, strictly speaking, "the
temple."[*] Even here there is no reason to believe
that the building had externally much beauty. No
fragments of architraves or capitals, no sculptured
ornaments of any kind, have been found among the
heaps of rubbish in which Chaldæan monuments are
three-parts buried. The ornaments which have been
actually discovered, are such as suggest the idea of
internal rather than external decoration; and they
render it probable that such decoration was, at least
in some cases, extremely rich. The copper nails and

---

[*] Mr. Loftus says—"I know of
nothing more exciting or impressive
than the first sight of one of these
great Chaldæan piles, looming in solitary grandeur from the surrounding
plains and marshes." (*Chaldæa and
Susiana,* p. 113.)

[*] See Herod. i. 181, where the
stages (πύργοι) are carefully distinguished from the temple (νηός) at
the summit.

blue enamelled tiles found high up in the Mugheir
mound, have been already noticed.[1] At Abu-Shahrein the ground about the basement of the second
story was covered with small pieces of agate, alabaster, and marble, finely cut and polished, from half
an inch to two inches long, and half an inch (or
somewhat less) in breadth, each with a hole drilled
through its back, containing often a fragment of a
copper bolt. It was also strewn less
thickly with small plates of pure gold,
and with a number of gold-headed or
gilt-headed nails,[2] used apparently to attach the gold
plates to the internal plaster or wood-work. These
fragments seem to attest the high ornamentation of
the shrine in this instance, which we have no
reason to regard as singular or in any way exceptional.

The Chaldæan remains which throw light upon
the domestic architecture of the people are few and
scanty. A small house was disinterred by Mr.
Taylor at Mugheir, and the plan of some chambers
was made out at Abu-Shahrein; but these are
hitherto the only specimens which can be confidently assigned to the Chaldæan period. The
house stood on a platform of sundried bricks, paved
on the top with burnt bricks. It was built in the
form of a cross, but with a good deal of irregularity,
every wall being somewhat longer or shorter than
the others. The material used in its construction
was burnt brick, the outer layer imbedded in
bitumen, and the remainder in a cement of mud.
Externally the house was ornamented with perpen-

---

[1] See above, page 90.   [2] *Journal of Asiatic Society*, vol. xv. p. 407.

dicular stepped recesses,[1] while internally the bricks
had often a thin coating of gypsum or enamel, upon
which characters were inscribed. The floors of the
chambers were paved with burnt brick, laid in
bitumen. Two of the doorways were arched, the
arch extending through the whole thickness of the
walls; it was semicircular, and was constructed with
bricks made wedge-shaped for the purpose. A good
deal of charred date-wood was found in the house,
probably the remains of rafters
which had supported the roof.[2]

The chambers at Abu-Shah-
rein were of sun-dried brick,
with an internal covering of fine
plaster, ornamented with paint.
In one the ornamentation consisted of a series of red, black,
and white bands, three inches in
breadth; in another was represented, but very rudely, the
figure of a man holding a bird
on his wrist, with a smaller
figure near him, in red paint.[3]
The favourite external ornamentation for houses seems to have
been by means of coloured cones
in terra cotta, which were imbedded in moist mud or plaster,
and arranged into a variety of
patterns.[4]

Terra cotta cone.   Actual size.

[1] Loftus, *Chaldæa and Susiana,*
p. 133.
[2] *Journal of Asiatic Society,* vol.
xv. pp. 265, 266.
[3] Ibid. p. 409, and p. 410.

[4] Loftus, *Chaldæa and Susiana,*
pp. 188-9. The building discovered
by Mr. Loftus (from which the above
representation is taken) was at Warka, and therefore might perhaps not

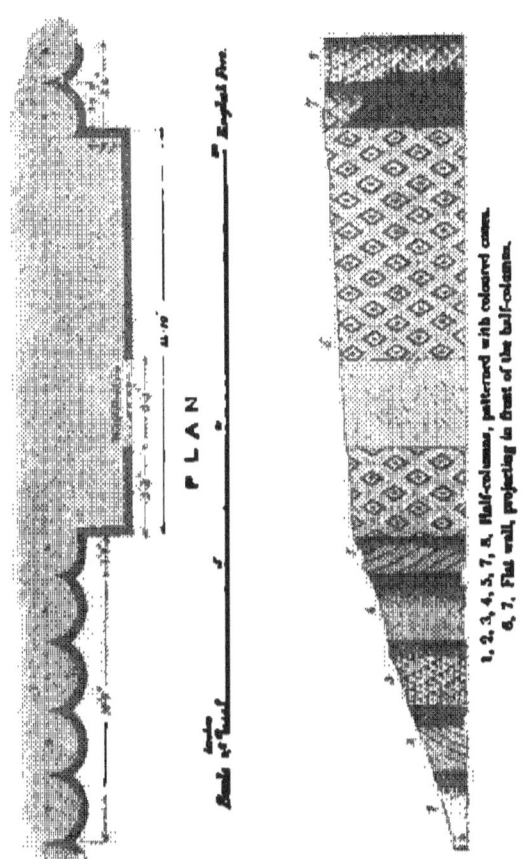

1, 2, 3, 4, 5, 7, 8, Half-columns, patterned with coloured cones.
6, 7, Flat wall, projecting in front of the half-columns.

But little can be said as to the plan on which
houses were built. The walls were generally of vast

in *Chaldæa*. The vast number of   purely Chaldæan ruins, sufficiently
similar cones, however, which occur   indicate the ornamentation to belong
at Abu-Shahrein (*Journal of As. So-*   to the first empire.
ciety, vol. xv. p. 411) and other

thickness, the chambers long and narrow, with the
outer doors opening directly into them. The rooms
ordinarily led into one another, passages being rarely

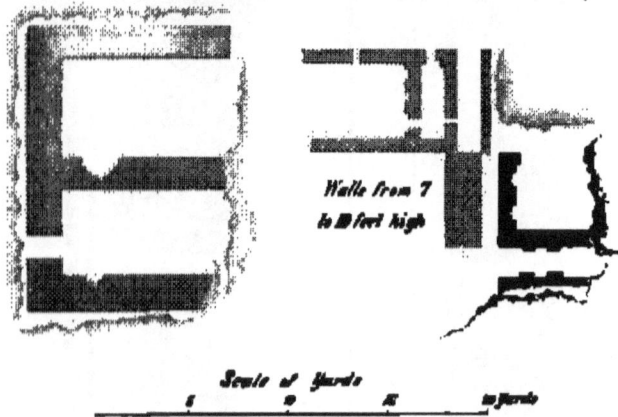

*Walls from 7
to 10 feet high*

Scale of Yards

found. Square recesses, sometimes stepped or den-
tated, were common in the rooms ; and in the
arrangement of these something of symmetry is
observable, as they frequently correspond to or face
each other. The roofs were probably either flat—
beams of palm-wood being stretched across from
wall to wall[5]—or else arched with brick.[6] No indication of windows has been found as yet ; but still
it is thought that the chambers were lighted by
them,[7] only they were placed high, near the ceiling
or roof, and thus do not appear in the existing ruins,

[5] Mr. Taylor found remnants of
these at Mugheir. (*Journal of As.
Soc.* vol. xv. p. 266.)

[6] Mr. Loftus believes that Chaldæan buildings were usually roofed
in this way. (*Chaldæa and Susiana,*
pp. 182, 183.) Mr. Taylor also believes that some of the chambers
which he excavated must have been
domed. (*Journal of As. Soc.* vol. xv.
p. 411.)

[7] Loftus, p. 182.

which consist merely of the lower portion of walls, seldom exceeding the height of seven or eight feet. The doorways, both outer and inner, are towards the sides rather than in the centre of the apartments—a feature common to Chaldæan with Assyrian buildings.

Next to their edifices, the most remarkable of the remains which the Chaldæans have left to after-ages, are their burial-places. While ancient tombs are of very rare occurrence in Assyria and Upper Babylonia, Chaldæa Proper abounds with them. It has been conjectured, with some show of reason, that the Assyrians, in the time of their power, may have made the sacred land of Chaldæa the general deposi-tory of their dead,[*] much in the same way as the Persians even now use Kerbela and Nedjif or Meshed Ali as special cemetery cities, to which thousands of corpses are brought annually.[*] At any rate, the quantity of human relics accumulated upon certain Chaldæan sites is enormous, and seems to be quite beyond what the mere population of the surrounding district could furnish. At Warka, for instance, ex-cepting the triangular space between the three principal ruins, the whole remainder of the platform, the whole space within the walls, and an unknown extent of desert beyond them, are everywhere filled with human bones and sepulchres.[1] In places coffins are piled upon coffins, certainly to the depth of 30, probably to the depth of 60 feet; and for miles on each side of the ruins the traveller walks upon a soil teeming with the relics of ancient, and now probably extinct, races. Sometimes these relics

---

[*] Loftus, p. 190.
[*] Ibid. pp. 64 and 65.
[1] Ibid. p. 199.

manifestly belong to a number of distinct and widely
separate eras; but there are places where it is otherwise. However we may account for it—and no
account has been yet given which is altogether satisfactory—it seems clear, from the comparative homo-
geneousness of the remains in some places, that they
belong to a single race, and if not to a single period,
at any rate to only two, or, at the most, three distinct periods, so that it is no longer very difficult to
distinguish the more ancient from the later relics.[1]
Such is the character of the remains at Mugheir,
which are thought to contain nothing of later date
than the close of the Babylonian period, B.C. 538;[2]
and such is, still more remarkably, the character of
the ruins at Abu-Shahrein and Tel-el-Lahm, which
seem to be entirely, or almost entirely, Chaldæan.
In the following account of the coffins and mode of
burial employed by the early Chaldæans, examples
will be drawn from these places only; since otherwise we should be liable to confound together the
productions of very different ages and peoples.

The tombs to which an archaic character most
certainly attaches are of three kinds—brick vaults,
clay coffins shaped like a dish-cover, and coffins in
the same material, formed of two large jars placed
mouth to mouth, and cemented together with bitumen. The brick vaults are found chiefly at Mugheir. They are seven feet long, three feet seven
inches broad, and five feet high, composed of sun-
dried bricks imbedded in mud, and exhibit a very

---

[1] Position of the relics *in situ*,
character of the tomb or coffin, and
apparent antiquity, or the reverse, of
the enclosed vessels and ornaments,
will commonly determine the age
without much uncertainty.
[2] Loftus, p. 134.

remarkable form and construction of the arch. The side walls of the vaults slope outwards as they ascend; and the arch is formed, like those in Egyptian buildings and Scythian tombs,[4] by each successive layer of bricks, from the point where the arch begins, a little overlapping the last, till the two sides of the roof are brought so near together that the aperture may be closed by a single brick. The floor of the

Brick vault at Mugheir.

vaults was paved with brick similar to that used for the roof and sides; on this floor was commonly spread a matting of reeds, and the body was laid upon the matting. It was commonly turned on its left side, the right arm falling towards the left, and the fingers resting on the edge of a copper bowl, usually placed on the palm of the left hand. The

[4] See the author's *Herodotus*, vol. III. p. 61.

head was pillowed on a single sun-dried brick. Various
articles of ornament and use were interred with each
body, which will be more particularly described hereafter. Food seems often to have been placed in the
tombs, and jars or other drinking vessels are universal.
The brick vaults appear to have been family sepulchres;
they often contain three or four bodies, and in one
case a single vault contained eleven skeletons.[1]

The clay coffins, shaped like a dish-cover, are
among the most curious of the sepulchral remains of
antiquity. On a platform of sun-dried brick is laid a
mat, exactly similar to those in common use among
the Arabs of the country at the present day; and
hereon lies the skeleton, disposed as in the brick
vaults, and surrounded by utensils and ornaments.
Mat, skeleton, and utensils are then concealed by a
huge cover in burnt clay, formed of a single piece,
which is commonly seven feet long, two or three feet
high, and two feet and a half broad at the bottom.
It is rarely that modern potters produce articles of
half the size. Externally the covers have commonly
some slight ornament, such as rims and shallow
indentations, as represented in the sketch (No. 1).
Internally they are plain. Not more than two skeletons have ever been found under a single cover; and
in these cases they were the skeletons of a male and
a female. Children were interred separately, under
covers about half the size of those for adults. Tombs
of this kind commonly occur at some considerable
depth. None were discovered at Mugheir nearer
the surface than seven or eight feet.[2]

The third kind of tomb, common both at Mugheir

[1] *Journal of the Asiatic Society,*   [2] Ibid. p. 269.
vol. xv. pp. 271-274.

No. 1.

No. 2.

a. Sun-dried brick under head.
b. Copper bowl.
c. Small cylinder of meteoric stone; remains of thread going round arm-bone.
d. Pieces of cylindrical meteoric stone.

e. Pieces of bamboo.
f. Jars and utensils for food and water, made of baked clay; remains of date-stones in the shallow dish.

and at Tel-el-Iahm,[1] is almost as eccentric as the preceding. Two large open-mouthed jars (*a* and *b*), shaped like the largest of the water-jars at present in use at Baghdad, are taken, and the body is disposed inside them with the usual accompaniments of dishes, vases, and ornaments. The jars average from two and a half feet to three feet in depth, and have a diameter of about two feet; so that they would readily contain a full-sized corpse if it was slightly bent at

Chaldæan jar-coffin.

the knees. Sometimes the two jars are of equal size, and are simply united at their mouths by a layer of bitumen (*d d*); but more commonly one is slightly larger than the other, and the smaller mouth is inserted into the larger one for a depth of three or four inches, while a coating of bitumen is still applied externally at the juncture. In each coffin there is an air-hole at one extremity (*c*), to allow the escape of the gases generated during decomposition.

Besides the coffins themselves, some other curious features are found in the burial-places. The dead are commonly buried, not underneath the natural surface of the ground, but in extensive artificial mounds, each mound containing a vast number of coffins. The coffins are arranged side by side, often in several layers; and occasionally strips of masonry, crossing each other at right angles, separate each set of coffins from its neighbours. The surface of the mounds is sometimes paved with brick; and a similar pavement often separates the layers of coffins one from another. But the most remarkable feature in the tomb-mounds is their system of drainage. Long

shafts of baked clay extend from the surface of the
mound to its base, composed of a succession of rings
two feet in diameter, and about a foot and a half in
breadth, joined together by thin layers of bitumen.
To give the rings additional strength, the sides have
a slight concave curve (see woodcut, 2 and 3); and,

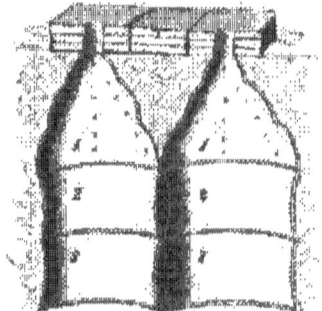

Section of drain.

still further to resist external pressure, the shafts are
filled from bottom to top with a loose mass of broken
pottery. At the top the shaft contracts rapidly by
means of a ring of a peculiar shape (see woodcut, 1);
and above this ring are a series of perforated bricks
leading up to the top of the mound, the surface of
which is so arranged as to conduct the rain-water
into these orifices. For the still more effectual drainage of the mound, the top-piece of the shaft immediately below the perforated bricks, and also the first
rings, are full of small holes to admit any stray
moisture; and besides this, for the space of a foot
every way, the shafts are surrounded with broken
pottery, so that the real diameter of each drain is
as much as four feet.' By these arrangements the

* *Journal of the Asiatic Society*, vol. xv. pp. 298, 299.

piles have been kept perfectly dry; and the consequence is the preservation, to the present day, not
only of the utensils and ornaments placed in the
tombs, but of the very skeletons themselves, which
are seen perfect on opening a tomb, though they
crumble to dust at the first touch.[*]

The skill of the Chaldæans as potters has received
considerable illustration in the foregoing pages. No
ordinary ingenuity was needed to model and bake
the large vases, and still larger covers, which were
the ordinary receptacles of the Chaldæan dead. The
rings and top-pieces of the drainage-shafts also exhibit much skill and knowledge of principles.
Hitherto, however, the reader has not been brought
into contact with any specimens of Chaldæan fictile
art which can be regarded as exhibiting elegance of

Chaldæan vases of the first period.

[*] Ibid. p. 272; Loftus, p. 210.
Mr. Taylor, however, qualifies this
latter statement. "Directly on opening these covers," he says, "were I
to attempt to touch the skulls or
bones, they would fall into dust
almost immediately; but I found,
on exposing them for a few days to
the air, that *they became quite hard,*
and could be handled with impu-
nity." It is to be regretted that
Mr. Taylor did not send any of the
skulls, when thus hardened, to England, as their examination would
have been important towards determining the ethnic character of the
race.

form, or indeed any sense of beauty as distinguished from utility. Such specimens are in fact somewhat scarce, but they are not wholly wanting. Among the vases and drinking-vessels with which the Chaldæan tombs abound, while the majority are characterised by a certain rudeness both of shape and material,[1] we occasionally meet with specimens of a higher character, which would not shrink from a comparison with the ordinary productions of Greek fictile art. A number of these are represented in the woodcut below, which exhibits several forms not hitherto published—some taken from drawings by Mr. Churchill, the artist who accompanied Mr. Loftus on his first journey; others drawn for the present work from vases now in the British Museum.

It is evident that, while the vases of the first group are roughly moulded by the hand, the vases and

Chaldæan vases, drinking-vessels, and amphora of the second period.

---

[1] The vases represented in the cut are in a coarse clay, mixed with chopped straw, which sometimes appears upon the surface.

I 2

Chaldæan lamps of the second period.

lamps of the second have been carefully shaped by
the aid of the potter's wheel. These last are formed
of a far finer clay than the earlier specimens, and
have sometimes a slight glaze upon them which adds
much to their beauty. ·

In a few instances the works of the Chaldæans in
this material belong to mimetic art, of which they
are rude but interesting specimens. Some of the
primitive graves at Senkareh yielded tablets of baked
clay, on which were represented, in low relief, sometimes single figures of men, sometimes groups, sometimes men in combination with animals. A scene in
which a lion is disturbed in his feast off a bullock, by
a man armed with a club and a mace or hatchet, possesses remarkable spirit, and, were it not for the
strange drawing of the lion's uplifted leg, might be
regarded as a very creditable performance. In
another, a lion is represented devouring a prostrate
human being; while a third exhibits a pugilistic
encounter after the most approved fashion of modern
England! It is perhaps uncertain whether these

tablets belong to the Chaldæan or to the Babylonian period; but on the whole their rudeness and simplicity favours the earlier rather than the later date.

The only other works having anything of an artistic character, that can be distinctly assigned to the primitive period, are a certain number of engraved cylinders, some of which are very curious. It is clearly established that the cylinders in question, which are generally of serpentine, meteoric stone, jasper, chalcedony, or other similar substance, were the seals or signets of their possessors, who impressed them upon the moist clay which formed the ordinary material for writing.[1] They are round, or nearly so,[2] and measure from half-an-inch to three inches in length; ordinarily they are about one-third of their length in diameter. A hole is bored through the stone from end to end, so that it could be worn upon a string; and cylinders are found in some of the earliest tombs which have been worn round the wrist in this way.[4] In early times they may have been impressed by the hand; but afterwards it was

Seal-cylinder on metal axis.

[1] Layard, *Nineveh and Babylon*, pp. 603, 600; Rawlinson's *Herodotus*, vol. i. p. 356; Birch's *Ancient Pottery*, vol. i. p. 114.

[2] Sometimes the sides are slightly concave, as in the above representation.

[4] *Journal of Asiatic Society*, vol. xv. p. 271.

common to place them upon a bronze or copper axis
attached to a handle, by means of which they were
rolled across the clay from one end to the other.[1]
The cylinders are frequently unengraved, and this
is most commonly their condition in the primitive
tombs; but there is some very curious evidence, from
which it appears that the art of engraving them was
really known and practised (though doubtless in rare
instances) at a very early date. The signet cylinder
of the monarch who founded the most ancient of the
buildings at Mugheir, Warka, Senkareh, and Niffer,
and who thus stands at the head of the monumental
kings, was in the possession of Sir R. Porter; and
though it is now lost, an engraving made from it is

Signet-cylinder of King Urukh.

preserved in his 'Travels.'[2] From this representation it would appear that the art had already made
considerable progress. The letters of the inscription,

---

[1] Mr. Layard found remains of
the bronze in one specimen. (Nineveh and Babylon, p. 600.) The
representation on p. 117 gives the
probable form of the bronze setting.
[2] Travels in Georgia, Persia, &c.,
vol. ii. pl. 79, fig. 6.

which gives the name of the king and his titles, are
somewhat rudely formed, as they are on the stamped
bricks of the period ;[1] but the figures appear to have
been as well cut, and as flowingly traced, as those of
a much later date.   It is possible that the artist employed by Sir R. Porter has given a flattering representation of his original ; otherwise the conclusion
must be that both mechanical and artistic skill had
reached a very surprising degree of excellence at the
most remote period to which Chaldæan records carry
us back.

It increases the surprise which we naturally feel
at the discovery of such a relic as the cylinder above
represented, to reflect upon the rudeness of the implements with which such results would seem to
have been accomplished.   In the primitive Chaldæan
ruins, the implements which have been discovered

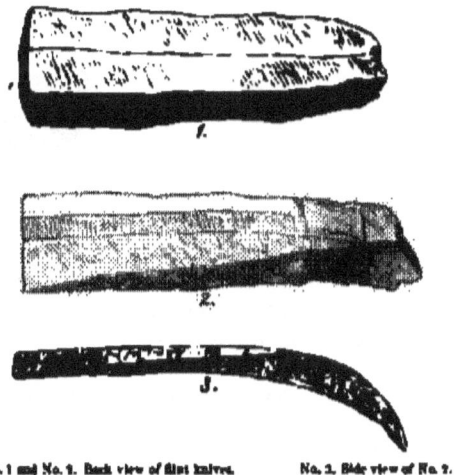

No. 1 and No. 2. Back view of flint knives.   No. 3. Side view of No. 2.

are either in stone or bronze. Iron in the early
times is seemingly unknown, and when it first appears is wrought into ornaments for the person.[*]
Knives of flint or chert, stone hatchets, hammers,
adzes, and nails, are common in the most ancient
mounds, which contain also a number of clay models,

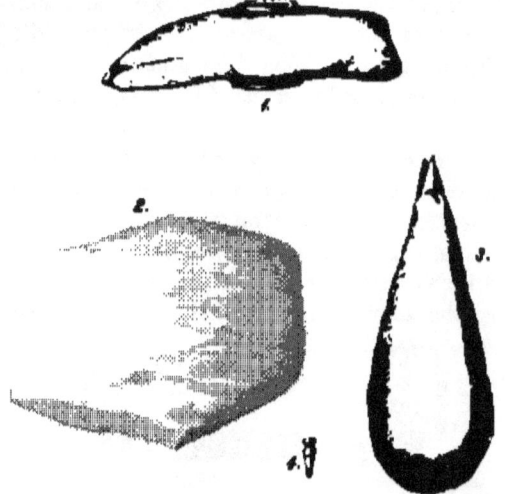

1. Stone hammer.   2. Stone hatchet.   3. Stone adze.   4. Stone nail.

the centres, as it is thought,[*] of moulds into which
molten bronze was run, and also occasionally the
bronze instruments themselves, as (in addition to
spear-heads and arrow-heads) hammers, adzes,
hatchets, knives, and sickles. It will be seen by the

[*] Bangles and rings. (See the
Journal of the Asiatic Society, vol.
xv. p. 415.)

[*] This view was taken by Mr.
Vaux in a paper read by him before
the Society of Antiquaries, January,
1860, which he has kindly put into
my hands. It may be questioned,
perhaps, whether these clay models
are not rather the representatives of
real weapons and implements, buried
in their stead by relatives too poor
to part with the originals.

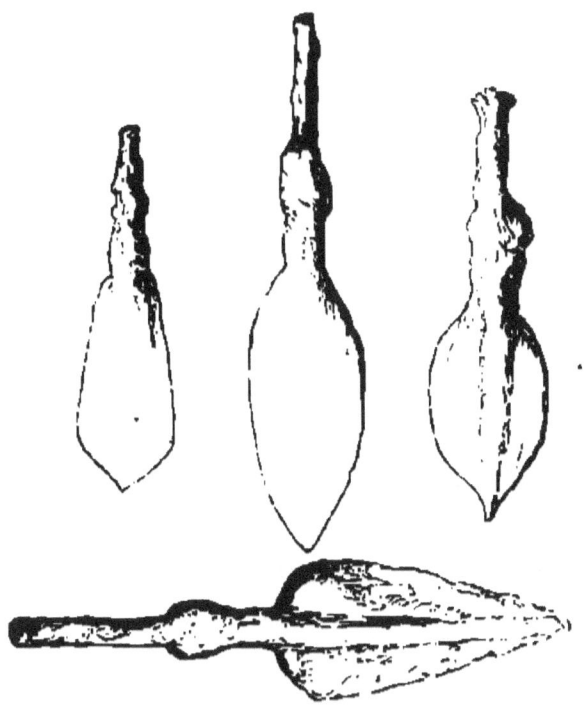

Chaldæan spear and arrow heads.

representations that these instruments are one and
all of a rude and coarse character.   The flint and
stone knives, axes, and hammers, which abound in
all the true Chaldæan mounds, are somewhat more
advanced indeed than those very primitive implements which have been found in the drift; but they
are of a workmanship at least as unskilled as that of
the ordinary stone celts of Western and Northern
Europe, which till the discoveries of M. Perthes were
regarded as the most ancient human remains in our

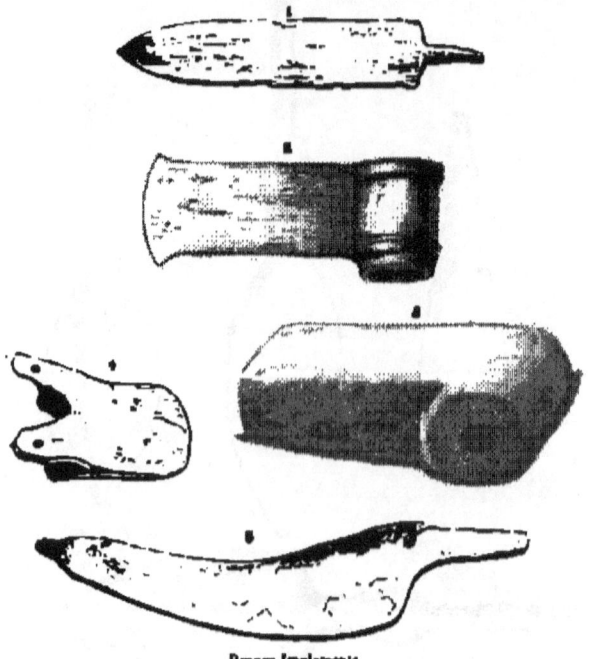

Bronze Implements.

1. Knife.   2. Hatchet.   3. Hammer.   4. Adze.   5. Sickle.

quarter of the globe. They indicate some practical
knowledge of the cleavage of silicious rocks, but
they show no power of producing even such finish
as the celts frequently exhibit. In one case only has
a flint instrument been discovered perfectly regular
in form, and presenting a sharp angular exactness.
The instrument, which is figured below, is a sort of

Flint Implement.

long, open parallelogram. Its use is uncertain ; but, according to a reasonable conjecture,[a] it may have been designed for impressing characters upon the moist clay of tablets and cylinders—a purpose for which it is excellently fitted.

The metallurgy of the Chaldæans, though indicative of a higher state of civilization and a greater knowledge of the useful arts than their stone weapons, is still of a somewhat rude character, and indicates a nation but just emerging out of an almost barbaric simplicity. Metal seems to be scarce, and not many kinds are found. There is no silver, zinc, or platinum; but only gold, copper, tin, lead, and iron. Gold is found in beads, ear-rings, and other

Ear-rings.

ornaments,[b] which are in some instances of a fashion that is not inelegant.[c] Copper occurs pure, but is more often hardened by means of an alloy of tin, whereby it becomes bronze, and is rendered suitable for implements and weapons.[d] Lead is rare, occurring

[a] *Journal of Asiatic Society*, vol. xv. p. 411.

[b] As fillets for the head. (Ibid. p. 273.)

[c] These ear-rings are given as Chaldæan, because they were found at Niffer among remains thought to be purely Chaldæan. At the same time it must be allowed that they very much resemble the Greek "Cupid ear-rings," of which there are so many in the British Museum.

[d] See above, pages 121 and 122.

only in a very few specimens, as in one jar or bottle,
and in what seems to be a portion of a pipe, brought
by Mr. Loftus from Mugheir. Iron, as already ob-

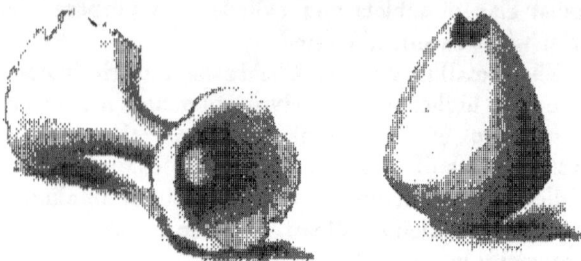

Leaden pipe and jar.

served, is extremely uncommon; and, when it occurs,
is chiefly used for the rings and bangles which seem
to have been among the favourite adornments of the

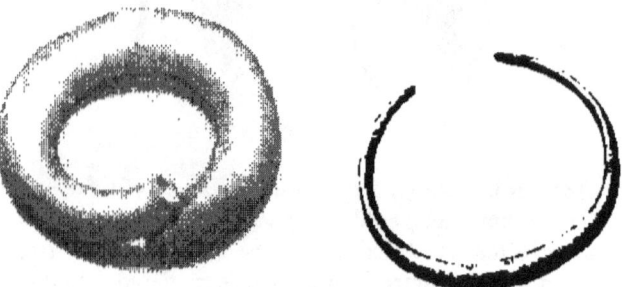

Bronze bangles.

people. Bronze is, however, even for these, the more
common material. It is sometimes wrought into thin
and elegant shapes, tapering to a point at either extremity; sometimes the form into which it is cast is
coarse and massive, resembling a solid bar twisted
into a rude circle. For all ordinary purposes of

utility it is the common metal used. A bronze or copper bowl is found in almost every tomb; bronze bolts remain in the pieces of marble used for tesselating;[3] bronze rings sometimes strengthen the cones used for ornamenting walls;[4] bronze weapons and instruments are, as we have seen, common; and in the same material have been found chains, nails, toe- and finger-rings, armlets, bracelets, and fishhooks.

No long or detailed account can be given of the textile fabrics of the ancient Chaldæans; but there is reason to believe that this was a branch of industry in which they particularly excelled. We know that as early as the time of Joshua a Babylonian garment had been imported into Palestine, and was of so rare a beauty as to attract the covetous regards of Achan, in common with certain large masses of the precious metals.[5] The very ancient cylinder figured above,[6] must belong to a time at least five or six centuries earlier; upon it we observe flounced and fringed garments, delicately striped, and indicative apparently of an advanced state of textile manufacture. Recent researches do not throw much light on this subject. The frail materials of which human apparel is composed can only under peculiar circumstances resist the destructive power of thirty or forty centuries; and consequently we have but few traces of the actual fabrics in use among the primitive people. Pieces of *linen* are said to have been found attaching to some

---

[3] See the small woodcut on page 103.
[4] See page 105; where a representation of this mode of ornamenting walls is given; and for the use of bronze rings, see *Journal of the Asiatic Society*, vol. xv. p. 411.
[5] Josh. vii. 21.   [6] See page 118.

of the skeletons in the tombs;[1] and the sun-dried
brick which supports the head is sometimes covered
with the remains of a " tasselled cushion of tapestry;"[2]
but otherwise we are without direct evidence either
as to the material in use, or as to the character of the
fabric. In later times Babylon was especially celebrated for its robes and its carpets.[3] Such evidence as
we have would seem to make it probable that both
manufactures had attained to considerable excellence
in Chaldæan times.

The only sciences in which the early Chaldæans
can at present be proved to have excelled are the
cognate ones of arithmetic and astronomy. On the
broad and monotonous plains of Lower Mesopotamia,
where the earth has little to suggest thought or please
by variety, the "variegated heaven," ever changing
with the hours and with the seasons, would early attract attention, while the clear sky, dry atmosphere,
and level horizon would afford facilities for observations, so soon as the idea of them suggested itself to
the minds of the inhabitants. The "Chaldæan learning" of a later age[4] appears to have been originated,
in all its branches, by the primitive people; in whose
language it continued to be written even in Semitic
times.

We are informed by Simplicius that Callisthenes,
who accompanied Alexander to Babylon, sent to
Aristotle from that capital a series of astronomical
observations, which he had found preserved there,

---

[1] Journal of the Asiatic Society,
vol. xv. p. 271.
[2] Ibid. l. s. c.

[3] Arrian. Exp. Alex. vi. 29; Athe-
næus, Deipnosoph. v. p. 107.
[4] Dan. i. 4.

extending back to a period of 1903 years from
Alexander's conquest of the city.[1] Epigenes related,
that these observations were recorded upon tablets of
baked clay,[2] which is quite in accordance with all we
know of the literary habits of the people. They must
have extended, according to Simplicius, as far back
as B.C. 2234, and would therefore seem to have been
commenced and carried on for many centuries by the
primitive Chaldæan people. We have no means of
determining their exact nature or value, as none
of them have been preserved to us: no doubt they
were at first extremely simple; but we have every
reason to conclude that they were of a real and substantial character. There is nothing fanciful, or (so
to speak) astrological, in the early astronomy of the
Babylonians. Their careful emplacement of their
chief buildings,[3] which were probably used from the
earliest times for astronomical purposes,[4] their invention of different kinds of dials,[5] and their division of
the day into those hours which we still use,[6] are all
solid, though not perhaps very brilliant, achievements. It was only in later times that the Chaldæans
were fairly taxed with imposture and charlatanism;

---

[1] This passage has often been referred to, but rarely quoted. Simplicius argues that the earlier writers
on astronomy have less value than
the later ones :—διὰ τὸ μήπω τὰς ὑπὸ
Καλλισθένους ἐκ Βαβυλῶνος πεμφθεί-
σας παρατηρήσεις ἀφικέσθαι εἰς τὴν
Ἑλλάδα, τοῦ Ἀριστοτέλους τοῦτο
ἐπισκήψαντος αὐτῷ· ἅστινας ἀγγείταις
ὁ Πορφύριος χιλίων ἐτῶν εἶναι καὶ
ἑπτακοσίων τριῶν, μέχρι τῶν χρόνων
Ἀλεξάνδρου τοῦ Μακεδόνος σωζομέ-
νας.

[2] Plin. H. N. vii. 56. " Epigenes
apud Babylonios DCCXX annorum ob-
servationes siderum coctilibus laterculis inscriptas docet."

[3] See above, page 96.

[4] This is distinctly asserted of the
great temple of Belus by Diodorus
(ii. 9, § 4). The careful emplacement of the earliest temples makes
it probable that they were applied to
similar uses.

[5] Herod. ii. 109.

[6] Ibid.

in the early ages they seem to have really deserved
the eulogy bestowed on them by Cicero.[*]

It may have been the astronomical knowledge of
the Chaldeans which gave them the confidence to
adventure on important voyages. Scripture tells us
of the later people, that " their cry was in the ships;"[*]
and the early inscriptions not only make frequent
mention of the "ships of Ur," but by connecting
these vessels with those of Ethiopia[*] seem to imply
that they were navigated to considerable distances.
Unfortunately we possess no materials from which
to form any idea either of the make and character
of the Chaldean vessels, or, of the nature of the
trade in which they were employed.   We may
perhaps assume that at first they were either canoes
hollowed out of a palm-trunk, or reed fabrics made
water-tight by a coating of bitumen.   The Chaldee
trading operations lay, no doubt, chiefly in the Persian
Gulf;[*] but it is quite possible that even in very
early times they were not confined to this sheltered
basin.   The gold, which was so lavishly used in decoration,[*] could only have been obtained in the necessary quantities from Africa or India; and it is
therefore probable that one, if not both, of these
countries was visited by the Chaldean traders.

Astronomical investigations could not be conducted
without a fair proficiency in the science of number.
It would be reasonable to conclude, from the admitted
character of the Chaldeans as astronomers, that they
were familiar with most arithmetical processes, even

[*] See the passage prefixed as a
motto to this chapter (supra, p. ++).
[*] Isaiah xliii. 14.
[*] Sir H. Rawlinson in the *Journal*

of the *Asiatic Soc.*, vol. xxvii. p. 185.
[*] See Heeren's *Asiatic Nations*,
vol. ii. p. 220, E. T.
[*] Supra, page 100.

had we no evidence upon the subject. Evidence
however, to a certain extent, does exist. On a tablet
found at Senkareh, and belonging *probably* to an early
period, a table of squares is given, correctly calculated from one to sixty.[1] The system of notation,
which is here used, is very curious. Berosus[2] informs
us that, in their computations of time, the Chaldæans
employed an alternate sexagesimal and centesimal
notation, reckoning the years by the *soss*, the *ner*, and
the *sar*—the *soss* being a term of 60 years, the *ner*
one of 600, and the *sar* one of 3600 (or 60 *sosses*).
It appears from the Senkareh monument, that they
occasionally pursued the same practice in mere numerical calculations, as will be evident from the following extract :—

EXTRACT from SENKAREH TABLE of SQUARES.

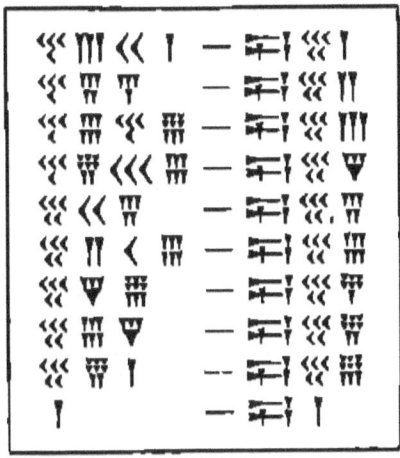

[1] See *Journal of the Asiatic Soc.*, vol. xv. p. 218; and compare Laftus's *Chaldæa and Susiana*, p. 256.

[2] Ap. Euseb. *Chron. Can.* i. t. p. 5, ed. Mai.

In Arabic numerals this table may be expressed as follows :—

Soss.	Units.		
43	21	=	51²
45	4	=	52²
46	49	=	53²
48	36	=	54²
50	25	=	55²
52	16	=	56²
54	9	=	57²
56	4	=	58²
58	1	=	59²
60	0	=	60²

The calculation is in every case correct; and the notation is by means of two signs—the simple wedge], and the arrowhead ⟨; the wedge representing the unit, the soss (60), and the sar (3600), while the arrowhead expresses the decades of each series, or the numbers 10 and 600.[*] The notation is cumbrous, but scarcely more so than that of the Romans. It would be awkward to use, from the paucity in the number of signs, which could scarcely fail to give rise to confusion,—more especially as it does not appear that there was any way of expressing a cypher. It is not probable that at any time it was the notation in ordinary use. Numbers were commonly expressed in a manner not unlike the Roman, as will be seen by the subjoined table. One, ten, a hundred, and a thousand had distinct signs. Fifty had the

---

[*] This is the ner of Berosus, which was a period of 600 years. Compare with this notation that of the Mexicans (Prescott, *History of the Conquest of Mexico*, vol. I. p. 91), where, besides the unit, the only numbers which had distinct signs were 20, 400, and 8000.

same sign as the unit—a simple wedge. The other
numbers were composed from these elements.

1	𒁹	11	𒌋𒁹	100	𒁹 𒈨
2	𒈫	12	𒌋𒈫	200	𒈫 𒈨
3	𒐈	20	𒎙	300	𒐈 𒈨
4	𒐉	30	𒌍	400	𒐉 𒈨
5	𒐋	40	𒐏	500	𒐋 𒈨
6	𒐌	50	𒐐	600	𒐌 𒈨
7	𒐌	60	𒐕	700	𒐌 𒈨
8	𒐌	70	𒐖	800	𒐌 𒈨
9	𒐌	80	𒐗	900	𒐌 𒈨
10	𒌋	90	𒐘	1000	𒁹 𒌋𒈨

CHAPTER VI.

MANNERS AND CUSTOMS.

CHALDÆA, unlike Egypt, has preserved to our day but few records of the private or domestic life of its inhabitants. Beyond the funereal customs, to which reference was made in the last chapter,[1] we can obtain from the monuments but a very scanty account of their general mode of life, manners, and usages. Some attempt, however, must be made to throw together the few points of this nature on which we have obtained any light from recent researches in Mesopotamia.

The ordinary dress of the common people among the Chaldæans seems to have consisted of a single garment, a short tunic, tied round the waist, and reaching thence to the knees, a costume very similar to that worn by the Madan Arabs at the present day.[2] To this may sometimes have been added an *abba*, or cloak, thrown over the shoulders, and falling below the tunic, about half-way down the calf of the leg.[3] The material of the former we may perhaps presume to have been linen, which best suits the climate, and is

---

[1] See above, pp. 107-114.

[2] Mr. Loftus makes this compari-son (*Chaldæa and Susiana*, p. 257). For representations of the costume are Loftus, pp. 257, 258, 260, and Rich (*Second Memoir*, pl. iii. fig. 13).

[3] See above, p. 116.

a material found in the ancient tombs.[1] The outer
cloak was most likely of woollen, and served to
protect hunters and others against the occasional
inclemency of the air. The feet were unprotected
by either shoes or sandals; on the head was worn a
skull-cap, or else a band of camel's hair[2]—the germ
of the turban which has now become universal
throughout the East.

The costume of the richer classes was more elaborate. A high mitre, of a very pe-
culiar appearance,[3] or else a low cap,
ornamented with two curved horns,
covered the head. The neck and arms
were bare. The chief garment was a
long gown or robe, extending from the
neck to the feet, commonly either striped
or flounced, or both; and sometimes
also adorned with fringe. This robe,
which was scanty according to modern notions, appears not to have been fastened by any girdle or
cincture round the waist, but to have
been kept in place by passing over
one shoulder, a slit or hole being
made for the arm on one side of
the dress only. In some cases the
upper part of the dress seems to
have been detached from the lower,
and to have formed a sort of
jacket, which reached about to the
hips.

---

[1] *Asiatic Journal*, vol. xv. p. 271.; given, page 118.
[2] Loftus, p. 259. Compare the central standing figure in the cy-linder of which a representation is [3] See the same cylinder, where two of the three standing figures wear the mitre in question.

The beard was commonly worn straight and long, not in crisp curls, as by the Assyrians. The hair was also worn long, either gathered together into a club behind the head, or depending in long spiral curls on either side the face and down the back. Ornaments were much affected, especially by the women. Bronze and iron bangles and armlets, bracelets of rings or beads, earrings, and rings for the toes, are common in the tombs, and few female skeletons are without them. The material of the ornaments is generally of small value. Many of the rings are formed by grinding down a small kind of shell;[1] the others are of bronze or iron. Agate beads, however, are not uncommon, and gold beads have been found in a few tombs, as well as some other small ornaments in the same material. The men seem to have carried generally an engraved cylinder in agate or other hard stone, which was used as a seal or signet, and was probably worn round the wrist.[2] Sometimes rings,[3] and even bracelets,[4] formed also a part of their adornment. The latter were occasionally in gold—they consisted of bands or fillets of the pure beaten metal, and were as much as an inch in breadth.

The food of the early Chaldæans consisted probably of the various esculents which have already been mentioned as products of the territory.[5] The chief support, however, of the mass of the population was, beyond a doubt, the dates, which still form the main

---

[1] Taylor in the *Journal of the Asiatic Society*, vol. xv. p. 272.

[2] At least this is the position which the signet cylinder always occupies in the tombs. (*Asiatic Journal*, vol. xv. p. 271.)

[3] Ibid. p. 415.

[4] See the sitting figure in the cylinder, page 119; and compare *As. Journ.* vol. xv. p. 273.

[5] See above, pp. 44, 45.

sustenance of those who inhabit the country. It is
clear that in Babylonia, as in Scythia,[3] the practice
existed of burying with a man a quantity of the food
to which he had been accustomed during life. In the
Chaldæan sepulchres a number of dishes are always
ranged round the skeleton, containing the *viaticum* of
the deceased person, and in these dishes are almost
invariably found a number of date-stones. They
are most commonly unaccompanied by any traces of
other kinds of food; occasionally, however, besides
date-stones, the bones of fish and of chickens have
been discovered, from which we may conclude that
those animals were eaten, at any rate by the upper
classes. Herodotus[4] tells us that in his day three
tribes of Babylonians subsisted on fish alone; and
the present inhabitants of Lower Mesopotamia make
it a principal article of their diet.[5] The rivers and
the marshes produce it in great abundance, while the
sea is also at hand, if the fresh-water supply should
fail. Carp and barbel are the principal fresh-water
sorts, and of these the former grows to a very great
size in the Euphrates. An early tablet represents a
man carrying a large fish by the head, which may
be a carp, though the species can scarcely be identified. There is evidence that the wild-boar was also
eaten by the primitive people; for Mr. Loftus found
a jaw of this animal, with the tusk still remaining,
lying in a shallow clay dish in one of the tombs.[6]
Perhaps we may be justified in concluding, from the
comparative rarity of any remains of animal food in

[3] Herod. iv. 71 (Author's Translation, vol. iii. pp. 61-63).
[4] Ibid. i. 200.
[5] Layard, *Nineveh and Babylon*,
ch. xxiv. p. 567.
[6] *Journal of the Asiatic Society*,
vol. xv. p. 272, note [1].

the early sepulchres, that the primitive Chaldæans subsisted *chiefly* on vegetable productions. The variety and excellence of such esculents are prominently put forward by Berosus in his account of the original condition of the country;[1] and they still form the principal support of those who now inhabit it.

We are told that Nimrod was "a mighty hunter before the Lord;"[2] and it is evident, from the account already given of the animals indigenous in Lower Mesopotamia,[3] that there was abundant room for the display of a sportsman's skill and daring when men first settled in that region. The Senkareh tablets show the boldness and voracity of the Chaldæan lion, which not only levied contributions on the settlers' cattle,[4] but occasionally ventured to attack man himself. We have not as yet any hunting scenes belonging to these early times; but there can be little doubt that the bow was the chief weapon used against the king of beasts, whose assailants commonly prefer remaining at a respectful distance from him.[5] The wild-boar may have been hunted in the same way, or he may have been attacked with the spear—a weapon equally well known with the bow to the early settlers.[6] Fish were certainly taken with the hook; for fish-hooks have been found in the tombs;[7] but probably they were also captured in nets, which are among the earliest of human inventions.[8]

---

[1] See the *Fragmenta Hist. Græc.* vol. ii. p. 496; Fr. 1, § 2.
[2] Gen. x. 9.
[3] See above, ch. ii. p. 49.
[4] See Loftus, *Chaldæa and Susiana,* p. 258.
[5] Ibid. ch. xx. p. 259.
[6] For representations of spearheads, vide supra, page 121.

[7] *Journal of Asiatic Society,* vol. xv. p. 272, note [4].
[8] See Wilkinson, *Ancient Egyptians,* 1st Series, vol. ii. p. 21; vol. iii. p. 55; and compare Sophocl. *Antig.* 347, where the invention of nets is united with that of ships, agriculture, and language.

A considerable portion of the primitive population must have been engaged in maritime pursuits. In the earliest inscriptions we find constant mention of the "ships of Ur," which appear to have traded with Ethiopia—a country whence may have been derived the gold, which—as has been already shown —was so largely used by the Chaldæans in ornamentation.[6] It would be interesting could we regard it as proved, that they traded also with the Indian peninsula; but the "rough logs of wood, *apparently teak*," which Mr. Taylor discovered in the great temple at Mugheir,[7] belong more probably to the time of its repair by Nabonidus than to that of its original construction by a Chaldæan monarch. The Sea-god was one of the chief objects of veneration at Ur and elsewhere; and Berosus appears to have preserved an authentic tradition, where he makes the primitive people of the country derive their arts and civilization from "the Red Sea."[8] Even if their commercial dealings did not bring them into contact with any more advanced people, they must have increased the intelligence, as well as the material resources, of those employed in them, and so have advanced their civilization.

Such are the few conclusions concerning the manners of the Chaldæans which alone we seem to have any right to form with our present means of information.

---

[6] See above, p. 103.

[7] *Journal of the Asiatic Society*, vol. xv. p. 264.

[8] *Fragm. Hist. Græc.* i. s. c. The "Red Sea" of Berosus, like that of Herodotus, is not our Red Sea, but the sea which washes the south of Asia, including both the Indian Ocean and the Persian Gulf. (See Herod. i. 1; Author's Translation, vol. i. p. 153, note [8].)

CHAPTER VII.

———

RELIGION.

'Ἀποτιλίσαι δὲ τὸν Βῆλον καὶ ἄστρα, καὶ ἥλιον, καὶ σελήνην, καὶ τοὺς πέντε πλανήτας.—BEROS. ap. Syncell. p. 58.

THE religion of the Chaldæans, from the very earliest times to which the monuments carry us back,
was, in its outward aspect, a polytheism of a very
elaborate character. It is quite possible that there
may have been esoteric explanations, known to the
priests and the more learned, which, resolving the
personages of the Pantheon into the powers of
nature, reconciled the apparent multiplicity of gods
with monotheism, or even with atheism.[1] So far,
however, as outward appearances were concerned, the
worship was grossly polytheistic. Various deities,
whom it was not considered at all necessary to trace
to a single stock, divided the allegiance of the people,
and even of the kings, who regarded with equal
respect, and glorified with equally exalted epithets,

———

[1] It appears from Eusebius (*Chron.
Can.* pars i. c. li.) and Syncellus
(*Chronograph.* vol. i. pp. 50-53) that
Berosus at any rate gave this turn to
the Babylonian mythology. What is
commonly reported of Pythagoras,
Democritus, and others, who are said
to have drawn their philosophies
from Chaldæan sources, would seem
to show that there was really such
an esoteric doctrine as is suggested
in the text. We cannot tell, however, which more nearly represented
it—the monotheism of the Samian,
or the atheism of the Abderite phi-
losopher.

some fifteen or sixteen personages. Next to these principal gods were a far more numerous assemblage of inferior or secondary divinities, less often mentioned, and regarded as less worthy of honour, but still recognised generally through the country. Finally, the Pantheon contained a host of mere local gods or genii, every town and almost every village in Babylonia being under the protection of its own particular divinity.

It will be impossible to give a complete account of this vast and complicated system. The subject is still but partially worked out by cuneiform scholars; the difficulties in the way of understanding it are great; and in many portions to which special attention has been paid it is strangely perplexing and bewildering.[1] All that will be attempted in the present place is to convey an idea of the general character of the Chaldæan religion, and to give some information with regard to the principal deities.

In the first place, it must be noticed that the religion was to a certain extent *astral*. The heaven itself, the sun, the moon, and the five planets, have each their representative in the Chaldæan Pantheon among the chief objects of worship. At the same time it is to be observed that the astral element is not universal, but partial; and that, even where it has place, it is but one aspect of the mythology, not by any means its full and complete exposition. The Chaldæan religion even here is far from being mere Sabæanism—the simple worship of the "host of heaven." The æther, the sun, the moon, and still

---

[1] See the Essay of Sir H. Rawlinson in the author's *Herodotus*, vol. i. p. 585; from which most of the views contained in this chapter are taken.

more the five planetary gods, are something above
and beyond those parts of nature. Like the classical Apollo and Diana, Mars and Venus, they are
real persons, with a life and a history, a power and
an influence, which no ingenuity can translate into a
metaphorical representation of phenomena attaching
to the air and to the heavenly bodies. It is doubtful,
indeed, whether this class of gods are really of astronomical origin, and not rather primitive deities,
whose characters and attributes were, to a great
extent, fixed and settled before the notion arose of
connecting them with certain parts of nature. Occasionally they seem to represent heroes rather than
celestial bodies; and they have all attributes quite
distinct from their physical or astronomical character.

Secondly, the striking resemblance of the Chaldæan system to that of the Classical Mythology
seems worthy of particular attention. This resemblance is too general, and too close in some respects,
to allow of the supposition that mere accident has
produced the coincidence. In the Pantheons of
Greece and Rome, and in that of Chaldæa, the same
general grouping is to be recognised; the same genealogical succession is not unfrequently to be traced;
and in some cases even the familiar names and
titles of classical divinities admit of the most curious
illustration and explanation from Chaldæan sources.
We can scarcely doubt but that, in some way or
other, there was a communication of beliefs—a passage in very early times, from the shores of the
Persian Gulf to the lands washed by the Mediterranean, of mythological notions and ideas. It is a
probable conjecture[1] that "among the primitive

[1] Sir H. Rawlinson, in the above-quoted Essay, p. 586.

tribes who dwelt on the Tigris and Euphrates, when
the cuneiform alphabet was invented and when such
writing was first applied to the purposes of religion,
a Scythic or Scytho-Arian race existed, who subsequently migrated to Europe, and brought with them
those mythical traditions, which as objects of popular
belief, had been mixed up in the nascent literature
of their native country," and that these traditions
were passed on to the classical nations, who were in
part descended from this Scythic or Scytho-Arian
people.[4]

The grouping of the principal Chaldæan deities is
as follows. At the head of the Pantheon stands a
god, Il or Ra, of whom but little is known. Next
to him is a Triad, *Ana*, *Bil* or *Belus*, and *Hea* or
Hoa, who correspond closely to the classical Pluto,
Jupiter, and Neptune. Each of these is accompanied
by a female principle or wife,—*Ana* by *Anat*, *Bil*
(or *Bel*) by *Mulita* or Beltis, and *Hea* or *Hoa* by
Davkina. Then follows a further Triad, consisting
of *Sin* or *Hurki*, the Moon-god ; *San* or *Sansi*, the
Sun ; and *Vul*,[5] the god of the atmosphere. The
members of this Triad are again accompanied by
female powers or wives,—*Vul* by a goddess called
Shala or *Tala*, *San* (the Sun) by *Gula* or *Anunit*,
and *Hurki* (the Moon) by a goddess whose name is

---

[4] It is now generally allowed that
a Scythic or Turanian race was the
first to people Europe. Of this race
we have still remnants in the Bas-
ques, Finns, Laps, and Esths or Estho-
nians upon the Baltic. The Etrus-
cans in Italy are perhaps of the
same stock. In Greece they probably
blended with the Pelasgi (Arians),
as they did also with the Celts in
several countries. The "lake-dwell-
ings" of Europe may be with great
probability assigned to them ; and
the flint-weapons in the drift are
perhaps traces of their burial-grounds.

[5] This name is very doubtful.
Mr. Fox Talbot renders it by Yem ;
M. Oppert by Ao ; Dr. Hincks by
Iv or Iva.

wholly uncertain, but whose common title is " the great lady." Such are the gods at the head of the Pantheon. Next in order to them we find a group of five minor deities, the representatives of the five planets,—Nin or Ninip (Saturn), Merodach (Jupiter), Nergal (Mars), Ishtar (Venus), and Nebo (Mercury). These together constitute what we have called the *principal* gods; after them are to be placed the numerous divinities of the second and third order.

These principal gods do not appear to have been connected, like the Egyptian and the classical divinities,[*] into a single genealogical scheme: yet still a certain amount of *relationship* was considered to exist among them. Ana and Bel, for instance, were brothers, the sons of Il or Ra; Vul was son of Ana; Hurki, the Moon-god, of Bel; Nebo and Merodach were sons of Hea or Hoa. Many deities, however, are without parentage, as not only Il or Ra, but Hea, San (the Sun), Ishtar, and Nergal. Sometimes the relationship alleged is confused, and even contradictory, as in the case of Nin or Ninip, who is at one time the son, at another the father of Bel, and who is at once the son and the husband of Beltis. It is evident that the genealogical aspect is not that upon which much stress is intended to be laid, or which is looked upon as having much reality. The great gods are viewed habitually rather as a hierarchy of co-equal powers, than as united by ties implying on the one hand pre-eminence and on the other subordination.

---

[*] These schemes themselves were probably not genealogical at first. In their genealogical shape they were an arrangement given after a while to separate and independent deities recognised in different places by distinct communities, or even by distinct races. (See Bunsen's *Egypt*, vol. iv. p. 66, B. Engl. Transl.)

We may now consider briefly the characters and attributes of the several deities, so far as they can be made out, either from the native records, or from classical tradition. And first, concerning the god who stands in some sense at the head of the Chaldaean Pantheon,

IL or RA.

The form *Ra* represents probably the native Chaldaean name of this deity, while *Il* is the Semitic equivalent. *Il*, of course, is but a variant of *El* (אל), the root of the well-known Biblical *Elohim* (אלהים) as well as of the Arabic *Allah*. It is this name which Diodorus represents under the form of *Elus* (Ἦλος),[1] and Sanchoniathon, or rather Philo-Byblius, under that of Elus (Ἦλος) or *Ilus* (Ἶλος).[2] The meaning of the word is simply "God," or perhaps "the god" emphatically. *Ra*, the Cushite equivalent, must be considered to have had the same force originally, though in Egypt it received a special application to the sun, and became the proper name of that particular deity. The word is lost in the modern Ethiopic. It formed an element in the native name of Babylon, which was *Ka-ra*, the Cushite equivalent of the Semitic *Bab-il*, an expression signifying "the gate of God."

Ra is a god with few peculiar attributes. He is a sort of fount and origin of deity, too remote from man to be much worshipped or to excite any warm interest. There is no evidence of his having had

---

[1] See Diod. Sic. ii. 30, § 3, where, however, there is a corrupt reading, the word Ἦλος being most absurdly replaced by Ἴλιον.

[2] See his fragments in Müller's *Fragm. Hist. Graec.* vol. iii. pp. 567 and 571; Fr. 2, § 14, and Fr. 6.

any temple in Chaldæa during the early times. A belief in his existence is implied rather than expressed in inscriptions of the primitive kings, where the Moon-god is said to be "brother's son of Ana, and eldest son of Bil, or Belus." We gather from this, that Bel and Ana were considered to have a common father; and later documents sufficiently indicate that that common father was Il or Ra. We must conclude from the name *Babil*, that Babylon was originally under his protection, though the god specially worshipped in the great temple there seems to have been in early times Bel, and in later times Merodach. The identification of the Chaldæan Il or Ra with Saturn, which Diodorus makes,[*] and which may seem to derive some confirmation from Philo-Byblius,[†] is certainly incorrect, so far as the planet Saturn, which Diodorus especially mentions, is concerned; but it may be regarded as having a basis of truth, inasmuch as Saturn was in one sense the chief of the gods, and was the father of Jupiter and Pluto, as Ra was of Bil and Ana.

ANA.

Ana, like *Il* and *Ra*, is thought to have been a word originally signifying "God," in the highest sense. The root occurs probably in the Annedôtus and Oannes of Berosus,[‡] as well as in Philo-Byblius's

---

[*] Loc. sup. cit. Ἴδιῳ τὸν ὑπὸ τῶν Ἑλλήνων Κρόνον ὀνομαζόμενον καλοῦσιν "Ἥλου.

[†] Κρόνος τοίνυν, ὃν οἱ Φοίνικες Ἴλον ἐπονομαγορεύουσι, βασιλεὺων τῆς χώρης, καὶ ὕστερον μετὰ τὴν τοῦ βίου τελευτὴν εἰς τὸν τοῦ Κρόνου ἀστέρα καθιερωθείς, κ.τ.λ. This, however,

professes to be Phœnician and not Babylonian mythology.

[‡] Fr. 1, § 3 and Fr. 6. Annedôtus (Ἀννήδωτος) is (perhaps) "given by Ana," or "given by God." Oannes is probably Hoa-ana; or "the god, Hoa."

Anobret.[3] In its origin it is probably Cushite; but
it was adopted by the Assyrians, who inflected the
word (which was indeclinable in the Chaldæan
tongue), making the nominative *Anu*, the genitive
Ani, and the accusative *Ana*.

Ana is the head of the first Triad, which follows immediately after the obscure god Ra. His position is
well marked by Damascius,[4] who gives the three gods,
Anus, Illinus, and Aüs, as next in succession to the
primeval pair, Assorus and Missara. He corresponds
in many respects to the classical Hades or Pluto,
who, like him, heads the triad to which he belongs.[5]
His epithets are chiefly such as mark priority and
antiquity. He is called "the old Ana," "the
original chief," perhaps in one place "the father of
the gods," and also "the Lord of spirits and demons."
Again, he bears a number of titles which serve to
connect him with the infernal regions. He is "the
king of. the lower world," the "Lord of darkness"
or "death," "the ruler of the far-off city," and the
like. The chief seat of his worship is *Huruk* or
Erech — the modern Warka — which becomes the
favourite Chaldæan burying city, as being under his
protection. There are some grounds for thinking
that one of his names was *Dis*.[6] If this was indeed
so, it would seem to follow, almost beyond a doubt,
that Dis, the lord of Orcus in Roman mythology,

---

[3] Fr. 6. Anobret ('Αναβρέτ) signifies "beloved by Ana."

[4] Damasc. *De Princip.* 125.

[5] Hesiod, *Theogon.* 455-457; Apollod. *Bibliothec.* I. 1, § 5, 6.

[6] A single wedge ▼, which according to Chaldæan numeration represents the number 60 (supra, p. 120),
is emblematic of the god Ana on the
notation tablets; and, as would be
expected from this fact, *Ana* is one
of the phonetic powers of ▼. Another of its powers is *Dis*; and hence
the conclusion is drawn that Dis was
probably another name of Ana. (See
the Essay of Sir H. Rawlinson in
the author's *Herodotus*, vol. i. p.
592.)

must have been a reminiscence brought from the East—a lingering recollection of *Dis* or Ana, patron god of Erech ('Ορέχ of the LXX.), the great city of the dead, the necropolis of Lower Babylonia. Further, curiously enough, we have, in connexion with this god, an illustration of the classical confusion between Pluto and Plutus; for Ana is "the layer-up of treasures"—the "lord of the earth" and of the "mountains," whence the precious metals are derived.

The worship of Ana by the kings of the Chaldaean series is certain. Not only did Shamas-vul, the son of Ismi-dagon, raise a temple to the honour of Ana and his son Vul at Kileh-Sherghat (or Asshur) about B.C. 1850—whence that city appears in later times to have borne the name of Telane,[1] or "the mound of Ana"—but Urukh himself mentions him as a god in the inscription quoted above;[2] and there is reason to believe that from at least as early a date he was recognised as the presiding deity at Erech or Warka. This is evident from the fact, that though the worship of Beltis superseded that of Ana in the great temple at that place from a very remote epoch, yet the temple itself always retained the title of *Bit-Ana* (or Beth-Ana), "the house of Ana;" and Beltis herself was known commonly as "the lady of *Bit-Ana*," from the previous dedication to this god of the shrine in question. Ana must also have been worshipped tolerably early at Nipur (*Niffer*), or that city could scarcely have acquired, by the time of Moses,[3] the

---

[1] Cf. Steph. Byz. ad voc. Τελάνη. Τελάνη, πόλις ἀρχαιοτάτη Συρίας (i. e. 'Ασσυρίας) ἣν φασι Νίνος πρὸ τῆς Νίνου κτίσεως.

[2] Gen. x. 10. The identification of Niffer with Calneh rests on the authority of the Talmud (see above, p. 25).

[3] Supra, page 144.

appellation of Calneh (Χαλάνη in the Septuagint translation), which is clearly *Kal-Ana*, "the fort of Ana."

Ana was supposed to have a wife, Anata, of whom a few words will be said below. She bore her husband a numerous progeny. One tablet shows a list of nine of their children, among which, however, no name occurs of any celebrity. But there are two sons of Ana mentioned elsewhere, who seem entitled to notice. One is the god of the atmosphere, Vul, of whom a full account will be hereafter given.[1] The other bears the name of *Martu*, and may be identified with the *Brathy* (Βραθὺ) of Sanchoninthon.[2] He represents "Darkness" or "the West," corresponding to the Erebus of the Greeks.

ANATA.

Anat or Anata has no peculiar characteristics. As her name is nothing but the feminine form of the masculine Ana, so she herself is a mere reflection of her husband. All his epithets are applied to her, with a simple difference of gender. She has really no personality separate from his, resembling Amente in Egyptian mythology, who is a mere feminine Ammon.[3] She is rarely, if ever, mentioned in the historical and geographical inscriptions.

---

[1] Infra, pp. 163-165.

[2] *Fragm. Hist. Gr.* vol. iii. p. 566. M. Bunsen having changed the reading of this name from Βραθὺ to Βαθὺ (on what authority I am not aware) proceeded to suggest that Βαθὺ, or rather ἐκ Βαθὺ, was a corruption of Τάβωρ, and that Mount Tabor was meant! (See his *Egypt*, vol. iv. pp. 205, 206, Engl. Tr.) The identification in the text assumes the MS. reading to be genuine.

[3] Bunsen's *Egypt*, vol. i. p. 378, E. T.; Wilkinson in the author's *Herodotus*, vol. ii. p. 285.

BIL or ENU.

Bil or Enu is the second god of the first Triad. He is the Illinus (*Il-Enu* or "God Enu") of Damascius.[4] His name, which seems to mean merely "lord,"[5] is usually followed by a qualificative adjunct, possessing great interest. It is proposed to read this term as *Nipru*, or in the feminine *Niprut*, a word which cannot fail to recall the Scriptural Nimrod, who is in the Septuagint Nebroth (Νεβρώθ). The term *nipru* seems to be formed from the root *napar*, which is in Syriac to "pursue," to "make to flee," and which has in Assyrian nearly the same meaning. Thus Bil-Nipru would be aptly translated as "the Hunter Lord," or "the god presiding over the chase," while, at the same time, it might combine the meaning of "the conquering Lord" or "the Great Conqueror."

On these grounds it is reasonable to conclude that we have, in this instance, an admixture of hero-worship in the Chaldæan religion. Bil-Nipru is probably the Biblical Nimrod, the original founder of the monarchy, the "mighty hunter" and conqueror. At the same time, however, that he is this hero deified, he represents also, as the second god of the first Triad, the classical Jupiter. He is "the supreme," "the father of the gods," "the pro-creator," "the Lord" *par excellence*, "the king of all the spirits," "the lord of the world," and again, "the lord of all the countries." There is some question whether he is altogether to be identified with

---

[4] *De Princip.* 125.
[5] *Bil* or *Bilu* is "lord" in the Assyrian and the Semitic Babylo-

nian: *Enu* is the corresponding Cushite or Hamitic term.

the Belus of the Greek writers, who in certain respects rather corresponds to Merodach.[*] When Belus, however, is called the first king,[1] the founder of the empire, or the builder of Babylon,[2] it seems necessary to understand Bil-Nipru or Bel-Nimrod. Nimrod, we know, built Babylon;[3] and Babylon was called in Assyrian times "the city of Bil-Nipru," while its famous defences—the outer and the inner wall—were known, even under Nebuchadnezzar, by the name of the same god.[4] Nimrod, again, was certainly the founder of the kingdom;[5] and, therefore, if Bil-Nipru is his representative, he would be Belus under that point of view.

The chief seat of Bel-Nimrod's worship was undoubtedly Nipur (Niffer) or Calneh. Not only was this city designated by the very same name as the god, and specially dedicated to him and to his wife Beltis, but Bel-Nimrod is called "Lord of Nipru," and his wife "Lady of Nipra," in evident allusion to this city or the tract wherein it was placed. Various traditions, as will be hereafter shown,[6] connect Nimrod with Niffer, which may fairly be regarded as his principal capital. Here then he would be naturally first worshipped upon his decease; and here seems to have been situated his famous temple called *Kharris-Nipra*, so noted for its wealth, splendour,

---

[*] The Jupiter Belus worshipped in the great temple at Babylon seems certainly to have been Merodach, who likewise represents the planet Jupiter. (See below, p. 168.)

[1] As by Abydenus (cf. Euseb. *Chron.* Can. i. 12, p. 30, and Mos. Choren. i. 4, p. 13), by Stephen (ad voc. Βαβυλών), and, perhaps we may say, by Herodotus (i. 7). Compare also Thallus (Fr. 2) and Mos.

Choren. (i. 6, and 9), who absolutely identifies Belus with Nimrod.

[2] Abyden. Fr. 8.

[3] Gen. x. 10.

[4] These walls were known respectively as the *Imgur-Bilu-Nipru*, and the *Nimitti-Bilu-Nipru*. (Sir H. Rawlinson in the author's *Herodotus*, vol. i. p. 590, and vol. ii. p. 580.)

[5] Gen. x. 10.

[6] Infra, pp. 104, 105.

and antiquity, which was an object of intense veneration to the Assyrian kings. Besides this celebrated shrine, he does not appear to have possessed many others. He is sometimes said to have had four "arks" or "tabernacles;" but the only places, besides Niffer, where we know that he had buildings dedicated to him, are Calah (Nimrud) and Durabo (Akkerkuf). At the same time he is a god almost universally acknowledged in the invocations of the Babylonian and Assyrian kings, in which he has a most conspicuous place. In Assyria he seems to be inferior only to Asshur; in Chaldæa to Ra and Ana.

Of Beltis, the wife of Bel-Nimrod, a full account will be given presently. Nin or Ninip—the Assyrian Hercules—was universally regarded as their son; and he is frequently joined with Bel-Nimrod in the invocations. Another famous deity, the Moon-god, Sin or Hurki, is also declared to be Bel-Nimrod's son in some inscriptions. Indeed, as " the father of the gods," Bel-Nimrod might evidently claim an almost infinite paternity.

The worship of Bel-Nimrod in Chaldæa extends through the whole time of the monarchy. It has been shown that he was probably the deified Nimrod, whose apotheosis would take place shortly after his decease. Urukh, the earliest monumental king, built him a temple at Niffer; and Durri-galazu, one of the latest, paid him the same honour at Akkerkuf. Urukh also frequently mentions him in his inscriptions in connexion with Hurki, the Moon-god, whom he calls his "eldest son."

BELTIS.

Beltis, the wife of Bel-Nimrod, presents a strong contrast to Anata, the wife of Ana. She is far more than the mere female power of Bel-Nimrod, being in fact a separate and very important deity. Her common title is "the *Great* goddess." In Chaldæa her name was Mulita [a] or Enuta—both words signifying "the Lady;" in Assyria she was Bilta or Bilta Nipruta, the feminine forms of Bil and Bilu-Nipru. Her favourite title was "the Mother of the Gods," or "the Mother of the Great Gods;" whence it is tolerably clear that she was the "Dea Syria" worshipped at Hierapolis under the Arian appellation of Mabog.[b] Though commonly represented as the wife of Bel-Nimrod, and mother of his son Nin or Ninip, she is also called "the wife of Nin," and in one place "the wife of Asshur." Her other titles are "the lady of Bit-Ana," "the lady of Nipur," "the Queen of the land" or "of the lands," "the great lady," "the goddess of war and battle," and "the queen of fecundity." She seems thus to have united the attributes of the Juno, the Ceres or Demeter,[c] the Bellona, and even the Diana of the classical nations; for she was at once the queen of

---

[a] Hence the Mylitta (Μύλιττα) of Herodotus (i. 131, 199), and perhaps the Molis (Μόλις) of Nic. Damascenus (*Fragm. Hist. Gr.* vol. iii. p. 361, note 16). It has been usual to derive these words from the Hebrew יָלַד, "generare;" but no similar root is found in either Assyrian or Babylonian. *Mul* in Hamitic Babylonian is the exact equivalent of *Bil* in Semitic Assyrian. Both signify "lord," while *Bilta* and *Mulita* signify "lady."

[b] *Mabog* is "the mother of the gods," from *mu* or *muta*, "mother," and *bugu*, "god" (Sclavonic *bog*).

[c] Etymologists have been puzzled by the name Rhea (Ῥέα)—one of the numerous appellatives of the "Great Goddess"—who is known also as Ceres, Cybele or Cybebe, Mater Dindymene, Magna Mater, Bona Dea, Dea Phrygia, Ops, Terra, and Tellus. Perhaps the explanation is to be found in the numerical symbol of this goddess, which was 15, pronounced as *Ri* by the Chaldæans.

heaven, the goddess who makes the earth fertile, the goddess of war and battle, and the goddess of hunting. In these latter capacities she appears, however, to have been gradually superseded by Ishtar, who sometimes even appropriates her higher and more distinctive appellations.

The worship of Beltis was wide-spread, and her temples were very numerous. At Erech (Warka) she was worshipped on the same platform, if not even in the same building, with Ana. At Calneh or Nipur (Niffer), she shared fully in her husband's honours. She had a shrine at Ur (Mugheir), another at Rubesi (Zerghul), and another outside the walls of Babylon. Some of these temples were very ancient, those at Warka and Niffer being built by Urukh, while that at Mugheir was either built or repaired by Ismi-dagon.

According to one record,[1] Beltis was a daughter of Ana. It was especially as "Queen of Nipur" that she was the wife of her son Nin. Perhaps this idea grew up out of the fact that at Nipur the two were associated together in a common worship. It appears to have given rise to some of the Greek traditions with respect to Semiramis, who was made to contract an incestuous marriage with her own son Ninyas, although no explanation can at present be given of the application to Beltis of that name.

HEA or HOA.

The third god of the first Triad was Hea or Hoa, the Aüs (Ἀός) of Damascius.[2] His appellation is

---

[1] The inscription on the open-mouthed lion, now in the British Museum. (See the author's *Hero-dotus*, vol. i. p. 625, note [*].)

[2] *De Princip.* l. s. c.

perhaps best rendered into Greek by the 'Ωη of
Helladius—the name given to the mystic animal,
half man, half fish, which came up from the Persian
Gulf to teach astronomy and letters to the first settlers on the Euphrates and Tigris.[*] It is perhaps
contained also in the word by which Berosus designates this same creature—Oannes ('Ωάννης)[1]—
which may be explained as *Hoa-ana*, or "the god
Hoa." There are no means of strictly determining
the precise meaning of the word in Babylonian; but
it is perhaps allowable to connect it, provisionally,
with the Arabic *Hiya*, which is at once "life" and
"a serpent," since, according to the best authority,
"there are very strong grounds for connecting Hea
or Hoa with the serpent of Scripture, and the Para-
disaical traditions of the tree of knowledge and the
tree of life."[2]

Hoa occupies, in the first Triad, the position which
in the classical mythology is filled by Poseidon or
Neptune, and in some respects he corresponds to him.
He is "the lord of the earth," just as Neptune is
γαιήοχος; he is "the king of rivers;" and he comes
from the sea to teach the Babylonians; but he is
never called "the lord of the sea." That title belongs to Nin or Ninip. Hoa is "the lord of the
abyss," or of "the great deep," which does not seem
to be the sea, but something distinct from it. His
most important titles are those which invest him
with the character, so prominently brought out in
Oë and Oannes,[3] of the god of science and know-

---

[*] Ap. Phot. *Bibliothec.* ccLXXXIX.
p. 1594.
[1] Beros. Fr. 1, § 3. Oannes has
been otherwise explained. It has
been thought to signify "given by

Aon."
[2] Sir H. Rawlinson in the author's
Herodotus, vol. i. p. 600.
[3] Cf. Hellad. l. s. c., and Beros.
Fr. 1, § 3. The latter writer gave

ledge. He is "the intelligent guide," or, according
to another interpretation, "the intelligent *fish*," [4]
"the teacher of mankind," "the lord of understanding." One of his emblems is the "wedge" or "arrow-
head," the essential element of cuneiform writing,
which seems to be assigned to him as the in-
ventor, or at least the patron, of the Chaldæan
alphabet.[5] Another is the serpent, which occupies so conspicuous a place among the symbols
of the gods on the black stones recording bene-
factions, and which sometimes appears upon
the cylinders. This symbol, here as elsewhere,
is emblematic of superhuman knowledge—a
record of the primeval belief that "the serpent was
more subtle than any beast of the field."[6] The stellar
name of Hoa was Kimmut; and it is suspected that
in this aspect he was identified with the constellation
Draco, which is perhaps the Kimah (כימה) of Scripture.[7] Besides his chief character of "god of knowledge," Hoa is also "god of life," a capacity in which
the serpent would again fitly symbolise him.[8] He
was likewise "god of glory," and "god of giving,"

---

the following account of Oannes—
Παραδιδόναι, φησί, τοῖς ἀνθρώποις
γραμμάτων καὶ μαθημάτων καὶ τεχνῶν
παντοδαπῶν ἐμπειρίαν, καὶ πόλεων
συνοικισμούς, καὶ ἱερῶν ἱδρύσεις,
καὶ νόμων εἰσηγήσεις, καὶ γεωμετρίαν
διδάσκειν, καὶ σπέρματα καὶ καρπῶν
συναγωγὰς ὑποδεικνύναι, καὶ συνόλως
πάντα τὰ πρὸς ἡμέρωσιν ἀνήκοντα
βίου παραδιδόναι τοῖς ἀνθρώποις
ἀπὸ δὲ τοῦ χρόνου ἐκείνου οὐδὲν
ἄλλο περισσὸν εὑρεθῆναι.

[4] Berosus and Helladius both agree
in regarding Hoa ("Ὡη or 'Ὡάννης) as
the Fish-God; but from the inscriptions it appears that the Fish-God

was really Nin or Ninip. (See below,
p. 167.)   [5] So Berosus, l. s. c.

[6] Gen. iii. 1.

[7] Job ix. 9; xxxviii. 31; Amos
v. 8. There seem to be no grounds
for our translating *Kimah* as "the
Pleiades." It is not even a plural.

[8] It is not perhaps altogether clear
why the serpent has been so frequently regarded as an emblem of
life. Some say, because serpents
are long-lived; others because the
animal readily formed a circle, and
a circle was the symbol of eternity.
But, whatever the reason, the fact
cannot be doubted.

being, as Berosus said, the great giver of good gifts to man.[1]

The monuments do not contain much evidence of the early worship of Hea. His name appears on a very ancient stone tablet brought from Mugheir (Ur); but otherwise his claim to be accounted one of the primeval gods must rest on the testimony of Berosus and Helladius, who represent him as known to the first settlers. He seems to have been the tutelary god of Is or Hit, which Isidore of Charax calls Aeipolis[1] (Ἀείπολις), or " Hea's city ;" but there is no evidence that this was a very ancient place. The Assyrian kings built him temples at Asshur and Calah.

Hea had a wife *Dav-Kina*, of whom a few words will be said presently. Their most celebrated son was Meroduch or Bel-Merodach, the Belus of Babylonian times. As Kimmut, Hea was also the father of Nebo, whose functions bear a general resemblance to his own.

DAV-KINA.

Dav-Kina, the wife of Hea, is clearly the Dauké or Davké (Δαύκη) of Damascius,[2] who was the wife of Aûs and mother of Belus (Bel-Merodach). Her name is thought to signify " the chief lady."[3] She

---

[1] See the passage cited at full length in note [4]. According to Assyrian notions, Hea did not confine his presents to men. One of the kings of Assyria says—"The senses of seeing, hearing, and understanding, which Hea allotted to the whole 4000 gods of heaven and earth, they in the fulness of their hearts granted to me."

[1] Mans. Parth. p. 6.

[2] *De Princip.* l. s. c. Τοῦ δὲ Ἀοῦ καὶ Δαύκης υἱὸν γενέσθαι τὸν Βῆλον.

[3] Sir H. Rawlinson in the author's *Herodotus*, vol. I. p. 601, note [4]. Movers and Bunsen derive Δαύκη from the Heb. דוק, " tunder," and interpret it " strife," comparing the Syriac *dauhat*. (See Bunsen's *Egypt*, vol. iv. pp. 155, 156.)

has no distinctive titles or important position in the
Pantheon, but, like Anata, takes her husband's epithets with a mere distinction of gender.

SIN or HURKI.

The first god of the second Triad is Sin or Hurki,
the moon-deity. It is in condescension to Greek
notions that Berosus inverts the true Chaldæan
order, and places the sun before the moon in his
enumeration of the heavenly bodies.[1] Chaldæan
mythology gives a very decided preference to the
lesser luminary, perhaps because the nights are more
pleasant than the days in hot countries. With respect to the names of the god, we may observe that
Sin, the Assyrian or Semitic term, is a word of
quite uncertain etymology, which, however, is found
applied to the moon in many Semitic languages;[2]
while Hurki, which is the Chaldæan or Hamitic
name, is probably from a root cognate to the Hebrew
'Ur, ‏אור‎, "vigilare," whence is derived the term
sometimes used to signify "an angel"[3]—'Ir, ‏עיר‎,
"a watcher."

The titles of Hurki are usually somewhat vague.
He is "the chief," "the powerful," "the lord of
spirits," "he who dwells in the great heavens;" or,
hyperbolically, "the chief of the gods of heaven and
earth," "the king of the gods," and even "the god
of the gods." Sometimes, however, his titles are
more definite and particular: as, firstly, when they

[1] Beros. Fr. 1, § 6.
[2] Sin is used for the Moon in
Mendæan and Syriac at the present
day. It is the name given to the
Moon-God in St. James of Sarug's list
of the idols of Harran; and it was
the term used for Monday by the
Sabæans as late as the 9th century.
[3] As in Daniel iv. 13, 17, and in
the Syriac liturgy.

belong to him in respect of his being the celestial
luminary—*e. g.* "the bright," "the shining," "the
lord of the month;" and, secondly, when they represent him as presiding over buildings and architecture,
which the Chaldæans appear to have placed under
his special superintendence.   In this connexion he is
called "the supporting architect," "the strengthener
of fortifications," and, more generally, "the lord of
building" (Bel-zuna).[1]   Bricks, the Chaldæan building material, were of course under his protection;
and the sign which designates them is also the sign
of the month over which he was considered to exert
particular care.[2]   His ordinary symbol is the crescent
or new moon, which is commonly represented as
large, but of extreme thinness ⌣ ; though not
without a certain variety in the forms ⌣   ⌣ .

The most curious and the most purely conventional
representations are a linear semicircle ⌣ , and an
imitation of this semicircle formed by three straight
lines[3] ⌣ .   The illuminated part of the moon's
disk is always turned directly towards the horizon,
a position but rarely seen in nature.

The chief Chaldæan temple to the moon-god was at
Ur or Hur (Mugheir), a city which probably derived
its name from him,[4] and which was under his special

---

[1] The term *zuna* may perhaps be
connected with the Heb. ⸢, "form."
Zanan is common in Assyrian for
"building."

[2] Sin is expressly called "the god
of the mouth Sivan of happy name;"
and it may be suspected that his
name is a mere contraction of Sivan.
The sign used for the mouth Sivan

is also the sign which represents
"bricks."

[3] These forms are taken chiefly
from the engravings of cylinders
published by the late Mr. Cullimore.

[4] It is not uncommon for the second syllable in an Assyrian or Babylonian god's name to be dropped
as unimportant.   We have both

protection. He had also shrines at Babylon and
Borsippa, and likewise at Calah and Dur-Sargina
(Khorsabad). Few deities appear to have been worshipped with such constancy by the Chaldæan kings.
His great temple at Ur was begun by Urukh, and
finished by his son Ilgi—the two most ancient of all
the monarchs. Later in the series we find him in
such honour that every king's name during some
centuries comprises the name of the moon-god in it.
On the restoration of the Chaldæan power he is
again in high repute. Nebuchadnezzar mentions
him with honour; and Nabonidus, the last native
monarch, restores his shrine at Ur, and accumulates
upon him the most high-sounding titles.[7]

The moon-god is called, in more than one inscription, the eldest son of Bel-Nimrod. He had a wife
(the moon-goddess) whose title was "the great lady,"
and who is frequently associated with him in the
lists. She and her husband were conjointly the
tutelary deities of Ur or Hur; and a particular portion of the great temple there was dedicated to her
honour especially. Her "ark" or "tabernacle,"
which was separate from that of her husband, was
probably, as well as his, deposited in this sanctuary.
It bore the title of "the lesser light," while his was
called, emphatically, "the light."

Ashur and *As*, both *Samsi* and *Sau*,
both *Ninip* and *Nin*, &c. Thus
we might expect to find both *Hur*
and *Hurki*. It is not perhaps a
proof of the connexion—but still it
is an argument in favour of it—to
find that when Ur changed its name
to Camarina (Eupolem. ap. Alex.
Polyhist. Fr. 3), the new appellation
was a derivative from another word
(*Kumar*, Arab.) signifying "the
moon." (Sir H. Rawlinson in the
author's *Herodotus*, vol. I. p. 616.)

[1] Nabonidus calls him "the chief
of the gods of heaven and earth, the
king of the gods, god of gods, he who
dwells in the great heavens," &c.

SAN or SANSI.

San or Sansi, the sun-god, was the second member of the second Triad. The main element of this name is probably connected with the root *shani*, שָׁנִי, which is in Arabic, and perhaps in Hebrew, "bright."[3] Hence we may perhaps compare our own word "sun" with the Chaldæan "San;" for "sun" is most likely connected etymologically with "sheen" and "shine." Shamas or Shemesh, שֶׁמֶשׁ, the Semitic title of the god, is altogether separate and distinct, signifying, as it does, the *ministering* office of the sun,[4] and not the brilliancy of his light. A trace of the Hamitic name appears in the well-known city Bethsan,[5] whose appellation is declared by Eugesippus to signify "domus Solis," "the house of the sun."[6]

The titles applied to the sun-god have not often much direct reference to his physical powers or attributes. He is called indeed, in some places, "the lord of fire," "the light of the gods," "the ruler of the day," and "he who illumines the expanse of heaven and earth." But commonly he is either spoken of in a more general way, as "the regent of all things," "the establisher of heaven and earth;" or, if special

[3] In Hebrew *shani*, שָׁנִי, is usually translated "scarlet," but some learned Jews suggest that the true meaning is bright. (See Newman's *Hebrew Lexicon* ad voc., and compare Gesenius.)

[4] From שָׁמַשׁ, "ministrare." (See Buxtorf ad voc.)

[5] Josh. xvii. 11; Judg. i. 27; 1 Sam. xxxi. 10, &c. The Hebrew form is בֵּית־שְׁאָן, *Beth-shean*, or בֵּית־שָׁן, *Beth-shan*. The LXX give Βαιθσάν, Βαιθσάν, Βαιθσύμ, and Βηθσάν. Josephus has Βήθσανα and Βηθσάνη. The Talmud contracts the word to *Bisan*, בֵּיסָן; and the existing name is *Beisân*. As Scythopolis this city was well known to the Greeks and Romans.

[6] See the small treatise of Eugesippus, *De Locis*, &c. In the folio edition of the Byzantine Historians (vol. xxiii. sub fin.). "Scythopolis civitas, Galilææ metropolis, quæ et Bethsan, id est, domus solis."

functions are assigned to him, they are connected
with his supposed "motive" power, as inspiring warlike thoughts in the minds of the kings, directing
and favourably influencing their expeditions; or
again, as helping them to discharge any of the other
active duties of royalty. San is "the supreme ruler
who casts a favourable eye on expeditions," "the
vanquisher of the king's enemies," "the breaker-up
of opposition." He "casts his motive influence"
over the monarchs, and causes them to "assemble
their chariots and warriors"—he goes forth with
their armies, and enables them to extend their dominions—he chases their enemies before them, causes
opposition to cease, and brings them back with
victory to their own countries. Besides this, he
helps them to sway the sceptre of power, and to rule
over their subjects with authority. It seems that,
from observing the manifest agency of the material
sun in stimulating all the functions of nature, the
Chaldæans came to the conclusion that the sun-god
exerted a similar influence on the minds of men, and
was the great motive agent in human history.

The chief seats of the sun-god's worship in Chaldæa appear to have been the two famous cities of
Larsa or Ellasar, and Sippara. The great temple
of the Sun, called Bit-Parra,[1] at the former place,
was erected by Urukh, repaired by more than one
of the later Chaldæan monarchs, and completely
restored by Nebuchadnezzar. At Sippara, the worship of the sun-god was so predominant, that Abydenus, probably following Berosus, calls the town

---

[1] It would seem from this name
that *Parra* was also a title under
which the Sun was known in Chaldæa in the early times. May not
this title be connected with the
Egyptian *Phra* or *Pi-ra*, "the sun,"
whence probably the Hebrew *Pha-
raoh*?

Heliopolis.[a] There can be little doubt that the Adrammelech, or "Fire-king,"[b] whose worship the Sepharvites (or people of Sippara) introduced into Samaria,[1] was this deity. Sippara is called *Tsipar sha Shama*, "Sippara of the Sun," in various inscriptions, and possessed a temple of the god which was repaired and adorned by many of the ancient Chaldæan kings, as well as by Nebuchadnezzar and Nabonidus.

The general prevalence of San's worship is indicated most clearly by the cylinders. Few comparatively of those which have any divine symbol upon them are without his. This symbol is either a simple circle $\bigcirc$, a quartered disk $\oplus$, or a four-rayed orb of a more elaborate character.

San or Sansi had a wife, Ai, Gula, or Anunit, of whom it now follows to speak.

AI, GULA, or ANUNIT.

Ai, Gula, or Anunit, was the female power of the sun, and was commonly associated with San in temples and invocations. Her names are of uncertain signification, except the second, Gula, which undoubtedly means "great," being so translated in the vocabularies.[c] It is suspected that the three

<hr />

[a] Abyden. Fr. 1; Syncell. vol. i. p. 70.

[b] Winer, *Realwörterbuch*, ad voc. "Adrammelech." Sir H. Rawlinson allows this derivation to be not improbable (Rawlinson's *Herodotus*, vol. i. p. 611), suggesting, however, another, from *edim*, "the arranger," and *melek* (ibid.).

[1] 2 Kings xvii. 31.

[c] *Gula* is rendered by *rabu* in the vocabularies, which is the Hebrew *rab*, רב, "a great one"—and thence "a doctor." It is probably connected with the Abyssinian *gudo*, "great;" but not with גדל, or at any rate only indirectly.

terms may have been attached respectively to the " rising," the " culminating," and the " setting sun,"[3] since they do not appear to interchange; while the name Gula is distinctly stated in one inscription to belong to the " great" goddess, " the wife of the *meridian* Sun." It is perhaps an objection to this view, that the male Sun, who is decidedly the superior deity, does not appear to be manifested in Chaldæa under any such threefold representation.[4]

As a substantive deity, distinct from her husband, Gula's characteristics are that she presides over life and over fecundity. It is not quite clear whether these offices belong to her alone, or whether she is associated in each of them with a sister goddess. There is a " Mistress of Life," who must be regarded as the special dispenser of that blessing; and there is a " Mistress of the Gods," who is expressly said to " preside over births." Concerning these two personages we cannot at present determine whether they are really distinct deities, or whether they are not rather aspects of Gula, sufficiently marked to be represented in the temples by distinct idols.[5]

Gula was worshipped in close combination with her husband, both at Larsa and Sippara. Her name appears in the inscriptions connected with both places; and she is probably the " Anammelech," whom the Sepharvites honoured in conjunction with

---

Ai may perhaps be the same word as the Agau (Abyssinian) *awi*, " light."

[4] Sir H. Rawlinson in the author's *Herodotus*, vol. i. p. 612.

[5] In Assyria such a threefold worship of the male Sun is found ; but even there we have no triple nomenclature.

[5] The only place where these two deities are clearly distinguished from Gula is in the list of the idols contained in the great temple of Bel-Merodach at Babylon. But for this notice, the names would certainly have been regarded as nothing more than titles of Gula.

Adrammelech, the "Fire-King."[*]   In later times
she had also temples independent of her husband,
at Babylon and Borsippa, as well as at Calah and
Asshur.

The emblem now commonly regarded as symboli-
zing Gula is the eight-rayed disk or orb, which frequently accompanies the orb with four rays in the
Babylonian representations.   In lieu of a disk, we
have sometimes an eight-rayed star ✳, and even
occasionally a star with six rays only ✶.   It is
curious that the eight-rayed star became at an early
period the universal emblem of divinity; but perhaps
we can only conclude from this the *stellar* origin of
the worship generally, and not any special pre-
eminence or priority of Anunit over other deities.

VUL or IVA.

The third member of the second Triad is the god
of the atmosphere, whose name it has been proposed
to render phonetically in a great variety of ways.[1]
On the whole the best rendering is now thought to
be *Vul*; and this is accordingly the name adopted in
these volumes.   Were *Iva* the correct articulation,

---

[*] No satisfactory explanation has
been given of the word Adrammelech.
If it represents the female power of
the sun, we must suppose that *Adar*
is an abbreviated form of Anunit,
and that *melek*, מֶלֶךְ, is for *malcah*,
מַלְכָּה, the Jews from contempt not
caring to be correct in the names of
false gods.

[1] M. Oppert calls this god *Ao*,
identifying him, apparently, with
the 'Aὸς of Damascius.   Mr. Fox
Talbot calls him *Iva* (*Inscription
of Tiglath-Pileser I*. passim).   Sir
H. Rawlinson on the whole prefers
Vul, but admits at the same time
that *Iva, Iien*, and *Air* or *Aûr* are
possible readings. (See the author's
Herodotus, vol. i. p. 600.)

we might regard the term as simply the old Hamitic
name for "the air," and illustrate it by the Arabic
hawa, ﻫﻮﺍ, which has still that meaning.

The importance of Vul in the Chaldæan mythology, and his strong positive character, contrast
remarkably with the weak and shadowy features of
Uranus, or Æther, in the classical system. Vul
indeed corresponds in great measure with the classical Zeus or Jupiter, being, like him, the real
"Prince of the power of the air," the lord of the
whirlwind and the tempest, and the wielder of the
thunderbolt. His standard titles are "the minister
of heaven and earth," "the Lord of the air," "he who
makes the tempest to rage." He is regarded as the
destroyer of crops, the rooter-up of trees, the scatterer
of the harvest. Famine, scarcity, and even their
consequence, pestilence, are assigned to him. He is
said to have in his hand a "flaming sword," with
which he effects his works of destruction; and this
"flaming sword," which probably represents lightning, becomes his emblem upon the tablets
and cylinders, where it is figured as a
double or triple bolt.* Vul again, as the
god of the atmosphere, gives the rain;
and hence he is "the careful and benefi-
cent chief," "the giver of abundance,"
"the lord of fecundity." In this capacity he is naturally chosen to preside over canals, the great fer-
tilizers of Babylonia; and we find among his titles

---

* Bolts of the kind represented, his conquests. (Sir H. Rawlinson
were also used as trophies of victory. | in the author's *Herodotus*, vol. I.
Tiglath-Pileser I. made one of cop- | p. 609.)
per and inscribed upon it a record of

"the lord of canals," and "the establisher of works of irrigation."

There is not much evidence of the worship of Vul in Chaldæa during the early times. That he must have been known appears from the fact of his name forming an element in the name of Shamas-Vul, son of Ismi-dagon, who ruled over Chaldæa about B.C. 1850.[1] It is also certain that this Shamas-Vul set up his worship at Asshur (Kileh-Sherghat) in Assyria, associating him there with his father Ana, and building to them conjointly a great temple.[2] Further than this we have no proof that he was an object of worship in the time of the first monarchy; though in the time of Assyrian preponderance, as well as in that of the later Babylonian Empire, there were few gods more venerated.

Vul is sometimes associated with a goddess, Shala or Tala, who is probably the Salambo or Salambas of the lexicographers.[3] The meaning of her name is uncertain;[4] and her epithets are for the most part obscure. Her ordinary title is *sarrut* or *sharrat*, "queen," the feminine of the common word *sar*, which means "Chief," "King," or "Sovereign."

BAR, NIN, or NINIP.

If we are right in regarding the five gods who stand next to the Triad formed of the Moon, the Sun, and the Atmosphere, as representatives of the five planets visible to the naked eye, the god Nin,

---

[1] See below, ch. viii. p. 207.
[2] See the *Inscription of Tiglath-Pileser I.* p. 62.
[3] Hesychius uses the form Σαλαμβώ, and calls the goddess "the Babylonian Venus." In the Ety- mologicum Magnum the form used is Σαλάμβας.
[4] The second element in Salambo or Salambas is probably *amma* (Heb. אם), "a mother."

or Ninip, should be Saturn. His names Bar, and
Nin, are respectively a Semitic and a Hamitic term
signifying "lord" or "master." Nin-ip, his full
Hamitic appellation, signifies "Nin, by name," or
"he whose name is Nin;" and similarly, his full
Semitic appellation seems to have been Barshem,
"Bar, by name," or "he whose name is Bar"—a
term which is not indeed found in the inscriptions,
but which appears to have been well known to the
early Syrians and Armenians,[1] and which was probably the origin of the title Barsemii, borne by the
kings of Hatra (*Hadhr* near Kileh-Sherghat) in
Roman times.[2]

In character and attributes the classical god,
whom Nin most closely resembles, is, however, not
Saturn, but Hercules. An indication of this connexion is perhaps contained in the Herodotean
genealogy, which makes Hercules an ancestor of
Ninus.[3] Many classical traditions, we must remember, identified Hercules with Saturn;[4] and it
seems certain that in the East at any rate this identification was common.[5] Nin, in the inscriptions, is
the god of strength and courage. He is "the lord
of the brave," "the champion," "the warrior who sub-
dues foes," "he who strengthens the heart of his
followers;" and again, "the destroyer of enemies,"

---

[1] See Mos. Choren. *Hist. Armen.*
I. 13, "Barsamum ob fortissimas res
gestas in Deos ascriptum ad longum
tempus Syri coluere." ii. 13, "Ti-
granes in Mesopotamiam descendit, et
nactus ibi Barsami statuam, quam
ex ebore et beryllo factam argento
ornaverat, deportari eam jubet, et in
Thordano oppido locari."
[2] Herodian. iii. 1, § 11.

[3] Herod. i. 7.
[4] Lydus, *De Mensibus*, iv. 46;
Athenag. *Leg. pro Christ.* xv. 6;
Damasc. *de Princip.*
[5] See the Memoir of M. Raoul
Rochette on the Assyrian Hercules
in the seventeenth volume of the
Mémoires de l'Institut, where this
point is abundantly proved.

"the reducer of the disobedient," "the exterminator of rebels," "he whose sword is good." In many respects he bears a close resemblance to Nergal or Mars. Like him, he is a god of battle and of the chace, presiding over the king's expeditions, whether for war or hunting, and giving success in both alike. At the same time he has qualities which seem wholly unconnected with any that have been hitherto mentioned. He is the true "Fish-God" of Berosus,[*] and is figured as such in the sculptures. In this point of view he is called "the god of the sea," "he who dwells in the deep," and again, somewhat curiously, "the opener of aqueducts." Besides these epithets he has many of a more general character, as "the powerful chief," "the supreme," "the first of the gods," "the favourite of the gods," "the chief of the spirits," and the like. Again, he has a set of epithets, which seem to point to his stellar character, very difficult to reconcile with the notion, that, as a celestial luminary, he was Saturn. We find him called "the light of heaven

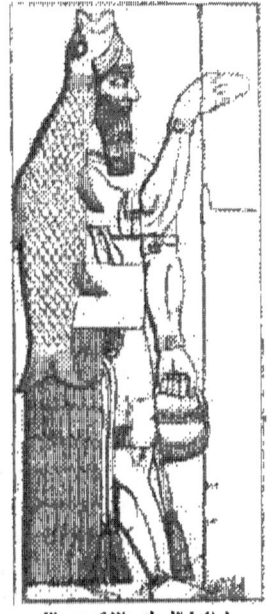

Figure of Nin, the Fish-God.

---

[*] Fr. 1, § 3. Τὸ μὲν ὅλον σῶμα ἔχον ἰχθύος, ὑπὸ δὲ τὴν κεφαλὴν παραπεφυκυῖαν ἄλλην κεφαλὴν ὑπο- | κάτω τῆς τοῦ ἰχθύος κεφαλῆς, καὶ πόδας ὁμοίως ἀνθρώπου, παραπεφυ- κότας δὲ ἐκ τῆς οὐρᾶς τοῦ ἰχθύος.

and earth," "he who, like the sun, the light of the
gods, irradiates the nations." These phrases appear to point to the Moon,
or to some very brilliant
star, and are scarcely re-
concilable with the notion
that he was the dark and
distant Saturn.

Nin's emblem in As-
syria is the Man-Bull, the
impersonation of strength
and power. He guards
the palaces of the Assyrian
kings, who reckon him
their tutelary god, and give
his name to their capital
city. We may conjecture
that in Babylonia his
emblem was the sacred
fish, which is often seen
under different forms upon

Nin's emblem, the Man-Bull.

the cylinders.

The monuments furnish no evidence
of the early worship of Nin in Chaldæa.
We may perhaps gather the fact from
Berosus' account of the Fish-God as an
early object of veneration in that region,[10]
as well as from the Hamitic etymology
of the name by which he was ordinarily
known even in Assyria.[1]

---

[10] The Fish-god (Oannes) comes
out of the Red Sea (Persian Gulf) to
instruct the settlers in Chaldæa.

[1] That the Assyrians commonly
used the Hamitic Nin, or Ninip, and

not the Semitic Bar, or Barshem, is
proved by the traditions concerning
Ninus, and by the name of their
capital city.

There he was always one of the most important deities. His temple at Nineveh was very famous, and is noticed by Tacitus in his "Annals;"[1] and he had likewise two temples at Calah (Nimrud), both buildings of some pretension.

It has been already mentioned[2] that Nin was the son of Bel-Nimrod, and that Beltis was both his wife and his mother. These relationships are well established, since they are repeatedly asserted. One tablet, however, inverts the genealogy, and makes Bel-Nimrod the son of Nin, instead of his father. The contradiction perhaps springs from the double character of this divinity, who, as Saturn, is the father, but, as Hercules, the son of Jupiter.

BEL-MERODACH.

Bel-Merodach is, beyond all doubt, the planet Jupiter, which is still called Bel by the Mendæans. The name Merodach is of uncertain etymology and meaning. It has been compared with the Persian *mardak*,[3] the diminutive of *mard* "a man," and with the Arabic *Mirrich*,[4] which is the name of the planet Mars. But, as there is every reason to believe that the term belongs to the Hamitic Babylonian, it is in vain to have recourse to Arian or Semitic tongues for its derivation. Most likely the word is a descriptive epithet, originally attached to the name Bel, in the same way as *Nipru*, but ultimately usurping its place and coming to be regarded as the proper name of the deity. It is doubtful whether any phonetic representative of Merodach has been found on the monu-

---

[1] Tacit. Ann. xii. 13.
[2] See above, page 151.
[3] Gesenius, *Lexicon Hebraicum*,

ad voc. "Merodach."
[4] Kitto's *Biblical Cyclopædia*, vol. ii. p. 328.

ments; if so, the pronunciation should, apparently,
be *Amarduk*, whence we might derive the Amordacia
(Ἀμορδακία) of Ptolemy.[5]

The titles and attributes of Merodach are of more
than usual vagueness. In the most ancient monuments which mention him, he seems to be called
"the old man of the gods,"[7] and "the judge"; he
also certainly has the *gates*, which in early times were
the seats of justice, under his special protection.
Thus he would seem to be the god of justice and
judgment—an idea which may have given rise to the
Hebrew name of the planet Jupiter, viz. *Sedek*, צדק,
"justitia." Bel-Merodach was worshipped in the
early Chaldæan kingdom, as appears from the Tel-
Sifr tablets. He was probably from a very remote
time the tutelary god of the city of Babylon;[8] and
hence, as that city grew into importance, the worship
of Merodach became more prominent. The Assyrian
monarchs always especially associate Babylon with
this god; and in the later Babylonian empire he
becomes by far the chief object of worship. It is his
temple which Herodotus describes so elaborately,[9] and
his image, which, according to the Apocryphal Daniel,
the Babylonians worshipped with so much devotion.[10]
Nebuchadnezzar calls him "the king of the heavens

---

[5] This is Ptolemy's name for a
district of Babylonia (see his *Geography*, v. 20). The Latin translator
renders it by Marodacus.

[7] So the Phœnicians worshipped
Bel as Βήλαθος, or בל ארץ, "the
old Bel" (Damasc. ap. Phot. *Bibliothec.* p. 343); and the Sabæans of
Harran called their Bel, "Bel, the
grave old man." (Chwolsohn, *Ssabier
und Ssabismus*, vol. ii. p. 30.)

[8] The Babylonian kings are fond
of including the word Merodach in
their names. As early as B.C. 1110,
we find a *Merodach-iddin-akki*, the
son of an *Irba-Merodach*. Afterwards we have Merodach-Baladan,
Mesessimordachus, Evil-Merodach,
&c.

[9] Herod. i. 181-183.   Compare
Diod. Sic. ii. 9.

[10] Apoc. Dan. xiv. 2.

and the earth," "the great lord," "the senior of the
gods," "the most ancient," "the supporter of sovereignty," "the layer-up of treasures," &c., and as-
cribes to him all his glory and successes.

We have no means of determining which among
the emblems of the gods is to be assigned to
Bel-Merodach; nor is there any sculptured
form which can be certainly attached to
him.   According to Diodorus, the great
statue of Bel-Merodach at Babylon was a
figure "standing and *walking*."[1]   Such a
form appears more often than any other
upon the cylinders of the Babylonians;
and it is perhaps allowable to conjecture
that it may represent this favourite deity.

ZIR-BANIT.

Bel-Merodach has a wife, with whom he is commonly associated, called Zir-banit.   She had a temple
at Babylon, probably attached to her husband's, and
is perhaps the Babylonian Juno (Hera) of Diodorus.[2]
The essential element of her name seems to be *Zir*,
which is an old Hamitic root, of uncertain meaning,
while the accompanying *banit* is a descriptive epithet,
which may be rendered by "genetrix."   Zir-banit
was probably the goddess whose worship the Babylonian settlers carried to Samaria, and who is called
Succoth-benoth in Scripture.[3]

NERGAL.

Nergal, the planet Mars, whose name still remains

[1] Diod. Sic. ii. 9, § 5 : Τὸ μὲν τοῦ
Διὸς ἄγαλμα ἱστηκὸς ἦν καὶ διαβε-
βηκός.
[2] Ibid. ii. 9, § 6.

[3] Succoth, "tents," is probably a
mistranslation of Zir, or Zirat, which
was confounded with *zarut*, a word
having that meaning.

under the form of Nerig in the astronomical system
of the Mendæans, is a god whose character and attributes are tolerably clear and definite. His name
is evidently compounded of the two Hamitic roots
nir " a man," and *gula* "great;" so that he is " the
great man," or " the great hero." He is the special
god of war and of hunting, more particularly of the
latter. His titles are " the king of battle," " the
champion of the gods," " the storm ruler," " the strong
begetter," " the tutelar god of Babylonia," and " the
god of the chace." He is usually coupled with Nin, who
likewise presides over battles and over hunting ; but
while Nin is at least his equal in the former sphere,
Nergal has a decided pre-eminence in the latter.

We have no evidence that Nergal was worshipped
in the primitive times. He is first mentioned by
some of the early Assyrian kings,[1] who regard him
as their ancestor. It is conjectured, that, like Bil-
Nipru, he represents the deified hero, Nimrod,[2] who
may have been worshipped in different parts of
Chaldæa under different titles.

The city peculiarly dedicated to Nergal was Cutha
or Tiggaba, which is constantly called his city in the
inscriptions. He was worshipped also at Turbisa,
near Nineveh, but in Tiggaba he was said to " live,"
and his shrine there was one of great celebrity. Hence
" the men of Cuth," when transported to Samaria by
the Assyrians, naturally enough " made Nergal their
god," carrying his worship with them into their new
country.[3]

It is probable that Nergal's symbol was the Man-

---

[1] As Tiglath-Pileser I., about B.C.
1100, and Sardanapalus, about B.C.
950.

[2] Sir H. Rawlinson in the author's
Herodotus, vol. i. p. 632.

[3] See 2 Kings xvii. 30.

Nergal's emblem, the Man-Lion.

Lion. *Nir* is sometimes used in the inscriptions in
the meaning of "lion"; and the Semitic name for
the god himself is "Aria"—the ordinary term for
the king of beasts both in Hebrew and in Syriac.
Perhaps we have here the true derivation of the
Greek name for the god of war, Ares ("Αρης),[1] which
has long puzzled classical scholars. The lion would
symbolize both the fighting and the hunting propen-
sities of the god, for he not only engages in combats
upon occasions, but often chases his prey and runs it
down like a hunter. Again, if Nergal is the Man-
Lion, his association in the buildings with the Man-
Bull, would be exactly parallel with the conjunction,
which we so constantly find, between him and Nin in
the inscriptions.

Nergal had a wife, called Laz, of whom, however,
nothing is known beyond her name. It is uncertain
which among the emblems of the gods appertains
to him.

ISHTAR or NANA.

Ishtar or Nana is the planetary Venus, and in
general features corresponds with the classical goddess. Her name Ishtar is that by which she was
known in Assyria, and the same term prevailed with
slight modifications among the Semitic races generally. The Phœnician form was Astarte, the Hebrew
Ashtoreth;[2] the present Mendæan form is Ashtar.

---

[1] The Sabeans of Harran, who
used generally the Babylonian appellations of the gods, applied the name
of *Ares* to the third day of the week
—the "dies Martis" of the Romans.
(Chwolsohn, *Ssabier und Ssabismus*,
vol. ii. p. 22.)

[2] 2 Kings xi. 5 and 33. Ashtoreth

(עַשְׁתֹּרֶת), "the goddess of the Sidonians" ('Ασταρτη of LXX.), is to
be distinguished from Ashtaroth
(עַשְׁתָּרוֹת), the plural form (vais
'Ασταρταις of LXX.), which seems
to be a generic word for "false god-
desses."

In Babylonia the goddess was known as Nana, which seems to be the Nannea of the second book of Maccabees,[9] and the Nani of the modern Syrians.[10] No satisfactory account can at present be given of the etymology of either name; for the proposal to connect Ishtar with the Greek ἀστήρ (Zend starann, Sanscrit tara, English star, Latin stella), though it has great names in its favour,[1] is not worthy of much attention.

Ishtar's aphrodisiac character, though it can scarcely be doubted, does not appear very clearly in the inscriptions. She is "the goddess who rejoices mankind," and her most common epithet is "Amrah," "the fortunate" or "the happy."[2] But otherwise her epithets are vague and general, insomuch that she is often scarcely distinguishable from Beltis. She is called "the mistress of heaven and earth," "the great goddess," "the queen of all the gods;" and again "the goddess of war and battle," "the queen of victory," "she who arranges battles," and "she who defends from attacks." She is also represented in the inscriptions of one king as the goddess of the chace.[3]

The worship of Ishtar was wide-spread, and her

---

[9] 2 Mac. i. 13–15.

[10] The name of Nani is given by the Syrian lexicographer Bar-Bahlul as one of the fifteen titles applied to the planet Venus by the Arabs. The word is also found further east, as in Affghanistan, where many places are called Bibi Nani, after "the lady Venus." The same origin may be assigned to the Greek "Nanæa," the name of a courtesan. (Athen. xiii. p. 576.)

[1] As Gesenius, Movers, and Fürst. Bunsen's argument against an Iranian derivation of the name of a Semitic god (Egypt's Place, vol. iv. p. 349, E. T.) is perfectly sound; but his suggestion that the true etymology of Ashtoreth is Ans-toreth, "the seat of the cow," seems scarcely entitled to acceptance.

[2] Compare the Roman notion by which the best throw on the dice was called "Venus," or "Jactus Venereus." (Plaut. Asin. v. ii. 55; Cic. de Div. ii. 50, &c.)

[3] This is her character in the records of Ashur-bani-pal, the son and successor of Esar-haddon.

shrines were numerous. She is often called "the queen of Babylon," and must certainly have had a temple in that city.[4] She had also temples at Asshur (Kileh-Sherghat), at Arbela, and at Nineveh. It may be suspected that her symbol was the naked female form, which is not uncommon upon the cylinders. She may also be represented by the rude images in baked clay so common throughout the Mesopotamian ruins, which are generally regarded as images of Mylitta.[5]

Ishtar is sometimes coupled with Nebo in such a way as to suggest the notion that she was his wife. This, however, can hardly have been her real position in the mythology, since Nebo had, as will presently appear, another wife, Varamit, whom there is no reason to believe identical with Ishtar. It is most probable that the conjunction is casual and accidental, being due to special and temporary causes.[6]

NEBO.

The last of the five planetary gods is Nebo, who

---

[4] Nebuchadnezzar speaks of having "made the way of Nana" in Babylon, by which he probably means a way or road to her temple. (See the Standard Inscription, as given in the author's *Herodotus*, vol. ii. p. 586.)

[5] Loftus, *Chaldæa and Susiana*, ch. xviii. p. 214; Layard, *Nineveh and its Remains*, vol. ii. ch. 7.

[6] The conjunction appears to belong only to the time of Nebuchadnezzar. Sir H. Rawlinson observes that, as Nebuchadnezzar never once mentions Varamit, the true wife of Nebo, in his inscriptions, it is evident she was out of favour with him, and that therefore Nana "may have been thrust temporarily into her place." (See the author's *Herodotus*, vol. i. p. 637.)

undoubtedly represents the planet Mercury. His
name is the same, or nearly so, both in Babylonian
and Assyrian;[1] and we may perhaps assign it a
Semitic derivation, from the root *nibbah*, נבה, " to
prophesy." It is his special function to preside over
knowledge and learning. He is called " the god who
possesses intelligence," " he who hears from afar,"
" he who teaches," or " he who teaches and instructs."
In this point of view, he of course approximates to
Hoa, whose son he is called in some inscriptions, and
to whom he bears a general resemblance. Like Hoa,
he is symbolized by the simple wedge or arrowhead,[2]
the primary and essential element of cuneiform writing, to mark his joint presidency with that god over
writing and literature. At the same time Nebo has,
like so many of the Chaldæan gods, a number of general titles, implying divine power, which, if they
had belonged to him only, would have seemed to
prove him the supreme deity. He is " the Lord of
lords, who has no equal in power," " the supreme
chief," " the sustainer," " the supporter," " the ever
ready," " the guardian over the heavens and the
earth," " the lord of the constellations," " the holder
of the sceptre of power," " he who grants to kings
the sceptre of royalty for the governance of their
people." It is chiefly by his omission from many
lists, and his humble place when he is mentioned

---

[1] The Babylonian form is *Nabiu*,
the Assyrian *Nabu*. The word forms
the initial element in Nabonassar,
Nabopolassar, Nebuchadnezzar, Nabonidus or Labynetus, Nebuzaradan,
and possibly in Laborosoarchod.

[2] In the great temple of Nebo at
Borsippa there is an interior chamber, which seems to have been a
chapel or oratory, all the bricks of
which are found to be stamped—in
addition to the ordinary legend of
Nebuchadnezzar—with the figure of
a wedge or arrow-head. It is probably with reference to this symbol
that Nebo received the name of *Tir*,
which is at once "an arrow," and
the name of the planet Mercury in
ancient Persian.

together with the really great gods, that we know
he was mythologically a deity of no very great
eminence.

There is nothing to prove the early worship of
Nebo. His name does not appear as an element in
any royal appellation belonging to the Chaldæan
series. Nor is there any reference to him in the
records of the primeval times. Still, as he is probably of Babylonian rather than Assyrian origin,[*]
and as an Assyrian king is named after him in the
twelfth century B.C.,[1] we may assume that he was not
unknown to the primitive people of Chaldæa, though
at present their remains have furnished us with no
mention of him. In later ages the chief seat of his
worship was Borsippa, where the great and famous
temple, known at present as the Birs-Nimrud, was
dedicated to his honour. He had also a shrine at
Calah (Nimrud), whence were procured the statues
representing him which are now in the British
Museum. He was in special favour with the kings
of the great Babylonian empire, who were mostly
named after him, and viewed him as presiding
over their house. His symbol has not yet been
recognised.

The wife of Nebo, as already observed, was Varn-
mit or Urmit—a word which perhaps means "exalted," from the root רם, "to be lifted up." No
special attributes are ascribed to this goddess, who

---

[*] When Nebo first appears in Assyria, it is as a foreign god, whose
worship is brought thither from Babylonia. His worship was never
common in the more northern country.

[1] This is the monarch whose name
is read as Mutaggil-Nebo, the grand-
father of Tiglath-Pileser I., who is
mentioned in that monarch's great
inscription. (p. 66.)

merely accompanies her husband in most of the places where he is mentioned by name.

Nebo (from a statue in the British Museum).

Such, then, seem to have been the chief gods worshipped by the early Chaldæans. It would be an endless as well as an unprofitable task to give

an account of the inferior deities. Their name is
"Legion;" and they are, for the most part, too vague
and shadowy for effective description. A vast number are merely local; and it may be suspected that
where this is the case the great gods of the Pantheon
come before us repeatedly, disguised under rustic
titles. We have, moreover, no clue at present to
this labyrinth, on which, even with greater knowledge, it would perhaps be best for us to forbear to
enter; since there is no reason to expect that we
should obtain any really valuable results from its
exploration.

A few words, however, may be added upon the
subject of the Chaldæan cosmogony. Although the
only knowledge that we possess on this point is derived from Berosus, and therefore we cannot be sure
that we have really the belief of the ancient people,
yet, judging from internal evidence of character, we
may safely pronounce Berosus' account not only
archaic, but in its groundwork and essence a primeval
tradition, more ancient probably than most of the
gods whom we have been considering.

"In the beginning," says this ancient legend, "all
was darkness and water, and therein were generated
monstrous animals of strange and peculiar forms.
There were men with two wings, and some even with
four, and with two faces; and others with two heads,
a man's and a woman's, on one body; and there
were men with the heads and the horns of goats, and
men with hoofs like horses, and some with the upper
parts of a man joined to the lower parts of a horse,
like centaurs; and there were bulls with human
heads, dogs with four bodies and with fishes' tails,
men and horses with dogs' heads, creatures with the

heads and bodies of horses, but with the tails of fish,
and other animals mixing the forms of various beasts.
Moreover, there were monstrous fish and reptiles and
serpents, and divers other creatures, which had borrowed something from each other's shapes; of all
which the likenesses are still preserved in the temple
of Belus.   A woman ruled them all, by name
Omorka, which is in Chaldee Thalatth, and in Greek
Thalassa (or ' the sea ').   Then Belus appeared, and
split the woman in twain; and of the one half of her
he made the heaven, and of the other half the earth;
and the beasts that were in her he caused to perish.
And he split the darkness, and divided the heaven
and the earth asunder, and put the world in order;
and the animals that could not bear the light
perished.   Belus, upon this, seeing that the earth
was desolate, yet teeming with productive power,
commanded one of the gods to cut off his head,[1] and
to mix the blood which flowed forth with earth, and
form men therewith, and beasts that could bear the
light.   So man was made, and was intelligent, being
a partaker of the divine wisdom.[2]   Likewise Belus
made the stars, and the sun and moon, and the five
planets."

It has been generally seen that this cosmogony

---

[1] There is a confusion here in Polyhistor, both as reported by Eusebius (Chron. Can. i. 2, pp. 11, 12)
and by Syncellus (Chronograph. vol.
i. p. 53), which can scarcely have belonged to his authority, Berosus.
Belus is first made to cut off his own
head, and " the other gods" are said
to have mixed his blood with earth
and formed man; but afterwards the
account contained in the text is
given.   It seems to me that the first

account is an interpolation in the
legend.
[2] I have placed this phrase a little
out of its order.   It occurs in the
passage, which appears to me inter-
polated, and which is perhaps rather
an explanation which Berosus gave
of the legend, than part of the legend itself.   However, Berosus has
no doubt here explained the legend
rightly.

bears a remarkable resemblance to the history of Creation contained in the opening chapters of the book of Genesis. Some have gone so far as to argue that the Mosaic account was derived from it.[4] Others, who reject this notion, suggest that a certain "old Chaldee tradition" was "the basis of them both."[5] If we drop out the word "Chaldee" from this statement, it may be regarded as fairly expressing the truth. The Babylonian legend embodies a primeval tradition, common to all mankind, of which an inspired author has given us the true groundwork in the first and second chapters of Genesis. What is especially remarkable is the fidelity, comparatively speaking, with which the Babylonian legend reports the facts. While the whole tone and spirit of the two accounts,[6] and even the point of view from which they are taken, differ,[7] the general outline of the narrative in each is nearly the same. In both we have the earth at first "without form and void," and "darkness upon the face of the deep." In both the first step taken towards creation is the separation of the mixed mass, and the formation of the heavens and the earth as the consequence of such separation. In both we have light mentioned before the creation of the sun and moon; in both we have

---

[4] So Niebuhr says (*Lectures on Ancient History*, vol. i. p. 16, E.T.), but without mentioning to what writers he alludes.

[5] Bunsen, *Egypt's Place in Universal History*, vol. iv. p. 365, E.T.

[6] The Chaldee narrative is extravagant and grotesque; the Mosaical is miraculous, as a true account of creation must be; but it is without unnecessary marvels, and its tone is sublime and solemn.

[7] In Genesis the point of view is the divine—"*In the beginning God created the heaven and the earth, and the Spirit of God moved upon the face of the waters.*" In the Chaldee legend the point of view is the physical and mundane, God being only brought in after a while as taking a certain part in creation.

the existence of animals before man ; and in both we
have a divine element infused into man at his birth,
and his formation " from the dust of the ground."
The only points in which the narratives can be said
to be at variance are points of order. The Babylonians apparently made the formation of man and
of the animals which at present inhabit the earth
simultaneous, and placed the creation of the sun,
moon, and planets after, instead of before, that of
men and animals. In other respects the Babylonian
narrative either adds to the Mosaic account, as in its
description of the monsters and their destruction, or
clothes in mythic language, that could never have
been understood literally, the truth which in Scripture is put forth with severe simplicity. The cleav-
ing of the woman Thalatth in twain, and the be-
heading of Belus, are embellishments of this latter
character; they are plainly and evidently mythological; nor can we suppose them to have been at
any time regarded as facts. The existence of the
monsters, on the other hand, may well have been an
actual belief. All men are prone to believe in such
marvels ; and it is quite possible, as Niebuhr supposes,[*] that some discoveries of the remains of mam-
moths and other monstrous forms embedded in the
crust of the earth, may have given definiteness
and prominency to the Chaldæan notions on this
subject.

Besides their correct notions on the subject of creation, the primitive Chaldæans seem also to have
been aware of the general destruction of mankind,

---

[*] *Lectures on Ancient History*, vol. i. p. 17, E. T.

on account of their wickedness,[1] by a Flood; and of
the rebellious attempt which was made soon after the
Flood to concentrate themselves in one place, instead
of obeying the command to "replenish the earth"[10]—
an attempt which was thwarted by means of the
confusion of their speech. The Chaldæan legends
embodying these primitive traditions were as follows :—

"God appeared to Xisuthrus (Noah) in a dream,
and warned him that on the fifteenth day of the
month Dæsius, mankind would be destroyed by a
deluge. He bade him bury in Sippara, the City of
the Sun, the extant writings, first and last; and build
a ship, and enter therein with his family and his
close friends; and furnish it with meat and drink;
and place on board winged fowl, and four-footed
beasts of the earth; and when all was ready, set sail.
Xisuthrus asked 'Whither he was to sail?' and was
told, 'To the gods, with a prayer that it might fare
well with mankind.' Then Xisuthrus was not disobedient to the vision, but built a ship five furlongs
(3125 feet) in length, and two furlongs (1250 feet) in
breadth; and collected all that had been commanded
him, and put his wife and children and close friends
on board. The flood came; and as soon as it ceased,
Xisuthrus let loose some birds, which, finding neither
food nor a place where they could rest, came back to
the ark. After some days he again sent out the
birds,[1] which again returned to the ark, but with feet

---

[1] This is not expressly stated in
the legend; but the divine warning
to Xisuthrus, and the stress laid by
Xisuthrus in his last words on the
worship of God, seem to imply such
a belief.

[10] Gen. ix. 1.
[1] So in Syncellus (*Chronograph.*
p. 54); but in the Armenian Eusebius we read "*other birds*" (*Chron.
Can.* i. 3, p. 15).

covered with mud. Sent out a third time, the birds returned no more, and Xisuthrus knew that land had reappeared: so he removed some of the covering of the ark, and looked, and behold! the vessel had grounded on a mountain. Then Xisuthrus went forth with his wife and his daughter, and his pilot,[2] and fell down and worshipped the earth,[3] and built an altar, and offered sacrifice to the gods; after which he disappeared from sight, together with those who had accompanied him. They who had remained in the ark and not gone forth with Xisuthrus, now left it and searched for him, and shouted out his name; but Xisuthrus was not seen any more. Only his voice answered them out of the air, saying, ' Worship God; for because I worshipped God, am I gone to dwell with the gods; and they who were with me have shared the same honour.' And he bade them return to Babylon, and recover the writings buried at Sippara, and make them known among men; and he told them that the land in which they then were was Armenia. So they, when they had heard all, sacrificed to the gods and went their way on foot to Babylon, and, having reached it, recovered the buried writings from Sippara, and built many cities and temples, and restored Babylon. Some portion of the ark still continues in Armenia, in the Gordiæan (Kurdish) Mountains; and persons scrape off the bitumen from it to bring away, and this they use as a remedy to avert misfortunes." [4]

---

[2] The Armenian translator turns the pilot (κυβερνήτης) into the "architect of the ship." M. Bunsen follows him (*Egypt*, &c., vol. iv. p. 371).

[3] This is plainly stated both in the Greek and in the Armenian. M. Bunsen has "threw himself upon the earth and prayed" (l. s. c.).

[4] I have inverted the order of this clause and the preceding one, to keep the connexion more clear.

"The earth was still of one language, when the
primitive men, who were proud of their strength
and stature, and despised the gods as their inferiors,
erected a tower of vast height, in order that they
might mount to heaven. And the tower was now
near to heaven, when the gods (or God) caused the
winds to blow and overturned the structure upon the
men, and made them speak with divers tongues;
wherefore the city was called Babylon."[*]

Here again we have a harmony with Scripture of
the most remarkable kind—a harmony not confined
to the main facts, but reaching even to the minuter
points, and one which is altogether most curious and
interesting. The Babylonians have not only, in
common with the great majority of nations, handed
down from age to age the general tradition of the
Flood, but they are acquainted with most of the particulars of the occurrence. They know of the divine
warning to a single man,[*] the direction to construct
a huge ship or ark,[*] the command to take into it a
chosen few of mankind only,[*] and to devote the chief
space to winged fowl and four-footed beasts of the
earth.[*] They are aware of the tentative sending out
of birds from it,[*] and of their returning twice,[*] but
when sent out a third time returning no more.[*]
They know of the egress from the ark by removal
of some of its covering,[*] and of the altar built

---

[*] Two separate versions of this legend have come down to us. They
come respectively from Abydenus
and Polyhistor. We have the words
of the authors in Euseb. *Prop. Ev.*
ix. 14, 15, and Syncell. *Chronograph.*
vol. i. p. 81. We have also a translation of their words in the Armenian Eusebius (*Chron. Can.* i. 4

and 8.)

[*] Gen. vi. 13.   [*] Ib. 14-16.
[*] Ib. verse 18.   [*] Ib. verse 20.
[*] Ib. viii. 7.   [*] Ib. 9-11.
[*] Ib. verse 12.
[*] Ib. verse 13: "Noah *removed
the covering of the ark,* and looked,
and, behold, the face of the earth
was dry."

and the sacrifice offered immediately afterwards.[4]
They know that the ark rested in Armenia;[5] that
those who escaped by means of it, or their descendants, journeyed towards Babylon;[6] that there a
tower was begun, but not completed, the building
being stopped by divine interposition and a miraculous confusion of tongues.[7]   As before, they are not
content with the plain truth, but must amplify and
embellish it.   The size of the ark is exaggerated to
an absurdity,[8] and its proportions are misrepresented
in such a way as to outrage all the principles of
naval architecture.[9]   The translation of Xisuthrus,
his wife, his daughter, and his pilot—a reminiscence
possibly of the translation of Enoch—is unfitly as
well as falsely introduced just after they have been
miraculously saved from destruction.   The story of
the Tower is given with less departure from the
actual truth.   The building is, however, absurdly
represented as an actual attempt to scale heaven;[10]
and a storm of wind is somewhat unnecessarily intro-

---

[4] Gen. viii. 20: "And Noah
builded an altar unto the Lord, and
took of every clean beast, and of
every clean fowl, and offered burnt
offerings upon the altar."

[5] Ib. verse 4: "And the ark
rested . . . upon the mountains of
Ararat." Ararat is the usual word
for Armenia in the Assyrian inscriptions.

[6] Gen. xi. 2.   [7] Ib. 4-9.

[8] The ark is made more than half
a mile long, whereas it was really
only 300 cubits, which is at the utmost 600 feet, or less than an eighth
of a mile.

[9] According to some writers, the
principles of naval architecture were
not concerned in the building of the
ark, since (as they say) "it was not
a ship, but a house" (Kitto's Bibli-

cal Cyclopædia, vol. i. p. 212). But
would "a floating house," not shaped
shipwise, have been safe amid the
winds and currents of so terrible a
crisis? The Chaldæans, despite the
absurd proportions that they assign
it, term the ark "a ship," and give
it "a pilot."

[10] The expression in Gen. xi. 4,
"a tower whose top may reach unto
heaven," is a mere common form of
Oriental hyperbole, applied to any
great height. (See Deut. i. 28, where
the spies are said to have brought
back word that the cities of the Canaanites were great, and "walled up
to heaven.") But in the Chaldee
version of the story we are told that
the men built the tower "in order
that they might mount to heaven"
(ὅπως εἰς τὸν οὐρανὸν ἀναβῶσιν).

duced to destroy the tower, which from the Scripture
narrative seems to have been left standing. It is
also especially to be noticed that in the Chaldæan
legends the whole interest is made narrow and local.
The flood appears as a circumstance in the history of
Babylonia; and the priestly traditionists, who have
put the legend into shape, are chiefly anxious to
make the event redound to the glory of their sacred
books, which they boast to have been the special
objects of divine care, and represent as a legacy from
the antediluvian ages. The general interests of
mankind are nothing to the Chaldæan priests, who
see in the story of the Tower simply a local etymology, and in the Deluge an event which made the
Babylonians the sole possessors of primeval wisdom.[1]

---

[1] Baron Bunsen observes with reason—" The general contrast between
the Biblical and the Chaldæ version
is very great. What a purely special
local character, legendary and fabulous, without ideas, does it display
in every point which it does not hold
in common with the Hebrew!"
(*Egypt's Place*, vol. iv. p. 374, E.T.)

CHAPTER VIII.

—

HISTORY AND CHRONOLOGY.

" The beginning of his kingdom was Babel, and Erech, and Accad, and
Calneh, in the land of Shinar."—Gen. x. 10.

THE establishment of a Cushite kingdom in Lower
Babylonia dates probably from (at least) the twenty-
third century before our era. A number of Greek
traditions[1] unite in assigning to the city of Babylon
an antiquity thus remote; and there is reason to
believe that the native historian, Berosus, intended
to represent the true Chaldæan kingdom as commencing from about this period. Unfortunately the
works of this great authority have been lost; and
even the general outline of his chronological scheme,

---

[1] Simplicius relates (*Comment. in
Aristot. de Cœlo,* ii. p. 123) that Callisthenes, the friend of Alexander,
sent to Aristotle from Babylon a
series of stellar observations made in
that city, which reached back 1903
years before the conquest of the
place by Alexander. (B.C. 331 + 1903
= B.C. 2234.) Philo-Byblius, according to Stephen (ad voc. Βαβυλών),
made Babylon to have been built 1002
years before Semiramis, whom he
considered contemporary with, or a
little anterior to, the Trojan War.
(*Fragm. Hist. Græc.* vol. iii. p. 563.)
We do not know his date for this
last event, but supposing it to be that
of the Parian Chronicle, B.C. 1216,
we should have B.C. 2220, or a little
earlier, for the building of the city,
according to him. Again, Ilumeus
and Critodemus are said by Pliny
(*H. N.* vii. 56) to have declared that
the Babylonians had recorded their
stellar observations upon bricks for
480 years before the era of Phoroneus. At least the passage may be
so understood. (See the *Journal of
Asiatic Society,* vol. xv. p. 222.)
Now the date of Phoroneus, according to Clinton (*F. H.* vol. i. p. 139),
is B.C. 1753; and B.C. 1753 + 480
gives B.C. 2233.

whereof some writers have left us an account,[1] is
to a certain extent imperfect; so that, in order to
obtain a definite chronology for the early times, we
are forced to have recourse, in some degree, to ingenuity and conjecture. Berosus declared that six
dynasties had reigned in Chaldæa since the great
flood of Xisuthrus, or Noah. To the first, which
consisted of 86 kings, he allowed the extravagant
period of 34,080 years. Evechius, the founder of
the dynasty, had enjoyed the royal dignity for 2400
years, and Chomasbélus, his son and successor, had
reigned 300 years longer than his father. The other
84 monarchs had filled up the remaining space of
28,980 years—their reigns thus averaging 345 years
apiece. It is clear that these numbers are unhis-
toric; and though it would be easy to reduce them
within the limits of credibility by arbitrary supposi-
tions—as, for instance, that the years of the narrative
represent months or days[2]—yet it may reasonably
be doubted whether we should in this way be doing
any service to the cause of historic truth. The
names Evechius and Chomasbélus seem mythic
rather than real; they represent personages in the
Babylonian Pantheon, and can scarcely have been
borne by men. It is likely that the entire series of
names partook of the same character, and that, if we
possessed them, their bearing would be found to be,
not historic, but mythological. We may parallel
this dynasty of Berosus, where he reckons kings'

[1] The most authentic account seems to be that which Eusebius copied from Polyhistor (*Chronica*, i. 4). Syncellus is far less to be trusted, on account of his elaborate systematizing.

[2] This view is taken by Mr. William Palmer in his Appendix on 'Babylonian and Assyrian Antiquities.' (See his *Egyptian Chronicles*, vol. ii. pp. 942, 943.)

reigns by the cyclical periods of *soses* and *ners*,
with Manetho's dynasties of Gods and Demigods in
Egypt, where the sum of the years is nearly as
great.[1]

It is necessary, then, to relegate to the domain of
myth this first dynasty of Berosus, and to regard the
historical portion of his scheme as commencing, at
the earliest, when the first period is closed, and kings
begin to reign whose longevity is not more than
human.

Now the scheme of Berosus, setting aside the first
period, is—according to the best extant authorities[2]
—as follows :—

(ii.)	Dynasty of	8 Median	kings	..	224	years.
(iii.)	„	11	„			
(iv.)	„	49 Chaldæan	„	..	458	„
(v.)	„	9 Arabian	„	..	245	„
(vi.)	„	45 Assyrian	„	..	526	„
(vii.)	„	Assyrian	„	..		
(viii.)	„	6 Chaldæan	„	..	87	„

It will be observed that this table contains various
lacunæ, which greatly impair its value, and render it
unavailable for chronological purposes, unless they
can be supplied. An ingenious German writer[3] has
successfully grappled with the difficulty, and produced a scheme which is at once so probable, so
consistent with history, and so agreeable to the
numerical fancies of the Babylonians, that we can
scarcely doubt its near approximation to that which
Berosus actually set forth. This writer begins by

---

[1] Manetho assigns 24,925 years to
the reigns of Gods, Demigods, and
Manes, who ruled Egypt before
Menes — the first historical king.
(See *Fragm. Hist. Gr.* vol. ii. p.
528.)

[2] Eusebius and Josephus.
[3] M. Gutschmid. (See his paper
in the *Rheinisches Museum*, vol. viii.
p. 252 et seqq.; and compare Brau-
dis's *Rerum Assyriarum Tempora
Emendata*, pp. 16, 17.)

supplying the latest deficiency. Assuming that the division between the earlier and the later Assyrian dynasty synchronises with the celebrated era of Nabonassar (B.C. 747), which is probable, but not certain, and taking the year B.C. 538 as the admitted date of the conquest of the last Chaldæan king by Cyrus, he obtains for the seventh or second Assyrian dynasty the term of 122 years—from B.C. 747 to B.C. 625.[1] Assuming next, that the year B.C. 2234, from which the Babylonians counted their stellar observations,[2] must be a year of note in Chaldæan history, and finding that it cannot well represent the first year of the second or Median dynasty, since in that case the *eleven* kings of the third dynasty would have reigned no more than 34 years,[3] he concludes that it must mark the expulsion of the Medes, and the accession of the third—which he regards as a native Chaldæan—dynasty. From his previous calculations it follows that the fourth dynasty began to reign B.C. 1976; between which and B.C. 2234 there are 258 years, a period which may very fairly be assigned to a series of eleven monarchs.[10] Thus much is to a great extent conjecture—reasonable conjecture, harmonising with historic facts: the proof now suddenly flashes on us. If the numbers

---

[1] The 87 years assigned to the six Chaldæan monarchs by Berosus, added to B.C. 538, give B.C. 625 for the accession of the 8th dynasty. This is the exact year in which Ptolemy's Canon places the accession of Nabopolassar.

[2] See above, p. 189, note [3].

[3] If the Medes began to reign in B.C. 2234, they would remain on the throne till B.C. 2010, between which and B.C. 1976—the presumed first year of the 4th dynasty—would be only 34 years.

[10] The average of their reigns would be 23½ years, somewhat less than that of the Median and Arabian reigns, though greater than that of the others. Some writers regard as authoritative the number 48, which is suggested in the margin of the Armenian Eusebius, to supply the blank in the text. (Palmer, p. 1828.) I cannot view it as more than a conjecture.

are taken in the way assigned, and then added to
the years of the first or purely mythical dynasty, the
sum produced is *exactly* 36,000 years—the next term
to the *sar* in the Babylonian system of cycles.[1] It is
impossible that this should be the result of chance.
The later Babylonians clearly contrived their mythical
number so that when added to those which they
viewed as historical the sum total should be a perfect
cyclical period.   The date B.C. 2234 for the accession
of the third dynasty may thus be regarded as certainly that which Berosus intended to assign, and as
most probably correct.   The other dates in the subjoined scheme, except the first and last, are more
doubtful; since they depend on the presumed syn-
chronism between the accession of the sixth (or second
Assyrian) dynasty, and the era of Nabonassar.

BABYLONIAN CHRONOLOGY, according to GUTSCHMID.

Dynasties of Berosus	Mythic.	I.	86 Chaldæans	Years. 34,080	B.C.	B.C.
	Historical	II.	8 Medes	224	2458	2234
		III.	11 [Chaldæans]	[258]	2234	1976
		IV.	49 Chaldæans	458	1976	1518
		V.	9 Arabians	245	1518	1273
		VI.	45 [Assyrians]	526	1273	747
		VII.	[8 Assyrians]	[122]	747	625
		VIII.	6 Chaldæans	87	625	538
				36,000		

---

[1] In the Babylonian system of notation the numbers 6 and 10 were
employed alternately. (See above,
p. 129.) Time was measured ordinarily by the *sos*, the *ner*, and the
sar — the *sos* being (10×6=) 60
years, the *ner* (60×10=) 600 years,
and the *sar* (600×6=) 3600 years.

The next term in this series would
evidently be (3600×10=) 36,000
years, and the term following (36,000
×6=) 216,000. Berosus actually
uses this last term, making his antediluvian period consist of 432,000,
or two such periods.

It appears, then, that Berosus commenced that
portion of his Chaldæan history, which has some
appearance of being authentic, with a Median dynasty
of eight kings, whose united reigns covered a space
of 224 years, and who were anterior to Alexander
by above twenty centuries.   The Medes, according
to him, were conquerors, who seized Babylon, super-
seding the Chaldæan dynasty by which the country
had been previously ruled, and exercising a tyran-
nical authority over the old inhabitants.[1] We can
scarcely doubt that this narrative represents a fact.
Traditions of foreign conquest may always be accepted as having a certain value ; since national
vanity positively forbids their invention by the
people who relate the conquest, and makes their
acceptance from any other quarter very unlikely.
What the exact value, however, of this particular
tradition may be, is uncertain. The appearance of
Medes in Chaldæa at so early a date surprises us ;
and it has been questioned whether Berosus intends
persons really belonging to that ethnic race, or only
a nation coming from the country which in his own
day was known as Media.[2] Again, it is perhaps
doubtful whether we ought to accept the conquest
and the previous Chaldæan occupation of the country
as facts, or whether we ought not rather to regard
the first or Median dynasty as merely representing
the sovereignty of a non-Chaldæan race in the
country before the arrival of the Cushite immi-

---

[1] "Post hos derepente Medos col-
lectis copiis Babylonem cepisse ait,
ibique de suis tyrannos constituisse."
(Euseb. Chron. l. 4, p. 18.) The
other kings are "reges," not "ty-
ranni."

[2] See Sir H. Rawlinson's paper on
the ' Early History of Babylonia '
in the Journal of the Asiatic Society,
vol. xv. p. 236; and compare the
author's Herodotus, vol. i. p. 403.

grants from Ethiopia, and consider these immigrants
as making their first lodgment not long before
B.C. 2234.   In this case the Median period would
not belong to the history of the Chaldæan race at
all, any more than that of the Roman dominion in
Britain does to the history of the Anglo-Saxons. †

Passing over the Median period, therefore, as one
concerning which scarcely anything has been made
out,[1] and the connexion of which with the Chaldæans
is in reality very doubtful, we may commence our
history of the latter people with the year B.C. 2234,
the traditional date for the founding of the Empire.
It was then, we may suppose, that Nimrod, the son
or descendant of Cush, set up a kingdom in Lower
Mesopotamia, which attracted the attention of surrounding nations.   The people, whom he led, came
probably by sea; at any rate, their earliest settle-
ments were on the coast; and Ur or Hur, on the
right bank of the Euphrates, at a very short distance from its embouchure, was the primitive capital.
The "mighty hunter" rapidly spread his dominion
inland, subduing or expelling the various tribes by
which the country was previously occupied.   His
kingdom extended northwards, at least as far as
Babylon, which (as well as Erech or Huruk, Accad,

---

[1] If we may trust Syncellus, the
first of Berosus' Median monarchs of
Babylon was Zoroaster! (Chronograph. p. 78, C.) This would seem
to imply a Magian people, worship-
pers of the elements, and probably
Scythic in race. It is a recent conjecture, that the Zoroastrian Medes
of Berosus were in reality the Barbar
or Akkad, a Turanian race, whose
proper seats were in Armenia, where
they are found in the Assyrian
period, but who at a very early date
conquered the Babylonian Cushites,
and mixed with them. (See above,
ch. iii. p. 69.) The other names
of kings which Syncellus has been
thought to assign to this dynasty
(Palmer, Egyptian Chronicles, vol.
ii. pp. 857, 858) belong probably
to the mythic dynasty of the 86
monarchs, from which Evechius and
Chomasbélus, who are joined with
them, are certainly taken.

and Calneh) was first founded by this monarch.[1] Further historical details of his reign are wanting; but the strength of his character and the greatness of his achievements are remarkably indicated by a variety of testimonies, which place him among the foremost men of the Old World, and guarantee him a never-ending remembrance. At least as early as the time of Moses his name had passed into a proverb. He was known as "the mighty hunter before the Lord"[2]—an expression which had probably a double meaning, implying at once skill and bravery in the pursuit and destruction of wild beasts, and also a genius for war and success in his aggressions upon men. In his own nation he seems to have been deified, and to have continued down to the latest times one of the leading objects of worship, under the title of *Bilu-Nipru* or Bel-Nimrod,[3] which may be translated "the god of the chace," or "the great hunter." One of his capitals, Calneh, which was regarded as his special city, appears afterwards to have been known by his name (probably as being the *chief* seat of his worship in the early times), and this name it still retains, slightly corrupted. In the modern Niffer we may recognise the Talmudical Nopher, and the Assyrian *Nipur*, which is *Nipru*, with a mere metathesis of the two final letters. The fame of Nimrod has always been rife in the country of his domination. Arab writers record a number of remarkable traditions, in which he plays a conspi-

---

[1] Gen. x. 10.
[2] Gen. x. 9: "He was a mighty hunter before the Lord; wherefore it is said, Even as Nimrod, the mighty hunter before the Lord."
[3] The Greek forms, Νεβρώδ and Νεβρώθ, serve to connect *Nipru* with נמרד. The native root is thought to be *namar*, "to pursue," or "cause to flee." (See the author's *Herodotus*, vol. i. p. 597.)

cuous part;[1] and there is little doubt but that it is in honour of his apotheosis that the constellation Orion bears in Arabian astronomy the title of *El Jabbar,* or "the giant."[2] Even at the present day his name lives in the mouth of the people inhabiting Chaldæa and the adjacent regions, whose memory of ancient heroes is almost confined to three —Nimrod, Solomon, and Alexander. Wherever a mound of ashes is to be seen in Babylonia or the adjoining countries, the local traditions attach to it the name of *Nimrud* or *Nimrod;*[3] and the most striking ruins now existing in the Mesopotamian valley, whether in its upper or its lower portion, are made in this way monuments of his glory.[4]

If the chronological scheme above set forth[5] be regarded as sufficiently established, the dynasty of Nimrod must be considered to have occupied the throne for a period somewhat exceeding two centuries and a half—from b.c. 2234 to b.c. 1976. It consisted, we are told, of eleven monarchs. The names of all these sovereigns are unrecorded by the classical writers, unless we may make an exception in favour of a certain Orchamus, who is mentioned

---

[1] Yacut declares that Nimrod attempted to mount to heaven on the wings of an eagle, and makes Niffer (Calneh) the scene of this occurrence. (*Lex. Geograph.* in voc. *Niffer.*) It is supposed that we have here an allusion to the building of the tower of Babel. The Koran contains a story of Nimrod's casting Abraham into a fiery furnace.

[2] The Arabic *Jabbar* represents the Hebrew גִּבּוֹר, which is the epithet applied to Nimrod in Gen. x. 9. The identification of Nimrod with Orion is noted by Greek writers.

(See John of Antioch, Fr. 3; *Pasch. Chron.* vol. i. p. 64; John of Malala, p. 17; Cedrenus, vol. i. p. 27; &c.) Orion is a "mighty hunter," even in Homer. (See Odyss. xi. 572-575.)

[3] *Journ. of Asiatic Soc.* vol. xv. p. 230.

[4] The great temple of Borsippa is known as the *Birs-i-Nimrud;* and the simple name *Nimrud* is given to probably the most striking heap of ruins in the ancient Assyria.

[5] See page 193.

by Ovid in his Metamorphoses as the seventh in
succession from Belus.[4] This classical notice would
have seemed unimportant, had it not accorded very
curiously with information obtained from the inscriptions. The excavations conducted by Mr. Loftus
and Mr. Taylor in the mounds of ancient Chaldæa
have brought to light a name very closely resembling that of Orchamus, which appears to have
belonged to one of the earliest kings of the country.
The *basement* platforms of all the most ancient buildings throughout the entire region are the work of a
certain Urukh or Urkham, who calls himself "King
of Ur (or Hur) and Kingi-Accad," and is thought to
be the first monarch of whom any remains have
been obtained.   Not only are his bricks found in a
lower position than any others, at the very foundations
of buildings, but they are of a rude and coarse make,
and the inscriptions upon them contrast most remarkably, in the simplicity of the style of writing used
and in their general archaic type, with the elaborate
and often complicated symbols of the later monarchs.[5]
The style of Urukh's buildings is also primitive and
simple in the extreme; his bricks are of many sizes,
and ill fitted together;[6] he belongs to a time when
even the baking of bricks seems to have been comparatively rare, for sometimes he employs only the
sun-dried material;[7] and he is altogether unac-
quainted with the use of lime mortar, for which his

[4] Metamorph. iv. 212, 213 :—

    "Regit Achæmenias urbes pater Orchamus,
      isque
    Septimus a prisci numeratur origine Beli."

Bel probably represents Nimrod,
whose worship as Bel-Nimrod has
been already mentioned.

[5] See Sir H. Rawlinson's remarks
in the author's *Herodotus*, vol. i. p.
425; and compare above, page 60.

[6] *Journal of Asiatic Society*, vol.
xv. pp. 261-263; Loftus, *Chaldæa
and Susiana*, p. 168.

[7] As in the Bowariyeh ruin at
Warka (Loftus, p. 167).

substitute is moist mud, or else bitumen. There can
be little doubt that he stands at the head of the present series of monumental kings, one of whom certainly reigned as early as B.C. 1860.[1] If we may
trust the statement of Ovid, that he was the seventh
monarch of his dynasty, we are entitled to place his
reign in the twenty-first century before our era—
from about B.C. 2093 to B.C. 2070.[2]

It is as a builder of gigantic works that Urukh is
chiefly known to us. The basement platforms of his
temples are of an enormous size; and though they
cannot seriously be compared with the Egyptian
pyramids, yet indicate the employment for many
years of a vast amount of human labour in a very
unproductive sort of industry. The Bowariyeh
mound at Warka is 200 feet square, and about 100
feet high.[10] Its cubic contents, as originally built,
can have been little, if at all, under 3,000,000 feet;
and above 30,000,000 of bricks must have been used
in its construction. Constructions of a similar character, and not very different in their dimensions, are
proved by the bricks composing them to have been
raised by the same monarch at Ur, Calneh or Nipur,
and Larancha or Larsa, which is perhaps Ellasar.[1]
It is evident, from the size and number of these
works, that their erector had the command of a vast
amount of naked human strength, and did not scruple
to employ that strength in constructions from which
no material benefit was derivable, but which were

---

[1] See below, page 207.
[2] These dates are drawn from
the amended scheme of Berosus
(supra, p. 193), by assigning to the
six kings preceding Urukh their due
proportion of the 258 years which
are presumed to belong to the dynasty. (As 11 : 258 :: 6 : 141
nearly, and B.C. 2234 — 141 = B.C.
2093.)
[10] Supra, pp. 94, 95.
[1] Gen. xiv. 1.

probably designed chiefly to extend his own fame
and perpetuate his glory. We may gather from
this that he was either an oppressor of his people,
like some of the Pyramid Kings in Egypt,[1] or else a
conqueror, who thus employed the numerous captives carried off in his expeditions. Perhaps the
latter is the more probable supposition; for the
builders of the great fabrics in Babylonia and Chaldœa do not seem to have left behind them any character of oppressiveness, such as attaches commonly
to those monarchs who have ground down their own
people by servile labour.

The great buildings of Urukh appear to have been
all designed for temples. They are carefully placed
with their angles facing the cardinal points,[2] and
are dedicated to the Sun, the Moon, to Belus (Bel-
Nimrod), or to Beltis. The temple at Mugheir was
built in honour of the Moon-god, Sin or Hurki, who
was the tutelary deity of the city. The Warka
temple was dedicated to Beltis. At Calneh or Nipur
Urukh erected two temples, one to Beltis and one to
Belus. At Larsa or Ellasar the object of his worship was the Sun-god, San or Sansi. He would thus
seem to have been no special devotee of a single
god, but to have divided out his favours very fairly
among the chief personages of the Pantheon.

It has been observed that both the inscriptions of
this king, and his architecture, are of a rude and
primitive type. Still in neither case do we seem to
be brought to the earliest dawn of civilisation or of
art. The writing of Urukh has passed out of the
first or hieroglyphic stage, and entered the second or

---

[1] Herod. ii. 124, 128; Arist. Pol. vii. 11.   [2] Loftus, *Chaldœa and Susiana*, p. 246.

transition one, when pictures are no longer attempted,
but the lines or wedges follow roughly the old outline of the objects.[4] In his architecture, again,
though there is much that is rude and simple, there
is also a good deal which indicates knowledge and
experience. The use of the buttress is understood ;
and the buttress is varied according to the material.[5]
The importance of sloping the walls of buildings
inwards to resist interior pressure is thoroughly
recognised.[6] Drains are introduced to carry off
moisture, which must otherwise have been very destructive to buildings composed mainly, or entirely,
of crude brick. It is evident that the builders
whom the king employs, though they do not possess
much genius, have still such a knowledge of the
most important principles of their art as is only
obtained gradually by a good deal of practice.
Indeed the very fact of the continued existence of
their works at the distance of forty centuries is sufficient evidence that they possessed a considerable
amount of architectural skill and knowledge.

We are further, perhaps, justified in concluding,
from the careful emplacement of Urukh's temples,
that the science of astronomy was already cultivated
in his reign, and was regarded as having a certain
connexion with religion. We have seen that the
early worship of the Chaldæans was to a great
extent astral[7]—a fact which naturally made the
heavenly bodies special objects of attention. If the

---

[4] Supra, page 80.

[5] Compare the slight buttresses, only 12 inches thick, supporting the Mugheir temple, which has a facing of burnt brick to the depth of ten feet, with the strong ones at Warka (where unburnt brick is the material used), which project seven feet and a half from the central mass. (Loftus, pp. 128, 129, and p. 169.)

[6] Ibid. p. 128.

[7] See above, ch. vii. p. 139.

series of observations, which Callisthenes sent to
Aristotle, dating from the very commencement of
the kingdom, was in reality a record, and not a
mere calculation backwards of the dates at which
certain celestial phenomena must have taken place,
astronomical studies must have begun at a period
long anterior to Urukh.

Nor must we omit to notice, if we would estimate
aright the condition of Chaldæan art under this
king, the indications furnished by his signet-cylinder.
So far as we can judge from the representation,
which is all that we possess of this relic, the drawing
on the cylinder was as good and the engraving as
well executed as any work of the kind, either of the
Assyrian or of the later Babylonian period. Apart
from the inscription, this work of art has nothing about
it that is rude or primitive. The elaboration of the
dresses and headgear of the figures has been already
noticed.[1] It is also worthy of remark, that the
principal figure sits on an ornamental throne or chair,
of particularly tasteful construction, two legs of
which appear to have been modelled after those of
the bull or ox. We may conclude, without much
danger of mistake, that in the time of the monarch
who owned this seal, dresses of delicate fabric and
elaborate pattern, and furniture of a *recherché* and
elegant shape, were in use among the people over
whom he exercised dominion.

Urukh appears to have been succeeded in the
kingdom by a son, whose name it is proposed to read
as Elgi or Ilgi. Of this prince our knowledge is
exceedingly scanty. It only appears, from inscrip-

---

[1] Supra, p. 125.

tions of a comparatively recent date, that he completed some of the buildings at Ur, which his father
had left unfinished, especially the great temple of
the Moon-God. If Urukh reigned from about B.C.
2093 to B.C. 2070, we may assign to Ilgi the years
included between B.C. 2070 and B.C. 2047.

If Urukh and his son Ilgi are rightly regarded as
the seventh and eighth kings of Berosus' second, or
first Chaldæan, dynasty, we may conclude from that
historian that they were followed by three other
monarchs of their race, who reigned from about
B.C. 2047 to B.C. 1976.* Of this period we do not
possess any monumental records. It appears, however, from the monuments, that, not very long after
the time of Urukh and Ilgi, a change of dynasty
took place in the country, the old Chaldæan line
being superseded by an Elamitic family,** which
reigned (like the former dynasty) at Ur, but possessed a far more extended dominion. Of this change
we seem to have a remarkable trace in the account
which Scripture gives of Chedor-laomer's Syrian
Expedition. Chedor-laomer is an Elamitic king;
yet he exercises paramount authority over the whole
of Lower Mesopotamia. Amraphel, King of Shinar,
Arioch, King of Larsa or Ellasar, and Tidal,[1] King
of the nomadic races, are his tributaries. Possessing
thus authority over the whole of the alluvial plain,
and being able to collect together a formidable army,

---

* These dates, except the last, have
nothing exact about them. They are
formed simply by assigning to each
of the eleven kings the number of
years which the kings of this dynasty
seem to have reigned on an average.

** Peculiarities in the form of
Kudur-Mabuk's letters seem to con-

nect him with Elam or Susiana.
An element too in his father's name
—khuk—appears in the name of
Tirkhak, a monumental Susan king,
which is unknown in the language
of Chaldæa.

[1] Gen. xiv. 1.

he resolves on an expedition up the Euphrates,
with the object of extending his dominion to the
Mediterranean Sea and to the borders of Egypt.
At first his endeavours are successful. Together
with his confederate kings, he marches as far as
Palestine, where he is opposed by the native princes,
Bera, king of Sodom, Birsha, king of Gomorrah,
Shinab, king of Admah, Shemeber, king of Zeboiim,
and the king of Bela or Zoar.[1] A great battle is
fought between the two confederated armies in
the vale of Siddim towards the lower end of the
Dead Sea.[2] The invaders are victorious; and for
twelve years, Bera and his allies were content to
own themselves subjects of the Elamitic king, whom
they "served" for that period.[4] In the thirteenth
year they rebelled: a general rising of the western
nations seems to have taken place;[5] and in order
tô maintain his conquests it was necessary for the
conqueror to make a fresh effort. Once more the
four eastern kings entered Syria, and, after various
successes against minor powers, engaged a second
time in the valley of Siddim with their old antago-
nists, whom they defeated with great slaughter; after
which they plundered the chief cities belonging to
them.[6] It was on this occasion that Lot, the nephew
of Abraham, was taken prisoner. Laden with booty

---

[1] Gen. xiv. 2.

[2] The scene of the battle seems to
have been that part of the plain
which was afterwards submerged,
when the area of the Dead Sea was
extended. Compare the expression
(Gen. xiv. 3), "All these were joined
together in the vale of Siddim, which
is the salt sea;" and see Mr.
Ffoulkes's article on GOMORRAH in
Dr. Smith's *Biblical Dictionary*, vol.

I. pp. 709, 710.

[4] "Twelve years they served
Chedor-laomer, and in the thirteenth
year they rebelled." (Gen. xiv. 4.)

[5] Among the nations chastised
by Chedor-laomer on his second
invasion we find the Rephaim or
"Giants," the Zuzim, the Emim,
the Horites, the Amorites, and the
Amalekites. (Gen. xiv. 5-7.)

[6] Gen. xiv. 8-11.

of various kinds, and encumbered with a number of
captives, male and female,[1] the conquering army set
out upon its march home, and had reached the neighbourhood of Damascus, when it was attacked and
defeated by Abraham, who with a small band
ventured under cover of night to fall upon the
retreating host, which he routed and pursued to
some distance.[2] The actual slaughter can scarcely
have been great; but the prisoners and the booty
taken had to be surrendered; the prestige of victory
was lost; and the result appears to have been that
the Mesopotamian monarch relinquished his projects,
and, contenting himself with the fame acquired by
such distant expeditions, made no further attempt to
carry his empire beyond the Euphrates.[3]

It has been thought by many, and among others
by the author of the present volumes,[4] that there
were grounds for identifying the great monarch, of
whom we have this account in Scripture, with a
certain monumental king, whose name has been read
upon the bricks as Kudur-mabuk, or Kudur-mapula.
This king appeared to synchronise with the probable
date of Abraham;[5] his name agreed in one element

---

[1] Gen. xiv. 16.

[2] May not the tradition, that
Abraham was king of Damascus
(Nic. Dam. Fr. 30), be connected
with this exploit? It could scarcely
have been grounded on the mere fact
that he had for steward a native of
that city. (Gen. xv. 2.)

[3] The expression in verse 17 of the
Authorized Version, "the slaughter
of Chedor-laomer, and of the kings
which were with him," is over-
strong. The Hebrew phrase נְכוֹת
does not mean more than "defeat"
or "overthrow."

[4] See Smith's *Dictionary of the
Bible*, ad voc. CHEDOR-LAOMER, and
Bampton Lectures, p. 58, 2nd edit.

[5] It is undoubtedly difficult to obtain from Scripture an exact date for
Abraham. Clinton places his death
in B.C. 1955, and consequently makes
him resident in Canaan from B.C.
2055 to B.C. 1955. Mr. Palmer brings
him into Canaan 80 years earlier—
in B.C. 2084, and places his death in
B.C. 1984. (*Egyptian Chronicles*, vol.
ii. p. 897.) Now Kudur-Mabuk was
certainly before Ismi-dagon, whose
date is fixed to the middle of the

with that of Chedor-laomer, and where it disagreed
the disagreement was thought to admit of explanation;[2] above all, he bore in his inscriptions a title,
Apda Martu, which it was proposed to translate as
"Ravager of the West," apparently in commemo-
ration of the very exploits described in Genesis. But
the progress of cuneiform discovery has not been
favourable to the proposed identification. The writer
whose authority is the greatest in this field of
inquiry,[1] is now of opinion that Kudur-mabuk, and
Chedor-laomer, though of one family, were distinct
persons. He finds reason to regard both names as
purely Hamite,[2] and as essentially distinct; he is
not certain of the real meaning of the expression,
Apda Martu; and he thinks it on the whole safest
at present to regard the first Kudur as the original
Susianian conqueror who established his dominion
over Chaldæa, and the second Kudur as a descendant of far inferior consequence. If this view be
taken we must enlarge the list of early Chaldæan
kings, and, regarding Chedor-laomer as the first
monarch of Berosus' second Chaldæan dynasty, place

---

nineteenth century B.C.; and if—as
is probable—he was the first king
of Berosus' third dynasty, and so
ascended the throne in B.C. 1976, his
expedition into Syria would synchronise exactly with Abraham's
date according to Clinton.

[2] The first element in the name—
Kudur—is fairly enough translite-
rated in the Hebrew Chedor, כְּדָר,
Mabuk, the other element, was
thought to be either the Hamitic
equivalent of *laomer*, or an unimportant part of the name which had
been dropped, and afterwards replaced by a descriptive epithet. (See

the author's *Herodotus*, vol. i. p.
436, note[1].)

[1] Sir H. Rawlinson. The views
of this scholar will shortly appear
in the second edition of the author's
Herodotus.

[2] The Hebrew כְּדָרְלָעֹמֶר is, it appears, well rendered by the Septuagint Χοδολλογομόρ. *Lagomer* is a
Susianian god, and *Kudur-Lagomer*
would be "the servant of Lagomer,"
a name formed according to known
analogies. The Hebrew ע has often
the force of a *g*, and is probably the
original form from which the Greek
γ was taken.

after him, probably as next successor, Sinti-shil-khak, the father of Kudur-mabuk, and then Kudur-mabuk himself, who thus becomes the sixth known monarch.

Kudur-Mabuk's bricks have been found at Mugheir, or Ur, only. He does not appear to have been a great builder. Though of a race, apparently, only cognate to that of the Chaldæans, he maintained their religion unchanged, adding to the old temples, and worshipping the gods under the same titles. He may be regarded as having reigned from about B.C. 1935 to B.C. 1910. He was probably succeeded by his son, Arid-Sin, who is mentioned on the bricks of his father. Arid-Sin may have reigned from about B.C. 1910 to B.C. 1890.

The next of the monumental kings must be placed about forty years later. Sennacherib, in a rock in-scription at Bavian, relates that in his tenth year (which was B.C. 692) he recovered from Babylon certain images of the gods which had been carried thither by *Merodach-iddin-akhi*, King of Babylon, after his defeat of Tiglath-Pileser, King of Assyria, 418 years previously. And the same Tiglath-Pileser relates, that he rebuilt a temple in Assyria, which had been taken down 60 years before, after it had lasted 641 years from its foundation by Shamas-Vul, son of Ismi-dagon.[1] It results from these numbers, that Ismi-dagon was king as early as B.C. 1850, or, probably, a little earlier.[2]

---

[1] See the author's *Herodotus*, vol. I. Essay vi. p. 433, note ¹.

[2] If Sennacherib's 10th year is B.C. 692, Tiglath-Pileser's defeat must have been in B.C. 1110. His restor-ation of the temple was certainly

earlier, for it was at the very begin-ning of his reign — say B.C. 1120. Add the 60 years during which the building had been in ruins and the 641 during which it had stood, and we have B.C. 1821 for the building

The monuments furnish little information concerning Ismi-dagon, beyond the evidence which they
afford of the extension of this king's dominion into
the upper part of the Mesopotamian valley, and
especially into the country known in later times as
Assyria.   The fact, that Shamas-Vul, the son of Ismi-
dagon, built a temple at Kileh-Sherghat, implies
necessarily that the Chaldæans at this time bore sway
in the upper region.   Shamas-iva appears to have
been, not the eldest, but the second son of the
monarch, and must be viewed as ruling over Assyria
in the capacity of viceroy, either for his father or his
brother.   Such evidence as we possess of the condition of Assyria about the period seems to show
that it was weak and insignificant, administered
ordinarily by Babylonian satraps or governors, whose
office was one of no great rank or dignity.[1]

In Chaldæa, Ismi-dagon was succeeded by a son,
whose name is read, with a good deal of uncertainty,
as Ibil-anu-duma.   This prince is known to us
especially as the builder of the great public ceme-
teries which now form the most conspicuous objects
among the ruins of Mugheir, and the construction
of which is so remarkable.[2]   He was followed in the
kingdom, apparently, by his son, Gunguna or Gurguna, of whom nothing but the name—which is
itself very doubtful—is recorded.   These monarchs
probably reigned from about B.C. 1825 to B.C. 1775.

Hitherto there has been no great difficulty in de-

---

of the original temple by Shamas-
Vul.   The date of his father's accession should be at least 30 years
earlier—or B.C. 1861.

[2] Three or four tablets of Babylonian satraps have been discovered

at Kileh-Sherghat.   The titles assumed are said to "belong to the
most humble class of dignities."
(Sir H. Rawlinson, in the author's
Herodotus, vol. i. p. 448, note [2].)

[3] See above, ch. v., pp. 109-111.

termining the order of the monumental kings, from
the position of their bricks in the principal Chaldæan
ruins and the general character of their inscriptions.
But the relative place occupied in the series by the
later monarchs is rendered very doubtful by their
records being scattered and unconnected, while their
styles of inscription vary but slightly. It is most un-
fortunate that no writer has left us a list corresponding in Babylonian history with that which Manetho
put on record for Egyptian; since we are thus compelled to arrange our names in an order which rests
on little more than conjecture.[1]

The monumental king who is thought to have approached the nearest to Gurguna, is Naram-sin, of
whom records have been discovered at Babylon, and
who is mentioned in a late inscription[2] as the builder
of a temple at Sippara or Sepharvaim, the modern
Mosaib. His date is probably about B.C. 1750. The
seat of his court may be conjectured to have been
Babylon, which had by this time risen into metropolitan consequence. It is evident, that, as time went
on, the tendency was to remove the seat of government and empire to a greater distance from the sea.
The early monarchs reign at Ur (Mugheir), and
leave no traces of themselves further north than
Niffer. Sin-shada holds his court at Erech (Warka),

---

[1] Berosus gave no doubt the complete list; but his names have not
been preserved to us. The brief
Chaldæan list in Syncellus (p. 169)
probably came from him; but the
names seem to have belonged to the
1st or mythical dynasty. (See above,
p. 195, note [4].) One might have
hoped to obtain some help from
Ctesias's Assyrian list, as it went
back at least as far as B.C. 2182, when

Assyria was a mere province of the
Chaldæan Empire. But it presents
every appearance of an absolute
forgery, being composed of Arian,
Semitic, Egyptian, and Greek appellations, with a sprinkling of terms
borrowed from geography.

[2] The fact is recorded by Nabonidus—the Labynetus of Herodotus
—on the famous Mugheir cylinder.

twenty-five miles above Mugheir; while Naram-sin is connected with the still more northern city of Babylon. We shall find a similar tendency in Assyria, as it rose into power. In both cases we may regard the fact as indicative of a gradual spread of empire *towards the north*, and of the advance of civilisation and settled government in that direction.

A king who disputes the palm of antiquity with Naram-sin, has left various records at Erech or Warka, which appears to have been his capital city. It is proposed to call him Sin-shada. He constructed, or rather re-built, the upper terrace of the Bowariyeh ruin, or great temple which Urukh raised at Warka to Beltis; and his bricks are found in the doorway of another large ruin (the *Wuswas*) at the same place; it is believed, however, that in this latter building they are not *in situ*, but have been transferred from some earlier edifice.[1] He may have reigned about B.C. 1700.

Several monarchs of the *Sin* series—i.e. monarchs into whose names the word *Sin*, the name of the Moon-god, enters as an element—now present themselves. The most important of them has been called Zur-sin. This king erected some buildings at Mugheir; but he is best known as the founder of the very curious town whose ruins bear at the present day the name of Abu-Shahrein. A description of the principal buildings at this site has been already given.[2] They exhibit certain improvements on the architecture of the earlier times, and appear to have been very richly ornamented, at least in parts. At

---

[1] Loftus, *Chaldæa and Susiana*, ch. xvi. p. 184.

[2] See above, pp. 100, 101.

the same time they contain among their *débris* remarkable proofs of the small advance which had as
yet been made in some of the simplest arts. Flint
knives and other implements, stone hatchets, chisels,
and nails are abundant in the ruins; and though the
use of metal is not unknown, it seems to have been
comparatively rare. When a metal is found, it is
either gold or bronze, no trace of iron appearing in
any of the Chaldæan remains. Zur-sin, and two or
three other monarchs of the *Sin* series, whose names
are imperfect or uncertain,[a] may be assigned to the
period included between B.C. 1700 and B.C. 1625.

Next in order to the kings of the *Sin* series may
be placed two monarchs, a father and a son—by name
Purna-puriyas and Durri-galazu—whose memorials
have been found in many parts of the country. These
kings had been already connected together by the
near resemblance of the legends on their bricks,[b]
though the bricks themselves were found at places
very remote from one another, when a fresh discovery at once showed the soundness of a judgment
based upon such resemblance, and established beyond
controversy the nature of the connexion existing between them. The signet of one of the two monarchs

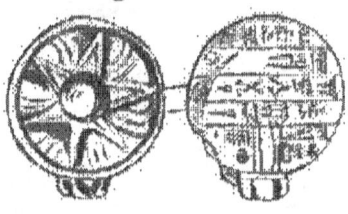

---

[a] It has been proposed to call one
of these kings Rim-sin. He has left
a very fine inscription on a small
black tablet, found at Mugheir.

[b] See the author's *Herodotus*, vol.
I. Essay vi. pp. 439, 440; and compare Loftus, p. 435.

was found at Baghdad, and the inscription upon this
remarkable relic made it evident that the monarchs
not only belonged to the same period and family, but
that one immediately followed the other, Purna-
puriyas being the father, and Durri-galazu his son
and successor in the kingdom.

The bricks of Purna-puriyas are found at Senkereh,
where he repaired the famous Temple of the Sun originally built by Urukh. Those of Durri-galazu have
been procured from Akkerkuf to the north-west of
Baghdad, from Mugheir or Ur, and from Mosaib or
Sippara. His signet, as already observed, was found
at Baghdad; and his name is thought to retain a place
even at the present day in the geographical nomenclature of the lower country, where there is a *Zergul*,[1]
a ruined town not far from Mugheir, to the east of
the Shat-el-Hie, near its junction with the Euphrates.
This place was probably one of his foundations.
Another was certainly the important city marked by
the striking ruin called Tel-Nimrud or Nimrud-Tepassé,
at Akkerkuf, of which a representation has been
given in a former chapter.[1] Purna-puriyas and Durri-galazu may be regarded as having reigned from
about B.C. 1625 to B.C. 1675.

The only other Chaldæan monarchs of whom legible records have been discovered are another father
and son, whose names are read as Khammurabi and

---

[1] The existence of this place has
had the curious effect of introduc-
ing into Ctesias's list of Assyrian
kings a single historical appellation.
In the latter part of his series, where
he flies for help to geography, the
name of Derkylus occurs — drawn
probably from this city. The other
instances of a geographic nomenclature are Arbelus (Arbela), Chalatis
(Calah), Ophrataeus (the Euphrates),
and Acraganes (a branch of the Euphrates, as in Abyden, Fr. 9, ad fin.).

[1] See ch. i. p. 28. It must not,
however, be supposed that this ruin
is a Chaldæan work. It is certainly
much later, and probably belongs to
Parthian times.

Samshu-iluna. They may be placed in the interval between B.C. 1575 and B.C. 1518, when the second Chaldæan dynasty (according to Berosus) terminated. Of Khammurabi we have numerous memorials. He repaired the Temple of the Sun at Senkereh; he built himself a palace at Kalwadha, or Chilmad, not far from Baghdad; numerous clay tablets dated in his reign have been found at Tel-Sifr; and tablets bearing his name and titles have been obtained at Babylon.[*] Like the other monarchs of the series, he is evidently king of the whole alluvial country, bearing sway alike in the low region about the mouth of the Euphrates and in the upper tract about Baghdad and Babylon. Of Samshu-iluna, his son, our notices are comparatively scanty. We know him merely from the Tel-Sifr clay tablets, some of which are dated in the reign of this monarch.

Modern research has thus supplied us with memorials of fifteen or sixteen kings, who ruled in the country properly termed Chaldæa at a very remote date. Their antiquity is evidenced by the character of their buildings and of their inscriptions, which are unmistakably rude and archaic. It is further indicated by the fact that they are the builders of certainly the most ancient edifices whereof the country contains any trace. A probable connexion of one of them [u] with the only king known from good authority to have reigned in the country during the

---

[*] One such tablet, which is reported to have been obtained on the site of Babylon, has been long in the British Museum; no authentic account, however, of the circumstances attending its discovery has been preserved. Another mutilated one, now in the Louvre, was brought from Babylon by the late French expedition.

[u] Kudur-Mabuk, who is at any rate to be connected with the Chedorlaomer of Scripture. (See above, pp. 206, 200.)

primitive ages confirms the conclusion drawn from
the appearance of the remains themselves; which is
further strengthened by a monumental date assigning another[11] of them, who is certainly not among the
earliest in the series, to the nineteenth century before our era. That the kings belong to one series,
or at most to two closely-connected ones, is evidenced
by the similarity of the titles which they use, by their
uninterrupted worship of the same gods, and by the
general resemblance of the language and mode of
writing which they employ.[12] That they are the
monarchs of whom Berosus spoke as Chaldæans, and
whom he arranged in two dynasties, as native rulers
intervening between a Median and an Arabian series,
may not be exactly proved; but it is in the highest
degree probable. If it be objected that Berosus, instead of fifteen kings, assigned to the dynasties in
question no fewer than sixty, according to the report
of Polyhistor, we may answer, in the first place, that
it has never been supposed by any one that the fifteen
or sixteen kings, of whom distinct mention has been
made in the foregoing account, are a complete list of
all the Chaldæan sovereigns. On the contrary, it is
plain that they are a very incomplete list, like that
which Herodotus gives of the kings of Egypt, or that
which the later Romans possessed of their early monarchs. The monuments themselves present no fewer
than ten other names of kings, belonging evidently

---

[11] Ismi-dagon. (See page 207.)

[12] Sir H. Rawlinson says:—" All
the kings whose monuments are
found in ancient Chaldæa used the
same language and the same form of
writing; they professed the same
religion, inhabited the same cities,
and followed the same traditions.

Temples built in the earliest times
received the veneration of successive
generations, and were repaired and
adorned by a long series of monarchs,
even down to the time of the Semitic
Nabonidus." (Rawlinson's *Herodotus*,
vol. i. Essay vi. p. 441.)

to the same series," which are too obscure or too illegible for transliteration. And there may of course have been many others of whom no traces remain, or of whom none have been as yet found. On the other hand, it is to be observed, that the number reported by Polyhistor is preposterous. If sixty consecutive monarchs held the Chaldæan throne between B.C. 2234 and B.C. 1518, they must have reigned on an average less than twelve years apiece. Nay, if forty-nine ruled between B.C. 1976 and B.C. 1518, covering a space of above four centuries and a half—which is what Berosus is made to assert—these later monarchs cannot even have reigned so long as *ten* years each, an average which may be pronounced quite impossible in a settled monarchy such as the Chaldæan. The probability would seem to be that Berosus has been misreported, his numbers having suffered corruption during their passage through so many hands, and being in this instance quite untrustworthy. We may conjecture that the actual number of reigns which he intended to allow his third dynasty was nineteen, or at the utmost twenty-nine, the former of which numbers would give the common average of twenty-four years, while the latter would produce the less usual but still possible one of sixteen years.

" See the author's *Herodotus*, vol. i. p. 440.

" See the fragments of this writer preserved by Eusebius (*Chron. Can.* pars i. c. 4).

' The words of Polyhistor are reported to us by Eusebius in a work (his *Chronicon*) the original of which is lost, and which we have only in an Armenian version. Polyhistor himself does not appear to have read the work of Berosus. He derives his knowledge of it from Apollodorus.

Thus we have Berosus at fifth hand —through Apollodorus, Polyhistor, Eusebius, and the Armenian translator. Hence the excellent advice of C. Muller—"Igitur cum per tot manus migraverint quæ ad nos perdurarunt fragmenta, haud miraberis variis modis verba Berosi deformata esse, cavendumque ne Beroso imputemus quæ sunt imputanda excerptoribus." (*Fragm. Hist. Gr.* vol. ii. p. 496.)

The monarchy, which we have had under review, is one no doubt rather curious from its antiquity than illustrious from its great names, or admirable for the extent of its dominions. Less ancient than the Egyptian, it claims the advantage of priority over every empire or kingdom which has grown up upon the soil of Asia. The Arian, Turanian, and even the Semitic tribes appear to have been in the nomadic condition, when the Cushite settlers in Lower Babylonia betook themselves to agriculture, erected temples, built cities, and established a strong and settled government. The leaven which was to spread by degrees through the Asiatic peoples was first deposited on the shores of the Persian Gulf at the mouth of the " Great River ;"[1] and hence civilisation, science, letters, art, extended themselves north-ward, and eastward, and westward. Assyria, Media, Semitic Babylonia, Persia, as they derived from Chaldæa the character of their writing,[2] so were they indebted to the same country for their general notions of government and administration, for their architecture, their decorative art, and still more for their science and literature. Each people no doubt modified in some measure the boon received, adding more or less of its own to the common in-heritance. But Chaldæa stands forth as the great parent and original inventress of Asiatic civilisation, without any rival that can reasonably dispute her claims.

---

[1] Gen. xv. 18 ; Deut. i. 7 ; Josh. i. 4.

[2] The alphabets, as well as the languages, of these various races differ ; but, as all assume the wedge as the ultimate element out of which their letters are formed, it seems almost certain that they learnt the art of writing from one another. If so, Chaldæa has on every ground the best claim to be regarded as the teacher of the others.

The great men of the Empire are Nimrod, Urukh, and Chedor-laomer. Nimrod, the founder, has the testimony of Scripture, that he was "a mighty one in the earth;"[4] "a mighty hunter;"[5] the establisher of a "kingdom," when kingdoms had scarcely begun to be known; the builder of four great and famous cities, "Babel, and Erech, and Accad, and Calneh, in the land of Shinar,"[6] or Mesopotamia. To him belongs the merit of selecting a site peculiarly fitted for the development of a great power in the early ages of the world,[7] and of binding men together into a community which events proved to possess within it the elements of prosperity and permanence. Whether he had indeed the rebellious and apostate character which numerous traditions, Jewish, Arabian, and Armenian,[8] assign to him; whether he was in reality concerned in the building of the tower related in the eleventh chapter of the Book of Genesis,[9] we have no means of positively determining. The language of Scripture with regard to Nimrod is laudatory rather than the contrary;[10] and it would seem to have been from a misapprehension of the *nexus* of the Mosaic narrative that

---

[4] Gen. x. 8.
[5] Ib. verse 9.
[6] Ib. verse 10.
[7] In later times, when civilisation was more advanced, less fruitful tracts may, by calling forth men's powers, have produced the most puissant races (see Herod. ix. ad fin.); but in the first ages only fertile regions could nurture and develop greatness. Elsewhere man's life was a struggle for bare existence.
[8] Josephus makes Nimrod the prime mover in the building of the tower (*Ant. Jud.* i. 4, § 2). The

Targums generally take the same view. Some of the Arabic traditions have been already mentioned. (Supra, p. 197, note [6].) The Armenian account will be found in Moses of Chorene, who, identifying Nimrod with Belus, proceeds to describe him as the chief of the Giants, by whom the tower was built, proud and fierce, and of insatiable ambition, engaged in perpetual wars with his neighbours. (*Hist. Armen.* i. 6-10.)

[9] Gen. xi. 1-9.

[10] Nimrod is called "a mighty one in the earth," and "a mighty hunter

the traditions above mentioned originated.[1] Nimrod, " the mighty hunter *before the Lord*," had not in the days of Moses that ill reputation which attached to him in later ages, when he was regarded as the great Titan or Giant, who made war upon the gods, and who was at once the builder of the tower, and the persecutor who forced Abraham to quit his original country. It is at least doubtful whether we ought to allow any weight at all to the additions and embellishments with which later writers, so much wiser than Moses, have overlaid the simplicity of his narrative.

Urukh, whose fame has been shown to have reached the Romans,[2] was the great Chaldæan *architect*. To him belongs, apparently, the conception of the Babylonian temple, with its rectangular base, carefully placed so as to present its angles to the four cardinal points, its receding stages, its buttresses, its drains, its sloped walls, its external staircases for ascent, and its ornamental shrine crowning the whole. At any rate, if he was not the first to conceive and erect such structures, he set the example of building them on such a scale and with such solidity as to secure their long continuance, and render them well nigh imperishable. There is no appearance in all Chaldæa, so far as it has been

---

before the Lord." Many commentators have observed that the phrase in italics is almost always used in a good sense, implying the countenance and favour of God, and his blessing on the work which is said to have been done " before " him, or " in his sight."

[1] Commentators seem generally to have supposed that the building, or attempt to build, described in Gen. xi. 1-9, is the building of Babel ascribed to Nimrod in Gen. x. 10. But this cannot be so: for in Gen. xi. we are told, " they *left off* to build the city." The truth seems to be that the tenth chapter is parenthetical, and the author in ch. xi. takes up the narrative from ch. ix., going back to a time not long after the Deluge.

[2] See above, page 198, note [4].

explored, of any building which can be even probably
assigned to a date anterior to Urukh. The attempted tower was no doubt earlier; and it *may*
have been a building of the same type;[3] but there is
no reason to believe that any remnant, or indeed any
trace, of this primitive edifice, has continued to exist
to our day. The structures of the most archaic
character throughout Chaldæa are, one and all, the
work of King Urukh; who was not content to adorn
his metropolitan city only with one of the new
edifices, but added a similar ornament to each of the
great cities within his empire.[4]

The great builder was followed shortly by the
great *conqueror*. Kudur-Lagamer, the Elamitic prince,
who, nearly twenty centuries before our era, having
extended his dominion over Babylonia and the adjoining regions, marched an army a distance of 1200
miles[5] from the shores of the Persian Gulf to the
Dead Sea, and held Palestine and Syria in subjection
for twelve years, thus effecting conquests which were
not again made from the same quarter till the time
of Nebuchadnezzar, fourteen hundred years afterwards, has a good claim to be regarded as one of
the most remarkable personages in the world's history
—being, as he is, the forerunner and prototype of all
those great Oriental conquerors who from time to
time have built up vast empires in Asia out of hete-
rogeneous materials, which have in a longer or a
shorter space successively crumbled to decay. At a

---

[3] See the article on the "Tower
of Babel" in Smith's *Dictionary of
the Bible*, vol. i. pp. 158-160.

[4] See above, page 109.

[5] The march would necessarily be
along the Euphrates to the latitude
(nearly) of Aleppo, and then down
Syria to the Dead Sea. This is 1200
miles. The direct distance by the
desert is not more than 800 miles;
but the desert cannot be crossed by
an army.

time when the kings of Egypt had never ventured
beyond their borders, unless it were for a foray in
Ethiopia,[a] and when in Asia no monarch had held
dominion over more than a few petty tribes, and a
few hundred miles of territory, he conceived the
magnificent notion of binding into one the manifold
nations inhabiting the vast tract which lies between
the Zagros mountain-range and the Mediterranean.
Lord by inheritance (as we may presume) of Elam,
the country intervening between the mountains and
the lower Tigris, he first made himself master of the
adjacent region of Chaldæa or Babylonia, absorbing
some portion into his own kingdom, while he left
others to be governed by tributary kings or viceroys;[b] after which he proceeded on his career of
conquest up the Euphrates and through Syria, into
Palestine. Successful here, he governed for twelve
years dominions extending near a thousand miles
from east to west, and from north to south probably
not much short of five hundred. It is true that he
was not able to *hold* this large extent of territory;
but the attempt and the success temporarily attending it are memorable circumstances, and were probably long held in remembrance through Western
Asia, where they served as a stimulus and incentive
to the ambition of later monarchs.

These, then, are the great men of the Chaldæan
empire. Its extent, as we have seen, varied greatly
at different periods. Under the kings of the first
dynasty—to which Urukh and Ilgi belonged—it was
probably confined to the alluvium, which seems then
to have been not more than 300 miles in length

---

[a] See the "Historical Essay" of
Sir G. Wilkinson, in the author's

[b] *Herodotus*, vol. II. pp. 341-351.

[b] *Supra*, p. 203.

along the course of the rivers,[8] and which is about 70 or 80 in breadth from the Tigris to the Arabian desert. At the commencement of the second dynasty it received a vast increase, being suddenly carried out on the one side to the Elamitic mountains, and on the other to the Mediterranean, by the accession and conquests of Chedor-laomer. On his Syrian defeat it again contracted, though to what extent we have no means of determining. It is probable that Elam or Susiana, and not unlikely that the Euphrates valley, for a considerable distance above Hit, remained subject to the Chaldæan monarchs after the loss of Syria and Palestine. Assyria seems certainly to have continued in this condition, or else to have been reduced shortly afterwards; for Ismi-dagon, whose son builds a temple at Kileh-Shergat, is the next monumental king to Chedor-laomer. There is reason to think that the subjection of Assyria continued to the very end of the dynasty, and that this region, whose capital was at Kileh-Sherghat, was administered by viceroys deriving their authority from the Chaldæan monarchs.[9] These monarchs, as has been already observed,[10] gradually remove their capital more and more northwards; by which it would appear as if their empire tended to progress in that direction.

The close of the second dynasty, and the downfal of the Chaldæan Empire, seem to have been the result of a great invasion. On the skirts of Chaldæa lay the vast Arabian desert — a tract containing above a million square miles[1]—which, despite its

---

[8] Compare ch. 1. p. 5.
[9] Supra, page 208, note[8].
[10] Page 209.

[1] Chesney, *Euphrates Expedition*, vol. II. p. 448.

arid and unproductive character, has always been a
nursery of nations—a place where they may grow
up to strength secretly, and whence they may issue
in hordes capable of laying prostrate fair and flourishing kingdoms.   Moreover, it may be suspected
that there has been at all times an important Arabian element in the population of Mesopotamia itself.
Just as, at the present day, we find Bedouin and
Jebour Arabs in the upper region between the Tigris
and Khabour rivers,[1] Zobeid and Affej Arabs between Babylon and Niffer,[2] Montefiks about Warka
and Senkereh,[3] Beni Lam and others in Khuzistan,
between the Tigris and the mountains,[4] so in Assyrian
times we have at least thirty distinct tribes of Arabs
among the dwellers upon the banks of the two great
rivers; while some are even represented as living
beyond the mountain barrier in Media.[5]   It is impossible to say how early this dispersion of the race
took place; it may have dated from times as ancient
as the Chaldæan Empire itself; or it may have been
connected with the very event with which we are
now dealing—the destruction of that empire by an
Arab conquest after it had lasted above seven centuries.   No details have reached us of the conquest
itself.   Indeed we do not possess any distinct statement that it was by force of arms the Arabians im-
posed their yoke upon the Chaldæan people.   The
brief summary of Berosus' narrative preserved to us
in Eusebius' does but say, that after the Chaldæan

[1] Layard, *Nineveh and Babylon,*
ch. xi. p. 235, &c.
[2] Lottus, *Chaldæa and Susiana,*
chs. ix. and x. pp. 89-91.
[3] Ibid. pp. 135-145.

[1] Ibid. pp. 328, 358, &c.
[2] See Sir H. Rawlinson's Essay in
the author's *Herodotus,* Vol. I. Essay
vi. p. 450.
[3] *Chron. Can. pars* i. c. iv.

dynasty, which held the throne for 458 years, there
followed a dynasty of nine Arab kings, who ruled
for 245 years. Still, as we can scarcely suppose that
the proud and high-spirited Chaldæans would have
submitted to a yoke so entirely foreign, as that of
Arabs must have been, without a struggle, it seems
necessary to presume a contest wherein the native
Hamitic race was attacked by a foreign Semitic
stock, and overpowered, so as to be forced to accept
a change of rulers. Thus, then, the Chaldæan kingdom perished. Crushed by a race of far inferior
civilisation, which has left no monuments, and barely
a trace of itself in the country,[*] the ancient Chaldæans—the stock of Cush, and people of Nimrod—
sank, about B.C. 1500, into comparative obscurity.
By Arabian and Assyrian influence they were gradually Semitized—assimilated, that is, to the stock
of nations to which the Jews, the northern Arabs,
the Aramæans or Syrians, the Phœnicians, and the
Assyrians belong. Their language fell into disuse,
and grew to be a learned tongue, studied by the
priests and the *literati*; their Cushite character was
lost, and they became, as a people, scarcely distinguishable from the Assyrians.[*] After seven centuries and a half of submission and insignificance, the
Chaldæans, however, began to revive and recover
themselves—they renewed the struggle for national

---

[*] The only relic hitherto discovered, which has been thought to
belong *possibly* to the Arab period, is
a brick found by Sir R. Ker Porter
at Hymar, and now in the British
Museum ; the legend on which
"bears such marks of originality as
may distinguish it from the general
Chaldæan series, and may thus fa-

vour its attribution to the Arabian
dynasty." (Sir H. Rawlinson in the
Essay above quoted, p. 449.)
[*] Hence Herodotus always regards
the Babylonians as Assyrians, and
Babylonia as a district of Assyria.
(See i. 106, 178, 188, 192, &c.; iii.
92 and 155.)

independence, and in the year B.C. 625 succeeded in establishing a second kingdom, which will be treated of in a later volume, as the fourth or Babylonian Monarchy. Even when this monarchy met its death at the hands of Cyrus the Great, the nationality of the Chaldæans was not swept away. We find them recognised under the Persians,[10] and even under the Parthians,[1] as a distinct people. When at last they cease to have a separate national existence, their name remains; and it is in memory of the successful cultivation of their favourite science by the people of Nimrod from his time to that of Alexander, that the professors of astronomical and astrological learning under the Roman Emperors receive, from the poets and historians of the time, the appellation of " Chaldæans."[2]

---

[10] Herod. vii. 63.
[1] Strab. xvi. 1, § 6; Plin. *H. N.* vi. 28.
[2] Juv. *Sat.* vi. 552; x. 94; Tacit.
Ann. ii. 27; iii. 22; vi. 20; &c., Sueton. *Vit. Vitell.* 14; *Vit. Domit.* 14.

THE SECOND MONARCHY.

ASSYRIA.

CHAPTER I.

DESCRIPTION OF THE COUNTRY.

"Τριημορίη ἡ Ἀσσυρίη χώρη τῇ δυνάμει τῆς ἄλλης Ἀσίης." Herod. i. 192.

THE site of the second—or great Assyrian—monarchy, was the upper portion of the Mesopotamian valley. The cities which successively formed its capitals lay, all of them, upon the middle Tigris; and the heart of the country was a district on either side that river, enclosed within the thirty-fifth and thirty-seventh parallels. By degrees these limits were enlarged; and the term, Assyria, came to be used, in a loose and vague way, of a vast and ill-defined tract extending on all sides from this central region. Herodotus[1] considered the whole of Babylonia to be a mere district of Assyria. Pliny[2] reckoned to it all Mesopotamia. Strabo[3] gave it, besides these regions,

---

[1] Herod. i. 106, 192; iii. 92. Ἀπὸ Βαβυλῶνος δὲ καὶ τῆς λοιπῆς Ἀσσυρίης.

[2] Plin. Hist. Nat. vi. 26. "Mesopotamia tota Assyriorum fuit."

[3] Strabo says: "The Assyrians adjoin on Persia and Susiana; for by this name they call Babylonia, and a vast tract of the surrounding country, including Aturia (which contains Nineveh) and Apollonias, and the Elymaeans, and the Parætacæ, and the district about Mount Zagros called Chalonitis, and the plain tracts near Nineveh—Dolomæné, and Calachené, and Chazené, and Adiabené—and the Mesopotamian nations about the Gordiæans, and the Mygdonians about Nisibis, as far as the passage of the Euphrates, and a great part of the country beyond the Euphrates (which is in possession of the

a great portion of Mount Zagros (the modern Kurdistan) and all Syria as far as Cilicia, Judæa, and Phœnicia.

If, leaving the conventional, which is thus vague and unsatisfactory, we seek to find certain natural limits which we may regard as the proper boundaries of the country, in two directions we seem to perceive an almost unmistakable line of demarcation. On the east the high mountain-chain of Zagros, penetrable only in one or two places, forms a barrier of the most marked character, and is beyond a doubt the natural limit for which we are looking. On the south a less striking, but not less clearly defined, line—formed by the abutment of the upper and slightly elevated plain on the alluvium of the lower valley[4]—separates Assyria from Babylonia, which is best regarded as a distinct country. In the two remaining directions, there is more doubt as to the most proper limit. Northwards, we may either view Mount Masius as the natural boundary, or the course of the Tigris from Diabekr to Til, or even perhaps the Armenian mountain-chain north of this portion of the Tigris, from whence that river receives its early tributaries.[5] Westward, we might confine Assyria to the country watered by the affluents of the Tigris,[6] or extend it so as to include the Khabour and its tributaries, or finally venture to carry it across the whole of Mesopotamia, and make it be

Araba), and the people now called by way of distinction Syrians, reaching to Cilicia, and Phœnicia, and Judæa, and to the sea over against the sea of Egypt and the gulf of Issus." (Geograph. xvi. 1, § 1.)

[4] Supra, p. 4.
[5] Supra, p. 12.

[6] This is the division adopted in the geographical essay, contained in vol. i. of the author's Herodotus (p. 569). It was thought most suitable to a general review of the geography of Western Asia; but is less adapted to a special account of the empire of the Assyrians.

bounded by the Euphrates. On the whole it is
thought that in both the doubtful cases the wider
limits are historically the truer ones. Assyrian
remains cover the entire country between the Tigris
and the Khabour, and are frequent on both banks of
the latter stream, giving unmistakable indications
of a long occupation of that region by the great
Mesopotamian people. The inscriptions show that
even a wider tract was in process of time absorbed
by the conquerors; and if we are to draw a line
between the country actually taken into Assyria, and
that which was merely conquered and held in subjection, we can select no better boundary than the
Euphrates westward, and northward the snowy mountain chain known to the ancients as Mons Niphates.

If Assyria be allowed the extent which is here
assigned to her, she will be a country, not only very
much larger than Chaldæa or Babylonia, but positively, of considerable dimensions. Reaching on the
north to the thirty-eighth, and on the south to the
thirty-fourth parallel, she had a length diagonally
from Diarbekr to the alluvium of 350 miles, and a
breadth between the Euphrates and Mount Zagros
varying from above 300 to 170 miles. Her area was
probably not less than 75,000 square miles, which is
beyond that of the German provinces of Prussia or
Austria, more than double that of Portugal, and not
much below that of Great Britain. She would thus
from her mere size be calculated to play an important part in history: and the more so, as during the
period of her greatness scarcely any nation, with
which she came in contact, possessed nearly so
extensive a territory.

Within the limits here assigned to Assyria, the

face of the country is tolerably varied. Possessing, on the whole, perhaps, a predominant character of flatness, the territory still includes some important ranges of hills, while on two sides it abuts upon lofty mountain-chains. Towards the north and east it is provided by nature with an ample supply of water ; rills everywhere flowing from the Armenian and Kurdish ranges, which soon collect into rapid and abundant rivers. The central, southern, and western regions are, however, less bountifully supplied ; for though the Euphrates washes the whole western and south-western frontier, it spreads fertility only along its banks ; and though Mount Masius sends down upon the Mesopotamian plain a considerable number of streams, they form in the space of 200 miles between Balis and Nimrud but two rivers, leaving thus large tracts to languish for want of the precious fluid. The vicinity of the Arabian and Syrian deserts is likewise felt in these regions, which, left to themselves, tend to acquire the desert character, and have occasionally been regarded as actual parts of Arabia.[1]

The chief natural division of the country is that made by the Tigris, which, having a course nearly from north to south, between Til and Samarah, separates Assyria into a western and an eastern district. Of these two, the eastern or that upon the left bank of the Tigris, although considerably the smaller, has always been the more important region. Comparatively narrow at first, it broadens as the course of the river is descended, till it attains about the thirty-fifth parallel a width of 130 or 140 miles.

----

[1] Xenophon, *Anab.* i. 5, § 1 ; Plin. *H. N.* v. 24 ; Strab. xvi. 1, § 26.

It consists chiefly of a series of rich and productive
plains, lying along the courses of the various tributaries which flow from Mount Zagros into the Tigris,
and often of a semi-alluvial character. These plains
are not, however, continuous. Detached ranges of
hills, with a general direction parallel to the Zagros
chain, intersect the flat rich country, separating the
plains from one another, and supplying small streams*
and brooks in addition to the various rivers, which,
rising within or beyond the great mountain barrier,
traverse the plains on their way to the Tigris. The
hills themselves—known now as the Jebel Maklub,
the Ain-es-sufra, the Karachok, &c.—are for the
most part bare and sterile. In form they are hog-
backed, and viewed from a distance have a smooth
and even outline; but on a nearer approach they
are found to be rocky and rugged. Their limestone sides are furrowed by innumerable ravines, and
have a dry and parched appearance, being even in
spring generally naked and without vegetation.
The sterility is most marked on the western flank,
which faces the hot rays of the afternoon sun; the
eastern slope is occasionally robed with a scanty
covering of dwarf oak or stunted brushwood.* In
the fat soil of the plains the rivers commonly run
deep and concealed from view,¹ unless in the spring
and the early summer, when through the rains and

---

* The most important of these is
the Khosr, or river of Koyunjik,
which, rising from the Ain Sifni
hills beyond the Jebel Maklub,
forces its way through that range,
and after washing Khorsabad, and
crossing the great plain, winds round
the eastern base of the mound at
Koyunjik, and then runs on the
Tigris. It is a narrow and sluggish
stream, but deep, and only fordable
about Koyunjik in a few places.
(See Layard's *Nineveh and Babylon*,
p. 77; and compare the view of the
ruins of Nineveh, infra, p. 318.)

² Layard, p. 222.
¹ Ibid, p. 223.

the melting of the snows in the mountains they are greatly swollen, and run bank full, or even overflow the level country.

The most important of these rivers are the following:—the Kurnib or Eastern Khabour, which joins the Tigris in lat. 37° 12'; the Greater Zab (Zab Ala), which washes the ruins of Nimrud, and enters the main stream almost exactly in lat. 36°; the Lesser Zab (Zab Asfal), which effects its junction about lat. 35° 15'; the Adhem, which is received a little below Samarah, about lat. 34°; and the Diyaleh, which now joins below Baghdad, but from which branches have sometimes entered the Tigris a very little below the mouth of the Adhem. Of these streams the most northern, the Khabour, runs chiefly in an untraversed country—the district between Julamerik and the Tigris. It rises a little west of Julamerik in one of the highest mountain districts of Kurdistan, and runs with a general south-westerly course to its junction with another large branch, which reaches it from the district immediately west of Amadiyeh; it then flows due west, or a little north of west, to Zakko, and bending to the north after passing that place, flows once more in a south-westerly direction until it reaches the Tigris. The direct distance from its source to its embouchure is about 80 miles; but that distance is more than doubled by its windings. It is a stream of considerable size, broad and rapid, at many seasons not fordable at all and always forded with difficulty.[*]

The Greater Zab is the most important of all the tributaries of the Tigris. It rises near Konia, in

the district of Karasu, about lat. 38° 20', long. 44°
30', a little west of the watershed which divides
the basins of Lakes Van and Urumiyeh. Its general
course for the first 150 miles is S.S.W., after which
for 25 or 30 miles it runs almost due south through
the country of the Tiyari. Near Amadiyeh it makes
a sudden turn, and flows S.E. or S.S.E. to its junction with the Rowandiz branch;[3] whence, finally, it
resumes its old direction, and runs south-west past
the Nimrud ruins into the Tigris. Its entire course,
exclusive of small windings, is above 350 miles, and
of these nearly 100 are across the plain country,
which it enters soon after receiving the Rowandiz
stream. Like the Khabour, it is fordable at certain
places and during the summer season; but even
then the water reaches above the bellies of horses.[4]
It is 20 yards wide a little above its junction
with the main stream.[5] On account of its strength
and rapidity the Arabs sometimes call it the "Mad
River."[6]

The Lesser Zab has its principal source near
Legwin,[7] about twenty miles south of Lake Urumiyeh,
in lat. 36° 40', long. 45° 25'. This source is to the
east of the great Zagros chain; and it might have
been supposed that the waters would necessarily flow
northward or eastward, towards Lake Urumiyeh, or
towards the Caspian. But the Legwin river, called
even at its source the Zei or Zab, flows from the

[3] Ainsworth, in the *Journal of
the Geographical Society*, vol. xi.
p. 70. Compare Mr. Layard's large
map at the end of his *Nineveh and
Babylon*.

[4] Layard, p. 160.

[5] Chesney, *Euphrates Expedition*,

vol. i. p. 24.

[6] Ibid. p. 22, note [5].

[7] See the account of its source
given by Sir H. Rawlinson, who was
the first European to explore this
region, in the *Journal of the Geographical Society*, vol. x. p. 31.

first westward, as if determined to pierce the mountain barrier. Failing, however, to find an opening
where it meets the range, the Little Zab turns south
and even south-east along its base, till about 25 or
30 miles from its source it suddenly resumes its
original direction, enters the mountains in lat. 36°
20′, and forces its way through the numerous parallel
ranges, flowing generally to the S.S.W., till it debouches upon the plain near Arbela in lat. 36° 10′,
long. 44° 40′, after which it runs S.W. and S.W. by
S. to the Tigris. Its course among the mountains is
from 80 to 90 miles, exclusive of small windings;
and it runs more than 100 miles through the plain.
Its ordinary width, just above its confluence with
the Tigris, is 25 feet.[*]

The Diyaleh, which lies mostly within the limits
that have been here assigned to Assyria, is formed
by the confluence of two principal streams, known
respectively as the Holwan, and the Shirwan, river.
Of these, the Shirwan seems to be the main branch.
This stream rises from the most eastern and highest
of the Zagros ranges, in lat. 34° 45′, long. 47° 40′
nearly. It flows at first west, and then north-west,
parallel to the chain, but on entering the plain of
Shahrizur, where tributaries join it from the north-
east and the north-west, the Shirwan changes its
course and begins to run south of west, a direction
which it pursues till it enters the low country, about
lat. 35° 5′, long. 45° 55′, near Semiram. Thence to
the Tigris it has a course, which in direct distance is
150 miles, and 200 if we include only main windings.[*]

---

[*] Chesney, vol. i. p. 25.
[*] See the map attached to Sir H.
Rawlinson's Memoir on the Atropa-
tenian Ecbatana, in the *Journal of
the Geographical Society,* vol. x.

The whole course cannot be less than 380 miles,
which is about the length of the Great Zab river.
The width attained, before the confluence with the
Tigris, is 60 yards,[1] or three times the width of the
Greater, and seven times that of the Lesser Zab.

On the opposite side of the Tigris, the traveller
comes upon a region far less favoured by nature
than that of which we have been lately speaking.
Western Assyria has but a scanty supply of water;
and unless the labour of man is skilfully applied to
compensate this natural deficiency, the greater part
of the region tends to be, for ten months out of the
twelve, a desert. The general character of the
country is level, but not alluvial. A line of mountains, rocky and precipitous, but of no great elevation, stretches across the northern part of the region,
running nearly due east and west, and extending
from the Euphrates at Rum-kaleh (lat. 37° 17',
long. 37° 50') to Til and Cholek upon the Tigris.
Below this, a vast slightly undulating plain extends
from the northern mountains to the Babylonian
alluvium, only interrupted about midway by a range
of low limestone hills called the Sinjar, which leaving
the Tigris near Mosul runs nearly from east to west
across central Mesopotamia, and strikes the Euphrates
half-way between Rakkeh and Kerkesiyeh, nearly in
long. 40°.

The northern mountain region, called by Strabo
"Mons Masius," and by the Arabs the Karajah Dagh
towards the west, and towards the east the Jebel
Tur, is on the whole a tolerably fertile country.[2] It

[1] Chesney, *Euphrates Expedition*,
vol. i. p. 35.

[2] This region has been traversed
by few, and described by fewer,
Europeans. The best account which
I have been able to find is that of

contains a good deal of rocky land; but has abundant
springs, and in many parts is well wooded. Towards
the west it is rather hilly than mountainous;[3] but
towards the east it rises considerably, and the cone
above Mardin is both lofty and striking.[4] The waters
flowing from the range consist, on the north, of a
number of small brooks, which after a short course
fall into the Tigris; on the south, of still more
numerous and more copious streams, which gradually
unite, and eventually form two rather important
rivers. These rivers are the Belik, known anciently
as the Bilecha,[5] and the Western Khabour, called
Habor in Scripture, and by the classical writers
Aborrhas or Chaboras.[6]

The Belik rises among the hills east of Orfa,
about long. 39°, lat. 37° 10'.[7] Its course is at first
somewhat east of south; but it soon sweeps round,
and passing by the city of Harran—the Haran of
Scripture and the classical Carrhæ[1]—proceeds nearly
due south to its junction, a few miles below Rakkah,
with the Euphrates. It is a small stream throughout
its whole course,[8] which may be reckoned at 100 or
120 miles.

The Khabour is a much more considerable river.

---

the elder Niebuhr. (See his *Voyage
en Arabie*, pp. 300-334.) On the
general fertility of the region, compare his *Description de l'Arabie*,
pp. 134, 135. Strabo's words are
well weighed, and just meet the
case—'Ἔστι δ' ἡ μὲν εὐπόριος εὐδαί-
μων ἰκανῶς xvi. i § 23.

[5] Niebuhr, *Voyage en Arabie*, pp.
321-334; Pocock, *Description of the
East*, vol. ii. pp. 158-163; Chesney,
Euphrates Expedition, vol. i. p. 107.

[6] Niebuhr, p. 317; Layard, *Ni-

neveh and Babylon*, p. 51.
[3] Ibid. Char. p. 3.
[4] Aborrhas by Strabo (xvi. i.
§ 27) and Procopius (*Bell. Pers. ii.
5); Chaboras (Χαβώρας) by Pliny
(xxx. 3), and Ptolemy (v. 18).
Other forms of the word are Abura
('Ἀβούρας, Isid. Char. p. 5), and
Aborn ('Ἀβόρα, Zosim. iii. 12).
[7] Plin. *H. N.* v. 24; Dio Cass.
xxxvii. 5; Strab. xvi. 1, § 23, &c.
[8] Chesney, *Euphrates Expedition*,
vol. i. p. 48.

It collects the waters which flow southward from at least two-thirds of the Mons Masius,[1] and has, besides, an important source, which the Arabs regard

The Khabour, from near Arban, looking north.

as the true " head of the spring,"[1] derived apparently from a spur of the Sinjar range.   This stream, which

[1] Ainsworth, *Travels in the Track of the Ten Thousand*, p. 79, note [1].   [1] *Has el Ain.* (Niebuhr, p. 316; Layard, p. 308; Ainsworth, p. 75.)

rises about lat. 36° 40,' long. 40,° flows only a little
south of east to its junction near Koukab with the
Jerujer or river of Nisibis, which comes down from
Mons Masius with a course not much west of south.
Both of these branches are formed by the union of a
number of streams. Neither of them is fordable for
some distance above their junction; and below it,
they constitute a river of such magnitude as to be
navigable for a considerable distance by steamers.[3]
The course of the Khabour below Koukab is tortuous;[3] but its general direction is S.S.W. The
entire length of the stream is certainly not less than
200 miles.

The country between the "Mons Masius" and the
Sinjar range is an undulating plain, from 60 to 70
miles in width, almost as devoid of geographical features as the alluvium of Babylonia. From a height
the whole appears to be a dead level;[4] but the traveller finds, on descending, that the surface, like that
of the American prairies and the Roman Campagna,
really rises and falls in a manner which offers a
decided contrast to the alluvial flats nearer the sea.
Great portions of the tract are very deficient in
water. Only small streams descend from the Sinjar
range, and these are soon absorbed by the thirsty
soil; so that except in the immediate vicinity of the
hills north and south, and along the courses of the
Khabour, the Belik, and their affluents, there is little
natural fertility, and cultivation is difficult. The
soil too is often gypsiferous; and its salt and nitrous
exudations destroy vegetation;[4] while at the same

[1] Ainsworth, l. s. c.   [3] Ibid. p. 51.
[2] Layard, p. 301.   [4] Ibid. p. 324.

time the streams and springs are from the same
cause for the most part brackish and unpalatable.[*]
Volcanic action probably did not cease in the region
very much, if at all, before the historical period.
Fragments of basalt in many places strew the plain;
and near the confluence of the two chief branches
of the Khabour, not only are old craters of volcanoes
distinctly visible, but a cone still rises from the centre
of one, precisely like the cones in the craters of Etna
and Vesuvius, composed entirely of loose lava, scoriæ,
and ashes, and rising to the height of 300 feet.

Koukab.

The name of this remarkable hill, which is Koukab,
is even thought to imply, that the volcano may have
been active within the time to which the traditions
of the country extend.[†]

---

[*] Layard, pp. 242, 325.
[†] Ibid. p. 308. *Koukab* is said to signify " a jet of fire or flame."

Sheets of water are so rare in this region, that the small lake of Khatouniyeh seems to deserve especial description. This lake is situated near the point where the Sinjar changes its character, and from a high rocky range subsides into low broken hills. It is of oblong shape, with its greater axis pointing nearly due east and west, in length about four miles, and in its greatest breadth somewhat less than three.[1] The banks are low and in part marshy, more especially on the side towards the Khabour, which is not more than ten miles distant.[2] In the middle of the lake is a hilly peninsula, joined to the mainland by a narrow causeway, and beyond it a small island covered with trees. The lake abounds with fish and waterfowl; and its water, though brackish, is regarded as remarkably wholesome both for man and beast.

The Sinjar range, which divides Western Assyria into two plains, a northern and a southern, is a solitary limestone ridge, rising up abruptly from the flat country, which it commands to a vast distance on both sides. The limestone, of which it is composed, is white, soft, and fossiliferous; it detaches itself in enormous flakes from the mountain-sides, which are sometimes broken into a succession of gigantic steps, while occasionally they present the columnar appearance of basalt.[3] The flanks of the Sinjar are seamed

---

[1] See Mr. Layard's maps at the end of his *Nineveh and Babylon*. For a general description of the lake, compare the same work, p. 324, with C. Niebuhr's *Voyage en Arabie*, p 316.

[2] A long swamp, called the Hol, extends from the lake to within a short distance of the Khabour (Lay-

ard, l. s. c). This is probably the Hull, or Hauli of some writers, which is represented as a tributary of the Khabour. (See Chesney, *Euphrates Expedition*, vol. i. p. 61; *Journal of Geographical Society*, vol. ix. p. 423, &c.)

[3] Layard, *Nineveh and Babylon*, p. 250.

with innumerable ravines, and from these small brooks issue, which are soon dispersed by irrigation,

Lake of Khatouniyeh.

or absorbed in the thirsty plains.[*] The sides of the mountain are capable of being cultivated by means

[*] Layard, *Nineveh and Babylon*, p. 256.   Compare *Nineveh and its Remains*, vol. I. p. 315, note.

of terraces, and produce fair crops of corn and excellent fruit; the top is often wooded with fruit-trees
or forest trees.[3]   Geographically, the Sinjar may be
regarded as the continuation of that range of hills
which shuts in the Tigris on the west, from Tekrit
nearly to Mosul, and then leaving the river strikes
across the plain in a direction almost from east to
west as far as the town of Sinjar, which is in long.
41° 52' east from Greenwich.   Here the mountains
change their course and bend to the south-west, till
having passed the little lake described above, they
somewhat suddenly subside,[4] sinking from a high
ridge into low undulating hills, which pass to the
south of the lake, and then disappear in the plain
altogether.   According to some, the Sinjar here terminates; but perhaps it is best to regard it as rising
again in the Abd-el-aziz hills,[5] which, intervening between the Khabour and the Euphrates, run on in the
same south-west direction from Arban to Zelabi.   If
this be accepted as the true course of the Sinjar, we
must view it as throwing out two important spurs.
One of these is near its eastern extremity, and runs
to the south-east, dividing the plain of Zerga from
the great central level.   Like the main chain, it is of
limestone; and, though low, has several remarkable
peaks which serve as landmarks from a vast distance.   The Arabs call it Kebritiyeh, or "the Sulphur range," from a sulphurous spring which rises
at its foot.[6]   The other spur is thrown out near
the western extremity, in lat. 36°, long. 40° 15'

---

[3] Layard, *Nineveh and Babylon*,
pp. 253-256.
[4] Ibid. p. 255.
[5] This is the view of Colonel

Chesney. (See his *Euphrates Expedition*, vol. i. p. 105.)
[6] Layard, *Nineveh and Babylon*,
p. 242, note, and p. 249.

nearly, and runs towards the north-west, parallel to
the course of the upper Khabour, which rises from
its flank at Ras-el-Ain.' The name of Abd-el-aziz is
applied to this spur, as well as to the continuation of
the Sinjar between Arban and Halebi. It is broken
into innumerable valleys and ravines,' abounding
with wild animals, and is scantily wooded with dwarf
oak. Streams of water abound in it.

South of the Sinjar range, the country resumes the
same level appearance which characterises it between the Sinjar and the Mons Masius. A low limestone ridge skirts the Tigris valley from Mosul to
Tekrit,' and near the Euphrates the country is sometimes slightly hilly;' but generally the eye travels
over a vast slightly undulating level, unbroken by
eminences, and supporting but a scanty vegetation.
The description of Xenophon a little exaggerates the
flatness, but is otherwise faithful enough :—" In these
parts the country was a plain throughout, as smooth
as the sea, and full of wormwood; if any other shrub
or reed grew there, it had a sweet aromatic smell;
but there was not a tree in the whole region."'
Water is still more scarce than in the plains north
of the Sinjar. The brooks descending from that
range are so weak that they generally lose themselves in the plain before they have run many miles.
In one case only do they seem sufficiently strong to

' Chesney, *Euphrates Expedition*,
p. 49.
' Layard, *Nineveh and Babylon*,
p. 312.
' Ibid. pp. 240, 241.
' Chesney, *Euphrates Expedition*,
pp. 52, 53. The hills in this region
are of chalk formation, as is the

Abd-el-aziz, according to the same
author. (Ibid. p. 105.)
' Xen. *Anab.* i. 5, § 1. Ἐν τούτῳ
δὲ τῷ τόπῳ ἦν μὲν ἡ γῆ πεδίον ἅπαν
ὁμαλὸν ὥσπερ θάλαττα, ἀψινθίου δὲ
πλῆρες· εἰ δέ τι καὶ ἄλλο ἐνῆν ὕλης ἢ
καλάμου, ἅπαντα ἦσαν εὐώδη, ὥσπερ
ἀρώματα· δένδρον δ' οὐδὲν ἐνῆν.

form a river. The Tharthar, which flows by the
ruins of El Hadhr, is at that place a considerable
stream, not indeed very wide, but so deep that horses
have to swim across it.[3] Its course above El Hadhr
has not been traced; but the most probable conjecture seems to be that it is a continuation of the
Sinjar river, which rises about the middle of the
range, in long. 41° 50', and flows south-east through
the desert. The Tharthar appears at one time to
have reached the Tigris near Tekrit,[4] but it now ends
in a marsh or lake to the south-west of that city.[5]

The political geography of Assyria need not occupy much of our attention. There is no native evidence that in the time of the great monarchy the
country was formally divided into districts, to which
any particular names were attached, or which were
regarded as politically separate from one another;
nor do such divisions appear in the classical writers
until the time of the later geographers, Strabo, Dionysius, and Ptolemy. If it were not that mention is
made in the Old Testament of certain districts within
the region which has been here termed Assyria, we
should have no proof that in the early times any
divisions at all had been recognized. The names,
however, of Padan-Aram, Aram-Naharaim, Gozan,
Halah, and (perhaps) Huzzab, designate in Scripture
particular portions of the Assyrian territory; and as
these portions appear to correspond in some degree
with the divisions of the classical geographers, we
are led to suspect that these writers may in many, if
not in most, cases have followed ancient and native

[3] *Journal of Geographical Society,*
vol. ix. p. 455.
[4] Chesney, p. 50.

[5] Ibid. p. 51; Layard, *Nineveh
and its Remains,* vol. i. p. 315,
note.

traditions or authorities. The principal divisions of
the classical geographers will therefore be noticed
briefly, so far at least as they are intelligible.

According to Strabo,[*] the district within which
Nineveh stood was called Aturia, which seems to be
the word Assyria slightly corrupted, as we know
that it habitually was by the Persians.[7] The neighbouring plain country he divides into four regions—
Dolomené, Calachené, Chazené, and Adiabené. Of
Dolomené, which Strabo mentions but in one place,
and which is wholly omitted by other authors, no
account can be given.[*] Calachené, which is perhaps
the Calaciné of Ptolemy,[*] must be the tract about
Calah (Nimrud), or the country immediately north
of the Upper Zab river. Chazené, like Dolomené, is
a term which cannot be explained.[1] Adiabené, on
the contrary, is a well-known geographical expression.[*] It is the country of the Zab or *Diab* rivers,[*]

[*] Strab. xvi. 1, § 1.

[7] The form Aturia ('Aτουρία) is used likewise by Arrian (*Exp. Al.* iii. 7), and by Stephen (ad voc. Nἴνος). Dio Cassius writes Atyria ('Aτυρία), and asserts that the τ was always used for the σ "by the barbarians" (lv. 26). It was cer- tainly so used by the Persians (see the *Behistun Inscription*, passim), but the Assyrians themselves, like the Jews and the Greeks, seem to have employed the σ.

[*] Dolomené is ingeniously con- nected by Mons. C. Muller with the Dolba of Arrian. (Fr. 11. See the *Fragment. Hist. Gr.* vol. iii. p. 588.) It is clear that the ethnic Δολβηνη (Steph. Bys. ad voc.) would easily pass into Δολομηνή. Dolba, according to Arrian, was a city in Adiabené.

[*] Ptol. vi. 1. As Ptolemy, how- ever, places Calaciné *above* Adia- bené, he may possibly intend it for

Chalonitis.

[1] Chazené was indeed mentioned by Arrian in his *Parthica*; and if we possessed that work, we should probably not find much difficulty in locating it. But the fragment in Stephen (ad voc. Xαζηνή) tells us nothing of its exact position. Ste- phen himself is clearly wrong in placing it on the *Euphrates*. Arrian probably included it in the territory of Dolba, which was with him a part of Adiabené. (See above, note[*], and compare the fragment of Ar- rian: 'Eν ταύτη τη 'Oλβία (leg. Δολβία vel Δολβαία) και τα πεδία της Xαζηνης σατραπειας επι μηκιστον ανεπταμενα.)

[*] See Strab. xvi. 1, § 1 and § 10; Plin. *H. N.* v. 12, vi. 13; Ptol. vi. 1; Arrian, Fr. 11-13; Pomp. Mel. i. 11; Solin. 48; Amm. Marc. xxiii. 20, &c.

[*] So Ammianus explains the

and either includes the whole of Eastern Assyria between the mountains and the Tigris,[4] or more strictly
is applied to the region between the Upper and
Lower Zab,[5] which consists of two large plains separated from each other by the Karachok hills. In this
way Arbelitis, the plain between the Karachok and
Zagros, would fall within Adiabené; but it is sometimes made a distinct region,[6] in which case Adiabené
must be restricted to the flat between the two Zabs,
the Tigris, and the Karachok. Chalonitis and Apolloniatis, which Strabo seems to place between these
northern plains and Susiana,[7] must be regarded as
dividing between them the country south of the
Lesser Zab, Apolloniatis (so called from its Greek
capital, Apollonia) lying along the Tigris, and Chalonitis along the mountains from the pass of Derbend
to Gilan.[8] Chalonitis seems to have taken its name
from a capital city called Chala,[9] which lay on the
great route connecting Babylon with the southern
Ecbatana, and in later times was known as Holwan.[1]

---

name — "Nos autem id dicimus,
quod in his terris amnes sunt duo
perpetui, quos et transivimus, Dia-
las et Adiabas, juncti navalibus
pontibus; ideoque intelligi Adiabe-
nam cognominatam, ut a flumini-
bus maximis Ægyptus, et India,
itidemque Hiberia et Bætica."
xxiii. 6.

[4] Pliny seems to give to Adiabené this extended signification,
when he says,—"Adiabenen Tigris
et montium sinus cingunt. At levâ
ejus regio Medorum est." (H. N.
vi. 9; compare ch. vi. 20.)

[5] Amm. Marc. l. s. c.

[6] As by Ptolemy (Geograph.
vi. 1).

[7] Strab. xv. 3, § 12; xvi. 1, § 1.

[8] The position of Chalonitis is
pretty exactly indicated by Strabo,

Polybius, and Isidore of Charax.
Strabo calls it τὴν περὶ τὸ Ζάγρον
ὄρος Χαλωνῖτιν (xvi. 1, § 1). Polybius connects it with the same
mountain range (v. 54, § 7). Isidore
distinctly places it between Apolloniatis and Media (Mans. Parth.
p. 5). See also Dionys. Perieg. i.
1015, and Plin. H. N. vi. 27.

[9] Isid. Mans. Parth. l. s. c. Tacitus probably intends the same city
by his "Halus" (Ann. vi. 41),
which he couples with Artemita.
It does not appear to have been
identical either with the Halah of
the Book of Kings, or with the Calah
of Genesis.

[1] The ruins of Holwan were visited by Sir H. Rawlinson in the
year 1836. For an account of them,
and for a notice of the importance

Below Apolloniatis,[1] and (like that district) skirting the Tigris, was Sittacené (so named from its capital, Sittacé[2]), which is commonly reckoned to Assyria,[3] but seems more properly regarded as Susianian territory. Such are the chief divisions of Assyria east of the Tigris.

West of the Tigris, the name Mesopotamia is commonly used, like the Aram-Naharaim of the Hebrews, for the whole country between the two great rivers. Here are again several districts, of which little is known, as Acabené, Tingené, and Ancobaritis.[4] Towards the north, along the flanks of Mons Masius from Nisibis to the Euphrates, Strabo seems to place the Mygdonians, and to regard the country as Mygdonia.[5] Below Mygdonia, towards the west, he puts Anthemusia, which he extends as far as the Khabour river.[6] The region south of the Khabour and the Sinjar he seems to regard as inhabited entirely by Arabs.[7] Ptolemy has, in lieu of the Mygdonia of Strabo, a district which he calls Gauzanitis;[8] and this name is on good grounds identified with the Gozan of Scripture[9]—the true original probably of the

---

of Holwan in Mahometan times, see the *Journal of the Geographical Soc.* vol. ix. pp. 35–40.

[1] Strabo identifies Sittacené with Apolloniatis (xv. 3, § 12); but from Ptolemy (vi. 1) and other geographers we gather that Sittacené was further down the river.

[2] Sittacé was first noticed by Hecatæus (Fr. 184). It was visited by Xenophon (*Anab.* ii. 4, § 13). Strabo omits all mention of it. We have notices of it in Pliny (*H. N.* vi. 27), and Stephen (ad voc. Σιττακη).

[3] Strab. xvi. 1, § 1, et passim:

Ptol. vi. 1.

[4] Ptol. v. 18.

[5] Strab. xvi. 1, § 1, and § 23.

[6] Ibid. § 27. Anthemusia derived its name from a city Anthemus (Steph. Byz.), or Anthemusias (Tacit. Isid.), built by the Macedonians between the Euphrates and the Belik.

[7] Strab. xvi. 1, § 26. Compare Plin. *H. N.* v. 24.

[8] Ptol. v. 18.

[9] 2 Kings xvii. 6; xviii. 11; xix. 12; 1 Chron. v. 26; Is. xxxvii. 12. The identification does not depend upon the mere resemblance of name;

"Mygdonia" of the Greeks.[1] Gozan appears to represent the whole of the upper country from which the longer affluents of the Khabour spring; while Halah, which is coupled with it in Scripture,[2] and which Ptolemy calls Chalcitis, and makes border on Gauzanitis, may designate the tract upon the main stream, as it comes down from Ras-el-Ain.[3] The region about the upper sources of the Belik has no special designation in Strabo, but in Scripture it seems to be called Padan-Aram,[4] a name which has been well explained as "the flat Syria," or "the country stretching out from the foot of the hills."[5] In the later Roman times it was known as Osrhoëné;[6] but this name was scarcely in use before the time of the Antonines.

The true heart of Assyria was the country close along the Tigris, from lat. 35° to 36° 30'. Within these limits were the four great cities, marked by the mounds at Khorsabad, Mosul, Nimrud, and Kileh-Sherghat, besides a multitude of places of inferior consequence. It has been generally supposed that

---

but upon that, combined with the mention of the Habor (or Khabour) as the river of Gozan, and the implied vicinity of Gozan to Haran (Harran) and Halah (Chalcitis).

[1] See the article on "Gozan" in Smith's *Biblical Dictionary*, vol. i. p. 720. The initial m (מ) in the word Mygdonia is probably a mere adjectival or participial prefix; while the d represents the Semitic z (ז), according to an ordinary phonetic variation.

[2] 2 Kings xvii. 6; xviii. 11; 1 Chron. v. 26.

[3] One of the mounds on this stream is still called Gla, or Kalah, by the Arabs. (See Layard's *Nin-*

eveh and Babylon, p. 312, note.)

[4] Gen. xxv. 20; xxviii. 2-7, &c. The name is only used in Genesis.

[5] Stanley, *Sinai and Palestine*, p. 129, note [1]. It is curious, however, that both Padan-Aram and Aram-Naharaïm recall the names of nations inhabiting these parts in the Assyrian times. The chief inhabitants of the Mons Masius mentioned by the early Assyrian kings are the Nairi; and across the Euphrates, towards Aleppo, there is a tribe called the Patena. Probably, however, both coincidences are accidental.

[6] Dio Cass. xl. 19; lxviii. 18, &c. Arrian, Fr. 2; Herodian, iii. 9, &c.

the left bank of the river was more properly Assyria than the right;[*] and the idea is so far correct, as that the left bank was in truth of primary value and importance,[*] whence it naturally happened that three out of the four capitals were built on that side of the river. Still the very fact that one early capital was on the right bank is enough to show that both shores of the stream were alike occupied by the race from the first; and this conclusion is abundantly confirmed by other indications throughout the region. Assyrian ruins, the remains of considerable towns, strew the whole country between the Tigris and Khabour, both north and south of the Sinjar range.[*] On the banks of the Lower Khabour are the remains of a royal palace,[*] besides many other traces of the tract through which it runs having been permanently occupied by the Assyrian people.[*] Mounds, probably Assyrian, are known to exist along the course of the Khabour's great western affluent;[*] and even near Seruj, in the country between Harran and the Euphrates, some evidence has been found not only of conquest but of occupation.[*] Remains are

<hr/>

[*] Ptolemy bounds Assyria by the Tigris (*Geograph.* vi. 1). Plloy identifies Adiabené with Assyria (*H. N.* v. 12). If the Hussab of Nahum is really "the Zab region" (Smith's *Biblical Dictionary*, sub voc.), that prophet would make the same identification. When Strabo (xvi. 1, § 1) and Arrian (*Exp. Alex.* iii. 7) place Aturia on the left bank of the Tigris only, they indicate a similar feeling.

[*] See above, pages 228 and 229.

[*] They are less numerous north of the Sinjar. (See Layard, *Nineveh and Babylon*, p. 252.) Still there are a certain number of ancient mounds in the more northern plain. (Ibid. pp. 334, 335; and compare *Nineveh and its Remains*, vol. i. p. 311.)

[*] At Arban. (*Nineveh and Babylon*, pp. 275, 276.)

[*] Ibid. pp. 297-300.

[*] Ibid. p. 312, and note.

[*] The colossal lions at this place, 12 feet long and 7 feet 3 inches high, are unmistakably Assyrian, and must have belonged to some large building. (See Chesney, *Euphrates Expedition*, vol. i. pp. 114, 115, whence the representation on the next page is taken.)

perhaps more frequent on the opposite side of the
Tigris; at any rate they are more striking and
more important. Bavian, Khorsabad, Shereef-Khan,

Nebbi-Yunus, Koyunjik,
and Nimrud, which have
furnished by far the most
valuable and interesting
of the Assyrian monu-
ments, all lie east of the
Tigris; while on the
west two places only
have yielded relics wor-

[Colossal lion, near Seru].

thy to be compared with these, Arban and Kileh-
Sherghat.

It is curious that in Assyria, as in early Chaldæa,
there is a special pre-eminence of *four* cities. An
indication of this might seem to be contained in
Genesis, where Asshur is said to have "builded
Nineveh, and the city Rehoboth, and Calah, and
Resen;" [*] but on the whole it is more probable that
we have here a mistranslation (which is corrected
for us in the margin [/]), and that three cities only are
ascribed by Moses to the great patriarch. In the
flourishing period of the empire, however, we actually find four capitals, of which the native names
seem to have been Ninua, Calah, Asshur, and Bit-
Sargina, or Dur-Sargina (the city of Sargon)—all
places of first-rate consequence. Besides these principal cities, which were the sole seats of government,
Assyria contained a vast number of large towns, few

---

[*] Gen. x. 11, 12.
[/] In the margin we have רְחֹבֹת עִיר, translated "the streets of the city," which is far better than the textual rendering. Had r'hoboth been the name of a place, the term 'ir would scarcely have been added.

of which it is possible to name, but so numerous
that they cover the whole face of the country with
their ruins.' Among them were Tarbisa, Arbil, and
Khazeh, in the tract between the Tigris and Mount
Zagros; Harran, Tel-Apni, and Amida, towards the
north-west frontier; Sirki (Circesium), at the confluence of the Khabour with the Euphrates; Anat
on the Euphrates, some way below this junction;
Tabiti, Magarisi, Shadikanni, Katni, Beth-Khalupi,
&c., in the district south of the Sinjar, between
the lower course of the Khabour and the Tigris.
Here again, as in the case of Chaldæa,' it is impossible at present to locate with accuracy all the
cities.   We must once more confine ourselves to
the most important, and seek to determine, either
absolutely or with a certain vagueness, their several
positions.

It admits of no reasonable doubt that the ruins
opposite Mosul are those of Nineveh. The name of
Nineveh is read on the bricks; and a uniform tradition, reaching from the Arab conquest to comparatively recent times,' attaches to the mounds themselves the same title. They are the most extensive
ruins in Assyria; and their geographical position
suits perfectly all the notices of the geographers and
historians with respect to the great Assyrian capital.'

***

* Layard, *Nineveh and its Remains*, vol. i. p. 314; *Nineveh and
Babylon*, pp. 245, 240, 312, 313,
&c.; *Journal of Asiatic Society*, vol.
xv. pp. 303, 304.

' See above, page 20.

' The early Arabian geographers
and historians mentioned the forts
of *Ninawi* to the east and of Mosul
to the west of the Tigris. (*As. Soc.*

Journ. vol. xli. p. 418, note '.) To
prove the continuity of the tradition, it would be necessary to quote
all travellers, from Benjamin of
Tudela to Mr. Layard, who disputes
its value, but does not deny it.

' See Herod. i. 193; Strab. xvi.
1, § 3; Ptol. vi. 1; Plin. vi. 13,
§ 16; Amm. Marc. xviii. 7; Eustath. ad Dionys. Perieg. 901.

As a subsequent chapter will be devoted to a description of this famous city,[1] it is enough in this place to observe that it was situated on the left or east bank of the Tigris, in lat. 36° 21', at the point where a considerable brook, the Khosr-su, falls into the main stream. On its west flank flowed the broad and rapid Tigris, the "arrow-stream," as we may translate the word;[2] while north, east, and south, expanded the vast undulating plain which intervenes between the river and the Zagros mountain-range. Midway in this plain, at the distance of from fifteen to eighteen miles from the city, stood boldly up the Jebel Maklub and Ain-sufra hills, calcareous ridges rising nearly 2000 feet[3] above the level of the Tigris, and forming by far the most prominent objects in the natural landscape.[4] Inside the Ain Sufra, and parallel to it, ran the small stream of the Gomel, or Ghazir, like a ditch skirting a wall, an additional defence in that quarter. On the south-east and south, distant about fifteen miles, was the strong and impetuous current of the Upper Zab, completing the natural defences of the position, which was excellently chosen to be the site of a great capital.

South of Nineveh, at the distance of about twenty miles by the direct route and thirty by the course of

[1] See below, ch. iv.

[2] No Strabo, xi. 14, § 8; Plin. H. N. vi. 27; Q. Curt. iv. 9, § 10, &c. There are, however, some difficulties attaching to this etymology. It is Arian, not Semitic—*tigra*, as "an arrow," standing connected with the Sanscrit *tij*, "to sharpen," Armenian *teg*, "a javelin," Persian *tigh*, "a blade," and *tir*, "an arrow." Yet it was used by the Jews, under the slightly corrupted form of *Dekel*,

(חֶדֶּקֶל), as early as Moses (Gen. ii. 14), and by the Assyrians about B.C. 1000. (*Journal of As. Soc.* vol. xiv. p. xov.) It is conjectured that there was a root *dik* in ancient Babylonian, of cognate origin with the Sanscrit *tij*, from which the forms *Dekel, Digla*, or *Diglath* were derived.

[3] Capt. Jones, in the *Journal of the As. Soc.* vol. xv. p. 290.

[4] Ibid. p. 299.

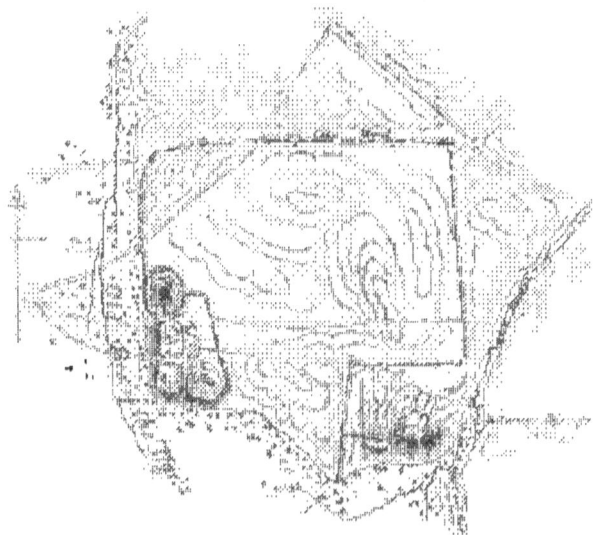

Plan of the Ruins at Nimrud (Calah).

the Tigris,' stood the second city of the empire, Calah,
the site of which is marked by the extensive ruins at
Nimrud.' Broadly, this place may be said to have
been built at the confluence of the Tigris with the
Upper Zab; but in strictness it was on the Tigris
only, the Zab flowing five or six miles further to the
south,' and entering the Tigris at least nine miles

---

[7] So Colonel Chesney (*Euphrates
Expedition*, vol. i. p. 21).

[8] Sir H. Rawlinson and Dr. Hincks
agree in reading the ancient name
of this city as Calah. At the same
time it is not to be denied that
there are difficulties in the identification. 1. Nimrud being only 20
miles from Nineveh, it is difficult
to find room for Resen, a "great
city" (Gen. x. 12) between them,

not to mention that there are no
important ruins in this position.
2. Calah, moreover, if it gave name
to Ptolemy's Calacine, should be
away from the river, for by placing
Calacine *above* Adiabené, he almost
certainly meant further from the
river.

[9] *Journal of As. Soc.* vol. xv.
p. 342. At the same time it must
be admitted that water from the

below the Nimrud ruins.[1] These ruins at present
occupy an area somewhat short of a thousand English acres,[2] which is little more than one-half of the
area of the ruins of Nineveh; but it is thought that
the place was in ancient times considerably larger,
and that the united action of the Tigris and some
winter streams has swept away no small portion
of the ruins.[3] They form at present an irregular
quadrangle, the sides of which face the four cardinal
points. On the north and east the rampart may still
be distinctly traced. It was flanked with towers
along its whole course,[4] and pierced at uncertain intervals by gates, but was nowhere of very great
strength or dimensions. On the south side it must
have been especially weak, for there it has disappeared altogether. Here, however, it seems probable that the Tigris and the Shor Derruh stream, to
which the present obliteration of the wall may be
ascribed, formed in ancient times a sufficient protection. Towards the west, it seems to be certain
that the Tigris (which is now a mile off) anciently
flowed close to the city.[5] On this side, directly
facing the river, and extending along it a distance of
600 yards,[6] or more than a third of a mile, was the
royal quarter, or portion of the city occupied by the
palaces of the kings. It consisted of a raised plat-

Zab was conducted into the city by
a canal and tunnel, of which more
will be said in another chapter.

[1] Chesney, l.s.c.

[2] Capt. Jones, in the *Journal of
the Asiatic Soc.* vol. xv. pp. 347-
351.

[3] Ibid. vol. xv. p. 347.

[4] Layard, *Nineveh and Babylon*,
p. 656.

[5] Ibid. l.s.c.; *As. Soc. Journal,*
vol. xv. pp. 342, 343.

[6] See Mr. Layard's "Plan" in
his *Nineveh and Babylon*, opp. p.
655. For the present state of the
ruins, see his *Nineveh and its Remains*, vol. i. opp. p. 331, and compare the chart (supra, p. 251), which
is reduced from Captain F. Jones's
Survey.

form, forty feet above the level of the plain, composed in some parts of rubbish, in others of regular layers of sun-dried bricks, and cased on every side with solid stone masonry, containing an area of sixty English acres, and in shape almost a regular rectangle, 560 yards long, and from 350 to 450 broad.[1] The platform was protected at its edges by a parapet, and is thought to have been ascended in various places by wide staircases, or inclined ways, leading up from the plain.[2] The greater part of its area is occupied by the remains of palaces constructed by various native kings, of which a more particular account will be given in the chapter on the architecture and other arts of the Assyrians.[3] It contains also the ruins of two small temples, and abuts at its north-western

angle on the most singular structure which has as yet been discovered among the remains of the Assyrian cities. This is the famous tower or pyramid which looms so conspicuously over the Assyrian plains, and which has always attracted the special

---

[1] The platform is not quite regular, being broader towards the south than towards the north, as will be seen in the plan.

[2] Layard, *Nineveh and Babylon*, p. 654.

[3] See below, chap. vi.

notice of the traveller.[1]   An exact description of this remarkable edifice will be given hereafter.   It appears from the inscriptions on its bricks to have been commenced by one of the early kings, and completed by another.   Its internal structure has led to the supposition that it was designed to be a place of burial for one or other of these monarchs.   Another conjecture is, that it was a watch-tower;[2] but this seems very unlikely, since no trace of any mode by which it could be ascended has been discovered.

Forty miles below Calah, on the opposite bank of the Tigris, was a third great city, the native name of which appears to have been Asshur.   This place is represented by the ruins at Kileh Sherghat, which are scarcely inferior in extent to those at Nimrud or Calah.[3]   It will not be necessary to describe minutely this site, as in general character it closely resembles the other ruins of Assyria.   Long lines of low mounds mark the position of the old walls, and show that the shape of the city was quadrangular.   The chief object is a large square mound or platform, two and a half

---

[1] Xenophon describes Calah, which he calls Larissa (compare the Lachism, לכיש, of the Samaritan Pentateuch), as "a vast deserted city, formerly inhabited by the Medes; it was," he says, "surrounded by a wall 25 feet broad, 100 feet high, and nearly seven miles in circumference, built of baked brick, with a stone basement to the height of 20 feet."   He then observes: "Παρ' αὐτὴν τὴν πόλιν ἦν πυραμὶς λιθίνη, τὸ μὲν εὗρος πλέθρου, τὸ δὲ ὕψος δύο πλέθρων." (Anab. iii. 4, § 9.) Ctesias, with his usual exaggeration, made the width nine stades, and the height eight stades, or nearly a

mile!   He placed the pyramid at Nineveh, and on the Euphrates! (See Diod. Sic. ii. 7, § 1.)   The imposing effect of the structure even now is witnessed to by Mr. Layard (Nineveh and its Remains, vol. i. p. 4); Colonel Rich (Kurdistan, vol. ii. p. 132); Colonel Chesney (Euphrates Expedition, vol. i. p. 21); and Captain Jones (As. Soc. Journal, vol. xv. pp. 348, 349).

[2] This is the opinion of Captain Jones (As. Soc. Journal, vol. xv. p. 349).

[3] See Layard, Nineveh and its Remains, vol. i. p. 5, and vol. ii. p. 44.

miles in circumference, and in places a hundred feet above the level of the plain, composed in part of sundried bricks, in part of natural eminences, and exhibiting occasionally remains of a casing of hewn stone, which may once have encircled the whole structure. About midway on the north side of the platform, and close upon its edge, is a high cone or pyramid. The rest of the platform is covered with the remains of walls and with heaps of rubbish, but does not show much trace of important buildings. This city has been supposed to represent the Biblical Resen; but the description of that place as lying " *between* Nineveh and Calah " seems to render the identification worse than uncertain.

The ruins at Kileh-Sherghat are the last of any extent towards the south, possessing a decidedly Assyrian character. To complete our survey, therefore, of the chief Assyrian towns, we must return northwards, and, passing Nineveh, direct our attention to the magnificent ruins on the small stream of the Khosr-su, which have made the Arab village of Khorsabad one of the best known names in Oriental topography. About nine miles from the north-east angle of the wall of Nineveh, in a direction a very little east of north, stands the ruin known as Khorsabad, from a small village which formerly occupied its summit [1]—the scene of the labours of M. Botta, who was the first to disentomb from among the mounds of Mesopotamia the relics of an Assyrian palace. The enclosure at Khorsabad is nearly square in shape, each side being about 2000 yards long.[2]

---

[1] Mr. Botta purchased and removed this village before he made his great excavations. (*Letters from* Nineveh, p. 57, note.)

[2] See Captain Jones's Survey, sheet I.

No part of it is very lofty, but the walls are on every side well marked. Their angles point towards the cardinal points, or nearly so; and the walls themselves consequently face the north-east, the north-west, the south-west, and the south-east. Towards the middle of the north-west wall, and projecting considerably beyond it, was a raised platform of the usual character; and here stood the great palace, which is thought to have been open to the plain, and on that side quite undefended.[1]

Four miles only from Khorsabad, in a direction a little west of north, are the ruins of a smaller Assyrian city, whose native name appears to have been Tarbisi, situated not far from the modern village of Sherif-khan. Here was a palace, built by Esar-haddon for one of his sons, as well as several temples and other edifices. In the opposite direction, at the distance of about twenty miles, is Keremlis, an Assyrian ruin, whose name cannot yet be rendered phonetically.[2] West of this site, and about half way between the ruins of Nineveh and Nimrud or Calah, is Selamiyah, a village of some size, the walls of which are thought to be of Assyrian construction.[3] We may conjecture that this place was the Resen, or Dasé,[4] of Holy Scripture, which is said to have been a large city, interposed between Nineveh and Calah.[5] In the same latitude, but considerably further to the

---

[1] Layard, *Nineveh and Babylon*, p. 657.

[2] The name is formed of two elements, the first meaning city, which would be *Dur* or *Beth*. The second element is the name of a god otherwise unknown to us; and this, being a mere monogram, cannot be represented phonetically.

[3] *Journal of Asiatic Society*, vol. xv. pp. 351 and 374.

[4] The LXX. interpreters have Δασή in the place of the Hebrew רֶסֶן. The Targums substitute the wholly different name of Tel-Assar (תֵּלְאַסָר).

[5] Gen. x. 12.

east, was the famous city of Arabil or Arbil,[1] known
to the Greeks as Arbela, and to this day retaining its
ancient appellation. These were the principal towns,
whose positions can be fixed, belonging to Assyria
Proper, or the tract in the immediate vicinity of
Nineveh.

Besides these places, the inscriptions mention a
large number of cities which we cannot definitely
connect with any particular site. Such are Zaban
and Zadu, beyond the lower Zab, probably somewhere in the vicinity of Kerkuk; Kurban, Tidu (?),
Napulu, Kapa, in Adiabene; Arabkha and Khapar-
khu, the former of which names recalls the Arra-
pachitis of Ptolemy,[2] in the district about Arbela;
Humkha, Sallat (?), Dur-Tila, Dariga, Lupdu, and
many others, concerning whose situations it is not
even possible to make any reasonable conjecture. The
whole country between the Tigris and the mountains
was evidently studded thickly with towns, as it is at
the present day with ruins;[4] but until a minute and
searching examination of the entire region has taken
place, it is idle to attempt an assignment to particular localities of these comparatively obscure names.

In Western Assyria, or the tract on the right bank
of the Tigris, while there is reason to believe that
population was as dense, and that cities were as
numerous, as on the opposite side of the river,[5] even

[1] Arbil is etymologically "the city of the four gods;" but it is not known which are the deities intended. This place is first mentioned in the reign of Shamas-Vul, the son of the Black Obelisk king, about B.C. 850.

[2] Geograph. vi. 1. Arapkha would be etymologically "the four fish," a name not very intelligible. It was certainly to the east of the Tigris, and probably not far from Arbela.

[4] Journal of Asiatic Soc. vol. xv. p. 304.

[5] Layard, Nineveh and its Remains, vol. i. p. 315; Nineveh and Babylon, pp. 245, 246.

fewer sites can be determinately fixed, owing to the
early decay of population in those parts, which seem
to have fallen into their present desert condition
shortly after the destruction of the Assyrian empire
by the conquering Medes. Besides Asshur, which is
fixed to the ruins at Kileh-Shergbat, we can only
locate with certainty some half-dozen places. These
are Nazibina, which is the modern Nisibin, the Nisibis
of the Greeks; Amidi, which is Amida or Diarbekr;
Haran,[*] which retains its name unchanged; Sirki,
which is the Greek Circesium,[†] now Kerkesiyeh;
Anat, now Anah, on an island in the Euphrates;
and Sidikan, now ' Arban, on the Lower Khabour.
The other known towns of this region, whose exact
position is more or less uncertain, are the following :—Tavnusir, which is perhaps Dunisir, near
Mardin; Guzana, or Gozan,[‡] in the vicinity of Nisibin; Razappa, or Rezeph, probably not far from
Harran; Tel-Apni, about Orfah or Ras-el-Ain; Tabiti
and Magarisi, on the Jerujer, or river of Nisibin;
Katni and Beth-Khalupi, on the Lower Khabour;
Tsupri and Nakarabani, on the Euphrates, between
its junction with the Khabour and Anah; and Khuzi-
rina, in the mountains near the source of the Tigris.
Besides these, the inscriptions contain a mention of
some scores of towns wholly obscure, concerning
which we cannot even determine whether they lay
west or east of the Tigris.

Such are the chief geographical features of Assyria.

---

* The name of Haran has not, I
believe, been found in the Assyrian
inscriptions; but it is mentioned in
Kings and Chronicles as an Assyrian
city. (2 Kings xix. 12; 1 Chron.
v. 26.)

† See Mr. Fox Talbot's *Assyrian
Texts Translated*, p. 31.

‡ See 2 Kings, l. s. c.

It remains to notice briefly the countries by which it was bordered.

To the east lay the mountain region of Zagros, inhabited principally, during the earlier times of the Empire, by the Zimri, and afterwards occupied by the Medes, and known as a portion of Media. This region is one of great strength, and at the same time of much productiveness and fertility. Composed of a large number of parallel ridges, Zagros contains, besides rocky and snow-clad summits, a multitude of fertile valleys, watered by the great affluents of the Tigris or their tributaries, and capable of producing rich crops with very little cultivation. The sides of the hills are in most parts clothed with forests of walnut, oak, ash, plane, and sycamore, while mulberries, olives, and other fruit-trees abound; in many places the pasturage is excellent; and thus, notwithstanding its mountainous character, the tract will bear a large population.[1] Its defensive strength is immense, equalling that of Switzerland before military roads were constructed across the High Alps. The few passes by which it can be traversed seem, according to the graphic phraseology of the ancients, to be carried up ladders;[2] they surmount six or seven successive ridges, often reaching the elevation of 10,000 feet,[3] and are only open during seven months of the year. Nature appears to have intended Zagros

---

[1] See Rich's *Kurdistan*, vol. i. pp. 48-102; Ker Porter, *Travels*, vol. ii. pp. 137-219; Ainsworth, *Travels*, vol. ii. pp. 163-326; Layard, *Nineveh and its Remains*, vol. i. pp. 163-235; *Nineveh and Babylon*, pp. 307-384, and 416-430; *Journal of Geographical Society*, vol. ix. pp. 20-56, &c.; Fraser, *Travels in Kurdistan*, vol. i. pp. 89-196; vol. ii. pp. 178-204.

[2] Diod. Sic. xix. 21, § 2. Compare Kinneir, *Persian Empire*, p. 74; and see also Ainsworth's *Researches*, pp. 224, 225.

[3] Layard, *Nineveh and Babylon*, p. 430; *Journal of Geographical Society*, vol. xvi. p. 49.

as a sevenfold wall for the protection of the fertile
Mesopotamian lowland from the marauding tribes
inhabiting the bare plateau of Iran.

North of Assyria lay a country very similar to the
Zagros region. Armenia, like Kurdistan, consists,
for the most part, of a number of parallel mountain
ranges,[3] with deep valleys between them, watered by
great rivers or their affluents. Its highest peaks, like
those of Zagros, ascend considerably above the snow-
line.[4] It has the same abundance of wood, especially
in the more northern parts; and though its valleys
are scarcely so fertile, or its products so abundant
and varied, it is still a country where a numerous
population may find subsistence. The most striking
contrast which it offers to the Zagros region is in the
direction of its mountain ranges. The Zagros ridges
run from north-west to south-east, like the principal
mountains of Italy, Greece, Arabia, Hindustan, and
Cochin China; those of Armenia have a course from
a little north of east to a little south of west, like the
Spanish Sierras, the Swiss and Tyrolese Alps, the
Southern Carpathians, the Greater Balkan, the
Cilician Taurus, the Cyprian Olympus, and the
Thian Chan. Thus the axes of the two chains are
nearly at right angles to one another, the triangular
basin of Van occurring at the point of contact, and
softening the abruptness of the transition. Again,
whereas the Zagros mountains present their gradual
slope to the Mesopotamian lowland, and rise in
higher and higher ridges as they recede from it, the
mountains of Armenia ascend at once to their full

---

[3] Layard, *Nineveh and Babylon,*
pp. 6, 7. Compare Strab. xi. 12, § 4.

[4] Chesney, *Euphrates Expedition,*
vol. i. p. 60; Layard, l. s. c.

height from the level of the Tigris, and the ridges
then gradually decline towards the Euxine. It follows from this last contrast, that, while Zagros in-
vites the inhabitants of the Mesopotamian plain to
penetrate its recesses, which are at first readily accessible, and only grow wild and savage towards the
interior, the Armenian mountains repel by presenting their greatest difficulties and most barren aspect
at once, seeming, with their rocky sides and snow-
clad summits, to form an almost insurmountable ob-
stacle to an invading host. Assyrian history bears
traces of this difference; for while the mountain
region to the east is gradually subdued and occupied
by the people of the plain, that on the north continues to the last in a state of hostility and semi-
independence.

West of Assyria (according to the extent which
has here been given to it), the border countries were,
towards the south, Arabia, and towards the north,
Syria. A desert region, similar to that which
bounds Chaldæa in this direction, extends along the
Euphrates as far north as the 36th parallel, approaching commonly within a very short distance of
the river. This has been at all times the country of
the wandering Arabs. It is traversed in places by
rocky ridges of a low elevation, and intercepted by
occasional *wadys*; but otherwise it is a continuous
gravelly or sandy plain,* incapable of sustaining a
settled population. Between the desert and the
river intervenes commonly a narrow strip of fertile
territory, which in Assyrian times was held by the
Tsukhi or Shuhites, and the Aramæans or Syrians.

---

* Niebuhr, *Description de l'Arabie*, p. 2.

North of the 36th parallel, the general elevation of the country west of the Euphrates rises. There is an alternation of bare undulating hills and dry plains, producing wormwood and other aromatic plants.[1] Permanent rivers are found, which either terminate in salt lakes or run into the Euphrates. In places the land is tolerably fertile, and produces good crops of grain, besides mulberries, pears, figs, pomegranates, olives, vines, and pistachio-nuts.[2] Here dwelt, in the time of the Assyrian Empire, the Khatti, or Hittites, whose chief city, Carchemish, appears to have occupied the site of Hierapolis, now Bambuk. In a military point of view, the tract is very much less strong than either Armenia or Kurdistan, and presents but slight difficulties to invading armies.

The tract south of Assyria was Chaldæa, of which a description has been given in an earlier portion of this volume.[3] Naturally, it was at once the weakest of the border countries and the one possessing the greatest attractions to a conqueror. Nature had indeed left it wholly without defence; and though art was probably soon called in to remedy this defect, yet it could not but continue the most open to attack of the various regions by which Assyria was surrounded. Syria was defended by the Euphrates—at all times a strong frontier; Arabia, not only by this great stream, but by her arid sands and burning climate; Armenia and Kurdistan had the protection of their lofty mountain ranges. Chaldæa was naturally without either land or water barrier; and

[1] Ainsworth, *Travels in the Track of the Ten Thousand*, p. 67; Pocock, *Description of the East*, vol. ii. pp. 150-172.

[2] Ainsworth, *Travels and Researches*, vol. i. pp. 306-358; Pocock, *Description, &c.*, vol. ii. p. 155.

[3] Supra, pp. 3-18.

the mounds and dykes whereby she strove to supply
her want were at the best poor substitutes for
Nature's bulwarks. Here again geographical features
will be found to have had an important bearing on
the course of history, the close connexion of the two
countries, in almost every age, resulting from their
physical conformation.

Chapter II.

CLIMATE AND PRODUCTIONS.

"Assyria, celebritate et magnitudine, et multiformi feracitate ditissima."
—Amm. Marc. xxiii. 6.

In describing the climate and productions of Assyria,
it will be necessary to divide it into regions; since
the country is so large and the physical geography
so varied, that a single description would necessarily
be both incomplete and untrue. Eastern Assyria has
a climate of its own, the result of its position at the
foot of Zagros. In Western Assyria we may distinguish three climates, that of the upper or mountainous country extending from Bir to Til and
Jezireh, that of the middle region on either side of
the Sinjar range, and that of the lower region immediately bordering on Babylonia. The climatic differences depend in part on latitude; but probably in a
greater degree on differences of elevation, distance or
vicinity of mountains, and the like.

Eastern Assyria, from its vicinity to the high and
snow-clad range of Zagros, has a climate at once
cooler and moister than Assyria west of the Tigris.
The summer heats are tempered by breezes from the
adjacent mountains, and though trying to the con-
stitution of an European, are far less oppressive than
the torrid blasts which prevail on the other side of
the river.[1] A good deal of rain falls in the winter,

[1] *Journal of Asiatic Society*, vol. xv. p. 209. Eastern Assyria is not, however, entirely free from the "torrid blasts," which are the curse of these countries. Mr. Layard ex- perienced at Koyunjik "the shr-

and even in the spring; while, after the rains are past, there is frequently an abundant dew,[1] which supports vegetation and helps to give coolness to the air. The winters are moderately severe.[2]

In the most southern part of Assyria, from lat. 34° to 35° 30′, the climate scarcely differs from that of Babylonia, which has been already described.[3] The same burning summers, and the same chilly, but not really cold, winters prevail in both districts; and the time and character of the rainy season is alike in each. The summers are perhaps a little less hot, and the winters a little colder than in the more southern and alluvial region; but the difference is inconsiderable and has never been accurately measured.

In the central part of Western Assyria, on either side of the Sinjar range, the climate is decidedly cooler than in the region adjoining Babylonia. In summer, though the heat is great, especially from noon to sunset,[4] yet the nights are rarely oppressive, and the mornings are enjoyable. The spring-time in this region is absolutely delicious;[5] the autumn is pleasant; and the winter, though cold and accompanied by a good deal of rain and snow,[6] is rarely prolonged and never intensely rigorous. Storms of thunder and lightning are frequent,[7] especially in

---

shis, or burning winds from the south, which occasionally swept over the country, driving in their short-lived fury everything before them." (Nineveh and Babylon, p. 364.)

[1] Journal of Asiatic Society, l. s. c.

[2] Ainsworth's Assyria, p. 32.

[3] Supra, pp. 35-38.

[4] Chesney, Euphrates Expedition, vol. i. p. 106.

See Mr. Layard's account of his visit to the Sinjar and the Khabour in 1850. (Nineveh and Babylon, pp. 234-836; cf. particularly pp. 246, 269, 273, and 324.)

[5] Chesney, l. s. c.

[6] Layard, Nineveh and its Remains, vol. i. p. 124, vol. ii. p. 54; Nineveh and Babylon, pp. 242, 243, and 294, 295; Rich's Kurdistan, vol. i. p. 10.

spring, and they are often of extraordinary violence : hailstones fall of the size of pigeon's eggs ;[*] the lightning is incessant ; and the wind rages with fury. The force of the tempest is, however, soon exhausted ; in a few hours' time it has passed away, and the sky is once more cloudless ; a delightful calm and freshness pervades the air, producing mingled sensations of pleasure and repose.[*]

The mountain tract, which terminates Western Assyria to the north, has a climate very much more rigorous than the central region. The elevation of this district is considerable,[*] and the near vicinity of the great mountain country of Armenia, with its eternal snows and winters during half the year, tends greatly to lower the temperature, which in the winter descends to eight or ten degrees below zero.[*] Much snow then falls, which usually lies for some weeks ; the spring is wet and stormy, but the summer and the autumn are fine ; and in the western portion of the region, about Harran and Orfah, the summer heat is great. The climate is here an "extreme" one, to use an expression of Humboldt's—the range of the thermometer being even greater than it is in Chaldæa, reaching nearly (or perhaps occasionally exceeding) 120 degrees.[*]

Such is the present climate of Assyria, west and east of the Tigris. There is no reason to believe that it was very different in ancient times. If irriga-

---

[*] Layard, *Nineveh and Babylon,* p. 204 ; Jones, *Journal of Asiatic Society,* vol. xv. p. 360.

[*] Layard, ibid. p. 243.

[*] Mr. Ainsworth estimates the average elevation at 1300 feet (*Assyria,* p. 20).

[*] Chesney, *Euphrates Expedition,* vol. i, p. 107.

[*] Colonel Chesney says : "The heat in summer is 110° under a tent." (*Euphrates Expedition,* l. s. c.) Mr. Ainsworth says the thermometer reaches 115° in the shade (p. 31).

tion was then more common and cultivation more widely extended, the temperature would no doubt have been somewhat lower and the air more moist. But neither on physical nor on historical grounds can it be argued, that the difference thus produced was more than slight. The chief causes of the remarkable heat of Mesopotamia—so much exceeding that of many countries under the same parallels of latitude—are its near vicinity to the Arabian and Syrian deserts, and its want of trees, those great refrigerators.[*] While the first of these causes would be wholly untouched by cultivation, the second would be affected in but a small degree. The only tree, which is known to have been anciently cultivated in Mesopotamia, is the date-palm; and as this ceases to bear fruit[*] about lat. 35°, its greater cultivation could have prevailed only in a very small portion of the country, and so would have affected the general climate but little. Historically, too, we find, among the earliest notices which have any climatic bearing, indications that the temperature and the consequent condition of the country were anciently very nearly what they now are. Xenophon speaks of the barrenness of the tract between the Khabour and Babylonia, and the entire absence of forage in as strong terms as could be used at the present day.[*] Arrian, following his excellent authorities, notes that

---

[*] Humboldt mentions three ways in which trees cool the air, viz., by cooling shade, by evaporation, and by radiation. "Forests," he says, "protect the ground from the direct rays of the sun, evaporate fluids elaborated by the trees themselves, and cool the strata of air in immediate contact with them by the radiation of heat from their perpendicular organs or leaves." (*Aspects of Nature*, vol. I, p. 127, E. T.)

[*] Chesney, *Euphrates Expedition*, vol. I, p. 100.

[*] Xen. *Anab.* i. 5, § 5. Οὐ γὰρ ἦν χόρτος, οὐδὲ ἄλλο δένδρον οὐδέν, ἀλλὰ ψιλὴ ἦν ἅπασα ἡ χώρα.

Alexander, after crossing the Euphrates kept close to the hills, "because the heat there was not so scorching as it was lower down, and because he could then procure green food for his horses."[1] The animals too which Xenophon found in the country are either such as now inhabit it,[2] or where not such, they are the denizens of hotter rather than colder climates and countries.[3]

The fertility of Assyria is a favourite theme with the ancient writers.[4] Owing to the indefiniteness of their geographical terminology, it is however uncertain, in many cases, whether the praise which they bestow upon Assyria is really intended for the country here called by that name, or whether it does not rather apply to the alluvial tract already described, which is more properly termed Chaldæa or Babylonia. Naturally Babylonia is very much more fertile than most parts of Assyria, which being elevated above the courses of the rivers, and possessing a saline and gypsiferous soil, tends in the absence of a sufficient water supply, to become a bare and arid desert. Trees are scanty in both regions except along the river courses; but in Assyria, even grass fails after the first burst of spring; and the plains, which for a few weeks have been carpeted with the tenderest verdure and thickly strewn with the brightest and loveliest flowers,[5] become, as the summer advances,

---

[1] Arrian, *Exp. Alex.* iii. 7.

[2] As bustards, antelopes, and wild asses.

[3] As the ostrich. It is curious that Heeren should regard the wild-ass as gone from Mesopotamia, and the ostrich as still occurring. (*As. Nat.* vol. I. pp. 132, 133, E. T.) His statement exactly inverts the truth.

[4] Herod. i. 193; Strab. xvi. 1, § 14; Dionys. Perieg. 992-999; Plin. *H. N.* vi. 26; Amm. Marc. xxiii. 6, &c.

[5] This peculiarity did not escape Dionysius, a native of Charax, on the Persian Gulf (Plin. *H. N.* vi. 27), who speaks feelingly of the "flowery pastures" (ποιης ενανθιας) of Mesopotamia (l. 1000).

yellow, parched, and almost herbless. Few things
are more remarkable than the striking difference
between the appearance of the same tract in Assyria
at different seasons of the year. What at one time
is a garden, glowing with brilliant hues and heavy
with luxuriant pasture, on which the most numerous
flocks can scarcely make any sensible impression, at
another is an absolute waste, frightful and oppressive
from its sterility.[4]

If we seek the cause of this curious contrast, we
shall find it in the productive qualities of the soil,
wherever there is sufficient moisture to allow of their
displaying themselves, combined with the fact,
already noticed, that the actual supply of water is
deficient. Speaking generally, we may say with truth,
as was said by Herodotus more than two thousand years
ago—that " but little rain falls in Assyria,"[5] and, if
water is to be supplied in adequate quantity to the
thirsty soil, it must be derived from the rivers. In most
parts of Assyria there are occasional rains during the
winter, and in ordinary years, frequent showers in
early spring. The dependance of the present inhabitants both for pasture and for grain, is on these.
There is scarcely any irrigation;[6] and though the
soil is so productive that wherever the land is cultivated, good crops are commonly obtained by means
of the spring rains, while elsewhere nature at once
spontaneously robes herself in verdure of the richest

Mr. Layard constantly alludes to
the wonderful beauty of the spring
flowers in the country at the foot of
the Sinjar. (*Nineveh and Babylon*,
pp. 268, 273, 301, &c.) Mr. Rich
notices the same features in the
country near Kerknk (*Kurdistan*,
vol. i. p. 47). Captain Jones remarks similarly of the tract in the
vicinity of Nimrud. (*Journal of
Asiatic Society*, vol. xv. pp. 372, 373.)

[4] Layard, *Nineveh and its Remains*, vol. ii. p. 70.

[5] Herod. i. 193. 71 γὴ ῥᾶν
Ἀσσυρίαν ὕεται μὲν ὀλίγῳ.

[6] Layard, ut supra, p. 69.

kind, yet no sooner does summer arrive than barrenness is spread over the scene; the crops ripen and
are gathered in; "the grass withereth, the flower
fadeth;"[1] the delicate herbage of the plains shrinks
back and disappears; all around turns to a uniform
dull straw-colour; nothing continues to live but what
is coarse, dry, and sapless; and so the land, which
was lately an Eden, becomes a desert.

Far different would be the aspect of the region,
were a due use made of that abundant water supply—
actually most lavish in the summer-time, owing to
the melting of the snows[2]—which nature has provided in the two great Mesopotamian rivers and their
tributaries. So rapid is the fall of the two main-
streams in their upper course, that by channels
derived from them, with the help perhaps of dams
thrown across them at certain intervals, the water
might be led to almost any part of the intervening
country, and a supply kept up during the whole
year. Or, even without works of this magnitude,
by hydraulic machines of a very simple construction,
the life-giving fluid might be raised from the great
streams and their affluents in sufficient quantity to
maintain a broad belt on either side of the river-
courses in perpetual verdure. Anciently, we know
that recourse was had to both of these systems. In
the tract between the Tigris and the Upper Zab,
which is the only part of Assyria that has been
minutely examined, are distinct remains of at least
one Assyrian canal, wherein much ingenuity and
hydraulic skill is exhibited, the work being carried
through the more elevated ground by tunnelling,

---

[1] Isaiah xl. 7.   [2] See above, p. 15.

and the canal led for eight miles contrary to the
natural course of every stream in the district.[1]
Sluices and dams, cut sometimes in the solid rock,
regulated the supply of the fluid at different seasons,
and enabled the natives to make the most economical
application of the great fertiliser. The use of the
hand-swipe was also certainly known, since it is mentioned by Herodotus,[2] and even represented upon
the sculptures. Very probably other more elaborate
machines were likewise em-
ployed, unless the general pre-
valency of canals superseded
their necessity. It is certain
that over wide districts, now
dependant for productive power
wholly on the spring rains, and

consequently quite incapable of sustaining a settled
population, there must have been maintained in
Assyrian times some effective water-system, whereby
regions that at present with difficulty furnish a few
months' subsistence to the wandering Arab tribes,
were enabled to supply to scores of populous cities
sufficient food for their consumption.[3]

We have not much account of the products of
Assyria Proper in early times. Its dates were of
small repute, being greatly inferior to those of
Babylon.[3] It grew a few olives in places,[4] and some
spicy shrubs,[5] which cannot be identified with any

[1] See the account of these works, given by Captain Jones in the *Journal of the Asiatic Society*, vol. xv. pp. 310, 311. Compare Layard, *Nineveh and its Remains*, vol. i. pp. 80, 81.

[2] Herodotus calls it *κηλώνιον* (i. 193).

[3] See Layard, *Nineveh and Ba-

bylon*, p. 241.

[3] Pliny speaks of the Assyrian dates as used chiefly for fattening pigs and other animals. (*Hist. Nat.* xiii. 4, sub fin.)

[4] As in Chalonitis. (Plin. *H. N.* vi. 27.)

[5] Strab. xvi. 1, § 24, sub fin.; Xen. *Anab.* i. 5, § 1.

certainty. Its cereal crops were good, and may
perhaps be regarded as included in the commendations
bestowed by Herodotus[*] and Strabo[*] on the grain
of the Mesopotamian region. The country was particularly deficient in trees, large tracts growing
nothing but wormwood and similar low shrubs,[*]
while others were absolutely without either tree or
bush.[*] The only products of Assyria which acquired
such note as to be called by its name were its silk[*]
and its citron trees. The silk, according to Pliny,
was the produce of a large kind of silkworm not
found elsewhere.[*] The citron trees obtained a very
great celebrity. Not only were they admired for
their perpetual fruitage, and their delicious odour;[*]
but it was believed that the fruit which they bore
was an unfailing remedy against poisons.[*] Numerous
attempts were made to naturalize the tree in other
countries; but up to the time when Pliny wrote,
every such attempt had failed, and the citron was
still confined to Assyria, Persia, and Media.[*]

It is not to be imagined that the vegetable products of Assyria were confined within the narrow
compass which the ancient notices might seem to

[*] Herod. i. 192. Mr. Layard remarks that the kinds of grain mentioned by Herodotus, sesame, millet,
wheat, and barley, still constitute
" the principal agricultural produce
of Assyria." (*Nineveh and its Remains*, vol. II. p. 428.)

[*] Strab. xvi. 1, § 14.

[*] Xen. *Anab.* i. 5, § 1.

[*] Ibid. i. 5, § 5. See the passage
quoted at length in note[*], page 260.

[*] Pliny speaks of "Assyrian
silk" as a proper dress for women.
(" Assyriâ tamen bombyce adhuc
fœminis cedimus." *H. N.* xi. 23.)

[*] Ibid. xi. 22.

[*] Ibid. xii. 3. "Odore præcellit
foliorum quoque, qui transit in
vestes unâ conditas arcetque anima-
lium noxia. Arbor ipsa omnibus
horis pomifera est, aliis cadentibus,
aliis maturescentibus, aliis verò sub-
nascentibus."

[*] Ibid. l. a. c. "Malus Assyria,
quam alii Medicam vocant, venenis
medetur." Compare Virg. *Georg.*
ii. 126; Solin. 49, &c.

[*] Plin. *H. N.* xii. 3; xvi. 32;
Solin. l. s. c.

indicate. Those notices are casual, and it is evident
that they are incomplete; nor will a just notion be
obtained of the real character of the region, unless
we take into account such of the present products as
may be reasonably supposed to be indigenous.
Now, setting aside a few plants of special importance
to man, the cultivation of which may have been introduced, such as tobacco, rice, Indian corn, and
cotton, we may fairly say that Assyria has no exotics,
and that the trees, shrubs, and vegetables now found
within her limits are the same in all probability as
grew there anciently. In order to complete our
survey, we may therefore proceed to inquire, what
are the chief vegetable products of the region at the
present time.

In the south the date-palm grows well as far as
Anah on the Euphrates and Tekrit on the Tigris.
Above that latitude it languishes, and ceases to give
fruit altogether about the junction of the Khabour
with the one stream and the Lesser Zab with the
other.[1] The unproductive tree, however, which the
Assyrians used for building purposes,[2] will grow and
attain a considerable size to the very edge of the
mountains.[3] Of other timber trees the principal are
the sycamore and the oriental plane, which are common
in the north; the oak, which abounds about Mardin[4]
(where it yields gall-nuts and the rare product
manna), and which is also found in the Sinjar and
Abd-el-Aziz ranges;[5] the silver poplar, which often

---

[1] Chesney, *Euphrates Expedition*,
vol. i. p. 107; Layard, *Nineveh and
its Remains*, vol. ii. p. 423.

[2] Strabo, xvi. 1, § 5; Plin. *H. N.*
xiii. 4.

[3] Chesney, l. s. c.; Layard, l. s. c.

[4] Niebuhr, *Voyage en Arabie*,
p. 323. Compare his *Description
de l'Arabie*, p. 128.

[5] Layard, *Nineveh and Babylon*,
pp. 256 and 312.

fringes the banks of the streams;[1] the sumac, which
is found on the Upper Euphrates;[2] and the walnut,
which is not uncommon between the foot of Zagros
and the outlying ranges of hills.[3] Of fruit-trees the
most important are the orange, lemon, pomegranate,
apricot, olive, vine, fig, mulberry, and pistachio-nut.
The pistachio-nut grows wild in the northern mountains, especially between Orfah and Diarbekr.[4] The
fig is cultivated with much care in the Sinjar.[5] The
vine is also grown in that region,[6] but bears better
on the skirts of the hills above Orfah and Mardin.[7]
Oranges, lemons, and pomegranates belong to the
southern part of the country, where it verges on
Babylonia.[8] The olive clothes the flanks of Zagros
in places.[9] Besides these rarer fruits, Assyria has
pears, apples, plums, cherries, wild and cultivated,
quinces, apricots, melons, and filberts.

The commonest shrubs are a kind of wormwood—
the apsinthium of Xenophon—which grows over
much of the plain extending south of the Khabour[10]—
and the tamarisk. Green myrtles, and oleanders with
their rosy blossoms, clothe the banks of some of the

[1] Chesney, p. 108.
[2] Ainsworth, Assyria, p. 34.
[3] Layard, Nineveh and Babylon, p. 366.
[4] Pocock, Description of the East, vol. II. pp. 158 and 163.
[5] It is grown on terraces, like the vine in Switzerland and on the banks of the Rhine. (Layard, Nin. and Babylon, pp. 254, 255.) Nie- buhr speaks of the Sinjar figs as in great request — "fort recherchés." (Voyage en Arabie, p. 315.)
[6] Layard, l. s. c. 'The vine is also cultivated near Kurkuk. (Rich, Kur- distan, vol. I. p. 50.)

[7] Pocock, vol. II. p. 158; Niebuhr, p. 318. The vine was at one time cultivated as low down as the com- mencement of the alluvium. See Amm. Mar. xxiv. 3 and 6.
[8] Layard, p. 472; Loftus, Chal- dæa and Susiana, p. 5; Rich, Kur- distan, vol. I. p. 20.
[9] Layard, Nineveh and its Re- mains, vol. ii. p 423; Nineveh and Babylon, pp. 123, 132.
[10] Ainsworth, Travels in the Track of the Ten Thousand, p. 76. Worm- wood abounds also near Jomeila, in the Kerkuk district (Rich, Kurdis- tan, vol I. p. 41.)

smaller streams between the Tigris and Mount
Zagros;[3] and a shrub of frequent occurrence is the
liquorice plant.[4] Of edible vegetables there is great
abundance. Truffles[5] and capers[6] grow wild; while
peas, beans, onions, spinach, cucumbers, and lentils are
cultivated successfully.[7] The carob (*Ceratonia Siliqua*)
must also be mentioned as among the rarer products
of this region.[8]

It was noticed above that manna is gathered in
Assyria from the dwarf oak. It is abundant in
Zagros, and is found also in the woods about Mardin,
and again between Orfah and Diarbekr. According
to Mr. Rich, it is not confined to the dwarf oak, or
even to trees and shrubs, but is deposited also on
sand, rocks, and stone.[9] It is most plentiful in wet
seasons, and especially after fogs;[1] in dry seasons it
fails almost totally. The natives collect it in spring
and autumn. The best and purest is that taken from
the ground; but by far the greater quantity is
obtained from the trees, by placing cloths under
them and shaking the branches. The natives use it
as food both in its natural state and manufactured
into a kind of paste. It soon corrupts; and in order
to fit it for exportation, or even for the storeroom
of the native housewife, it has to undergo the process of boiling.[2] When thus prepared, it is a gentle
purgative; but, in its natural state and when fresh,

[3] Layard, *Nin. and Bab.* pp. 216 and 366.
[4] Chesney, l. s. c.
[5] Layard, p. 315.
[6] Chesney, l. s. c.
[7] See for most of these the account of Colonel Chesney (l. s. c.).
Lentils are mentioned by Niebuhr
(*Voyage en Arabie*, p. 295); cucum-

bers by Mr. Layard (*Nin. and Bab.*
p. 224).
[8] Chesney, l. s. c.
[9] Rich, *Kurdistan*, vol. i. p. 149.
Compare Chesney, *Euphrates Exp.*
vol. i. p. 123.
[1] Chesney, l. s. c. Compare Niebuhr, *Description de l'Arabie*, p. 128.
[2] Chesney, p. 124.

it may be eaten in large quantities without any unpleasant consequences.[3]

Assyria is far better supplied with minerals than
Babylonia. Stone of a good quality, either limestone, sandstone, or conglomerate, is always at hand;
while a tolerable clay is also to be found in most
places. If a more durable material is required,
basaltic rock may be obtained from the Mons Masius
—a substance almost as hard as granite.[4] On the
left bank of the Tigris a soft grey alabaster abounds,
which is easily cut into slabs, and forms an excellent
material for the sculptor.[5] The neighbouring mountains of Kurdistan contain marbles of many different
qualities; and these could be procured without much
difficulty by means of the rivers. From the same
quarter it was easy to obtain the most useful metals.
Iron, copper, and lead, are found in great abundance
in the Tiyari Mountains within a short distance of
Nineveh;[6] where they crop out upon the surface, so
that they cannot fail to be noticed. Lead and copper
are also obtainable from the neighbourhood of
Diarbekr.[7] The Kurdish Mountains may have supplied other metals. They still produce silver and
antimony,[8] and it is possible that they may anciently
have furnished gold and tin. As their mineral
riches have never been explored by scientific persons,
it is very probable that they may contain many other
metals besides those which they are at present known
to yield.[9]

---

[3] Niebuhr, p. 129.

[4] Layard, Nin. and its Remains, vol. ii. p. 310.

[5] Ibid. pp. 313, 314. This is the material universally employed for the bas-reliefs.

[6] Ibid. vol. i. p. 223; vol. ii. p. 415.

[7] Chesney, vol. i. p. 108.

[8] Layard, Nin. and its Remains, vol. ii. pp. 417-410.

[9] Mr. Rich observed traces of iron

Among the mineral products of Assyria—bitumen, naphtha, petroleum, sulphur, alum, and salt, have also to be reckoned. The bitumen pits of Kerkuk, in the country between the Lesser Zab and the Adhem, are scarcely less celebrated than those of Hit;[1] and there are some abundant springs of the same character close to Nimrud, in the bed of the Shor Derreh torrent.[2] The Assyrian palaces furnish sufficient evidence that the springs were productive in old times; for the employment of bitumen as a cement, though not so frequent as in Babylonia, is yet occasionally found in them.[3] With the bitumen are always procured both naphtha and petroleum;[4] while at Kerkuk there is an abundance of sulphur also.[5] Salt is obtained from springs in the Kerkuk country;[6] and is also formed in certain small lakes lying between the Sinjar and Babylonia.[7] Alum is plentiful in the hills about Kifri.[8]

The most remarkable wild animals of Assyria are the following:—the lion, the leopard, the lynx, the wild-cat, the hyæna, the wild-ass, the bear, the deer, the gazelle, the ibex, the wild-sheep, the wild-boar, the jackal, the wolf, the fox, the beaver, the porcupine, the badger, and the hare. The Assyrian lion

---

in more places than one. (*Kurdistan*, vol. i. pp. 176 and 222.)

[1] See Niebuhr's *Voyage en Arabic*, p. 275; Ker Porter, *Travels*, vol. ii. pp. 440-442; Rich, *Kurdistan*, vol. i. p. 51; *First Memoir on Babylon*, p. 63.

[2] Layard, *Nin. and Bab.* p. 202; Jones, *Journal of Asiatic Society*, vol. xv. p. 371. The position of the chief springs is marked in the plan, supra, p. 251. There are other naphtha springs near Kifri. (Rich, *Kurdistan*, vol. i. p. 20.)

[3] In his first work Mr. Layard doubted the use of bitumen as a cement in Assyria (*Nineveh and its Remains*, vol. ii. pp. 278, 279); but subsequently he found some traces of its employment (*Nin. and Bab.* p. 203, &c.). M. Botta represents the use of it as common both at Khorsabad and Koyunjik (*Letters from Nineveh*, p. 43).

[4] See above, p. 49.

[5] Ker Porter, *Travels*, vol. ii. p. 441.

[6] Rich, *Kurdistan*, vol. i. p. 27.

[7] Layard, *Nineveh and Babylon*, p. 256.

[8] Rich, p. 20.

is of the maneless kind, and in general habits resembles the lion of Babylonia. The animal is comparatively rare in the eastern districts, being seldom
found on the banks of the Tigris above Baghdad,
and never above Kileh-Sherghat.[1]   On the Euphrates

Assyrian Lion, from Nimrud.

it has been seen as high as Bir; and it is frequent
on the banks of the Khabour, and in the Sinjar.[1]
It has occasionally that remarkable peculiarity—so
commonly represented on the sculptures—a short
horny claw at the extremity of the tail in the middle
of the ordinary tuft of hair.[2] The ibex or wild
goat—also a favourite subject with the Assyrian
sculptors—is frequent in Kurdistan, and moreover
abounds on the highest ridges of the Abd-el-Aziz
and the Sinjar, where it is approached with difficulty
by the hunter.[3] The gazelle, wild-boar, wolf, jackal,
fox, badger, porcupine, and hare, are common in the
plains, and confined to no particular locality. Bears
and deer are found on the skirts of the Kurdish hills.

[1] Layard, *Nin. and its Remains*,
vol. ii. p. 48.
[2] Ibid. l. s. c., note. For its fre-
quency in old times see Amm. Marc.
xviii. 7.

[2] Layard, pp. 426, 429.
[3] Layard, *Nineveh and its Remains*, p. 431. Compare *Nin. and
Bab.* pp. 256 and 312.

The leopard, hyæna, lynx, and beaver are comparatively rare. The last-named animal, very un-

Ibex, or Wild-Goat, from Nimrud.

common in Southern Asia, was at one time found in large numbers on the Khabour; but in consequence of the value set upon its musk bag, it has been hunted almost to extermination, and is now very seldom seen. The Khabour beavers are said to be a different species from the American. Their tail is not large and broad, but sharp and pointed; nor do they build houses, or construct dams across the stream, but live in the banks, making themselves large chambers above the ordinary level of the floods, which are entered by holes beneath the water-line.[4]

The rarest of all the animals which are still found in Assyria, is the wild ass (*Equus hemionus*). Till the present generation of travellers, it was believed

[4] *Nin. and Bab.* pp. 296, 297. Beavers are also found in the Zohab river, a tributary of the Diyaleh.

to have disappeared altogether from the region, and
to have "retired into the steppes of Mongolia and
the deserts of Persia."[5] But a better acquaintance
with the country between the rivers has shown, that
wild asses, though uncommon, still inhabit the tract

Wild Ass.

where they were seen by Xenophon.[6] They are
delicately made, in colour varying from a greyish-
white in winter to a bright bay, approaching to
pink, in the summer-time; they are said to be remarkably swift. It is impossible to take them when
full grown; but the Arabs often capture the foals,
and bring them up with milk in their tents. They
then become very playful and docile; but it is found
difficult to keep them alive; and they have never,
apparently, been domesticated. The Arabs usually
kill them and eat their flesh.[7]

[5] Heeren's *Asiatic Nations*, vol. i.
p. 132, E. T.

[6] *Anab.* i. 5, § 2. Xenophon
speaks of them as numerous in his
day. He calls them "the most
common animal" for some distance
below the Khabour.

[7] Layard, *Nin. and its Remains*,
vol. i. pp. 323, 324; *Nin. and Bab.*
p. 270; Ainsworth, *Travels*, p. 77.

It is probable that all these animals, and some others, inhabited Assyria during the time of the Empire. Lions of two kinds, with and without manes, abound in the sculptures, the former, which do not now exist in Assyria, being the more common. They are represented with a skill and a truth which shows the Assyrian sculptor to have been familiar not only with their forms and proportions, but with their natural mode of life, their haunts, and habits. The leopard is far less often depicted, but appears sometimes in the ornamentation of utensils, and is

Leopard, from Nimrud.

frequently mentioned in the inscriptions. The wild ass is a favourite subject with the sculptors of the later Empire, and is represented with great spirit,

Wild Ass, from Koyunjik.

though not with complete accuracy. The ears are too short, the head is too fine, the legs are not fine enough, and the form altogether approaches too nearly to the type of the horse. The deer, the gazelle, and the ibex, all occur frequently; and though the forms are to some extent conventional, they are not wanting in spirit. Deer are apparently of two kinds. That which is most commonly found appears to represent the grey deer, which is the only species existing at present within the confines of Assyria.* The other sort is more deli-

Gazelle, from Nimrud.

Stag and Hind, from Koyunjik.

* The deer which the army of Julian found in such numbers on the left bank of the Euphrates, a little above Anah, were probably of this species. (Amm. Marc. xxiv. 1.)

cate in shape, and spotted, seeming to represent the
fallow deer, which is not now known in Assyria or
the adjacent countries. It sometimes appears wild,
lying among the reeds;
sometimes tame, in the
arms of a priest or of a
winged figure. There is
no representation in the
sculptures of the wild boar;
but a wild sow and pigs
are given in one bas-relief,[*]
sufficiently indicating the

Fallow Deer, from Koyunjik.

Assyrian acquaintance with this animal. Hares are
often depicted, and with much truth; generally they
are carried in the hands of men, but sometimes they
are being devoured by vultures or eagles.[1] No re-

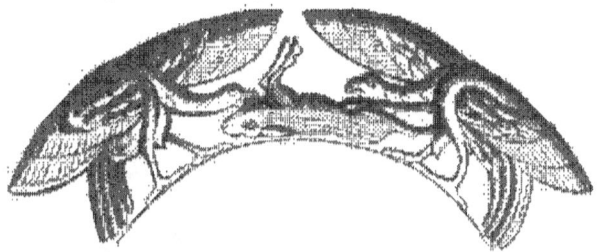

Hare and Eagles, from Nimrud.

presentations have been found of bears, wild-cats,
hyænas, wolves, jackals, wild-sheep, foxes, beavers,
porcupines, or badgers.

---

[*] Supra, p. 60. Both this seal and the above representation of a fallow-deer, belong to the decorations of Sennacherib's palace at Koyunjik. They are given by Mr. Layard in his "Second Series" of the *Monuments of Nineveh*, pl. 12.

[1] This representation is on one of the beautiful bronze plates or dishes which were brought by Mr. Layard from Nimrud, and are now in the British Museum. The dish is represented in the *Monuments of Nineveh*, second series, pl. 62.

There is reason to believe that two other animals, which have now altogether disappeared from the country, inhabited at least some parts of Assyria during its flourishing period. One of these is the wild bull—often represented on the bas-reliefs as a beast of chase, and perhaps mentioned as such in the inscriptions.[2] This animal, which is sometimes depicted as engaged in a contest with the lion,[3] must have been of vast strength and boldness. It is often hunted by the king, and appears to have been considered nearly as noble an object of pursuit as the lion. We may presume, from the practice in the adjoining country, Palestine,[4] that the flesh was eaten as food.

Hare, from Khorsabad.

Chase of Wild Ox, from Nimrud.

The other animal, once indigenous, but which has now disappeared, was called by the Assyrians the

---

[2] See the *Inscriptions of Tiglath-Pileser I.*, pp. 53, 54, where both Sir H. Rawlinson and Dr. Hincks understand the wild-bull to be intended. Dr. Hincks reads the word used as *Rim*, which would clearly be identical with the Hebrew רֵם, or רְאֵם, translated in our version "unicorn," and sometimes thought to be an antelope, but understood by Gesenius to designate "the wild buffalo." (See his *Lexicon* in voc.)

[3] Layard, *Monuments of Nineveh*, first series, pl. 46 and 48.

[4] Deut. xiv. 5.

mithin, and is thought to have been the tiger. Tigers
are not now found nearer to Assyria than the country
south of the Caspian, Ghilan, and Mazanderan; but
as there is no conceivable reason why they should
not inhabit Mesopotamia, and as the *mithin* is constantly joined with the lion, as if it were a beast of
the same kind, and of nearly equal strength and
courage, we may fairly conjecture that the tiger is
the animal intended. If this seem too bold a theory,
we must regard the *mithin* as the larger leopard,[1] an
animal of considerable strength and ferocity, which,
as well as the hunting leopard, is still found in the
country.[2]

The birds at present frequenting Assyria are
chiefly the following:—The bustard (which is of two
kinds—the great and the middle-sized), the egret, the
crane, the stork, the pelican, the flamingo, the red
partridge, the black partridge or francolin, the parrot,
the Seleucian thrush (*turdus Seleucus*), the vulture,
the falcon or hunting-hawk, the owl, the wild swan,
the bramin goose, the ordinary wild goose, the wild
duck, the teal, the tern, the turtle-dove, the nightin-
gale, the plover, and the snipe.[3] There is also a large
kite or eagle, called "agab," or "the butcher," by
the Arabs, which is greatly dreaded by fowlers, as it
will attack and kill the falcon no less than other birds.

We have little information as to which of these
birds frequented the country in ancient times. The

---

[1] This animal is now called the
nimr. The smaller or hunting-
leopard (now called *fuhad*), is the
nimr of the Assyrians, an animal of
which the Inscriptions make frequent
mention.

[2] Sir H. Rawlinson brought a
specimen of the larger leopard, which
he had tamed, from Baghdad to
England, and presented it to the
Clifton Zoological Gardens. Many
visitors will remember *fuhad*, who
died in the Gardens in 1858 or 1859.

[3] The authorities for this list are
Mr. Layard and Colonel Chesney.
(See the *Euph. Expedition*, vol. I.
pp. 107, 108; and *Nineveh and Babylon*, passim.)

Assyrian artists are not happy in their delineation
of the feathered tribe; and though several forms of
birds are represented upon the sculptures of Sargon
and elsewhere, there are but three which any writer
has ventured to identify—the vulture, the ostrich,
and the partridge.   The vulture is commonly represented flying in the air, in attendance upon the march

Vulture, from Nimrud.

and the battle—sometimes devouring, as he flies, the entrails
of one of Assyria's enemies.
Occasionally he appears upon
the battle-field, perched upon
the bodies of the slain, and

pecking at their eyes or their vitals.*   The ostrich,
which we know from Xenophon to have been a

Vulture feeding on Corpse (Koyunjik).

former inhabitant of the
country on the left bank
of the Euphrates,* but
which has now retreated
into the wilds of Arabia,
occurs frequently upon

cylinders, dresses, and utensils; sometimes stalking
along apparently unconcerned; sometimes hastening

Ostrich, from a cylinder.

at full speed, as if pursued by the
hunter, and, agreeably to the description of Xenophon, using its wing for a
sail.*   The partridge is
still more common than
either of these.   He is
evidently sought as food
We find him carried in

Ostrich, from Khorsabad.

---

* See especially the *Monuments of
Nineveh*, second series, pl. 46.
* *Anab.* l. s. c.

* Ταῖς πτέρυξιν, ἄρασα, ὥσπερ
ἱστίῳ, χρωμένη.   *Anab.* i. 5, § 3.

the hand of sportsmen returning from the chace, or see him flying above their heads as they beat the coverts,[1] or finally observe him pierced by a successful shot, and in the act of falling a prey to his pursuers.[2]

Partridges, from Khorsabad.

The other birds represented upon the sculptures, though occasionally possessing some marked peculiarities of form or habit, have not yet been identified with any known species. They are commonly represented as haunting the fir-woods, and often as perched upon the trees.[3] One appears, in a sculpture of Sargon's, in the act of climbing the stem of a tree, like the nut-hatch or the woodpecker.[4] Another has

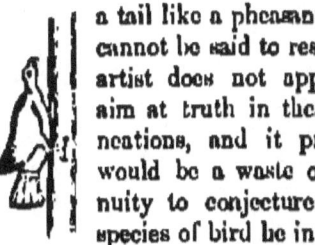

a tail like a pheasant, but in other respects cannot be said to resemble that bird. The artist does not appear to aim at truth in these delineations, and it probably would be a waste of ingenuity to conjecture which species of bird he intended.

We have no direct evidence that bustards inhabited Mesopotamia in Assyrian times; but as they have certainly been abundant in that region from

---

[1] *Monuments of Nineveh*, second series, pl. 32.
[2] Botta, *Monumens de Ninive*,
[3] Ibid. Plates 109 to 112.
[4] Ibid. Pl. 110.
vol. ii. pl. 111.

the time of Xenophon[*] to our own, there can be
little doubt that they existed in some parts of Assyria
during the Empire. Considering their size, their peculiar appearance, and the delicacy of their flesh, it
is remarkable that the Assyrian remains furnish no
trace of them.   Perhaps, as they are extremely shy,
they may have been comparatively rare in the country
when the population was numerous, and when the
greater portion of the tract between the rivers was
brought under cultivation.

Assyrian Garden and Fish-pond (Koyunjik).

[*] Anab. I. a. c.

The fish most plentiful in Assyria are the same as in Babylonia,[*] namely, barbel and carp. They abound not only in the Tigris and Euphrates, but also in the lake of Khutaniyeh, and often grow to a great size.[†] Trout are found in the streams which run down from Zagros;[‡] and there may be many other sorts which have not yet been observed. The sculptures represent all the waters, whether river, pond, or marsh, as full of fish;[§] but the forms are for the most part too conventional to admit of identification.

The domestic animals now found in Assyria are camels, horses, asses, mules, sheep, goats, oxen, cows, and dogs. The camels are of three colours—white, yellow, and dark brown or black.[‖] They are probably all of the same species, though commonly distinguished into camels proper, and *delouls* or

Bactrian, or two-humped Camel, from Nimrud.

dromedaries; the latter differing from the others as the English race-horse from the cart-horse. The Bactrian or two-humped camel, though known to the ancient Assyrians,[¶] is not now found in the country.

---

[*] See above, p. 51.
[†] Chesney, *Euphrates Expedition*, vol. i. p. 108 ; Layard, *Nineveh and Babylon*, p. 325.
[‡] Rich, *Kurdistan*, vol. i. p. 143.

[¶] See Woodcut on opposite page.
[‖] Layard, *Nineveh and Babylon*, p. 265.
[§] The Bactrian camel is, I believe, only represented on the famous

The horses are numerous, and of the best Arab blood.
Small in stature, but of exquisite symmetry and wonderful powers of endurance, they are highly prized
throughout the East,[3] and constitute the chief wealth
of the wandering tribes who occupy the greater portion of Mesopotamia. The sheep and goats are also
of good breeds, and produce wool of an excellent

Mesopotamian Sheep (after Layard).

quality.[4] The cows and oxen cannot be commended.[5]
The dogs kept are chiefly greyhounds,[6] which are
used to course the hare and the gazelle.

Loading a Camel (Koyunjik).

It is probable that
in ancient times the
animals domesticated
by the Assyrians were
not very different from
these. The camel ap-
pears upon the monu-
ments both as a beast
of burthen and also
as ridden in war, but
only by the enemies of the Assyrians. The horse

<hr>

Black Obelisk, where it appears
among the presents sent to the king
from foreign countries.

[4] The young colts fetch prices
varying from 50l. to 150l. A thousand pounds is no uncommon price
for a well-known mare. Mr. Layard
mentions a case where a Sheikh

refused for a favourite mare no less
a sum than 1200l. (Nin. and Bab.
p. 327.)

[5] Chesney, Euphrates Expedition,
vol. i. p. 108.

[6] Ibid. l. s. c.

[7] Layard, Nineveh and Babylon,
p. 246.

is used both for draught and for riding, but seems never degraded to ignoble purposes.' His breed is good, though he is not so finely or delicately made as the modern Arab. The head is small and well shaped, the nostrils large and high, the neck arched, but somewhat thick, the body compact, the loins strong, the legs moderately slender and sinewy. The ass is not found; but the mule appears, some-

Head of an Assyrian Horse (Koyunjik).

times ridden by women, sometimes used as a beast of burthen, sometimes employed in drawing a cart.

Assyrian Horse, from Nimrud.

' The horse draws chariots and not carts. He is never used as a beast of burthen.

Mule ridden by two women (Koyunjik).

Loaded Mule (Koyunjik).

Cart drawn by Mules (Koyunjik).

No. I.

Dog modelled in clay, from the palace of Asshur-bani-pal, Koyunjik.

No. II.

Dog in relief, on a clay tablet.

Cows, oxen, sheep, and goats are frequent; but
they are foreign rather than Assyrian, since they
only occur among the spoil taken from conquered
countries. The dog is frequent on the later sculptures; and has been found modelled in clay, and also
represented in relief on a clay tablet. Their character
is that of a large mastiff or hound, and there is abundant evidence that they were employed in hunting.[*]

If the Assyrians domesticated any bird, it would
seem to have been the duck. Models of the duck are

common, and seem gene-
rally to have been used
for weights.[*] The bird
is ordinarily represented
with its head turned upon
its back, the attitude of
the domestic duck when
asleep. The Assyrians

Assyrian Duck (Nimrud).

seem to have had artificial ponds or stews, which are
always represented as full of fish, but the forms are
conventional, as has been already observed.[*] Considering the size to which the carp and barbel
actually grow at the present day, the ancient representations are smaller than might have been
expected.

---

[*] Dogs are constantly represented
as engaged in the chase upon the
sculptures of Asshurbanipal (Sardanapalus III.). A number of his
hounds were found modelled in clay
at Koyunjik. They have each their
name inscribed on them, which is
always a term indicative of their
hunting prowess. The woodcut
(No. I.) on page 293 is taken from
one of them.

[*] Layard, *Nin. and Bab.* pp. 600,
601.

[*] Supra, p. 280.

Chapter III.

THE PEOPLE.

"The Assyrian was a cedar in Lebanon, fair of branches, and with a shadowing shroud, and of an high stature; and his top was among the thick boughs. . . . . Not was any tree in the garden of God like unto him in his beauty."—Ezek. xxxi. 3 and 8.

The ethnic character of the ancient Assyrians, like that of the Chaldæans, was in former times a matter of controversy. When nothing was known of the original language of the people beyond the names of certain kings, princes, and generals, believed to have belonged to the race, it was difficult to arrive at any determinate conclusion on the subject. The ingenuity of etymologists displayed itself in suggesting derivations for the words in question,[1] which were sometimes absurd, sometimes plausible, but never more than very doubtful conjectures. No sound historical critic could be content to base a positive view on any such unstable foundation, and nothing remained but to decide the controversy on other than linguistic considerations.

Various grounds existed on which it was felt that a conclusion could be drawn. The Scriptural genealogies[2] connected Asshur with Aram, Eber, and Joktan, the allowed progenitors of the Aramæans or Syrians, the Israelites or Hebrews, and the northern

[1] See Prichard's *Physical History of Mankind*, vol. iv. pp. 563, 564, where some of the supposed derivations are given.

[2] Gen. x. 21-31 ; 1 Chr. i. 17-23.

or Joktanian Arabs. The languages, physical type,
and moral characteristics of these races were well
known; they all belonged evidently to a single
family—the family known to ethnologists as the
Semitic. Again, the manners and customs, especially
the religious customs, of the Assyrians connected
them plainly with the Syrians and Phœnicians,
with whose practices they were closely allied.[*]
Further, it was observed that the modern Chaldæans
of Kurdistan, who regard themselves as descendants
of the ancient inhabitants of the neighbouring Assyria, still speak a Semitic dialect.[*] These three
distinct and convergent lines of testimony were sufficient to justify historians in the conclusion, which
they commonly drew,[*] that the ancient Assyrians belonged to the Semitic family, and were more or less
closely connected with the Syrians,[*] the (later) Babylonians, the Phœnicians, the Israelites, and the
Arabs of the northern portion of the peninsula.

Recent linguistic discoveries have entirely confirmed the conclusion thus arrived at. We now
possess in the engraved slabs, the clay tablets, the
cylinders, and the bricks, exhumed from the ruins of
the great Assyrian cities, copious documentary evi-

---

[*] See this argument urged by Dr.
Prichard, *Physical Hist. of Mankind*, vol. iv. pp. 507, 568.

[*] The elder Niebuhr was the first
to report this fact. (See his *Voyage
en Arabie*, p. 285.) It was commonly disbelieved till Mr. Ainsworth
confirmed the statement.

[*] See B. G. Niebuhr's *Lectures on
Ancient History*, vol. i. p. 12, E. T.;
Grote, *History of Greece*, vol. iii. p.
403; Bunsen, *Essay on Ethnology*
(1847), p. 20.

[*] Niebuhr went so far as to identify the Assyrians with the Syrians;
but here he fell into a mistake. The
Aramæans were probably as distinct
from the Assyrians as any other
Semitic race. Niebuhr was misled
by the Greek fancy that the names,
"Assyrian" and "Syrian," were
really identical. (See Herod. vii.
63.) But these names had, in truth,
an entirely distinct origin. Syria
(more properly *Tyria*) was the name
given by the Greeks to the country
about *Tsur* or Tyre, צֹר. Assyria
was the correspondent term to Asshur, אשור,—the native, as well as
the Hebrew, name of the tract upon
the middle Tigris.

dence of the character of the Assyrian language,
and (so far as language is a proof) of the ethnic
character of the race. It appears to be doubted by
none, who have examined the evidence,[1] that the
language of these records is Semitic. However imperfect the acquaintance which our best Oriental
archæologists have as yet obtained with this ancient
and difficult form of speech, its connexion with the
later Babylonian, the Hebrew, and the Arabic does
not seem to admit of a doubt.

Another curious confirmation of the ordinary belief
is to be found in the physical characteristics of the
people, as revealed to us by the sculptures. Few
persons in any way familiar with these works of art
can have failed to remark the striking resemblance
to the Jewish physiognomy which is presented by the
sculptured effigies of the Assyrians. The forehead
straight but not high, the full brow, the eye large
and almond-shaped, the aquiline nose, a little coarse

Assyrians (Nimrud).

at the end, and unduly depressed, the strong, firm,
mouth, with lips somewhat over thick, the well-formed
chin—best seen in the representations of eunuchs—

<hr />

[1] See Bunsen's *Philosophy of His-* | Müller, *Languages of the Seat of*
tory, vol. iii. pp. 193-216; Max | *War*, p. 25, 2nd Ed.

the abundant hair and ample beard, both coloured as black,—all these recall the chief peculiarities of the Jew, more especially as he appears in southern countries. They are less like the traits of the Arab, though to them also they bear a considerable resemblance. Chateaubriand's description of the Bedouin—"la tête ovale, le front haut et arqué, le nez *aquilin*, les yeux *grands* et *coupés en amandes*, le régard humide et singulièrement doux"*—would serve in many respects equally well for a description of the physiognomy of the Assyrians, as they appear upon the monuments. The traits, in fact, are for the most part common to the Semitic race generally, and not distinctive of any particular subdivision of it. They are seen now alike in the Arab, the Jew, and the Chaldæan of Kurdistan; while anciently they not only characterised the Assyrians, but probably belonged also to the Phœnicians, the Syrians, and other minor Semitic races. It is evident, even from the mannered and conventional sculptures of Egypt, that the physiognomy was regarded as characteristic of the western Asiatic

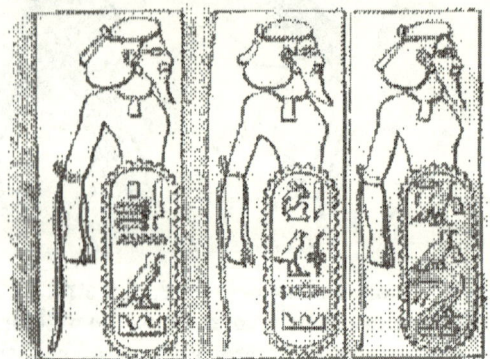

Mesopotamian captives, from an Egyptian monument.

* *Itinéraire*, vol. i. p. 421.

races. Three captives on the monuments of Amenophis III.,[*] represented as belonging to the Patana
(people of Bashan ?), the Asuru (Assyrians), and the
Karakamishi (people of Carchemish), present to us
the same style of face, only slightly modified by
Egyptian ideas.

While in face the Assyrians appear thus to have
borne a most close resemblance to the Jews, in shape
and make they are perhaps more nearly represented
by their descendants, the Chaldæans of Kurdistan.
While the Oriental Jew has a spare form and a
weak muscular development, the Assyrian, like the
modern Chaldæan,[1] is robust, broad-shouldered, and
large-limbed. Nowhere have we a race represented to
us monumentally of a stronger or more muscular type
than the ancient Assyrian. The great brawny limbs

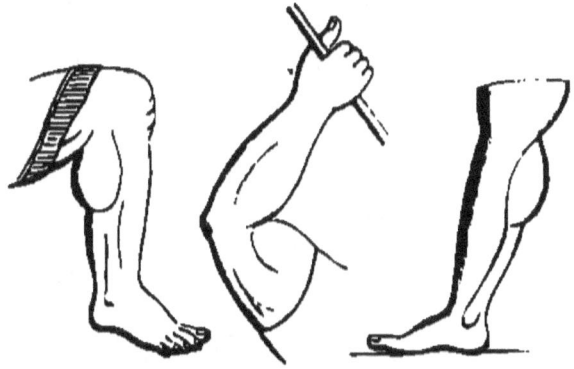

are too large for beauty; but they indicate a physical power, which we may well believe to have belonged to this nation—the Romans of Asia—the

* Lepsius, *Denkmäler*, Abtheil iii.
Bl. 88.

' Rich, *Residence in Kurdistan*,
vol. i. p. 278.

resolute and sturdy people which succeeded in imposing its yoke upon all its neighbours.

If from physical we proceed to mental characteristics, we seem again to have in the Jewish character the best and closest analogy to the Assyrian. In the first place there is observable in each a strong and marked prominency of the religious principle. Inscriptions of Assyrian kings begin and end, almost without exception, with praises, invocations, and prayers to the principal objects of their adoration. All the monarch's successes, all his conquests and victories, and even his good fortune in the chase,[1] are ascribed continually to the protection and favour of guardian deities. Wherever he goes, he takes care to "set up the emblems of Asshur," or of "the great gods;" and forces the vanquished to do them homage. The choicest of the spoil is dedicated as a thank-offering in the temples. The temples themselves are adorned, repaired, beautified, enlarged, increased in number, by almost every monarch. The kings worship in them in person,[2] and offer sacrifices.[3] They embellish their palaces, not only with representations of their own victories and hunting expeditions, but also with religious figures—the emblems of some of the principal deities,[4] and with scenes in which are portrayed acts of adoration.

---

[1] See especially the Tiglath-Pileser cylinder, where such expressions as these occur:—"Under the auspices of Ninip, my guardian deity, I killed four wild bulls, strong and fierce." "Under the auspices of Ninip, 120 lions fell before me" (pp. 54-57).

[2] "As he (Sennacherib) was worshipping in the house of Nisroch his god" (2 Kings xix. 37).

[3] Tiglath-Pileser I. speaks of sacri-ficing as a part of the kingly office. (*Inscription*, &c. p. 70.)

[4] See above, pp. 167, 168, 173. According to Ammianus Marcellinus, the later inhabitants of the country were far less religious, and confined their pictured and sculptured representations to battles and hunting-pieces. ("Nec enim apud eos pingitur vel fingitur aliud præter varias bestiarum, cædes et bella," xxiv. 6.)

Their signets, and indeed those of the Assyrians generally,[*] have a religious character. In every way religion seems to hold a marked and prominent place in the thoughts of the people, who fight more for the honour of their gods than even of their king, and aim at extending their belief as much as their dominion.

Again, combined with this prominency of the religious principle, is a sensuousness—such as we observe in Judaism continually struggling against a higher and purer element—but which in this less favoured branch of the Semitic family reigns uncontrolled, and gives to its religion a gross, material, and even voluptuous character. The ideal and the spiritual find little favour with this practical people, which, not content with symbols, must have gods of wood and stone whereto to pray, and which in its complicated mythological system, its priestly hierarchy, its gorgeous ceremonial, and finally in its lascivious ceremonies,[†] is a counterpart to that Egypt, from which the Jew was privileged to make his escape.

The Assyrians are characterised in Scripture as "a fierce people."[‡] Their victories seem to have been owing to their combining individual bravery and hardihood with a skill and proficiency in the arts of war not possessed by their more uncivilised neighbours. This bravery and hardihood were kept up, partly (like that of the Romans) by their perpetual wars, partly by the training afforded to their manly qualities by the pursuit and destruction of wild animals. The lion—the king of beasts—

---

[*] Layard, *Nineveh and its Remains*, vol. ii. p. 421; *Nin. and Bab.*, pp. 603–605.

[†] See below, ch. viii.
[‡] Isaiah xxxiii. 19.

abounded in their country,[1] together with many
other dangerous and ferocious animals. Unlike the
ordinary Asiatic, who trembles before the great
beasts of prey and avoids a collision by flight if possible,[1] the ancient Assyrian sought out the strongest
and fiercest of the animals, provoked them to the
encounter, and engaged with them in hand-to-hand
combats. The spirit of Nimrod, the "mighty hunter
before the Lord," not only animated his own people,
but spread on from them to their northern neighbours;
and, as far as we can judge by the monuments,
prevailed even more in Assyria than in Chaldæa
itself. The favourite objects of chase with the Assyrians seem to have been the lion and the wild-bull,
both beasts of vast strength and courage, which could
not be attacked without great danger to the bold
assailant.

No doubt the courage of the Assyrians was tinged
with ferocity. The nation was "a mighty and a
strong one, which, as a tempest of hail and a destroying storm, as a flood of mighty waters overflowing,
cast down to the earth with the hand."[2] Its capital
might well deserve to be called "a bloody city," or
"a city of bloods."[3] Few conquering races have
been tender-hearted, or much inclined to spare; and
undoubtedly carnage, ruin, and desolation followed
upon the track of an Assyrian army, and raised feelings of fear and hatred among their adversaries.

[*] "Inter arundineta Mesopotamiæ
fluminum et fruteta leones vagantur
innumeri." Amm. Marc. xviii. 7.
Tiglath-Pileser I. claims to have
slain in all 800 lions. (Inscription,
&c. p. 50.)

[1] Loftus, Chaldæa and Susiana,
pp. 261, 262.

[2] Isaiah xxviii. 2.

[3] Nahum iii. 1. "Woe to the
bloody city,"—or, as the margin
gives it — "Woe to the city of
bloods!" (דמים עיר הוי).

But we have no reason to believe that the nation was especially bloodthirsty or unfeeling. The mutilation of the slain — not by way of insult, but in proof of their slayer's prowess [1] — was indeed practised among them; but otherwise there is little indication of any barbarous—much less of any really cruel—usages. The Assyrian listens to the enemy who asks for quarter, he prefers making prisoners to slaying; he is very terrible in the battle and the assault, but afterwards he forgives and spares. Of course in some cases he makes exceptions. When a town has rebelled and been subdued, he impales some

Capture of a city (Nimrud).

[1] Probably a reward was given for heads, as has often been the fashion with Orientals. Sometimes scribes are represented as taking account of them. (See Layard, *Nin. and its Remains*, vol. ii. p. 184)

of the most guilty;[1] and in two or three instances prisoners are represented[2] as led before the king by a rope fastened to a ring which passes through the under lip, while now and then one appears in the

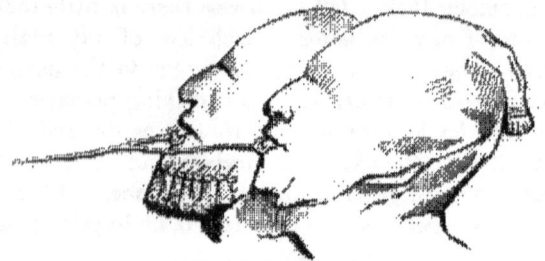

Captives of Sargon (Khorsabad).

act of being flayed with a knife.[1] But, generally, captives are either released, or else transferred, without unnecessary suffering,[2] from their own country

Captive Women in a cart (Nimrud).

to some other portion of the empire. There seems even to be something of real tenderness in the treatment of captured women,

---

[1] Mr. Layard has, I think, expressed himself too strongly when he says that on the capture of a town "an indiscriminate slaughter appears to have succeeded; and that the prisoners were either impaled or carried away as slaves." (*Nin. and its Remains*, vol. ii. p. 374.) It appears, by the inscriptions, that towns were frequently spared, and that the bulk of the inhabitants were generally left in the place.

[2] Botta, *Monument de Ninive*, Pl. 83 and 118.

[1] Botta, *Monument de Ninive*, vol. ii. Pl. 120; Layard, *Monuments of Nineveh*, Second Series, Pl. 47. Is it quite certain that these unfortunates are alive? The Persians and Scythians sometimes flayed men after death, in order to make use of their skins (Herod. iv. 64; v. 25).

[2] Captives are occasionally represented as urged onwards by blows, like tired cattle; and they are sometimes heavily fettered. But in each case the usage is exceptional.

who are never manacled, and are often allowed to
ride on mules,[1] or in carts.

 The worst feature in the character of the Assyrians was their treachery. "Woe to thee that
spoilest, though thou wast not spoiled, and dealest
treacherously, though they dealt not treacherously
with thee!" is the denunciation of the evangelical
prophet.[2] And in the same spirit the author of
"the Burthen of Nineveh" declares that city to be
"full of lies and robbery"[3]—or, more correctly,
"full of lying and violence."[4] Falsehood and
treachery are commonly regarded as the vices of the
weak, who are driven to defend themselves against
superior strength by the weapon of cunning; but
they are perhaps quite as often employed by the
strong, as furnishing short cuts to success, and even,
where the moral standard is low, as being in themselves creditable.[5] It certainly was not necessity
which made the Assyrians covenant-breakers; it
seems to have been in part the wantonness of power
—because they "despised the cities and regarded no
man;"[6] perhaps, it was in part also their imperfect
moral perception, which may have failed to draw the
proper distinction between craft and cleverness.

 Another unpleasant feature in the Assyrian character—but one at which we can feel no surprise—
was their pride. This is the quality which draws
forth the sternest denunciations of Scripture, and is

---

[1] See above, p. 202.
[2] Isaiah, xxxiii. 1.
[3] Nahum, iii. 1.
[4] Mr. Vance Smith renders, "full
of treachery and violence;" which is
probably the real meaning. But the
word used is מִרְמָה "mendacium,"

not בֶּגֶד "perfidia."
[5] See Thucyd. iii. 83.
[6] Isaiah xxxiii. 8; "He hath
broken the covenant, he hath despised the cities, he regardeth no
man."

expressly declared to have called down the Divine judgments upon the race.[*] Isaiah, Ezekiel, and Zephaniah alike dwell upon it.[⸸] It pervades the inscriptions. Without being so rampant or offensive as the pride of some Orientals—as, for instance, the Chinese—it is of a marked and decided colour : the Assyrian feels himself infinitely superior to all the nations with whom he is brought into contact; he alone enjoys the favour of the gods; he alone is either truly wise or truly valiant; the armies of his enemies are driven like chaff before him; he sweeps them away, like heaps of stubble; either they fear to fight, or they are at once defeated; he carries his victorious arms just as far as it pleases him, and never under any circumstances admits that he has suffered a reverse. The only merit that he allows to foreigners is some skill in the mechanical and mimetic arts, and his acknowledgment of this is tacit rather than express, being chiefly known from the recorded fact that he employs foreign artists to ornament his edifices.

According to the notions which the Greeks derived from Ctesias,[⸸] and passed on to the Romans, and through them to the moderns generally, the greatest defect in the Assyrian character—the besetting sin of their leading men—was luxuriousness of living and sensuality. From Ninyas to Sardana-

---

* Ezek. xxxi. 10, 11 ; "*Because thou hast lifted up thyself in height*, and he hath shot up his top among the thick boughs, and his heart is lifted up in his height ; I have *therefore* delivered him into the hand of the mighty one of the heathen ; he shall surely deal with him ; I have driven him out for his wickedness."

⸸ Isaiah x. 7-14, xxxvii. 24-28 ; Ezek. xxxi. 10 ; Zeph. ii. 15.

* Some idea of notable luxuriousness attaching to the Assyrians is, perhaps, earlier than Ctesias. (See *Aristoph. Aves*, 938, ed. Bothe.) Did it come from the Ἀσσύριοι λόγοι of Herodotus ?

palus—from the commencement to the close of the
empire—a line of voluptuaries, according to Ctesias
and his followers, held possession of the throne; and
the principle was established from the first, that
happiness consisted in freedom from all cares or
troubles, and unchecked indulgence in every species
of sensual pleasure.[a]   This account, intrinsically
suspicious, is now directly contradicted by the authentic records which we possess of the warlike character and manly pursuits of so many of the kings.
It probably, however, contains a germ of truth.   In
a flourishing kingdom, like Assyria, luxury must
have gradually advanced; and when the empire fell
under the combined attack of its two most powerful
neighbours, no doubt it had lost much of its pristine
vigour.   The monuments lend some support to the
view that luxury was among the causes which produced the fall of Assyria; although it may be questioned whether, even to the last, the predominant
spirit was not warlike and manly, or even fierce and
violent.   Among the many denunciations of Assyria
in Scripture, there is only one which can even be
thought to point to luxury as a cause of her down-
fall; and that is a passage of very doubtful interpretation.[1]   In general it is her violence, her treachery,
and her pride that are denounced.   When Nineveh
repented in the time of Jonah, it was by each man
" turning from his evil way and from the *violence*
which was in their hands."[2]   When Nahum an-

---

[a] See Diod. Sic. ii. 21, § 2.

[1] Nahum, iii. 4; " Because of the
multitude of the whoredoms of the
wellfavoured harlot, the mistress of
witchcrafts, that selleth nations
through her whoredoms, and families
through her witchcrafts, Behold, I
am against thee, saith the Lord."
Idolatry is probably the " whore-
dom " here intended.

[2] Jonah iii. 8.

nounces the final destruction, it is on "the *bloody*
city, full of lies and *robbery*."[3] In the emblematic
language of prophecy, the *lion* is taken as the fittest
among animals to symbolise Assyria, even at this
late period of her history.[4] She is still "the lion
that did tear in pieces enough for his whelps, and
strangled for his lioness, and filled his holes with
prey, and his dens with ravin." The favourite national emblem, if it may be so called,[5] is accepted as
the true type of the people, and blood, ravin, and
robbery are their characteristics in the mind of the
Hebrew prophet.

In mental power the Assyrians certainly deserve
to be considered as among the foremost of the Asiatic
races. They had not perhaps so much originality as
the Chaldæans, from whom they appear to have
derived the greater part of their civilisation ; but in
many respects it is clear that they surpassed their
instructors, and introduced improvements which gave
a greatly increased value and almost a new character
to arts previously discovered. The genius of the
people will best be seen from the accounts, hereafter
to be given, of their language, their arts, and their
system of government. If it must be allowed that
these have all a certain smack of rudeness and primitive simplicity, still they are advances upon aught
that had previously existed—not only in Mesopotamia
—but in the world. Fully to appreciate the Assyrians we should compare them with the much-lauded

---

[3] Nahum iii. 1
[4] Nahum ii. 11-13.
[5] The frequent occurrence of the
lion on the monuments, either in the
natural form or with a human head,
seems to justify this expression. It
must be admitted, however, that the
standards bear a different emblem.
See below, ch. vii.

Egyptians, who in all important points are very
decidedly their inferiors.   The spirit and progressive
character of their art offers the strongest contrast to
the stiff, lifeless, and unchanging conventionalism of
the dwellers on the Nile.   Their language and
alphabet are confessedly in advance of the Egyptian.[*]
Their religion is more earnest and less degraded.
In courage and military genius their superiority is
very striking; for the Egyptians are essentially an
unwarlike people.   The one point of advantage to
which Egypt may fairly lay claim, is the grandeur
and durability of her architecture.   The Assyrian
palaces, magnificent as they undoubtedly were, must
yield the palm to the vast structures of Egyptian
Thebes.[']   No nation, not even Rome, has equalled
Egypt in the size and solemn grandeur of its buildings.   But, except in this one respect, the great
African kingdom must be regarded as inferior to her
Asiatic rival—which was indeed "a cedar in Lebanon, exalted above *all* the trees of the field—fair in
greatness and in the length of his branches—so that
all the trees that were in the garden of God envied
him, and not one was like unto him in his beauty."[*]

[*] See Bunsen's *Philosophy of History*, vol. iii. p. 192; *Egypt*, vol. iv.
pp. 144, 638, &c.

['] Denon says of Thebes, with
equal force and truth:—"On est
fatigué d'écrire, on est fatigué de
lire, on est épouvanté de la pensée
d'une telle conception; on ne peut
croire, même après l'avoir vu, à la

réalité de l'existence de tant de constructions réunies sur un même
point, à leurs dimensions, à la con-
stance obstinée qu'a exigée leur
fabrication, aux dépenses incalcu-
lables de tant de somptuosité."
Egypte, vol. ii. p. 226.

[*] Ezek. xxxi. 3-9.

CHAPTER IV.

THE CAPITAL.

" Fuit et Ninus, imposita Tigri, ad solis occasum spectans, quondam clarissima."—PLIN. H. N. vi. 13.

THE site of the great capital of Assyria had generally been regarded as fixed with sufficient certainty
to the tract immediately opposite Mosul, alike by
local tradition and by the statements of ancient
writers,[1] when the discovery by modern travellers of
architectural remains of great magnificence at some
considerable distance from this position, threw a
doubt upon the generally received belief, and made
the true situation of the ancient Nineveh once more
a matter of controversy. When the noble sculptures
and vast palaces of Nimrud were first uncovered, it
was natural to suppose that they marked the real site ;
for it seemed unlikely that any mere provincial city
should have been adorned by a long series of monarchs
with buildings at once on so grand a scale and so
richly ornamented. A passage of Strabo, and
another of Ptolemy,[2] were thought to lend confirma-

---

[1] The local tradition is strikingly
marked by the Mahometan belief
that on the smaller of the two mounds
opposite Mosul is " the tomb of
Jonah ;" whence the name Nebbi-
Yunus. The most important of the
ancient authorities is Xenophon
(Anab. iii. 4, § 10-12).

[2] See Layard's Nineveh and its
Remains, vol. ii. p. 242. Neither

passage is correctly represented by
Mr. Layard. Ptolemy distinctly
places Nineveh—not on the Lycus,
as Mr. Layard says—but on the
Tigris (Geograph. vi. 1); and Strabo,
though he does not actually do the
same, certainly does not anywhere
say that it was " near the junction
of the two rivers." He says that
the Lycus divided Aturia from Ar-

tion to this theory, which placed the Assyrian capital nearly at the junction of the Upper Zab with the Tigris; and for a while the old opinion was displaced, and the name of Nineveh was attached very generally in this country to the ruins at Nimrud.

Shortly afterwards a rival claimant started up in the regions further to the north. Excavations carried on at the village of Khorsabad showed, that a magnificent palace and a considerable town had existed in Assyrian times at that site.. In spite of the obvious objection that the Khorsabad ruins lay at the distance of fifteen miles from the Tigris, which according to every writer of weight[2] anciently washed the walls of Nineveh, it was assumed by the excavator that the discovery of the capital had been reserved for himself, and the splendid work representing the Khorsabad bas-reliefs and inscriptions, which was published in France under the title of "Monument de Ninive," caused the reception of M. Botta's theory in many parts of the Continent.

After a while an attempt was made to reconcile the rival claims by a theory, the grandeur of which gained it acceptance, despite its improbability. It was suggested that the various ruins, which had hitherto disputed the name, were in fact all included within the circuit of the ancient Nineveh; which was described as a rectangle, or oblong square, eighteen miles long and twelve broad. The remains at Khorsabad, Koyunjik, Nimrud, and Keremlis marked

---

helitia, and that Nineveh was situated in the middle of the former district (xvi. 1, § 3).

[2] Herod. i. 193; Nic. Dam. Fr. 9; Arrian. *Hist. Ind.* 12; Plin.

H. N. vi. 13; Eustath. ad Dionys. Perieg. 988; &c. It is perhaps by a slip of the pen that Diodorus places Nineveh on the Euphrates (ii. 3).

the four corners of this vast quadrangle,[1] which contained an area of 216 square miles—about ten times that of London! In confirmation of this view was urged, first, the description in Diodorus,[2] derived probably from Ctesias, which corresponded (it was said) both with the proportions and with the actual distances; and next, the statements contained in the book of Jonah,[3] which (it was argued) implied a city of some such dimensions. The parallel of Babylon, according to the description given by Herodotus,[4] might fairly have been cited as a further argument; since it might have seemed reasonable to suppose that there was no great difference of size between the chief cities of the two kindred empires.

Attractive, however, as this theory is from its grandeur, and harmonious as it must be allowed to be with the reports of the Greeks, we have nevertheless to reject it on two grounds, the one historical and the other topographical. The ruins of Khorsabad, Keremlis, Nimrud, and Koyunjik bear on their bricks distinct local titles; and those titles are found attaching to distinct cities in the historical inscriptions. Nimrud, as already observed, is Calah; and Khorsabad is Dur-Sargina, or "the city of Sargon." Keremlis has also its own appellation, Dur- * * *, "the city of the God 工." Now the Assyrian writers do not consider these places to be parts of Nineveh, but speak of them as distinct and sepa-

---

[1] See Layard's *Nineveh and its Remains*, vol. ii. p. 247.

[2] Diodorus (l. s. c.) made Nineveh an oblong square 140 stades (18¼ miles) long, and 90 stades (11¼ miles) broad. Nimrud is eighteen miles from Koyunjik, and about twelve from Keremlis. (Layard, l. s. c.)

[3] Ch. iii. ver. 3, and ch. iv. ver. 11.

[4] Book i. ch. 178.

rate cities. Calah for a long time is the capital,
while Nineveh is mentioned as a provincial town.
Dur-Sargina is built by Sargon, not at Nineveh,
but "*near to* Nineveh." Scripture, it must be remembered, similarly distinguishes Calah as a place
separate from Nineveh and so far from it that there
was room for "a great city" between them.[1] And
the geographers, while they give the name of Aturia
or Assyria Proper to the country about the one
town,[2] call the region which surrounds the other by
a distinct name, Calachené.[3] Again, when the
country is closely examined, it is found, not only
that there are no signs of any continuous town over
the space included within the four sites of Nimrud,
Keremlis, Khorsabad, and Koyunjik, nor any remains
of walls or ditches connecting them,[4] but that the four
sites themselves are as carefully fortified on what, by
the theory we are examining, would be the inside of
the city as in other directions.[5] It perhaps need
scarcely be added, unless to meet the argument
drawn from Diodorus, that the four sites in question
are not so placed as to form the "oblong square" of
his description,[6] but mark the angles of a rhombus
very much slanted from the perpendicular.

---

[1] Gen. x. 11, 12. We must understand the expression "a great
city," as qualified by the circumstances under which it is used—a
great city according to the size of
cities in the primeval times. The
city in question may probably have
occupied the site of the ruins at Se-
lamiyeh.

[2] Strab. xvi. 1, §1; Arrian. *Exp.
Alex.* iii. 7; Plin. *H. N.* v. 12.

[3] Supra, p. 243.

[1] See the careful surveys of Capt.
Jones, published by the Royal
Asiatic Society. (*Journal*, vol. xv.)

[2] See the plans of the ruins at
Nimrud and Koyunjik (pp. 251 and
316). Koyunjik, according to the
hypothesis, would occupy the north-
west angle of the town, and its
southern and eastern sides would thus
be within the town; but the *chief*
defences are those on the east.

[4] Diod. Sic. ii. 3.

The argument derived from the book of Jonah deserves more attention than that which rests upon the authority of Diodorus and Ctesias. Unlike Ctesias, Jonah saw Nineveh while it still stood; and though the writer of the prophetical book may not have been Jonah himself,[*] he probably lived not very many years later.[*] Thus his evidence is that of a contemporary, though (it may be) not that of an eye-witness; and, even apart from the inspiration which guided his pen, he is entitled to be heard with the utmost respect. Now the statements of this writer, which have a bearing on the size of Nineveh, are two. He tells us, in one place, that it was "an exceeding great city, of three days' journey;"[*] in another, that "in it were more than 120,000 persons who could not discern between their right hand and their left."[*] These passages are clearly intended to describe a city of a size unusual at the time; but both of them are to such an extent vague and indistinct, that it is impossible to draw from either separately, or even from the two combined, an exact definite notion. "A city of three days' journey" may be one which it requires three days to traverse from end to end, or one which is three days' journey in circumference, or, lastly, one which

---

[*] It has been remarked that "the writer of the book of Jonah nowhere identifies himself with the prophet." (Vance Smith, *Prophecies on Nineveh*, p. 252.) "On the contrary, he rather carefully keeps himself distinct, speaking of Jonah always in the third person, and not *suggesting, by a single word or implication,* that he ever thought of being regarded as, at the same time, both writer and subject of the narrative." All this is undoubtedly true, but it does not establish the negative.

[*] The position of the book in the Hebrew Canon, between Amos and Micah, shows that its date was regarded as falling between Uzziah (B.C. 808) and Hezekiah (B.C. 697). Nineveh was not destroyed till B.C. 625.

[*] Jonah iii. 3.

[*] Ibid. iv. 11.

cannot be thoroughly visited and explored by a prophet commissioned to warn the inhabitants of a coming danger in less than three days' time. Persons not able to distinguish their right hand from their left may (if taken literally) mean children, and 120,000 such persons may therefore indicate a total population of 600,000; or, the phrase may perhaps with greater probability be understood of moral ignorance, and the intention would in that case be, to designate by it all the inhabitants. If Nineveh was in Jonah's time a city containing a population of 120,000, it would sufficiently deserve the title of "an exceeding great city;" and the prophet might well be occupied for three days in traversing its squares and streets. We shall find hereafter that the ruins opposite Mosul have an extent more than equal to the accommodation of this number of persons.

The weight of the argument from the supposed parallel case of Babylon must depend on the degree of confidence which can be reposed in the statement made by Herodotus, and on the opinion which is ultimately formed with regard to the real size of that capital. It would be improper to anticipate here the conclusions, which may be arrived at hereafter, concerning the real dimensions of " Babylon the Great;" but it may be observed that grave doubts are entertained in many quarters as to the ancient statements on the subject, and that the ruins do not cover much more than one twenty-fifth of the space which Herodotus assigns to the city.

We may, therefore, without much hesitation, set aside the theory which would ascribe to the ancient Nineveh dimensions nine or ten times greater than those of London, and proceed to a description of the

group of ruins believed by the best judges to mark
the true site.

The ruins opposite Mosul consist of two principal
mounds, known respectively as Nebbi-Yunus and
Koyunjik. The Koyunjik mound, which lies to the
north-west of the other, at the distance of 900 yards,
or a little more than half a mile, is very much the
more considerable of the two. Its shape is an
irregular oval, elongated to a point towards the
north-east, in the line of its greater axis. The surface is nearly flat; the sides slope at a steep angle,
and are furrowed with numerous ravines,. worn in

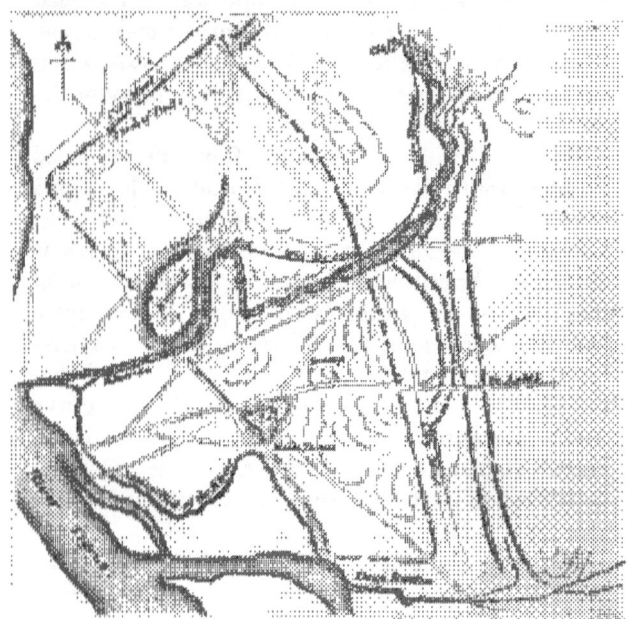

RUINS OF NINEVEH.
1. Palace of Sennacherib.   2. Supposed Tomb of Jonah.

the soft material by the rains of some thirty centuries. The greatest height of the mound above the plain is towards the south-eastern extremity, where it overhangs the small stream of the Khosr; the elevation in this part being about ninety-five feet. The area covered by the mound is estimated at a hundred acres, and the entire mass is said to contain 14,500,000 tons of earth. The labour of a man would scarcely excavate and place in position more than 120 tons of earth in a year; it would require therefore the united exertions of 10,000 men for twelve years, or 20,000 men for six years, to complete the structure.[1]   On this artificial eminence were raised in ancient times the palaces and temples of the Assyrian monarchs, which are now imbedded in the *débris* of their own ruins.

The mound of Nebbi-Yunus is at its base nearly triangular. It covers an area of about forty acres. It is loftier, and its sides are more precipitous than Koyunjik, especially on the west, where it abutted upon the wall of the city. The surface is mostly flat, but is divided about the middle by a deep ravine, running nearly from north to south, and separating the mound into an eastern and a western portion. The so-called tomb of Jonah is conspicuous on the north edge of the western portion of the mound, and about it are grouped the cottages of the Kurds and Turcomans to whom the site of the ancient Nineveh belongs. The eastern portion of the mound forms a burial-ground, to which the bodies of Mahometans are brought from considerable distances. The mass of earth is calculated at six and a half

---

[1] See the *Journal of the Asiatic Society*, vol. xv. p. 320, note [2].

millions of tons; so that its erection would have
given full employment to 10,000 men for the space
of five years and a half.

Khour-So and Mound of Nebbi-Yunus.

These two vast mounds—the platforms on which
palaces and temples were raised—are both in the same
line, and abutted, both of them, on the western wall
of the city. Their position in that wall is thought
to have been determined, not by chance, but by
design; since they break the western face of the
city into three nearly equal portions.[t] The entire
length of this side of Nineveh was 13,600 feet, or

---

[t] Capt. Jones notes that from the
N.W. angle of the city to the centre
of the Koyunjik mound, from that
to the centre of the Nebbi-Yunus
mound, and from the centre of the
Nebbi-Yunus mound to the N.W.
angle of the city, are exactly equal
distances. (*Journal of Asiatic Society*, vol. xv. p. 325.)

somewhat more than two and a half miles. Anciently
it seems to have immediately overhung the Tigris,
which has now moved off to the west, leaving a
plain nearly a mile in width between its eastern edge
and the old rampart of the city. This rampart followed, apparently, the natural course of the river-
bank ; and hence, while on the whole it is tolerably
straight, in the most southern of the three portions
it exhibits a gentle curve, where the river evidently
made a sweep, altering its course from south-east
nearly to south.

The western wall at its northern extremity
approaches the present course of the Tigris, and is
here joined, exactly at right angles, by the northern,
or rather the north-western, rampart, which runs in
a perfectly straight line to the north-eastern angle
of the city, and is said to measure exactly 7000 feet.[3]
This wall is again divided, like the western, but
with even more preciseness, into three equal portions. Commencing at the north-eastern angle, one-
third of it is carried along comparatively high
ground, after which for the remaining two-thirds
of its course it falls by a gentle decline towards the
Tigris. Exactly midway in this slope the rampart is
broken by a road, adjoining which is a remarkable
mound, covering one of the chief gates of the city.[4]

At its other extremity the western wall forms a
very obtuse angle with the southern, which impends
over a deep ravine formed by a winter torrent, and
runs in a straight line for about 1000 yards, when
it meets the eastern wall, with which it forms a
slightly acute angle.

[3] *Journal of Asiatic Society,* vol.
xv. p. 322.　　[4] *Journal of Asiatic Society,* vol.
xv. p. 323.

It remains to describe the eastern wall, which is the longest, and the least regular of the four. This barrier skirts the edge of a ridge of conglomerate rock, which here rises somewhat above the level of the plain, and presents a slightly convex sweep to the north-east. At first it runs nearly parallel to the western, and at right angles to the northern wall; but, after pursuing this course for about three-quarters of a mile, it is forced by the natural convexity of the ridge to retire a little, and curving gently inwards it takes a direction much more southerly than at first, thus drawing continually nearer to the western wall, whose course is almost exactly south-east. The entire length of this wall is 16,000 feet, or above three miles. It is divided into two portions, whereof the southern is somewhat the longer, by the stream of the Khosr-su; which, coming from the north-west, finds its way through the ruins of the city, and then runs on across the low plain to the Tigris.

The enceinte of Nineveh forms thus an irregular trapezium, or a "triangle with its apex abruptly cut off to the south."[1] The breadth, even in the broadest part—that towards the north—is very disproportionate to the length, standing to it as four to nine, or as 1 to 2·25. The town is thus of an oblong shape, and so far Diodorus truly described it;[2] though his dimensions greatly exceed the truth. The circuit of the walls is somewhat less than eight miles, instead of being more than *fifty*; and the area which they include is 1800 English acres, instead of being 112,000!

---

[1] *Journal of the Asiatic Society,* vol. xv. p. 324.

[2] Diod. Sic. ii. 3, § 2.

It is reckoned that in a populous Oriental town we may compute the inhabitants at nearly, if not quite, a hundred per acre. This allows a considerable space for streets, open squares, and gardens; since it assigns but one individual to every space of fifty square yards. According to such a mode of reckoning, the population of ancient Nineveh, within the enceinte here described, may be estimated at 175,000 souls. No city of Western Asia is at the present day so populous.

In the above description of the ramparts surrounding Nineveh, no account has been given of their width or height. According to Diodorus the wall wherewith Ninus surrounded his capital was 100 feet high, and so broad that three chariots might drive side by side along the top. Xenophon, who passed close to the ruins on his retreat with the Ten Thousand, calls the height 150 feet, and the width 50 feet.[1] The actual greatest height at present seems to be 46 feet;[2] but the *débris* at the foot of the walls are so great, and the crumbled character of the walls themselves is so evident, that the chief modern explorer inclines to regard the computation of Diodorus as probably no exaggeration of the truth.[3] The width of the walls, in their crumbled condition, is from 100 to 200 feet.

The mode in which the walls were constructed seems to have been the following. Up to a certain

---

[1] *Anab.* lii. 4, § 10. I assume that the Mespila of Xenophon is identical with the ruins opposite Mosul. There does not seem to be any reasonable doubt of this. (See Ainsworth, *Travels in the Track of the Ten Thousand*, p. 140; *Journal of Asiatic Society*, vol. xv. p. 332.)

[2] *Journal of Asiatic Society*, vol. xv. p. 322.

[3] Layard, *Nineveh and Babylon*, p. 660, "The remains still existing of these fortifications almost confirm the statement of Diodorus Siculus, that the walls were a hundred feet high," &c.

height—fifty feet, according to Xenophon [1]—they
were composed of neatly-hewn blocks of a fossiliferous
limestone, smoothed and polished on the outside.[2]
Above this, the material used was sun-dried brick.
The stone masonry was certainly ornamented along
its top by a continuous series of battlements or gra-

dines in the same material ;[3] and it is not unlikely
that a similar ornamentation crowned the upper

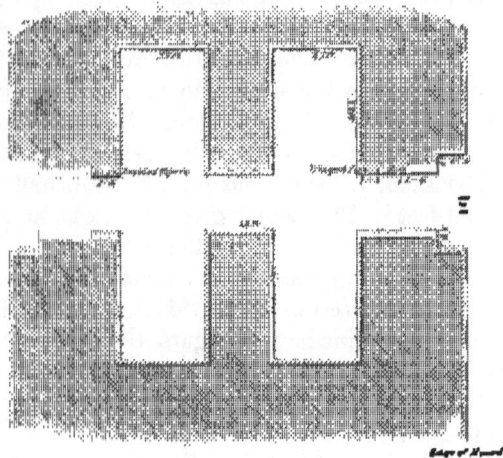

Gate in the North Wall, Nineveh.

[1] *Anab.* iii. 4, § 10. The excavations have not yet tested this
statement of Xenophon's; but, as
his estimate of twenty feet is cx-
actly correct for the stone basement
of the walls of Nimrud (Larissa), we
may fairly assume that he probably
did not much miscalculate here.
(Cf. *Anab.* iii. 4, § 7, with Layard's
Nineveh and Babylon. pp. 123, 125.)

[2] Λίθου ξεστοῦ κογχυλιάτου.
(*Anab.* iii. 4, § 10.) Mr. Ainsworth
remarks that this fossiliferous stone
is the common building material at
Mosul, but "does not occur far to
the north or to the south, being succeeded by wastes of gypsum."
(*Travels in the Track of the Ten
Thousand,* p. 140.)

[3] Layard, *Nin. and Bab.* p. 658.

brick structure.[1] The wall was pierced at irregular
intervals by gates, above which rose lofty towers;
while towers, probably of lesser elevation, occurred
also in the portions of the wall intervening between
one gate and another. A gate in the north-western
rampart has been cleared by means of excavation,
the form and construction of which will best appear
from the annexed ground-plan. It seems to have
consisted of three gateways, whereof the inner and
outer were ornamented with colossal human-headed
bulls and other figures, while the central one was
merely panelled with slabs of alabaster. Between the
gateways were two large chambers, 70 feet long by
23 feet wide, which were thus capable of containing
a considerable body of soldiers. The chambers and
gateways are supposed to have been arched over,
like the castle gates on the bas-reliefs. The gates
themselves have wholly disappeared ; but the *débris*
which filled both the chambers and the passages
contained so much charcoal that it is thought they
must have been made, not of bronze, like the gates
of Babylon,[2] but of wood. The ground within the
gateway was paved with large slabs of limestone,
still bearing the marks of chariot wheels.[3]

The castellated rampart which thus surrounded
and guarded Nineveh did not constitute by any
means its sole defence. Outside the stone basement
wall lay on every side a water barrier, consisting on
the west and south of natural river courses; on the
north and east, of artificial channels into which water
was conducted from the Khosr-su. The northern

---

[1] Layard, *Nin. and Bab.* p. 658, note.   [2] Herod. i. 179.
[3] Layard, *Nin. and Bab.* pp. 120-123.

and eastern walls were skirted along their whole
length by a broad and deep moat, into which the
Khosr-su was made to flow by occupying its natural
bed with a strong dam, carried across it in the line
of the eastern wall and at the point where the stream
now enters the enclosure. On meeting this obstruction, of which there are still some remains, the waters
divided, and while part flowed to the south-east, and
reached the Tigris by the ravine immediately to the
south of the city, which is a natural watercourse,
part turned at an acute angle to the north-west, and,
washing the remainder of the eastern and the whole
of the northern wall, gained the Tigris at the north-
west angle of the city, where a second dam kept it at a
sufficient height. Moreover, on the eastern face,
which appears to have been regarded as the weakest,
a series of outworks were erected for the further defence of the city. North of the Khosr, between the
city wall and that river, which there runs parallel to
the wall, and forms a sort of second or outer moat,
there are traces of a detached fort of considerable
size, which must have greatly strengthened the
defences in that quarter. South and south-east of
the Khosr, the works are still more elaborate. In
the first place, from a point where the Khosr leaves
the hills and debouches upon comparatively low
ground, a deep ditch, 200 feet broad, was carried
through compact silicious conglomerate for upwards
of two miles, till it joined the ravine which formed
the natural protection of the city upon the south.
On either side of this ditch, which could be readily
supplied with water from the Khosr at its northern
extremity, was built a broad and lofty wall; the
eastern one, which forms the outermost of the de-

fences, rises even now a hundred feet above the
bottom of the ditch on which it adjoins.   Further,
between this outer barrier and the city moat was
interposed a species of semi-lune, guarded by a double
wall and a broad ditch, and connected (as is thought)
by a covered way with Nineveh itself.[1]   Thus the
city was protected on this, its most vulnerable side,
towards the centre by five walls and three broad and
deep moats ; towards the north, by a wall, a moat,
the Khosr, and a strong outpost ; towards the south,
by two moats and three lines of rampart.   The
breadth of the whole fortification on this side is
2200 feet, or not far from half a mile.[2]

Such was the site, and such were the defences, of
the capital of Assyria.   Of its internal arrangements
but little can be said at present, since no general
examination of the space within the ramparts has
been as yet made, and no ancient account of the
interior has come down to us.   We can only see that
the side of the city which was most fashionable was
the western, which immediately overhung the Tigris ;
since here were the palaces of the kings, and here
seem also to have been the dwellings of the richer
citizens ; at least, it is on this side, in the space intervening between Koyunjik and the northern rampart,
that the only very evident remains of edifices—besides
the great mounds of Koyunjik and Nebbi-Yunus—
are found.[3]   The river was no doubt the main at-
traction ; but perhaps the western side was also
considered the most secure, as lying furthest from

---

[1] *Journal of Asiatic Society*, vol.
xv. p. 322.
[2] Layard, *Nin. and Bab.* p. 660,
note.

[3] See the plan (supra, p. 316) ;
and compare the *Journal of the
Asiatic Society*, vol. xv. p. 323.

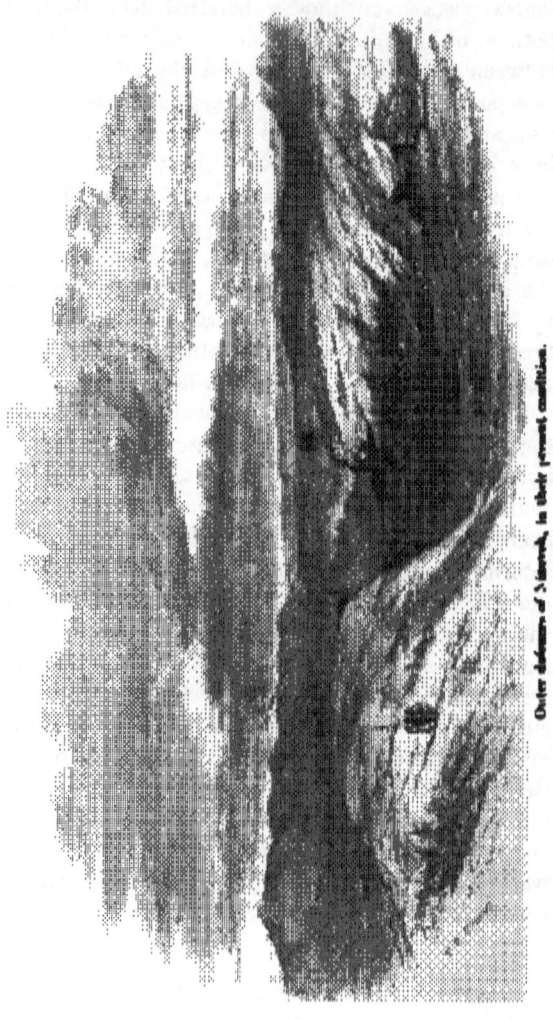

Outer chamber of Nimrud, in their present condition.

the quarter whence alone the inhabitants expected
to be attacked, namely, the east.   It is impossible at
present to give any account of the character of the
houses or the direction of the streets.   Perhaps the
time may not be far distant when more systematic
and continuous efforts will be made by the enterprise
of Europe to obtain full knowledge of all the remains
which still lie buried at this interesting site.   No
such discoveries are indeed to be expected as those
which have recently startled the world; but patient
explorers would still be sure of an ample reward,
were they to glean after Layard in the field from
which he swept so magnificent a harvest.

CHAPTER V.

LANGUAGE AND WRITING.

" Γράμματα 'Ασσύρια." Herod. iv. 87.

THERE has never been much difference of opinion
among the learned with regard to the language
spoken by the Assyrians. As the Biblical genealogy
connected Asshur with Eber and Aram,[1] while the
Greeks plainly regarded the Syrians, Assyrians, and
Babylonians as a single race,[2] it was always supposed
that the people thus associated must have possessed
a tongue allied, more or less closely, to the Hebrew,
the Syriac, and the Chaldee. These tongues were
known to be dialectic varieties of a single form of
speech—the Semitic; and it was consequently the
general belief, before any Assyrian inscriptions had
been disinterred, that the Assyrian language was of
this type, either a sister tongue to the three above-
mentioned, or else identical with some one of them.
The only difficulty in the way of this theory was
the supposed Medo-Persic or Arian character of a

---

[1] Gen. x. 21-25.
[2] See Herod. vii. 63, and 140;
Æsch. *Pers.* 86; Xen. *Cyrop.* v. 4,
§ 51, &c. ; Scylax, *Peripl.* p. 80;
Dionys. Perieg. 772 ; Strab. xvi. 1, §
2 ; Arrian, Fr. 48; Plin. *H. N.* v. 12 ;

Mela, i. 11, for the confusion of Assyrians with Syrians. For the close
connexion and almost identification
of the Babylonians with the Assyrians, see Herod. i. 106, 178 ; iii. 92 ;
Strab. l. s. c. ; &c.

certain number of Assyrian royal names; but this
difficulty was thought to be sufficiently met by a
suggestion that the ruling tribe might have been of
Median descent, and have maintained its old national
appellatives, while the mass of the population belonged to a different race.[3] Recent discoveries have
shown that this last suggestion was needless, as the
difficulty which it was intended to meet does not
exist. The Assyrian names, which either *history* or
the monuments have handed down to us, are Semitic,
and not Arian.   It is only among the fabulous accounts of the Assyrian Empire put forth by Ctesias
that Arian names, such as Xerxes, Arius, Arma-
mithres, Mithræus, &c., are to be found.

Together with the true names of the Assyrian
kings, the mounds of Mesopotamia have yielded up
a mass of documents in the Assyrian language, from
which it is possible that we may one day acquire as
full a knowledge of its structure and vocabulary as
we possess at present of Greek or Latin. These
documents have confirmed the previous belief that
the tongue is Semitic.   They consist, in the first
place, of long inscriptions upon the slabs of stone
with which the walls of palaces were panelled, sometimes occupying the stone to the exclusion of any
sculpture, sometimes carried across the dress of
figures, always carefully cut and generally in good
preservation.[4] Next in importance to these memorials are the hollow cylinders, or more strictly speaking, hexagonal or octagonal prisms, made in ex-

[3] Prichard, *Physical History of
Mankind*, vol. iv. p. 568.
[4] Occasionally the slabs have been
purposely defaced and rendered illegible, probably by kings of another
dynasty.

tremely fine and thin terracotta,[1] which the Assyrian
kings used to deposit at the corners of temples,
inscribed with an account of their chief acts and
with numerous religious invocations. These cylinders vary from a foot and a half to three feet in
height, and are covered closely with a small writing,

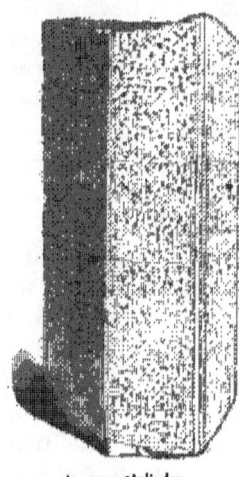

Assyrian Cylinder.

which it often requires a good
magnifying glass to decipher.
A cylinder of Tiglath-Pileser
I. (about B.C. 1180) contains
thirty lines in a space of six
inches, or five lines to an inch,
which is as close as the type
of the present volume. This
degree of closeness is exceeded
on a cylinder of Asshur-bani-
pal's (about B.C. 660), where
the lines are six to the inch,
or as near together as the type
of the Edinburgh Review. If
the complexity of the Assyrian
characters be taken into account, and if it be remem-
bered that the whole inscription was in every case
impressed by the hand, this minuteness must be
allowed to be very surprising. It is not favourable
to legibility; and the patience of cuneiform scholars
has been severely tried by a mode of writing which
sacrifices everything to the desire of crowding the
greatest possible quantity of words into the smallest
possible space. In one respect, however, facility of
reading is consulted, for the inscriptions on the

[1] Birch, *Ancient Pottery*, p. 144.

cylinders are not carried on in continuous lines round all the sides, but are written in columns, each column occupying a side. The lines are thus tolerably short; and the whole of a sentence is brought before the eye at once.

Besides slabs and cylinders, the written memorials of Assyria comprise inscribed bulls and lions, stone obelisks, clay tablets, and engraved seals. The seals generally resemble those of the Chaldæans, which have been already described;[*] but are somewhat more elaborate, and more varied in their character.

Assyrian Seals.

They do not very often exhibit any writing; but occasionally they are inscribed with the name of their

---

[*] See above, " First Monarchy," ch. iv. p. 85, and ch. v. pp. 117-119.

owner,' while in a few instances they show an inscription of some length. The clay tablets are both
numerous and curious. They are of various sizes,
ranging from nine inches long by six and a half
wide, to an inch and a half long by an inch wide, or
even less.* Sometimes they are entirely covered

Assyrian Clay Tablets.

with writing; while sometimes they exhibit on a
portion of their surface the impressions of seals,
mythological emblems, and the like. Some thousands of them have been recovered; and they are
found to be of the most varied character. Many are
historical, still more mythological; some are linguistic, some geographic, some again astronomical.
It is anticipated that, if they can be deciphered, we
shall obtain a complete encyclopædia of Assyrian
science, and shall be able by this means to trace a

large portion of the knowledge of the Greeks to an
Oriental source.   Here is a mine almost unworked,
from which patient and cautious investigators may
one day extract the most valuable literary treasures.
The stone obelisks are but few, and are mostly in a
fragmentary condition.   One alone is perfect—the
obelisk in black basalt, discovered by Mr. Layard at
Nimrud, which has now for many years been in the

Black Obelisk, from Nimrud.

British Museum.   This monument is sculptured on
each of its four sides, in part with writing and in
part with bas-reliefs.   It is about seven feet high,

and two feet broad at the base, tapering gently
towards the summit, which is crowned with three
low steps, or gradines. The inscription, which occupies the upper and lower portion of each side, and is
also carried along the spaces between the bas-reliefs,
consists of 210 clearly cut lines, and is one of the
most important documents that has come down to us.
It gives an account of various victories gained by
the monarch who set it up, and of the tribute
brought him by several princes.[*] The inscribed lions
and bulls are numerous. They commonly guard the
portals of palaces, and are raised in a bold relief on
alabaster slabs. The writing does not trench upon
the sculpture, but covers all those portions of the
slabs which are not occupied by the animal. It is
usually a full account of some particular campaign,
which was thus specially commemorated, giving in
detail what is far more briefly expressed in the
obelisk and slab inscriptions.[']

This review of the various kinds of documents
which have been discovered in the ancient cities of
Assyria, seems to show that two materials were principally in use among the people for literary purposes,
namely, stone and moist clay. The monarchs used
the former most commonly, though sometimes they
condescended for some special object to the coarser
and more fragile material. Private persons in their
business transactions, literary and scientific men in
their compositions, employed the latter, on which it
was possible to write rapidly with a triangular

---

[*] See the translation by Dr. Hincks
in the *Dublin University Magazine*
for October, 1853.

['] *Journal of Asiatic Society*, vol.
xii. p. 441.

instrument, and which was no doubt far cheaper than the slabs of fine stone, which were preferred for the royal inscriptions. The clay documents, when wanted for instruction or as evidence, were carefully baked; and thus it is that they have come down to us, despite their fragility, often in as legible a condition, with the letters as clear and sharp, as any legend on marble, stone, or metal that we possess belonging to Greek, or even to Roman times. The best clay, skilfully baked, is a material quite as enduring as either stone or metal;[1] resisting many influences better than either of those materials.

It may still be asked, did not the Assyrians use other materials also? Did they not write with ink of some kind on paper, or leather, or parchment? It is certain that the Egyptians had invented a kind of thick paper many centuries before the Assyrian power arose;[2] and it is further certain that the later Assyrian kings had a good deal of intercourse with Egypt. Under such circumstances, can we suppose that they did not import paper from that country? Again, the Persians, we are told, used parchment for their public records.[3] Are not the Assyrians, a much more ingenious people, likely to have done the same, at any rate to some extent? There is no direct evidence by which these questions can be determinately answered. No document on any of the materials suggested has been found. No ancient author states that the Assyrians or the Babylonians

---

[1] Birch, *Ancient Pottery*, vol. i. p. 2.
[2] Wilkinson in the author's *Herodotus*, vol. ii. p. 320, § 33.
[3] Diod. Sic. ii. 32. As Diodorus' sole authority here is the untrustworthy Ctesias, no great dependence can be placed on his statement.

used them.[1] Had it not been for one piece of indirect
evidence, it would have seemed nearly certain that
they were not employed by the Mesopotamian races.
In some of the royal palaces, however, small lumps of
fine clay have been found, bearing the impressions
of seals, and exhibiting traces of the string by which
they were attached to documents, while the documents themselves, being of a different material, have
perished.[2] It seems probable that in these instances
some substance like paper or parchment was used;
and thus we are led to the conclusion that, while clay
was the most common, and stone an ordinary writing
material among the Assyrians, some third substance,
probably Egyptian paper, was also known, and was
used occasionally, though somewhat rarely, for public
documents.

We may now proceed to consider the style and
nature of the Assyrian writing. Derived evidently
from the Chaldæan, it is far less archaic in type, presenting no pictorial representations of objects, and
but a few characters where the pictorial representation can be traced. It is in no case wholly rectilinear; and indeed preserves the straight line only

in a very few characters, as in for " house,"

---

[1] This is not a mere negative argument, since statements of the nature
of the material used do occur, and
accord with the monumental facts.
Epigenes, for instance, spoke of the
Babylonians recording their astronomical observations upon baked
tiles (" coctilibus laterculis," Plin.
H. N. vii. 56), and the historians
of Alexander mentioned a stone inscription of Sardanapalus (Arr. *Exp.
Al.* ii. 5; Strab. xiv. 5, § 9). The
eastern tradition that Seth wrote the
history and wisdom of antediluvian
times on burnt and unburnt brick
(Layard, *Nin. and Bab.* p. 347, note),
has a similar bearing.

[2] Layard, p. 154; Botta, *Lettres
from Nineveh*, p. 27. For a representation of the mark of the string
see above, p. 331.

for "gate," for "temple, altar,"

and for "fish," all which are in the later inscriptions superseded by simpler forms. The wedge
may thus be said to be almost the sole element of the
writing—the wedge, however, under a great variety
of forms — sometimes greatly elongated, as thus

, sometimes contracted to a triangle ,

sometimes broadened out , sometimes doubled in

such a way as to form an arrow-head , and placed
in every direction—horizontal, perpendicular, and
diagonal.

The number of characters is very great. Sir H.
Rawlinson, in the year 1851, published a list of 246,
or including variants, 366 characters, as occurring in
the inscriptions known to him.[1] M. Oppert, in 1858,
gave 318 forms as those "most in use."[2] Of course
it is at once evident that this alphabet cannot represent elementary sounds. The Assyrian characters
do, in fact, correspond, not to letters, according to
our notion of letters, but to syllables. These syllables are either mere vowel sounds, such as we
represent by our vowels and diphthongs, or such

---

[1] *Journal of Asiatic Society*, vol.
xiv.
[2] *Expédition scientifique en Mex-*

potamie, tom. ii. livre i. Appendice.
Catalogue des signes les plus usités,
pp. 107-120.

sounds accompanied by one or two consonants. The
vowels are not very numerous. The Assyrians recognise three only as fundamental—*a*, *i*, and *u*.
Besides these they have the diphthongs *ai*, nearly
equivalent to *e*, and *au*, nearly equivalent to *o*.[*] The
vowels *i* and *u* have also the powers, respectively, of
y and *v*.

The consonant sounds recognised in the language
are sixteen in number. They are the labial, guttural, and dental *tenues*, *p*, *k*, *t*; the labial, guttural,
and dental *mediæ*, *b*, *g*, *d*; the guttural and dental
aspirates, *kh* (= Heb. n) and *th* (= Greek θ); the
liquids *l*, *m*,[*] *n*, *r*; and the sibilants *s*, *sh* (= Heb. ש),
ts (= Heb. צ), and *z*. The system here is nearly
that of the Hebrews, from which it differs only by
the absence of the simple aspirate n,[*] of the guttural ע,
and of the aspirated פ (*ph*). It has no sound which
the Hebrew has not.

From these sounds, combined with the simple
vowels, comes the Assyrian syllabarium, to which,
and not to the consonants themselves, the characters
were assigned. In the first place, each consonant
being capable of two combinations with each simple
vowel, could give birth naturally to six simple syllables, each of which would be in the Assyrian
system represented by a character. Six characters,
for instance, entirely different from one another,
represented *pa, pi, pu, ap, ip, up*; six others, *ka, ki,*

---

[*] The vowels must be sounded as
in Italian, A as *a* in "vast"—E as
a in "face"—I as *e* in "me"—O as
o in "host"—U as *u* in "rude."

[*] The Assyrians confounded the
sounds of m and v, as the Greeks did

those of μ and β. (See Buttmann's
Lexilogus, p. 64, and p. 189, E. T.)

[*] There is a character representing
the soft breathing '; but none, apparently, for the rough breathing '.

ku, ak, ik, uk; six others again, *ta, ti, tu, at, it, ut.*
If this rule were carried out in every case the sixteen consonant sounds would, it is evident, produce
96 characters. The actual number, however, formed
in this way, is only 75, since there are seven of the
consonants which only combine with the vowels in
one way. Thus we have, *ba, bi, bu,* but not *ab, ib, ub;*
ga, gi, gu, but not *ag, ig, ug;* and so on. The sounds
regarded as capable of only one combination are the
mediæ, b, g, d; the aspirates *kh* and *th;* and the
sibilants *ts* and *z.*

Such is the first and simplest syllabarium : but
the Assyrian system does not stop here. It proceeds
to combine with each simple vowel sound two consonants, one preceding the vowel and the other following it. If this plan were followed out to the utmost
possible extent, the result would be an addition to
the syllabarium of 768 sounds, each having its
proper character, which would raise the number of
characters to between eight and nine hundred!
Fortunately for the student, phonetic laws and other
causes have intervened to check this extreme luxuriance ; and the combinations of this kind which are
known to exist, instead of amounting to the full
limit of 768, are under 150. The known Assyrian
alphabet is, however, in this way raised from 80, or,
including variants, 100, to between 240 and 250
characters.

Further, there is another kind of character, quite
different from these, which Orientalists have called
"determinatives." Certain classes of words have a
sign prefixed or suffixed to them, most commonly the
former, by which their general character is indicated.
The names of gods, of men, of cities, of tribes, of

wild animals, of domestic animals, of metals, of months, of the points of the compass, and of dignities, are thus accompanied. The sign prefixed or suffixed may have originally represented a word; but when used in the way here spoken of, it is believed that it was not sounded, but served simply to indicate to the reader the sort of word which was placed before him. Thus a single perpendicular

wedge, **Y**, indicates that the next word will be the

name of a man; such a wedge, preceded by two

horizontal ones, **⟫─Y** , tells us to expect the appel-

lative of a god; while other more complicated combinations are used in the remaining instances. There are about ten or twelve characters of this description.

Finally, there are a certain number of characters which have been called "ideographs," or "monograms." Most of the gods, and various cities and countries are represented by a group of wedges, which is thought not to have a real phonetic force, but to be a conventional sign for an idea, much as the Arabic numerals, 1, 2, 3, &c., are non-phonetic signs representing the ideas, one, two, three, &c. The known characters of this description are between twenty and thirty.

The known Assyrian characters are thus brought up nearly to three hundred! There still remain a considerable number which are either wholly unknown, or of which the meaning is known, while the phonetic value cannot at present be determined. M. Oppert's Catalogue contains fourteen of the former and fifty-nine of the latter class.

It has been already observed, that the monumental evidence accords with the traditional belief in regard to the character of the Assyrian language, which is unmistakably Semitic. Not only does the vocabulary present constant analogies to other Semitic dialects, but the phonetic laws and the grammatical forms are equally of this type. At the same time the language has peculiarities of its own, which separate it from its kindred tongues, and constitute it a distinct form of Semitic speech, not a mere variety of any known form. It is neither Hebrew, nor Arabic, nor Phœnician, nor Chaldee, nor Syriac, but a sister tongue to these, having some analogies with all of them, and others, more or fewer, with each. On the whole, its closest relationship seems to be with the Hebrew, and its greatest divergence from the Aramaic or Syriac, with which it was yet, locally, in immediate connection.

To attempt anything like a full illustration of these statements in the present place would be manifestly unfitting. It would be to quit the province of the historian and archæologist, in order to enter upon that of the comparative philologer or the grammarian. At the same time a certain amount of illustration seems necessary, in order to show that the statements above made are not mere theories, but have a substantial basis.

The Semitic character of the vocabulary will probably be felt to be sufficiently established by the following lists :—

NOUNS SUBSTANTIVE.

Abu, "a father." Compare Heb. אָב, אֲבִי; Arabic *abu.*

Ummu, "a mother." Comp. Heb. אֵם, and Arabic *um.*

Akhu, "a brother." Comp. Heb. אָח, אֲחִי.

Pal or *bal,* "a son." Comp. Syriac *bar,* and perhaps Heb. בֵּן.

Ilu, "God." Comp. Heb. אֵל, אֱלוֹהַּ; Arabic *Allah.*

Sarru, "a king." Comp. Heb. שַׂר.

Mulik, "a prince." Comp. Heb. מֶלֶךְ, and Arabic *malik.*

Bilu, "a lord." Comp. Heb. בַּעַל.

Nisu, "a man." Comp. Heb. אֱנוֹשׁ, "a mortal," and Chald. נָשִׁים, "women."

Dayan, "a judge." Comp. Heb. דִּין, from דָּן, *judicare.*

Sumu, "a name." Comp. Heb. שֵׁם.

Sami, "heaven." Comp. Heb. שָׁמַיִם, "the heavens."

Irtsit, "the earth." Comp. Heb. אֶרֶץ.

Shamas, "the sun." Comp. Heb. שֶׁמֶשׁ.

Tsin, "the moon." Comp. Syriac *sin.*

Marrat, or *warrat,* "the sea." Comp. Arabic *bahr,* "a lake" (?). Or may be the root be מַר, "bitter"? Comp. Lat. *marr, a-marus.*

Nahar, "a river." Comp. Heb. נָהָר, and Arabic *nahr.*

Yumu, "day." Comp. Heb. יוֹם.

Ramu, "the world." Comp. Heb. עוֹלָם.

'Ir, "a city." Comp. Heb. עִיר.

Bit, "a house." Comp. Heb. בַּיִת.

Bab, "a gate." Comp. Chald. בָּבָא, and Arabic *bab.*

Lisan, "a tongue," or "language." Comp. Heb. לָשׁוֹן, Chald. לִשָּׁן.

Asr, "a place." Comp. Chald. אֲתַר.

Mitu, "death." Comp. Heb. מוּת.

Susu, "a horse." Comp. Heb. סוּס.

ADJECTIVES.

Rabu, "great." Comp. Heb. רַב; whence the well-known Rabbi (רַבִּי), "a great one, a doctor."

Tabu, "good." Comp. Chald. טָב, and Heb. טוֹב.

Basha, "bad." Comp. Heb. מֵבִישׁ, "a base one," from בּוּשׁ, "to be ashamed."

Madut, "many." Comp. Heb. מְאֹד, "exceedingly."

Ruk, "far, wide." Comp. Heb. רָחוֹק.

NUMERALS.

[The forms marked with an asterisk are conjectural.]

Ishtin, " one " (masc.).   Comp. Heb. עֶשְׁתֵּי, in עֶשְׁתֵּי־עָשָׂר, " eleven."

Ikhit, " one " (fem.).   Comp. Heb. אַחַת.

Shamii, " two " (masc.)   Comp. Heb. שְׁנֵי, שָׁנִי.

Khalakal, " three " (masc.).   Comp. Heb. שְׁלֹשָׁה.

Shilash, " three " (fem.).   Comp. Heb. שָׁלֹשׁ.

Arbai, " four " (masc.).   Comp. Heb. אַרְבָּעָה.

Arba, " four " (fem.).   Comp. Heb. אַרְבַּע.

Khamshat, " five " (masc.).   Comp. Heb. חֲמִשָּׁה.

Khamish, " five " (fem.).   Comp. Heb. חָמֵשׁ.

Shashat, " six " (masc.).   Comp. Heb. שִׁשָּׁה.

Shash, " six " (fem.).   Comp. Heb. שֵׁשׁ.

Shibit, " seven " (masc.).   Comp. Heb. שִׁבְעָה.

Shibi, " seven " (fem.).   Comp. Heb. שֶׁבַע.

Shamnat,* " eight " (masc.).   Comp. Heb. שְׁמֹנָה.

Tishit,* " nine " (masc.).   Comp. Heb. תִּשְׁעָה.

Tishi,* " nine " (fem.).   Comp. Heb. תֵּשַׁע.

Iarit, " ten " (masc.).   Comp. Heb. עֲשָׂרָה.

Iari, " ten " (fem.).   Comp. Heb. עֶשֶׂר.

Iarai, " twenty."   Comp. Heb. עֶשְׂרִים.

Shilushmi, " thirty."   Comp. Heb. שְׁלֹשִׁים.

Irba'ai, " forty."   Comp. Heb. אַרְבָּעִים.

Khamshai, " fifty."   Comp. Heb. חֲמִשִּׁים.

Shishai, " sixty."   Comp. Heb. שִׁשִּׁים.

Shibai, " seventy."   Comp. Heb. שִׁבְעִים.

Shamnai,* " eighty."   Comp. Heb. שְׁמֹנִים.

Tishai, " ninety."   Comp. Heb. תִּשְׁעִים.

Mai, or *Mi*, " a hundred."   Comp. Heb. מֵאָה.

PRONOUNS.

[The forms marked with an asterisk are conjectural.]

Anaku, " I."   Heb. אָנֹכִי.

Atta, " thou " (masc.).   Heb. אַתָּה.

Atti,* " thou " (fem.).   Heb. אַתְּ.

Shu, " he."   Heb. הוּא.

Shi, " she."   Heb. הִיא.

Anakhni(?), " we."   Heb. אֲנַחְנוּ.

Attun,* " ye " (masc.).   Heb. אַתֶּם.

Attin, " ye " (fem.). Heb. אַתֵּן.
Shunnu, or *Shun,* " they " (masc.). Heb. הֵמָּה, הֵם.
Shinat, or *Shin,* " they " (fem.). Heb. הֵנָּה, הֵן.
Mu, " who, which." Heb. מַה.
Ulla, " that." Heb. אֵלֶּה, " these."

VERBS.

Alak, " to go." Heb. הָלַךְ.
Bakhar, " to collect." Comp. Heb. בָּחַר, " to select."
Bana, " to create, to build." Heb. בָּנָה.
Dann, " to give," in Niphal, *nadan.* Heb. נָתַן.
Din, " to judge." Heb. דִּין.
Duk, " to kill." Comp. Heb. דָּקַק, " to beat small;" דּוּךְ, " to pound or bruise." Chald. דּוּךְ.
'Ibir, " to pass, cross." Heb. עָבַר.
'Irash, " to make." Comp. Chald. עֲבַד.
'Irish, " to ask, pray." Comp. Heb. אֲרֶשֶׁת, " a request, desire."
Natzar, " to guard." Heb. נָצַר.
Nazz, " to leap." Heb. נָזָה.
Nazal, " to flow, sink, descend." Heb. נָזַל.
Pakad, " to entrust." Heb. פָּקַד.
Saga, " to grow, become great." Heb. שָׂגָה.
Shakan, " to dwell." Heb. שָׁכַן.
Shatar, " to write." Comp. Chald. שְׁטָר, " a written contract."
Tsabat, " to hold, possess." Comp. Heb. צֶבֶת, " a bundle;" Arab. *tsubut,* " to hold tight;" Chald. צְבַת, " tongs."

ADVERBS, CONJUNCTIONS, &c.

U, " and." Heb. וֹ or וּ.
La or *ul,* " not." Heb. לֹא.
Lapani, " before the face of." Heb. לִפְנֵי.
Tsilli, " by favour of." Heb. צֵל.
'Ilat, " except." Chald. אֶלָּא.
Adi, " until." Heb. עַד.
Ki, " if." Heb. כִּי.

It remains to notice briefly some of the chief grammatical laws and forms. There is one remarkable difference between the Assyrian language and the Hebrew, namely, that the former has no article. In this it resembles the Syriac, which is likewise deficient in this part of speech.

Assyrian nouns, like Hebrew ones, are all either masculine or feminine. Feminine nouns end ordinarily in -at or -it, as Hebrew ones in -eth, -ith, -uth, or -ah. There is a dual number, as in Hebrew, and it has the same limited use, being applied almost exclusively to those objects which form a pair. The plural masculine is commonly formed by adding -i or -ani to the singular—terminations which recal the Hebrew addition of ‏ים‎; but sometimes by adding -ut or -uti, to which there is no exact analogy in Hebrew.[1] The plural feminine is made by changing -it into -et, and -āt into -āt, or (if the word does not end in t), by adding -āt. Here again there is resemblance to, though not identity with, the Hebrew, which forms the feminine plural in -oth (‏ות‎).

Assyrian, like Hebrew, adjectives, agree in gender and number with their substantives. They form the feminine singular in -āt, the plural masculine in -i and -ut, the plural feminine in -āt and -et.

In Assyrian, as in all other Semitic languages, the possessive pronouns are expressed by suffixes. These suffixes are, for the first person singular, -ya, or -iya (Heb. ‏ִי‎); for the second person singular masculine, -ka (Heb. ‏ְךָ‎); for the second person singular feminine, -ki (Heb. ‏ֵךְ‎); for the third person singular masculine, -shu (Heb. ‏וֹ‎); for the third person singu-

---

[1] The nearest approach to an analogy is to be found in those Hebrew nouns which adopt the feminine termination for their plurals, as ‏אָב‎ "a father," ‏אָבוֹת‎ "fathers." But in Assyrian the masculine plural termination -ut is not identical with the feminine, which is -et or -at.

lar feminine, -sha (Heb. אּ;); for the first person
plural, -n (Heb. ט-); for the second person plural
masculine, -kun (Heb. כֻן); for the second person
plural feminine, -kin (Heb. כֵן); for the third person
plural masculine, -shun (Heb. ס;); for the third person
plural feminine, -shin (Heb. ן;). The resemblance, it
will be seen, is in most cases close, though in only
one is there complete identity.

Assyrian verbs have five principal, and four
secondary, voices. Only two of these—the *kal* and
the *niphal*—are exactly identical with the Hebrew.
The *puel*, however, corresponds nearly to the Hebrew
piel, and the *aphel* to the Hebrew *hiphil*. In addition to these we find enumerated the *shaphel*, the
iphtal, the *iphta'al*, the *istaphal*, and the *itaphal*.
Several of these are well known forms in Chaldee.

It is peculiar to Assyrian to have no distinctions
of tense. The same form of the verb serves for the
present, the past, and the future. The only distinctions of mood are an imperative and an infinitive,
besides the indicative. There is also, in each voice,
one participle.

The verbs are conjugated by the help of pronominal suffixes and prefixes, chiefly the latter, like the
future (present) tense in Hebrew. The suffixes and
prefixes are nearly identical with those used in
Hebrew.

For further particulars on this interesting subject
the student is referred to the modest but excellent
work of M. Oppert, entitled 'Elémens de la Gram-
maire Assyrienne,'[4] from which the greater portion
of the above remarks are taken.

---

[4] " *Elémens, &c.,*" par M. Jules Oppert. Paris, Imprimerie Impériale, 1860.

CHAPTER VI.

ARCHITECTURE AND OTHER ARTS.

" Architecti multarum artium solertes."—Mos. Chor. (De Assyriis) I. 15.

THE luxury and magnificence of the Assyrians, and
the advanced condition of the arts among them which
such words imply, were matters familiar to the Greeks
and Romans; who, however, had little ocular evidence of the fact, but accepted it upon the strength
of a very clear and uniform tradition.   More fortunate than the nations of classical antiquity, whose
comparative proximity to the time proved no advantage to them, we possess in the exhumed remains of
this interesting people a mass of evidence upon the
point, which, although in many respects sadly incomplete, still enables us to form a judgment for ourselves upon the subject, and to believe—on better
grounds than they possessed—the artistic genius and
multiform ingenuity of the Assyrians.   As architects,
as designers, as sculptors, as metallurgists, as en-
gravers, as upholsterers, as workers in ivory, as glass-
blowers, as embroiderers of dresses, it is evident that
they equalled, if they did not exceed, all other Oriental nations.   It is the object of the present chapter
to give some account of their skill in these various
respects.   Something is now known of them all; and
though in every case there are points still involved
in obscurity, and recourse must therefore be had upon
occasion to conjecture, enough appears certainly made

out to justify such an attempt as the present, and to supply a solid groundwork of fact valuable in itself, even if it be insufficient to sustain in addition any large amount of hypothetical superstructure.

The architecture of the Assyrians will naturally engage our attention at the outset. It is from an examination of their edifices that we have derived almost all the knowledge which we possess of their progress in every art; and it is further as architects that they always enjoyed a special repute among their neighbours. Hebrew and Armenian united with Greek tradition in representing the Assyrians as notable builders at a very early time. When Asshur "went forth out of the land of Shinar," it was to build cities, one of which is expressly called "a great city."[1] When the Armenians had to give an account of the palaces and other vast structures in their country, they ascribed their erection to the Assyrians.[2] Similarly, when the Greeks sought to trace the civilisation of Asia to its source, they carried it back to Ninus and Semiramis, whom they made the founders, respectively, of Nineveh and Babylon,[3] the two chief cities of the early world.

Among the architectural works of the Assyrians, the first place is challenged by their palaces. Less religious, or more servile, than the Egyptians and the Greeks, they make their temples insignificant in comparison with the dwellings of their kings, to which indeed the temple is most commonly a sort of appendage. In the palace their art culminates—there every effort is made, every ornament lavished. If the architecture of the Assyrian palaces be fully con-

---

[1] Gen. x. 12.   [2] Mos. Choren. i. 15.   [3] Diod. Sic. ii. 3 and 5.

sidered, very little need be said on the subject of
their other buildings.

The Assyrian palace stood uniformly on an artificial
platform. Commonly this platform was composed of
undried bricks in regular layers; but occasionally the
material used was merely earth or rubbish, excepting
towards the exposed parts—the sides and the surface—
which were always either of brick or of stone. In most
cases the sides were protected by massive stone masonry, carried perpendicularly from the natural ground

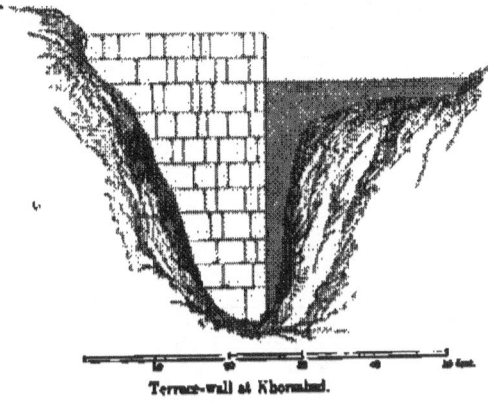

Terrace-wall at Khorsabad.

to a height somewhat exceeding that of the platform,
and either made plain at the top or else crowned with
stone battlements cut into gradines. The pavement
consisted in part of stone slabs, in part of kiln-dried
bricks of a large size, often as much as two feet square.
The stone slabs were sometimes inscribed, sometimes
ornamented with an elegant pattern. (See next
page.) Occasionally the terrace was divided into
portions at different elevations, which were connected
by staircases or inclined planes. The terrace commu-

nicated in the same way with the level ground at its
base, being (as is probable) sometimes ascended in a
single place, sometimes in several. These ascents
were always on the side where the palace adjoined
upon the neighbouring town, and were thus protected
from hostile attack by the town-walls. Where the
palace abutted upon the walls or projected beyond

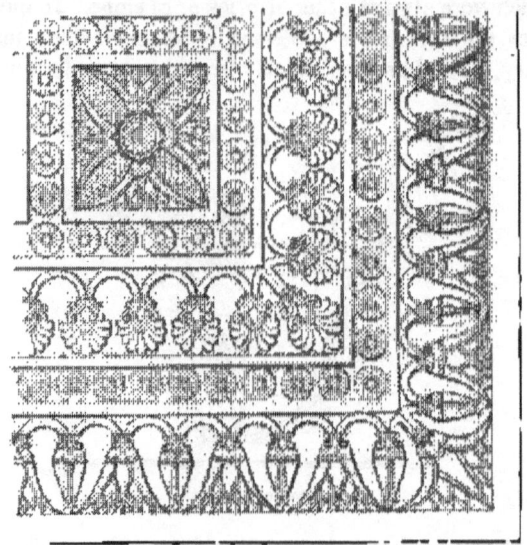

Pavement-slab, from the Northern Palace, Koyunjik.

them—and the palace was always placed at the edge
of a town, for the double advantage, probably, of a
clear view and of fresh air—the platform rose perpendicularly or nearly so; and generally a water
protection, a river, a moat, or a broad lake, lay at its
base, thus rendering attack, except on the city side,
almost impossible.

The platform appears to have been, in general

shape, a rectangle, or where it had different elevations, to have been composed of rectangles. The
mound of Khorsabad, which is of this latter character,
resembles a gigantic T.

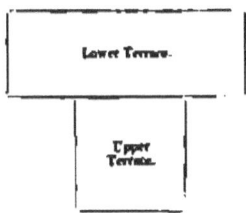

It must not be supposed, however, that the rectangle
was always exact. Sometimes its outline was broken
by angular projections and indentations, as in the annexed plan (p. 352),[1] where the shaded parts represent
actual discoveries. Sometimes it grew to be irregular, by the addition of fresh portions, as new kings
arose who determined on fresh erections. This is the
case at Nimrud, where the platform broadens towards
its lower or southern end,[3] and still more at Koyunjik
and Nebbi Yunus,[4] where the rectangular idea has
been so overlaid as to have almost wholly disappeared. Palaces were commonly placed near one
edge of the mound—more especially near the river
edge—probably for the better enjoyment of the prospect, and of the cool air over the water.

The palace itself was composed of three main elements, courts, grand halls, and small private apartments. A palace has usually from two to four courts,
which are either square or oblong, and vary in size

---

[1] The plan is borrowed, by per-
mission, from Mr. Fergusson's excellent work, *The Palaces of Nineveh
and Persepolis Restored.* Mr. Fergusson remarks that this feature of

alternate projection and indentation
is found also in the Persepolitan
platform (see p. 239).
[3] See the plan, supra, p. 251.
[4] See above, p. 316.

according to the general scale of the building. In
the north-west palace at Nimrud, the most ancient of
the edifices yet explored, one court only has been
found, the dimensions of which are 120 feet by 90.
At Khorsabad, the palace of Sargon has four courts.

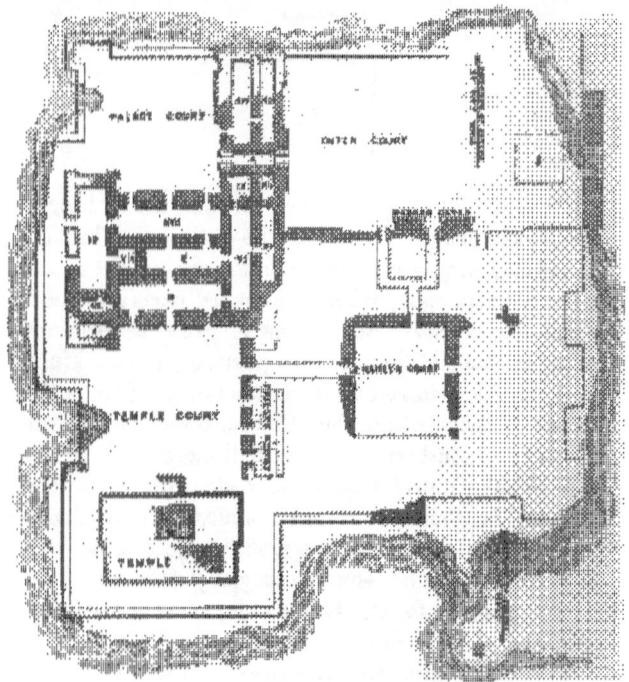

Plan of the Palace of Sargon, Khorsabad (after Fergusson).

Three of them are nearly square, the largest measuring 180 feet each way, and the smallest about 120 feet;
the third is oblong, and must have been at least 250
feet long and 150 feet wide. The palace of Sennacherib at Koyunjik, a much larger edifice than the

palace of Sargon, has also three courts, which are respectively 93 feet by 84, 124 feet by 90, and 154 feet by 125. Esar-haddon's palace at Nimrud has a court 220 feet long and 100 wide.[1] These courts were all paved either with baked bricks of large size, or with stone slabs, which were frequently patterned.[2] Sometimes the courts were surrounded with buildings; sometimes they abutted upon the edge of the platform: in this latter case they were protected by a stone parapet, which (at least in places) was six feet high.

The grand halls of the Assyrian palaces constitute their most remarkable feature. Each palace has commonly several. They are apartments narrow for their length, measuring from three to five times their own width, and thus having always somewhat the appearance of galleries. The scale upon which they are built is, commonly, magnificent. In the palace of Sardanapalus I. at Nimrud, the earliest of the discovered edifices, the great hall was 160 feet long by nearly 40 broad. In Sargon's palace at Khorsabad the size of no single room was so great; but the number of halls was remarkable, there being no fewer than five of nearly equal dimensions. The largest was 116 feet long, and 33 wide; the smallest 87 feet long, and 25 wide. The palace of Sennacherib at Koyunjik contained the most spacious apartment yet exhumed. It was immediately inside the great portal, and extended in length 180 feet, with a uniform width of 40 feet. In one instance only, so far as appears, was an attempt made to exceed this width. In the

---

[1] Mr. Layard calls this court a "hall" (*Nineveh and Babylon*, p. 654); but no one can compare his plan of Esar-haddon's Nimrud palace (No. 3, opp. p. 655) with M. Botta's plans of Khorsabad, and his own plans of Koyunjik, without seeing at once that the great space is really an inner court. How does Mr. Layard suppose that his "hall," one hundred feet wide, was roofed?

[2] See the woodcut on p. 350.

palace of Esar-haddon, the son of Sennacherib, a hall was designed, intended to surpass all former ones. Its length was to be 165 feet, and its width 62; consequently it would have been nearly one-third larger than the great hall of Sennacherib, its area exceeding 10,000 square feet. But the builder who had designed this grand structure appears to have been unable to overcome the difficulty of carrying a roof over so vast an expanse. He was therefore obliged to divide his hall by a wall down the middle; which, though he broke it in an unusual way into portions, and kept it at some distance from both ends of the apartment, still had the actual effect of subdividing his grand room into four apartments of only moderate size. The halls were paved with sun-burnt brick. They were ornamented throughout by the elaborate sculptures, now so familiar to us, carried generally in a single, but sometimes in a double line, round the four walls of the apartment. The sculptured slabs rested on the ground, and clothed the walls to the height of 10 or 12 feet. Above, for a space which we cannot positively fix, but which was certainly not less than four or five feet,[1] the crude brick wall was continued, faced here with burnt brick enamelled on the side towards the apartment, pleasingly and sometimes even brilliantly coloured.[2] The whole height of the walls was probably from 15 to 20 feet.

Hall of Esar-haddon's Palace, Nimrud.

(Scale of 10 ft. to an inch.)

---

[1] As much as four feet of the wall has sometimes been found standing (Fergusson's *Palaces*, p. 207).

[2] See the specimens of enamelled bricks in Mr. Layard's *Monuments of Nineveh*, 1st Series, Plates 84 to 86.

By the side of the halls, or at their ends, and opening into them, or sometimes collected together into groups, with no hall near, are the smaller chambers of which mention has been already made. These chambers are in every case rectangular: in their proportions they vary from squares to narrow oblongs, 90 feet by 17, 85 by 16, 80 by 15, and the like. When they are square, the side is never more than about 25 feet. They are often as richly decorated as the halls, but sometimes are merely faced with plain slabs or plastered; while occasionally they have no facing at all, but exhibit throughout the crude brick. This, however, is unusual.

The number of chambers in a palace is very great. In Sennacherib's palace at Koyunjik, where great part of the building remains still unexplored, the excavated chambers amount to sixty-eight—all, be it remembered, upon the ground floor. The space covered by them and by their walls exceeds 100,000 square yards. As Mr. Fergusson observes, "the imperial palace of Sennacherib is, of all the buildings of antiquity, surpassed in magnitude only by the great palace-temple of Karnak; and when we consider the vastness of the mound on which it was raised, and the richness of the ornaments with which it was adorned, it is by no means clear that it was not as great, or at least as expensive, a work as the great palace-temple at Thebes."[1] Elsewhere the excavated apartments are less numerous; but in no case is it probable that a palace contained on its ground floor fewer than forty or fifty chambers.

The most striking peculiarity which the ground-plans of the palaces disclose is the uniform adoption

---

[1] *Handbook of Architecture*, vol. i. p. 176.

throughout of straight and parallel lines. No plan
exhibits a curve of any kind, or any angle but
a right angle. Courts, chambers, and halls, are, in
most cases, exact rectangles; and even where any
variety occurs, it is only by the introduction of
squared recesses or projections, which are moreover
shallow and infrequent. When a palace has its own
special platform, the lines of the building are further
exactly parallel with those of the mound on which
it is placed; and the parallelism extends to any other
detached buildings that there may be anywhere
upon the platform.[3] When a mound is occupied
by more palaces than one, sometimes this law still
obtains, as at Nimrud,[4] where it seems to embrace
at any rate the greater number of the palaces;
sometimes, as at Koyunjik,[5] the rule ceases to be
observed, and the ground-plan of each palace seems
formed separately and independently, with no reference to any neighbouring edifice.

Apart from this feature, the buildings do not
affect much regularity.[6] In courts and façades, to
a certain extent, there is correspondence; but in
the internal arrangements, regularity is decidedly
the exception. The two sides of an edifice never
correspond; room never answers to room; doorways are rarely in the middle of walls: where a
room has several doorways they are seldom oppo-

---

[3] See the plan of Sargon's palace
at Khorsabad, supra, p. 352.

[4] See the plan of the Nimrud platform in Layard's Nineveh and Babylon, opp. p. 655. According to it,
all the palaces on the platform would
have their walls parallel to one another and to the sides of the platform; but Captain Jones's survey
shows that the platform itself is ir-

regular, so that Mr. Layard's representation cannot be wholly trusted.

[5] The walls of the palace excavated by Mr. Loftus are not parallel
with those of the edifice exhumed by
Mr. Layard.

[6] Compare the observations of M.
Botta, Monument de Ninive, vol. v.
p. 64.

site to one another, or in situations at all corresponding.

There is a great awkwardness in the communications. Very few corridors or passages exist in any of the buildings. Groups of rooms, often amounting to ten or twelve, open into one another; and we find comparatively few rooms to which there is any access, except through some other room. Again, whole sets of apartments are sometimes found, between which and the rest of the palace all communication is cut off by thick walls. Another peculiarity in the internal arrangements is the number of doorways in the larger apartments, and their apparently needless multiplication. We constantly find two or even three doorways leading from a court into a hall, or from one hall into a second. It is difficult to see what could be gained by such an arrangement.

The disposition of the various parts of a palace will probably be better apprehended from an exact account of a single building than from any further general statements. For this purpose it is necessary to select a specimen from among the various edifices that have been disentombed by the labours of recent excavators. The specimen should be, if possible, complete; it should have been accurately surveyed, and the survey should have been scientifically recorded; it should further stand single and separate, that there may be no danger of confusion between its remains and those of adjacent edifices. These requirements, though nowhere exactly met, are very nearly met by the building at Khorsabad, which stands on a mound of its own, unmixed with other edifices, has been most carefully examined, and most excellently represented and described, and which, though not completely

excavated, has been excavated with a nearer approach
to completeness than any other edifice in Assyria.
The Khorsabad building—which is believed to be a
palace built by Sargon, the son of Sennacherib—will
therefore be selected for minute description in this
place, as the palace most favourably circumstanced,
and the one of which we have, on the whole, the
most complete and exact knowledge.[1]

The situation of the town, whereof the palace of
Sargon formed a part, has been already described in
a former part of this volume.[2] The shape, it has been
noted, was square, the angles facing the four cardinal
points. Almost exactly in the centre of the north-
west wall occurs the palace platform, a huge mass of
crude brick, from 20 to 30 feet high, shaped like a T,
the upper limb lying within the city walls, and the
lower limb (which is at a higher elevation) projecting beyond the line of the walls to a distance of at
least 500 feet. At present there is a considerable
space between the ends of the wall and the palace
mound;[3] but anciently it is probable that they either
abutted on the mound, or were separated from it
merely by gateways. The mound, or at any rate
the part of it which projected beyond the walls, was
faced with hewn stone,[4] carried perpendicularly from
the plain to the top of the platform and even beyond,
so as to form a parapet protecting the edge of the
platform. On the more elevated portion of the
mound—that which projected beyond the walls—

---

[1] See Fergusson's *Palaces*, pp. 234, 235.

[2] *Supra*, pp. 255, 256.

[3] The Khosr-Su, which runs on this side of the Khorsabad ruins, often overflows its banks, and pours its waters against the palace mound. The gaps north and south of the mound may have been caused by its violence.

[4] See the woodcut, *supra*, p. 349.

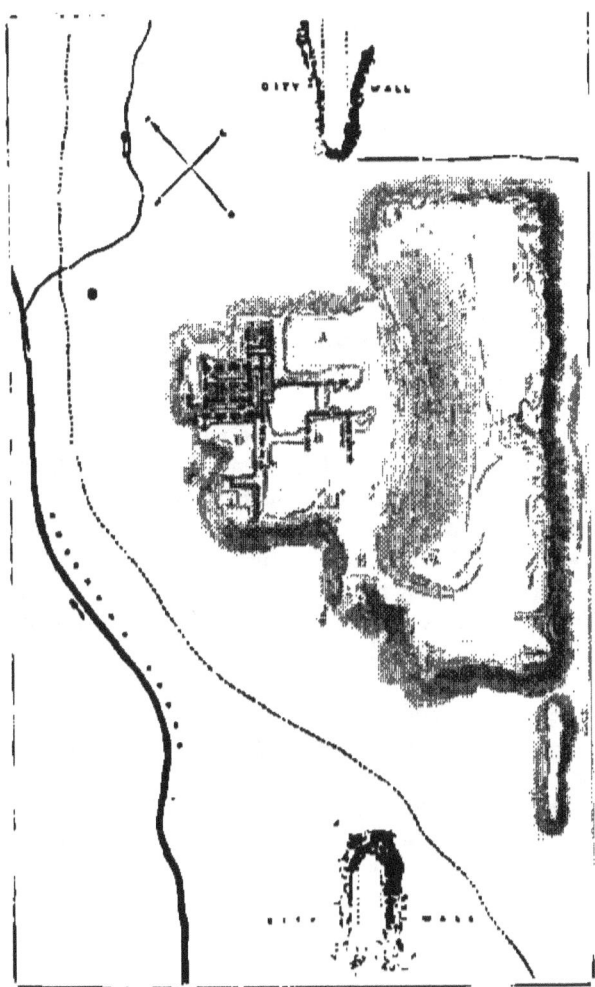

Plan of the Palace of Sargon, Khorsabad.

stood the palace, consisting of three groups of buildings, the principal group lying towards the mound's
northern angle.   On the lower portion of the
platform were several detached buildings, the most
remarkable being a huge gateway, or propylæum,
through which the entrance lay to the palace from
the city. Beyond and below this, on the level plain of
the city, the first or outer portals were placed,[1] giving
entrance to a court in front of the lower terrace.

A visitor approaching the palace, had in the first
place to pass through these portals.   They were
ornamented with colossal human-headed bulls on
either side, and probably spanned by an arch above,
the archivolte being covered with enamelled bricks
disposed in a pattern.   Received within the portals,
the visitor found himself in front of a long wall of
solid stone masonry, the revêtement of the lower terrace, which rose from the outer court to a height of at
least twenty feet.   Either an inclined way, or a flight
of steps—probably the latter—must have led up from
the outer court to this terrace.   Here the visitor
found another portal or propylæum of a magnificent
character.   Midway in the south-east side of the
lower terrace, and about fifty feet from its edge, stood
this grand structure, a gateway ninety feet in width,
and at least twenty-five in depth, having on each side
three winged bulls of gigantic size, two of them fifteen
feet high, and the third nineteen feet.   Between the
two smaller bulls, which stood back to back, presenting their sides to the spectator, was a colossal figure

---

[1] These portals were discovered by M. Place, M. Botta's successor at Mosul. I cannot find that any re-presentations of them have been published.

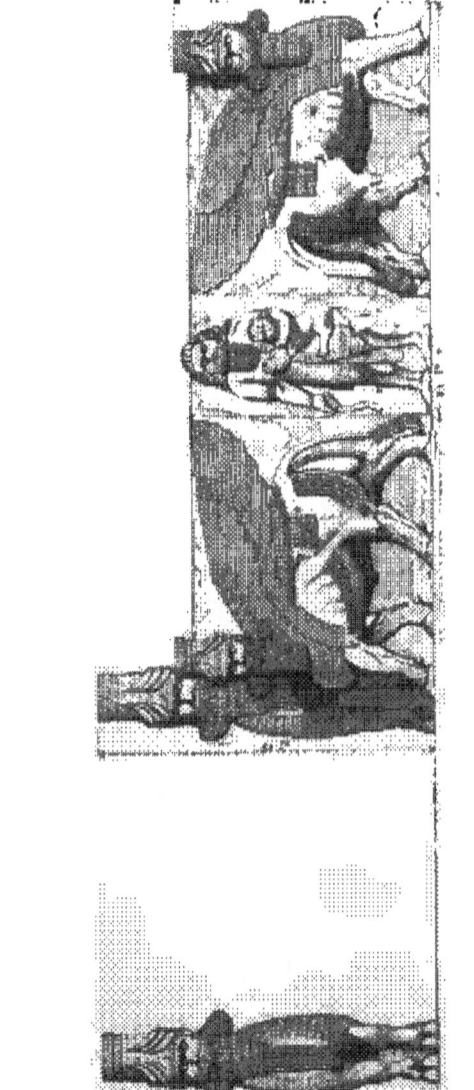

Remains of Propylaea, or outer gateway, Khorsabad.

strangling a lion—the Assyrian Hercules, according
to most writers. The larger bulls stood at right
angles to these figures, withdrawn within the portal,
and facing the spectator. The space between the
bulls, which is nearly twenty feet, was (it is probable)
arched over.[2] Perhaps the archway led into a chamber, beyond which was a second archway and an
inner portal, as marked in Mr. Fergusson's plan; but
this is at present uncertain.[3]

Besides the great portal, the only buildings as yet
discovered on this lower platform, are a suite of not
very extensive apartments. They are remarkable for
their ornamentation. The walls are neither lined with
slabs, nor yet (as is sometimes the case) painted; but
the plaster of which they are composed is formed
into sets of half pillars or reedings, separated from
one another by pilasters with square sunk panels.[4]
The former kind of ornamentation is found also in
lower Chaldæa, and has been already represented;[5]
the latter is peculiar to this building. It is suggested
that these apartments formed the quarters of the
soldiers who kept watch over the royal residence.[6]

About 300 feet from the outer edge of the lower
terrace, the upper terrace seems to have commenced.
It was raised probably about ten feet above the lower
one. The mode of access has not been discovered,
but is presumed to have been by a flight of steps,
not directly opposite the propylæum, but somewhat

[2] The widest Assyrian arch actually discovered is carried across a
space of about 15 feet (infra, p. 378).
[3] Mr. Fergusson argues for the
existence of a chamber and a second
gateway, from the analogy of the
Persepolitan ruins (*Palaces of Nine-*
veh, p. 246); but this analogy cannot be depended on.
[4] Fergusson, *Handbook of Archi-*
tecture, vol. i. p. 172.
[5] Supra, p. 105.
[6] Fergusson, *Handbook,* l. s. c.

to the right, whereby entrance was given to the great
court, into which opened the main gateways of the
palace itself.   The court was probably 350 feet long
by 160 or 170 feet wide.   The visitor, on mounting
the steps, perhaps passed through another propylæum
(*b* in the plan); after which, if his business was with
the monarch, he crossed the full length of the court,
leaving a magnificent triple entrance, which is
thought to have led to the king's *hareem*, on his left,
and making his way to the public gate of the palace,
which fronted him when he mounted the steps.   The
hareem portal, which he passed, resembled in the main
the great propylæum of the lower platform; but,
being triple, it was still more magnificent, exhibiting
two other entrances on either side of the main one,
guarded each by a single pair of winged bulls of the
smaller size.   Along the *hareem* wall, from the gateway to the angle of the court, was a row of sculptured
bas-reliefs, ten feet in height, representing the
monarch with his attendant guards and officers.

King and attendants, Khorsabad.

The façade occupying the end of the court was of inferior grandeur.   Sculptures similar to those along the
hareem wall adorned it; but its centre showed only a
single gateway, guarded by one pair of the larger
bulls, fronting the spectator, and standing each in a
sort of recess, the character of which will be best un-

derstood by the accompanying ground-plan.   Just
inside the bulls was the great door of the palace, a
single door made of wood—apparently of mulberry[1]—

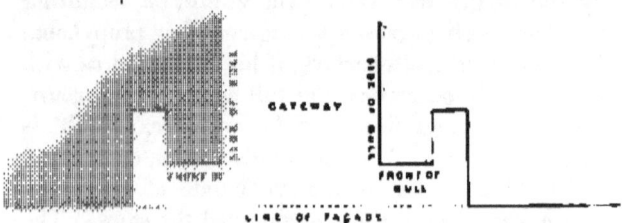

opening inwards, and fastened on the inside by a
bolt at bottom, and also by an enormous lock.   This
door gave entrance into a passage, 70 feet long and
about 10 feet wide, paved with large slabs of stone, and
adorned on either side with inscriptions and with a
double row of sculptures, representing the arrival of
tribute and gifts for the monarch.   All the figures
here faced one way, towards the inner palace court,
into which the passage led.   M. Botta believes that
the passage was uncovered;[2] while Mr. Fergusson[3]
imagines that it was vaulted throughout.   It must in
any case have been lighted from above; for it would
have been impossible to read the inscriptions, or even
to see the sculptures, merely by the light admitted at
the two ends.

From the passage in question—one of the few in
the edifice—no doorway opened out either on the
right hand or on the left.   The visitor necessarily
proceeded along its whole extent, as he saw the
figures proceeding in the sculptures, and, passing

---

[1] Botta, *Monument de Ninive*, vol.   [2] Ibid. p. 69.
v. p. 48.   [3] *Palaces of Nineveh*, p. 259.

through a second portal, found himself in the great inner court of the palace, a square of about 150 or 160 feet, enclosed on two sides—the south-east and the south-west—by buildings, on the other two sides reaching to the edge of the terrace, which here gave upon the open country. The buildings on the south-east side, looking towards the north-west, and adjoining the gateway by which he had entered, were of comparatively minor importance. They consisted of a few chambers suitable for officers of the court, and were approached from the court by two doorways, one on either side of the passage through which he had come. To his left, looking towards the north-east, were the great state apartments, the principal part of the palace, forming a façade, of which some idea may perhaps be formed from the representation overleaf. The upper part of this representation is indeed purely conjectural; and when we come to consider the mode in which the Assyrian palaces were roofed and lighted, we shall perhaps find reason to regard it as not very near the truth; but the lower part, up to the top of the sculptures, the court itself, and the various accessaries, are correctly given, and furnish the only *perspective* view of this part of the palace which has been as yet published.

The great state apartments consisted of a suite of ten rooms. Five of these were halls of large dimensions; one was a long and somewhat narrow chamber, and the remaining four were square or slightly oblong apartments of minor consequence. All of them were lined throughout with sculptures. The most important seem to have been three halls *en suite* (VIII. V. and II. in the plan), which " are, both in their external and internal decorations, by far the most splendid

South-West Court of Sargon's Palace at Khorsabad, restored. (After Fergusson.)

of the whole palace." [1]   The first lay just within the
north-east façade, and ran parallel to it.   It was entered by three doorways, the central one ornamented
externally with two colossal bulls of the largest size,
one on either side within the entrance, and with two
pairs of smaller bulls, back to back, on the projecting
pylons; the side ones guarded by winged genii,
human or hawk-headed.   The length of the chamber
was 116 feet 6 inches, and
its breadth 33 feet.   Its
sculptures represented the
monarch receiving prison-
ers, and either personally
or by deputy punishing
them. [2] We may call it,
for distinction's sake, "the
Hall of Punishment."

King punishing prisoners, Khorsabad.

The second hall (V. in the plan) ran parallel with
the first, but did not extend along its whole length.
It measured from end to end about 86 feet, and from
side to side 21 feet 6 inches.   Two doorways led into
it from the first chamber, and two others led from
it into two large apartments.   One communicated
with a lateral hall (marked VI. in the plan), the
other with the third hall of the suite which is here
the special object of our attention.   This third hall
(II. in the plan) was of the same length as the first,
but was less wide by about three feet.   It opened by
three doorways upon a square court, which has been

[1] *Palaces of Nineveh*, p. 261.
[2] In one case the monarch is in
the act of driving a spear or javelin
into the head of a captive with one
hand, while with the other he holds
him by a thong attached to a ring
passed through his under lip.   In
another case an executioner flays a
captive (or criminal) who is fastened
to a wall.

called "the Temple Court," from a building on one side of it, which will be described presently.

The sculptures of the second and third halls represented in a double row, separated by an inscribed space about two feet in width, chiefly the wars of the monarch, his battles, sieges, reception of captives and of spoil, &c. The monarch himself appeared at least four times, standing in his chariot, thrice in calm

Sargon in his war-chariot, Khorsabad.

procession, and once shooting his arrows against his enemies. Besides these, the upper sculptures on one side exhibited sacred ceremonies.

Placed at right angles to this primary suite of three halls were two others, one (IV. in the plan) [3] of

---

[3] This hall opened on the north-western terrace, and stood so near its edge that two of its sides have fallen away. Internally it was adorned with a single row of sculptures, representing the king receiving prisoners.

dimensions little, if at all, inferior to those of the
largest (No. VIII.), the other (VI. in the plan)' nearly
of the same length, but as narrow as the narrowest
of the three (No. V.). Of these two lateral halls the
former communicated directly with No. VIII., and
also by a narrow passage room (III. in the plan) with
No. II. The other had direct communication both
with No. II. and No. V., but none with No. VIII.
With this hall (No. VI.) three smaller chambers were
connected (Nos. IX. XI. and XII.); with the other
lateral hall, two only (Nos. III. and VII.). One
chamber attached to this block of buildings (I. in the
plan) opened only on the Temple Court. It has
been suggested that it contained a staircase;² but of
this there is no evidence.

The Temple Court—a square of 180 feet—was occupied by buildings on three sides, and open on one
only—that to the north-west. The state apartments
closed it in on the north-east, the temple on the south-
west; on the south-east it was bounded by the range
of buildings called " Priests' Rooms " in the plan,
chambers of less pretension than almost any that
have been excavated. The principal façade here was
that of the state apartments, on the north-east. On
this, as on the opposite side of the palace, were
three portals; but the two fronts were not of equal
magnificence. On the side of the Temple Court a
single pair of bulls, facing the spectator, guarded the
middle portal; the side portals exhibited only figures
of genii, while the spaces between the portals were

' The sculptures here were all
traceable. The king occurred three
times, with the sacred flower in his

left hand, receiving presents or tribute.
² Fergusson's *Palaces*, p. 263.

occupied, not with bulls, but merely with a series of human figures, resembling those in the first or outer court, of which a representation has been already given. Two peculiarities marked the south-east façade. In the first place, it lay in a perfectly straight line, unbroken by any projection, which is very unusual in Assyrian architecture. In the second place, as if to compensate for this monotony in its facial line, it was pierced by no fewer than five door-ways, all of considerable width, and two of them garnished with bulls, namely, the second and the fourth. The bulls of the second gateway were of the larger, those of the fourth were of the smaller size; they stood in the usual manner, a little withdrawn within the gateways and looking towards the spectator.

Of the curious building which closed in the court on the third or south-west side, which is believed to have been a temple,[*] the remains are unfortunately very slight. It stood so near the edge of the terrace that the greater part of it has fallen into the plain. Less than half of the ground-plan is left, and only a few feet of the elevation. The building may originally have been a square, or it may have been an oblong, as represented in the plan. It was approached from the court by a flight of stone steps, probably six in number, of which four remain in place. This flight of steps was placed directly opposite to the central door of the south-west palace façade. From the level of the court to that of the top of the steps, a height of about six feet, a solid platform of crude brick was raised as a basis for the temple; and this

---

* Botta, *Monument de Ninive*, vol. v. p. 53; Fergusson, *Palaces of* | *Nineveh*, p. 202; Layard, *Nineveh and Babylon*, p. 130.

was faced, probably throughout its whole extent, with
a solid wall of hard black basalt, ornamented with a
cornice in grey limestone, of which the accompanying woodcuts are representations.   Above this

 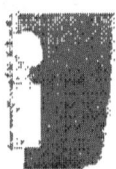

the external work has disappeared.   Internally, two
chambers may be traced, floored with a mixture of
stones and chalk; and round one of these are some
fragments of bas-reliefs, representing sacred subjects,
cut on the same black basalt as that by which the
platform is cased, and sufficient to show that the
same style of ornamentation prevailed here as in the
palace.

The principal doorway on the north-west side of
the Temple Court communicated, by a passage, with
another and similar doorway (*d* on the plan), which
opened into a fourth court, the smallest and least
ornamented of those on the upper platform.   The
mass of building, whereof this court occupied the
centre, is believed to have constituted the *hareem* or
private apartments of the monarch.[1]   It adjoined
the state apartments at its northern angle, but had
no direct communication with them.   To enter it
from them the visitor had either to cross the Temple
Court and proceed by the passage above indicated,
or else to go round by the great entrance (X. in

---

[1] Fergusson, *Palaces of Nineveh*, p. 254; Layard, *Nineveh and Babylon*, p. 646.

the plan) and obtain admission by the grand
portals on the south-west side of the outer court.
These latter portals, it is to be observed, are so
placed as to command no view into the *Hareem* Court,
though it is opposite to them. The passages by
which they gave entrance into that court must have
formed some such angles as those marked by the
dotted lines in the plan, the result being that
visitors, while passing through the outer court,
would be unable to catch any sight of what was
going on in the *Hareem* Court, even if the great
doors happened to be open. Those admitted so far
into the palace as the Temple Court were more
favoured or less feared. The doorway (*d*) on the
south-east side of the *Hareem* Court is exactly opposite
the chief doorway on the north-west side of the
Temple Court, and there can be no reasonable doubt
that a straight passage connected the two.

It is uncertain whether the *Hareem* Court was surrounded by buildings on every side, or open towards
the south-west. M. Botta believed that it was
open;[*] and the analogy of the other courts would
seem to make this probable. It is to be regretted,
however, that this portion of the great Khorsabad
ruin still remains so incompletely examined. Consisting of the private apartments, it is naturally less
rich in sculptures than other parts; and hence it
has been comparatively neglected. The labour
would, nevertheless, be well employed which should
be devoted to this part of the ruin, as it would
give us (what we do not now possess) the *complete*
ground-plan of an Assyrian palace. It is earnestly

---

[*] *Monument de Ninive*, vol. v. p. 42; and compare the plan, vol. i. pl. 6,

to be hoped that future excavators will direct their
efforts to this easily attainable and interesting
object.

The ground-plans of the palaces, and some sixteen
feet of their elevations, are all that fire and time
have left us of these remarkable monuments.   The
total destruction of the upper portion of every palatial building in Assyria, combined with the want
of any representation of the royal residences upon
the bas-reliefs, reduces us to mere conjecture with
respect to their height, to the mode in which they
were roofed and lighted, and even to the question
whether they had or had not an upper story.   On
these subjects various views have been put forward by persons entitled to consideration; and to
these it is proposed now to direct the reader's
attention.

In the first place, then, had they an upper story?
Mr. Layard and Mr. Fergusson decide this question
in the affirmative.   Mr. Layard even goes so far
as to say that the fact is one which "can no longer
be doubted." [*]   He rests this conclusion on two
grounds—first, on a belief that "upper chambers" are mentioned in the Inscriptions, and
secondly, on the discovery by himself, in Sennacherib's palace at Koyunjik, of what seemed to be
an inclined way, by which he supposes that the
ascent was made to an upper story.   The former of
these two arguments must be set aside as wholly
uncertain.   The interpretation of the architectural
inscriptions of the Assyrians is a matter of far too
much doubt at present to serve as a groundwork

--- --- ---

[*] *Nineveh and Babylon*, p. 660.

upon which theories can properly be raised as to
the plan of their buildings. With regard to the
inclined passage, it is to be observed that it did
not appear to what it led. It may have conducted
to a gallery looking into one of the great halls, or
to an external balcony overhanging an outer court;
or it may have been the ascent to the top of a
tower, whence a look-out was kept up and down
the river. Is it not more likely that this ascent
should have been made for some exceptional purpose, than that it should be the only specimen left
of the ordinary mode by which one half of a palace
was rendered accessible? It is to be remembered
that no remains of a staircase, whether of stone or of
wood, have been found in any of the palaces, and
that there is no other instance in any of them even
of an inclined passage.[1] Those who think the palaces
had second stories, believe these stories to have
been reached by staircases of wood, placed in various
parts of the buildings, which were totally destroyed
by the conflagrations in which the palaces perished.
But it is at least remarkable that no signs have
been found in any existing walls of rests for the
ends of beams, or of anything implying staircases. Hence M. Botta, the most careful and the
most scientific of recent excavators, came to a very
positive conclusion that the Khorsabad building had
had no second story,[2] a conclusion which it would
not, perhaps, be very bold to extend to Assyrian
edifices generally.

---

[1] The inclined passage of Asshur-
bani-pal's palace at Kovunjik was
not in the palace, but led from the
level of the city up to it.

[2] *Monument de Ninive*, vol. v.
p. 62.

It has been urged by Mr. Fergusson that there
must have been an upper story because, otherwise,
all the advantage of the commanding position of
the palaces, perched on their lofty platforms, would
have been lost.[1] The platform at Khorsabad was
protected, in the only places where its edge has been
laid bare, by a stone wall or parapet *six feet in height*.
Such a parapet continued along the whole of the
platform would effectually have shut out all prospect
of the open country both from the platform itself,
and also from the gateways of the palace, which
are on the same level. Nor could there well be
any view at all from the ground-chambers, which
had no windows, at any rate within fifteen feet of
the floor. To enjoy a view of anything but the
dead wall skirting the mound, it was necessary
(Mr. Fergusson thinks) to mount to a second story,
which he ingeniously places, not over the ground-
rooms, but on the top of the outer and party walls,
whose structure is so massive that their area falls
(he observes) but little short of the area of the ground-
rooms themselves.[2]

This reasoning is sufficiently answered, in the
first place, by observing that we do not know
whether the Assyrians appreciated the advantage
of a view or raised their palace platforms for any
such object. They may have constructed them for
security only, or for greater dignity and greater
seclusion. They may have looked chiefly to comfort,
and have reared them in order to receive the benefit
of every breeze, and at the same time to be above
the elevation to which gnats and mosquitoes com-

---

[1] *Palaces of Nineveh*, p. 275.   [2] Ibid.

monly rise.[5] Or there may be a fallacy in concluding, from the very slight data furnished by the
excavations of M. Botta,[6] that a palace platform
was, in any case, skirted along its whole length by
a six-foot parapet. Nothing is more probable than
that in places the Khorsabad parapet may have been
very much lower than this; and elsewhere it is not
even ascertained that any parapet at all edged the
platform. On the whole we seem to have no right
to conclude, merely on account of the small portions
of parapet wall uncovered by M. Botta, that an
upper story was a necessity to the palaces. If the
Assyrians valued a view, they may easily have made
their parapets low in places: if they cared so little
for it as to shut it out from all their halls and
terraces, they may not improbably have dispensed
with the advantage altogether.

The two questions of the roofing and lighting
of the Assyrian palaces are so closely connected
together that they will most conveniently be treated
in combination. The first conjecture published on
the subject of the roofing was that of M. Flandin,
who suggested that the chambers generally—in the
great halls, at any rate—had been ceiled with a
brick vault. He thought that the complete filling
up of the apartments to the height of fifteen or twenty
feet was thus best explained; and he believed that
there were traces of the fallen vaulting in the _débris_
with which the apartments were filled. His conjecture was combated, soon after he put it forth, by

---

[5] That this was one of the objects
held in view by the Babylonians
when they erected their Temple platforms, is conjectured by M. Fresnel.
(_Journal Asiatique_, Juin, 1853, pp.
528–531.)

[6] The parapet wall was observed
at most in two places. (See the
shaded parts, marked _a a_ on the
plan, p. 352.)

M. Botta,[1] who gave it as his opinion—first, that
the walls of the chambers, notwithstanding their
great thickness, would have been unable, considering
their material, to sustain the weight, and (still more
to bear) the lateral thrust, of a vaulted roof; and,
secondly, that such a roof, if it had existed at all,
must have been made of baked brick or stone—crude
brick being too weak for the purpose—and when it
fell must have left ample traces of itself within the
apartments, whereas, in none of them, though he
searched, could he find any such traces. On this
latter point M. Botta and M. Flandin—both eye-
witnesses—were at variance. M. Flandin believed
that he had seen such traces, not only in numerous
broken fragments of burnt brick strewn through all
the chambers, but in occasional masses of brickwork
contained in some of them—actual portions, as he
thought, of the original vaulting. M. Botta, however, observed—first, that the quantity of baked
brick within the chambers was quite insufficient for
a vaulted roof; and, secondly, that the position of
the masses of brickwork noticed by M. Flandin was
always towards the sides, never towards the centres
of the apartments; a clear proof that they had fallen
from the upper part of the walls above the sculptures, and not from a ceiling covering the whole
room. He further observed that the quantity of
charred wood and charcoal within the chambers, and
the calcined appearance of all the slabs, were phenomena incompatible with any other theory than
that of the destruction of the palace by the conflagration of a roof mainly of wood.[2]

---

[1] *Monument de Ninive*, vol. v. pp. 66–67.   [2] Ibid. p. 68.

To these arguments of M. Botta may be added another from the improbability of the Assyrians being sufficiently advanced in architectural science to be able to construct an arch of the width necessary to cover some of the chambers. The principle of the arch was, indeed, as will be hereafter shown,[9] well known to the Assyrians; but hitherto we possess no proof that they were capable of applying it on a large scale. The widest arch which has been found in any of the buildings is that of the Khorsabad town-gate uncovered by M. Place,[10] which spans a space of (at most) fourteen or fifteen feet. But the great halls of the Assyrian palaces have a width of twenty-five, thirty, and even forty feet. It is at any rate uncertain whether the constructive skill of their architects could have grappled successfully with the difficulty of throwing a vault over so wide an interval as even the least of these.

M. Botta, after objecting, certainly with great force, to the theory of M. Flandin, proceeded to suggest a theory of his own. After carefully reviewing all the circumstances, he gave it as his opinion that the Khorsabad building had been roofed throughout with a flat, earth-covered roofing of wood. He observed that some of the buildings on the bas-reliefs had flat roofs, that flat roofs are still the fashion of the country, and that the *débris* within the chambers were exactly such as a roof of that kind would be likely, if destroyed by fire, to have produced.[1] He further noticed that on the

floors of the chambers in various parts of the palace,
there had been discovered stone rollers, closely
resembling those still in use at Mosul and Baghdad,
for keeping close-pressed and hard the earthen
surface of such roofs ; which rollers had, in all
probability, been applied to the same use by the
Assyrians, and, being kept on the roofs, had fallen
through during the conflagration.[1]

The first difficulty which presented itself here was
one of those regarded as most fatal to the vaulting
theory, namely, the width of the chambers. Where
flat timber roofs prevail in the East, their span
seems never to exceed twenty-five feet.[2] The ordinary chambers in the Assyrian palaces might, undoubtedly, therefore, have been roofed in this way,
by a series of horizontal beams laid across them
from side to side, with the ends resting upon the
tops of the side walls. But the great halls seemed
too wide to have borne such a roofing without
supports. Accordingly, M. Botta suggested that in
the greater apartments a single or a double row
of pillars ran down the middle, reaching to the
roof and sustaining it.[3] His theory was afterwards
warmly embraced by Mr. Fergusson, who endea-
voured to point out the exact position of the pillars
in the three great halls of Sargon at Khorsabad.[4]
It seems, however, a strong and almost a fatal
objection to this theory, that no bases of pillars
have been found within the apartments, nor any
marks on the brick floors of such bases or of the

---

[1] *Monument de Ninive*, vol. v. p.
72.
[3] Fergusson, *Palaces of Nineveh*,
p. 276.
[2] *Monument, &c.,* vol. v. p. 69.
[4] *Palaces of Nineveh*, p. 262 ;
Handbook of Architecture, p. 171.

pressure of the pillars.   M. Botta states that he made
a careful search for bases, or for marks of pillars, on
the pavement of the north-east hall (No. VIII.) at
Khorsabad, but that he *entirely failed to discover any.*
This negative evidence is the more noticeable as stone
pillar-bases have been found in wide doorways,
where they would have been less necessary than in
the chambers, as pillars in doorways could have had
but little weight to sustain.

M. Botta and Mr. Fergusson, who both suppose
that in an Assyrian palace the entire edifice was
roofed in, and only the courts left open to the sky,
suggest two very different modes by which the
buildings may have been lighted.   M. Botta brings
light in from the roof by means of wooden *louvres,*
such as are still employed for the purpose in
Armenia and parts of India,' whereof he gives a

---

* *Monument de Ninive,* p. 70.
Compare Layard, *Nineveh and Babylon,* pp. 649, 650.   It must further
be noted, as throwing considerable
doubt on the whole spirit of Mr.
Fergusson's Assyrian restorations,
that their essence consists in giving
a thoroughly columnar character,
both internally and externally, to
Assyrian buildings, whereas one of
the most remarkable features in the
remains is the almost entire absence
of the column.   A glance at the restoration already given from Mr.
Fergusson (supra, p. 366), or at that,
by the same ingenious gentleman,
which forms the frontispiece to Mr.
Layard's *Nineveh and Babylon,* will
show the striking difference, and (as
it seems to me) the want of harmony
in his restorations between the basement story of a palace, which is all
that we can reconstruct with any
certainty, and the entire remainder
of the edifice.   Mr. Fergusson sup-

ports his view that the column was
really thus prominent in Assyrian
buildings by the analogy of Susa
and Persepolis; but the columnar
edifices at those places are on an entirely different plan from that of an
Assyrian palace.   Those buildings
had no solid walls at all (Loftus,
Chaldæa and Susiana, pp. 374, 375),
but lay entirely open to the air;
they were mere groves of pillars
supporting a flat roof—convenient
summer residences.   The evidence
of the remains seems to be that there
was a strong contrast between Assyrian and Persian architecture, the
latter depending almost wholly on
the column, and elaborating it as
much as possible; the former scarcely
allowing the column at all, and
leaving it almost in its primitive condition of a mere post.   (See below,
p. 388.)

' Fergusson, *Palaces of Nineveh,*
p. 260.

Armenian louvre (after Botta).

representation as above. Mr. Fergusson introduces light from the sides, by supposing that the
roof did not rest directly on the walls, but on rows
of wooden pillars placed along the edge of the walls
both internally towards the apartments and externally towards the outer air. The only ground for
this supposition, which is of a very startling character, seems to be the occurrence in a single bas-
relief, representing a city in Armenia, of what is
regarded as a similar arrangement. But it must be
noted that the lower portion of the building, represented overleaf, bears no resemblance at all to the
same part of an Assyrian palace, since in it perpendicular lines prevail, whereas, in the Assyrian
palaces, the lower lines were almost wholly horizontal; and that it is not even certain that the upper
portion, where the pillars occur, is an arrangement

for admitting light, since it may be merely an ornamentation.

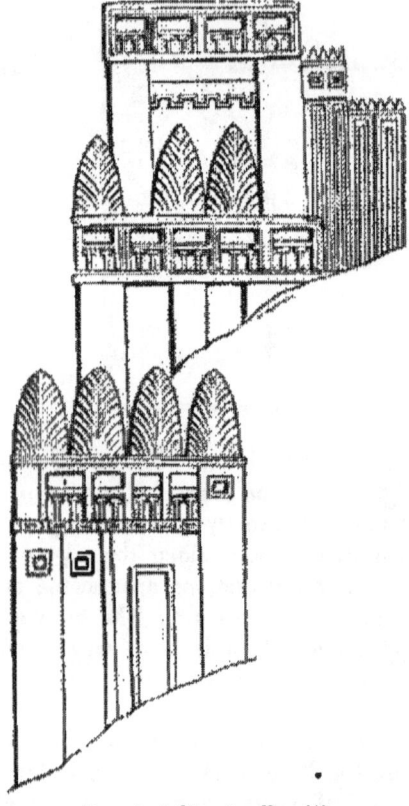

(Armenian buildings from Koyunjik).

Tho difficulties attaching to every theory of roofing and lighting which places the whole of an Assyrian palace under covert, has led some to suggest that the system actually adopted in the larger

apartments was that *hypæthral* one which is generally believed to have prevailed in the Greek
temples,[1] and which was undoubtedly followed in
the ordinary Roman house.   Mr. Layard was the
first to put forward the view that the larger halls,
at any rate, were uncovered, a projecting ledge, sufficiently wide to afford shelter and shade, being
carried round the four sides of the apartment, while
the centre remained open to the sky.[2]   The objections taken to this view are—first, that far too
much heat and light would thereby have been admitted into the palace; secondly, that in the rainy
season far too much rain would have come in for
comfort; and, thirdly, that the pavement of the
halls, being mere sun-dried brick, would, under such
circumstances, have been turned into mud.[3]   If these
objections are not removed, they would be, at any
rate, greatly lessened by supposing the roofing to
have extended to two-thirds or three-fourths of
the apartment, and the opening to have been
comparatively narrow.   We may also suppose that
on very bright and on very rainy days carpets or
other awnings were stretched across the opening,
which furnished a tolerable defence against the
weather.

On the whole, our choice seems to lie—so far as

[1] Mr. Fergusson disallows the hypæthral system even here (*True
Principles of Beauty*, p. 381); but
later writers do not seem converted
by his arguments. (See the article
on TEMPLUM in Smith's *Dictionary
of Greek and Roman Antiquities*,
p. 1105, 2nd edition; and compare
Mr. Falkener's *Dædalus*, Introduction, pp. 18-20.)

[2] *Nineveh and its Remains*, vol.
i. p. 260. Compare *Nineveh and
Babylon*, p. 647; and see also the
restoration of an Assyrian interior in
his *Monuments of Nineveh*, 1st series,
17. 2, from which the illustration overleaf is taken.

[3] Fergusson, *Palaces of Nineveh*,
p. 270.

Interior of an Assyrian Palace, restored (after Layard).

the great halls are concerned—between this theory
of the mode in which they were roofed and lighted,
and a supposition from which archæologists have
hitherto shrunk, namely, that they were actually
spanned from side to side by beams.   If we remember
that the Assyrians did not content themselves with
the woods produced in their own country, but habitually cut timber in the forests of distant regions, as
for instance of Amanus, Hermon, and Lebanon, which
they conveyed to Nineveh, we shall perhaps not
think it impossible that they may have been able to
accomplish the feat of roofing in this simple fashion
even chambers of thirteen or fourteen yards in width.
Mr. Layard observes that rooms of *almost* equal width
with the Assyrian halls are to this day covered in
with beams laid horizontally from side to side in
many parts of Mesopotamia, although the only timber
used is that furnished by the indigenous palms and
poplars.[1]   May not more have been accomplished in
this way by the Assyrian architects, who had at their
disposal the lofty firs and cedars of the above-men-
tioned regions?

If the halls were roofed in this way, they may have
been lighted by *louvres*;[2] or the upper portion of the
walls, which is now destroyed, may have been pierced
by windows, which are of frequent occurrence, and
seem generally to be somewhat high placed, in the
representations of buildings upon the sculptures.   (See
overleaf.)

It might have been expected that the difficulties
with respect to Assyrian roofing and lighting which

[1] *Nineveh and its Remains*, vol. ii.
pp. 259, 260.

[2] Such as that represented above,
p. 381.

have necessitated this long discussion, would have received illustration, or even solution from the forms of buildings which occur so frequently on the bas-reliefs.

Assyrian castle (Nimrud obelisk).

But this is not found to be the actual result. The forms are rarely Assyrian, since they occur commonly in the sculptures which represent the foreign campaigns of the kings; and they have the appearance of being to a great extent conventional, being nearly the same, whatever country is the object of attack. In the few cases where there is ground for regarding the building as native and not foreign, it is never palatial, but belongs either

No. I.
Assyrian altar (?), from a bas-relief, Khorsabad.

to sacred or to domestic architecture. Thus the monumental representations of Assyrian buildings which have come down to us, throw little or no light on the construction of their palaces. As, however, they have an interest of their own, and will serve to illustrate in some degree the domestic and sacred architecture of the people, some of the most remarkable of them will be here introduced.

The representation (No. I.) is from a slab at Khorsabad. It is placed on the summit of a hill, and is regarded by M. Botta as an altar. No. II. is from the same slab. It stands at the foot of the hill crowned

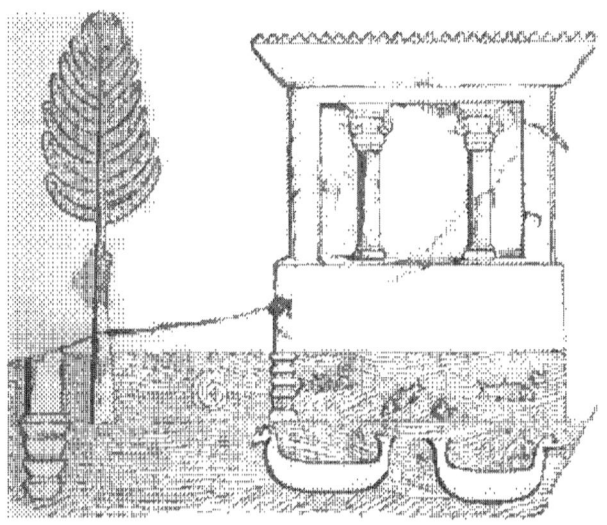

No. II. Assyrian temple (Khorsabad).

by No. I. It has been called a "fishing pavilion;"[4] but it is most probably a small temple, since it bears a good deal of resemblance to other representations which are undoubted temples, as (particularly) to No. III., which is from Lord Aberdeen's black stone, and is there accompanied by a priest, a sacred tree, and an ox for sacrifice.[5] The representation (No. IV.) is also thought to be a temple. It is of earlier date than any of the others, being taken from a slab belonging to the

No. III.
Assyrian temple,
from Lord Aberdeen's
black stone.

---

[4] Fergusson, *Handbook of Architecture*, p. 179.
[5] See the representation in Mr.

Fergusson's *Palaces of Nineveh Restored*, p. 298. This black stone is of the time of Esar-haddon.

North-west Palace at Nimrud, and is remarkable in
many ways. First, the want of symmetry is curious,
and unusual. Irregu-
lar as are the palaces
of the Assyrian kings,
there is for the most
part no want of regu-
larity in their sacred
buildings. The two
specimens above ad-
duced are proof of this;
and such remains of
actual temples as exist
are in accordance with
the sculptures in this particular. The right-hand
aisle in No. IV., having nothing correspondent to it
on the other side, is thus an anomaly in Assyrian
sacred architecture. The patterning of the pillars
with chevrons is also remarkable; and their capitals

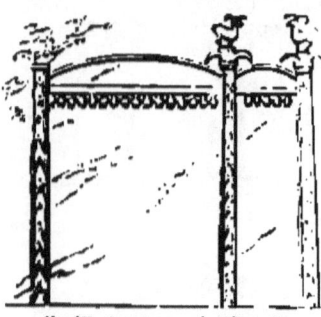

No. IV. Assyrian temple (Nimrud).

No. V. Assyrian temple (North Palace, Koyunjik).

are altogether unique.[*] No. V. is a temple of a more elaborate character. It is from the sculptures of *Asshur-bani-pal*, the son of Esar-haddon, and possesses several features of great interest. The body of the temple is a columnar structure, exhibiting at either corner a broad pilaster surmounted by a capital composed of two sets of volutes placed one over the other. Between the two pilasters are two pillars resting upon very extraordinary rounded bases, and crowned by capitals not unlike the Corinthian. We might have supposed the bases mere figments of the sculptor, but for an independent evidence of the actual employment by the Assyrians of rounded pillar-bases. Mr. Layard discovered at Koyunjik a set of "circular pedestals," whereof he gives the subjoined representation. They appeared to form part of a double line of similar objects, extending from the edge of the platform to an entrance of the palace, and probably (as Mr. Layard suggests) supported the wooden pillars of a co-

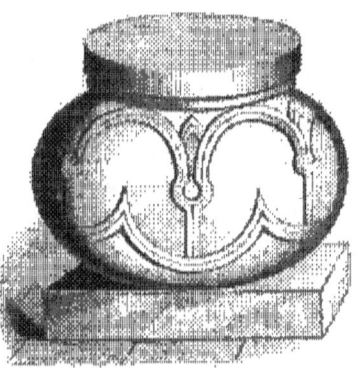

Circular pillar-base (Koyunjik).

vered way by which the palace was approached on this side. Above the pillars the temple (No. V.) exhibits a heavy cornice or entablature projecting

---

[*] On this print, see below, p. 416.

considerably, and finished at the top with a row
of gradines. At one side of this main building is
a small chapel or oratory, also finished with gradines, against the wall of which is a representation
of a king, standing in a species of frame arched
at the top. A road leads straight up to this royal
tablet, and in this road within a little distance
of the king stands an altar. The temple occupies
the top of a mound, which is covered with trees
of two different kinds, and watered by rivulets.
On the right is a " hanging garden," artificially elevated to the level of the temple by means of masonry
supported on an arcade, the arch here used being not
the round arch but a pointed one. No. VI. (opposite) is
unfortunately very imperfect, the entire upper portion
having been lost. Even, however, in its present mutilated state it represents by far the most magnificent
building that has yet been found upon the bas-reliefs.
The façade, as it now stands, exhibits four broad
pilasters and four pillars, alternating in pairs, excepting that, as in the smaller temples, pilasters occupy
both corners. In two cases, the base of the pilaster
is carved into the figure of a winged bull, closely resembling the bulls which commonly guarded the outer
gates of palaces. In the other two the base is plain
—a piece of negligence, probably, on the part of the
artist. The four pillars all exhibit a rounded base,
nearly though not quite similar to that of the pillars
in No. V.; and this rounded base in every case rests
upon the back of a walking lion. We might perhaps
have imagined that this was a mere fanciful or mythological device of the artist's, on a par with the representations at Bavian, where figures, supposed to be
Assyrian deities, stand upon the backs of animals

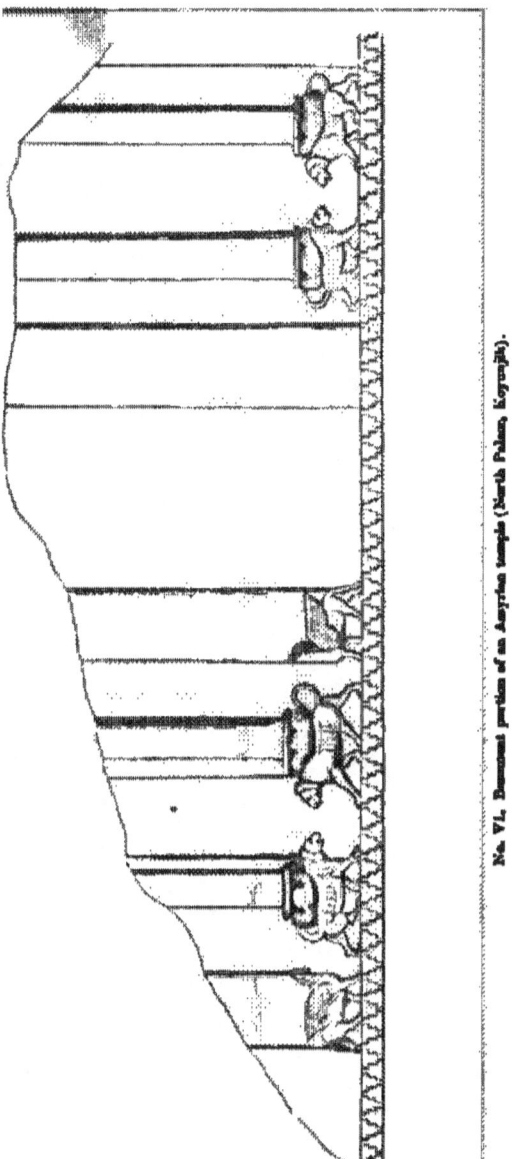

No. VI. Restored portion of an Assyrian temple (North Palace, Koyunjik).

resembling dogs.' But one of M. Place's architectural discoveries seems to make it possible, or even probable, that a real feature in Assyrian building is here represented. M. Place found the arch of the town gateway, which he exhumed at Khorsabad, to

Porch of the Cathedral, Trent.

spring from the backs of the two bulls which guarded it on either side.' Thus the lions at the base of the pillars may be real architectural forms as well as the winged bulls which support the pilasters. The lion was undoubtedly a sacred animal, emblematic of divine power, and specially assigned to Nergal, the Assyrian Mars, the god at once of war and of hunting. His introduction on the exteriors of buildings was common in Asia Minor ; but no other example occurs of his being made to support a pillar, excepting in the so-called Byzantine architecture of Northern Italy.

No. VIIa (opposite) introduces us to another kind

' See Layard's *Monuments of Nineveh*, 2nd series, PL 51 ; and compare *Nineveh and Babylon*, p. 208. A similar treatment of divine figures is common upon the Cylinders. (See Cullimore's *Cylinders*, Nos. 10, 20, 30, 55, 96, &c.)

' *Journal Asiatique*, Août, 1853, p. 150 ; Fergusson, *Handbook of Architecture*, vol. i. p. 173.

of Assyrian temple, or perhaps it should rather be said
to another feature of Assyrian temples—common to
them with Babylonian—the tower or *ziggurat*. This

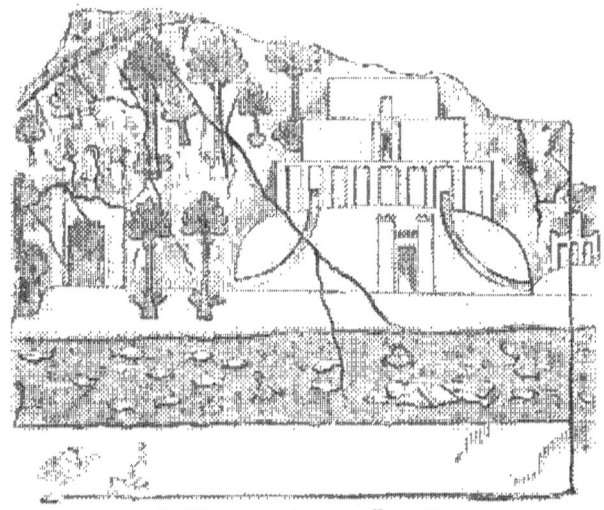

No. VII a. Tower of a temple (Koyunjik).

appears to have been always built in stages, which
probably varied in number—never, however, so far
as appears, exceeding seven.
The sculptured example before
us, which is from a bas-relief
found at Koyunjik, distinctly
exhibits four stages, of which
the topmost, owing to the
destruction of the upper portion of the tablet, is imperfect.
It is not unlikely that in this
instance there was above the
fourth a fifth stage, consisting of a shrine like that

No. VII b.
Tower of temple (restored).

which at Babylon crowned the great temple of Belus.[*]
The complete elevation would then have been nearly
as in No. VII*b*.

The following features are worthy of remark in
this temple. The basement story is panelled with
indented rectangular recesses, as was the case at
Nimrud,[1] and at the Birs;[2] the remainder are plain,
as are most of the stages in the Birs temple. Up
to the second of these squared recesses on either side
there runs what seems to be a road or path, which
sweeps away down the hill whereon the temple stands
in a bold curve, each path closely matching the
other. The whole building is perfectly symmetrical,
except that the panelling is not quite uniform in width
nor arranged quite regularly. On the second stage,
exactly in the middle, there is evidently a doorway,
and on either side of it a shallow buttress or pilaster.
In the centre of the third story, exactly over the
doorway of the second, is a squared niche. In front
of the temple, but not exactly opposite its centre, may
be seen the propylæa, consisting of a squared doorway placed under a battlemented wall, between two
towers also battlemented. It is curious that the
paths do not lead to the propylæa, but seem to curve
round the hill.

Remains of *ziggurats* similar to this have been discovered at Khorsabad, at Nimrud, and at Kileh-
Sherghat. The conical mound at Khorsabad explored by M. Place, was found to contain a tower in
seven stages;[3] that of Nimrud, which is so striking

---

[*] Herod. i. 181.
[1] See the illustration, infra, p. 390.
[2] *Journal of the Asiatic Society,*
vol. xvii. p. 13.

[4] Fergusson, *Handbook of Architecture,* p. 172. I have been unable
to obtain any detailed account of this
building.

an object from the plain,[4] and which was carefully
examined by Mr. Layard, presented no positive proof
of more than a single stage; but, from its conical
shape, and from the general analogy of such towers,
it is believed to have had several stages.   Mr. Layard
makes their number five, and crowns the fifth with a
circular tower terminating in a heavy cornice;[5] but

for this last there is no authority at all, and the actual
number of the stages is wholly uncertain.   The base
of this *ziggurat* was a square, 167 feet 6 inches each
way, composed of a solid mass of sun-dried brick, faced
at bottom to the height of twenty feet with a wall of
hewn stones, more than eight feet and a half in thickness.   The outer stones were bevelled at the edges,
and on the two most conspicuous sides the wall was

[4] Rupra, p. 253.
[5] *Nineveh and Babylon*, plan opp.

p. 128; *Monuments of Nineveh*, 2nd
series, frontispiece.

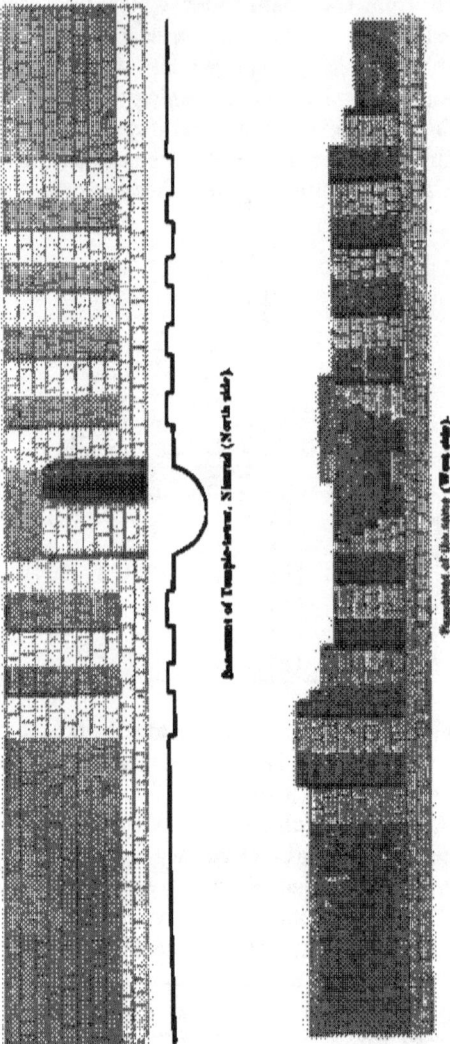

ornamented with a series of shallow recesses (see opposite page), arranged without very much attention to
regularity. The other two sides, one of which abutted
on and was concealed by the palace mound, while the
other faced towards the city, were perfectly plain. At
the top of the stone masonry was a row of gradines,
such as are often represented in the sculptures as
crowning an edifice.[6] Above the stone masonry the
tower was continued at nearly the same width, the
casing of stone being simply replaced by one of burnt
brick of inferior thickness. It is supposed that the
upper stages were constructed in the same way. As
the actual present height of the ruin is 140 feet, and
the upper stages have so entirely crumbled away, it
can scarcely be supposed that the original height fell
much short of 200 feet.[7]

The most curious of the discoveries made during
the examination of this building, was the existence
in its interior of a
species of chamber
or gallery, the true
object of which still
remains wholly un-
explained. This gal-
lery was 100 feet
long, 12 feet high,
and no more than
six feet broad. It
was arched or vault-
ed at top, both the

side walls and the vaulting being of sun-dried brick.
Its position was exactly half-way between the tower's

[6] See woodcut, No. V. on p. 388.
[7] Layard, *Nineveh and Babylon*, p. 129; comp. Diod. Sic. ii. 7.

northern and southern faces, and with these it ran
parallel, its height in the tower being such that its
floor was exactly on a level with the top of the
stone masonry, which again was level with the
terrace or platform, whereupon the Nimrud palaces
stood. There was no trace of any way by which
the gallery was intended to be entered; its walls
showed no signs of inscription, sculpture, or other
ornament; and absolutely nothing was found in it.
Mr. Layard, prepossessed with an opinion derived
from several confused notices in the classical writers,[*]
believed the tower to be a sepulchral monument,
and the gallery to be the tomb in which was
originally deposited " the embalmed body of the
king."[*]   To account for the complete disappearance,
not only of the body, but of all the ornaments and
vessels found commonly in the Mesopotamian tombs,
he suggested that the gallery had been rifled in times
long anterior to his visit; and he thought that he found
traces, both internally and externally, of the tunnel
by which it had been entered. But certainly, if this
long and narrow vault was intended to receive a
body, it is most extraordinarily shaped for the purpose. What other sepulchral chamber is there any-

---

[*] Xenophon and Ctesias both
noticed this remarkable edifice.
(*Anab.* iii. 4, § 9.) Xenophon calls
it a " pyramid," but shows that it
more resembled a tower by saying
that its height (200 ft.) was double
its width at the base, which he estimates at 100 ft. He gives no account
of the purpose for which it was intended. Ctesias, who enormously
exaggerates its size, making it 10
stadia wide and 9 stadia (more than
a mile) high, was the first to give it
a sepulchral character. He said that
it was built by Semiramis over the
body of her husband, Ninus. He
placed it, however, if we may believe
Diodorus (ii. 7), at Nineveh, and upon
the Euphrates! Next to these writers,
Amyntas, one of the historians of
Alexander, noticed the edifice. He
called it the tomb of Sardanapalus;
and, like Ctesias, placed it at Nineveh (ap. Athen. *Deipn.* xii. 4, § 11).
Ovid no doubt intended the same
building by his "busta Nini," which,
however, according to him, lay in
the vicinity of Babylon (*Metamorph.*
iv. 88).

[*] *Nineveh and Babylon*, p. 129.

where of so enormous a length? Without pretend-
ing to say what the real object of the gallery was,[1] we
may feel tolerably sure that it was not a tomb. The
building which contained it was a temple-tower, and
it is not likely that the religious feelings of the Assyrians would have allowed the application of a religious edifice to so utilitarian a purpose.

Besides the *ziggurat* or tower, which may commonly have been surmounted by a chapel or shrine,
an Assyrian temple had always a number of basement chambers, in one of which was the principal
shrine of the god. This was a square or slightly

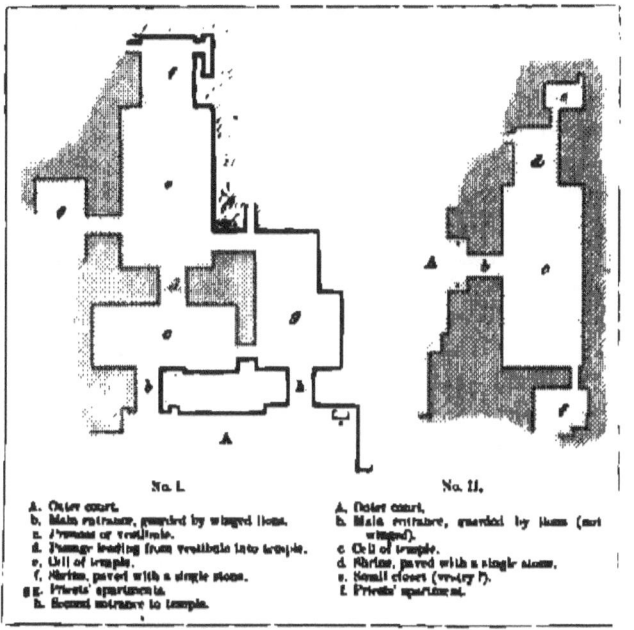

No. I.   No. II.

A. Outer court.
b. Main entrance, guarded by winged lions.
c. Passage or vestibule.
d. Passage leading from vestibule into temple.
e. Cell of temple.
f. Shrine, paved with a single stone.
g. Priests' apartments.
h. Second entrance to temple.

A. Outer court,
b. Main entrance, guarded by lions (not winged).
c. Cell of temple.
d. Shrine, paved with a single stone.
e. Small closet (vestry?).
f. Priests' apartment.

[1] It may perhaps have had a religious bearing; and similar galleries
may perhaps exist under all temple-
towers.

oblong recess at the end of an oblong apartment, raised somewhat above its level; it was paved (sometimes, if not always) with a single slab, the weight of which must occasionally have been as much as thirty tons.[3] One or two small closets opened out from the shrine, in which it is likely that the priests kept the sacerdotal garments and the sacrificial utensils.[1] Sometimes the cell of the temple, or chamber into which the shrine opened, was reached through another apartment, corresponding to the Greek *pronaos*. In such a case, care seems to have been taken so to arrange the outer and inner doorways of the vestibule, that persons passing by the outer doorway should not be able to catch a sight of the shrine.[4] Where there was no vestibule, the entrance into the cell or body of the temple seems to have been placed at the side, instead of at the end, probably with the same object.[5] Besides these main parts of a temple, a certain number of chambers are always found, which appear to have been priests' apartments.

The ornamentation of temples, to judge by the few specimens which remain, was very similar to that of palaces. The great gateways were guarded by colossal bulls (?) or lions (see opposite), accompanied by the usual sacred figures, and sometimes covered with inscriptions. The entrances and some portions of the chambers were ornamented with the customary sculptured slabs, representing here none but religious subjects. No great proportion of the

---

[3] The single slab which filled the recess (*f* in ground-plan, No. 1.) in the greater of the two Nimrud temples, was 21 ft. long, 16 ft. 7 in. broad, and 1 ft. 1 in. thick. It contained thus 375 cubic feet of stone, and must have weighed nearly, if not quite, 30 tons. (See Layard's *Nineveh and Babylon*, p. 352.)

[1] Ibid. p. 357.

[4] Note the position of the doorways, *b* and *d*, in ground-plan, No. 1.

[5] See ground-plan, No. II., entrance *h*.

Entrance to smaller temple, Nimrud.

interior, however, was covered in this way, the walls
being in general only plastered and then painted
with figures or patterns. Externally, enamelled
bricks were used as a decoration wherever sculptured slabs did not hide the crude brick.[4]

Much the same doubts and difficulties beset the
subjects of the roofing and lighting of the temples as
those which have been discussed already in connexion with the palaces. Though the span of the
temple-chambers is less than that of the great palace
halls, still it is considerable, sometimes exceeding thirty
feet.[5] No effort seems made to keep the temple-
chambers narrow, for their width is sometimes as
much as two-thirds of their length. Perhaps therefore they were hypæthral, like the temples of the
Greeks. All that seems to be certain is that what
roofing they had was of wood,[6] which at Nimrud was
cedar, brought probably from the mountains of Syria.

Of the domestic architecture of the Assyrians we
possess absolutely no specimen. Excavation has been
hitherto confined to the most elevated portions of
the mounds which mark the sites of cities, where it
was likely that remains of the greatest interest would
be found. Palaces, temples, and the great gates
which gave entrance to towns, have in this way seen
the light; but the humbler buildings, the ordinary
dwellings of the people, remain buried beneath the
soil, unexplored and even unsought for. In this
entire default of any actual specimen of an ordinary
Assyrian house, we naturally turn to the sculptured
representations which are so abundant and represent
so many different sorts of scenes. Even here, how-

[4] Layard, *Nineveh and Babylon*,
p. 359.
[5] The chamber marked * in ground-
plan, No. 1. (p. 350), was 47 ft. long
by 31 ft. wide. (Ibid. p. 352.)
[6] Layard, ibid. p. 357.

ever, we obtain but little light. The bulk of the
slabs exhibit the wars of the kings in foreign countries, and thus place before us foreign rather than
Assyrian architecture. The processional slabs, which
are another large class, contain rarely any building
at all, and, where they furnish one, exhibit to us a
temple rather than a house. The hunting scenes,
representing wilds far from the dwellings of man,
afford us, as might be expected, no help. Assyrian
buildings, other than temples, are thus most rarely
placed before us. In one case indeed we have an
Assyrian city, which a foreign enemy is passing;
but the only edifices represented are the walls and
towers of the exterior and the temple (No. VI. p. 391)
whose columns rest upon lions. In one other we
seem to have an unfortified Assyrian village;[1] and

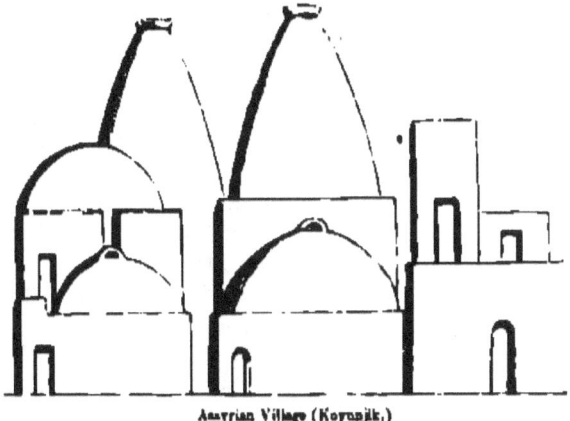

Assyrian Village (Koyunjik.)

from this single specimen we are forced to form our
ideas of the ordinary character of Assyrian houses.

[1] Layard, Monuments of Nineveh, Pl. 17.

It is observable here, in the first place, that the houses have no windows, and are, therefore, probably lighted from the roof; next, that the roofs are very curious, since, although flat in some instances, they consist more often either of hemispherical domes, such as are still so common in the East, or of steep and high cones, such as are but seldom seen anywhere. Mr. Layard finds a parallel for these last in certain villages of Northern Syria, where all the houses have conical roofs, built of mud, which present a very singular appearance.[1] Both

Village near Aleppo.

the domes and the cones of the Assyrian example have evidently an opening at the top, which may have admitted as much light into the houses as was thought necessary. The doors are of two kinds, square at the top, and arched; they are placed commonly towards the sides of the houses. The houses themselves seem to stand separate though in close juxtaposition.

The only other buildings of the Assyrians which appear to require some notice are the fortified enceintes of their towns. The simplest of these consisted of a single battlemented wall, carried in lines nearly

[1] Layard, *Nineveh and Babylon,* p. 112. The representation is of a village in the neighbourhood of Aleppo.

or quite straight along the four sides of the place,
pierced with gates and guarded at the angles, at the
gates, and at intervals along the curtain, with projecting towers, raised not very much higher than
the walls, and (apparently) square in shape.   In the

Assyrian battlemented wall.

sculptures we sometimes find the battlemented wall
repeated twice or thrice in lines placed one above the
other, the intention being to represent the defence of
a city by two or three walls, such as we have seen
existed on one side of Nineveh.[1]

The walls were often, if not always, guarded by
moats.   Internally they were, in every case, constructed of crude brick; while externally it was
common to face them with hewn stone, either from
top to bottom, or at any rate to a certain height.
At Khorsabad the stone revêtement of one portion
at least of the wall was complete; at Nimrud (Calah)
and at Nineveh itself it was partial, being carried at
the former of those places only to the height of twenty
feet.[2]   The masonry at Khorsabad was of three kinds.
That of the palace mound, which formed a portion of
the outer defence, was composed entirely of blocks
of stone, square-hewn and of great size, the length of
the blocks varying from two to three yards, while
the width was one yard and the height from five to
six feet.   The masonry was laid somewhat curiously.

The blocks (A A) were placed alternately long-wise
and end-wise against the crude brick (B), so as not
merely to lie against it, but to penetrate it with
their ends in many places.[1] Care was also taken
to make the angles especially strong, as will be
seen by the accompanying section.

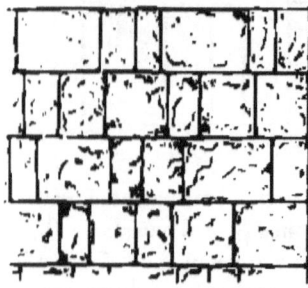
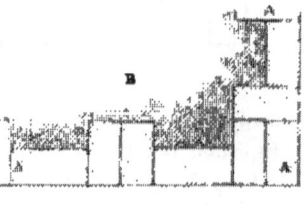

Masonry of platform wall, Khorsabad.   Section of same.

The rest of the defences at Khorsabad were of an
inferior character.   The wall of the town had a width
of about forty-five feet, and its basement, to the
height of three feet, was constructed of stone; but
the blocks were neither so large, nor were they hewn
with the same care as those of the palace platform.
The angles, indeed, were of squared stone; but even
there the blocks measured no more than three feet

[1] M. Botta says: "Cette muraille
était construite en blocs de pierre
calcaire très-dure, venant des mon-
tagnes voisines; ces blocs ont la
forme de parallélipipèdes rectangles
d'une coupe régulière, et sont dis-
posés par assises, de manière à pré-
senter alternativement au dehors leur
face la plus large et une de leurs extrémités ; c'est-à-dire que tous étant
posés de champ, l'un tapisse le massif, puis un et quelquefois deux
autres continuent l'assise par leurs

extrémités, la même alternative se
répétant dans toute la longueur de
celle-ci.   Il en résulte qu'étant tous
de même longueur, ceux qui pré-
sentent une extrémité au dehors dé-
passent à l'intérieur la ligne des
autres, et s'encastrent dans le massif
de briques.   Cette disposition avait
pour but de lier solidement l'amas
terreux intérieur au revêtement ex-
térieur." (Monument de Ninive, vol.
v. p. 31.)

in length and a foot in height: the rest of the masonry consisted of small polygonal stones, merely smoothed on their outer face, and roughly fitting together in a manner recalling the Cyclopian walls of Greece and Italy.[1] They were not united by any cement. Above the stone basement was a massive structure of crude brick, without any facing either of burnt brick or of stone.

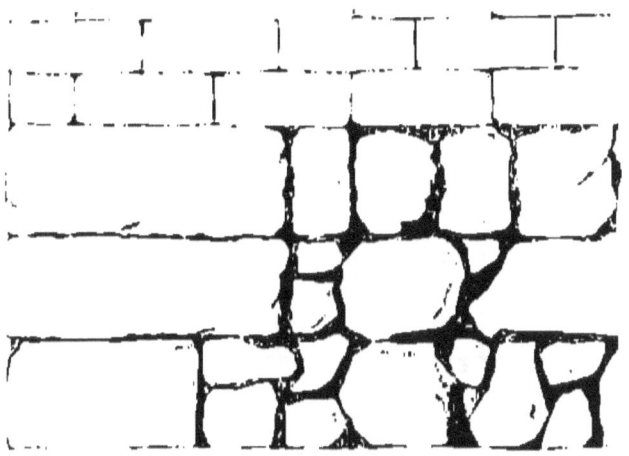

Masonry of town-wall (Khorsabad).

The third kind of masonry at Khorsabad was found outside the main wall, and may have formed either part of the lining of the moat or a portion of a tower, which may have projected in advance of the wall at this point. It was entirely of stone.

[1] M. Botta makes this comparison (*Monument de Ninive*, l. s. c.). His representation, however, differs in two main points from the ordinary Cyclopian style: 1. the horizontal course seems to be maintained throughout; and 2. the stones do not fit into each other at all closely or with any exactness.

The lowest course was formed of small and very irregular polygonal blocks roughly fitted together; above this came two courses of carefully squared stones more than a foot long, but less than six inches in width, which were placed end-wise, one over the other, care being taken that the joints of the upper tier should never coincide exactly with those of the lower. Above these was a third course of hewn stones, somewhat smaller than the others, which were laid in the ordinary manner. Here the construction, as discovered, terminated; but it was evident, from the *débris* of hewn stones at the foot of the wall, that originally the courses had been continued to a much greater height.[*]

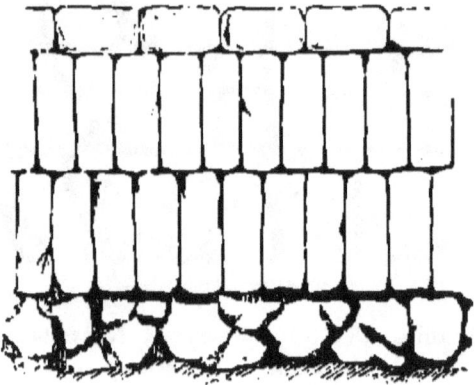

Masonry of tower or moat (Khorsabad).

In this description of the buildings raised by the Assyrians it has been noticed more than once that they were not ignorant of the use of the arch.[†] The old notion that the round arch was a discovery of

---

[*] Botta, *Monument de Ninive*, vol. v. p. 31.   [†] Supra, pp. 378, 380, &c.

the Roman, and the pointed of the Gothic architects, has gradually faded away with our ever-
increasing knowledge of the actual state of the
ancient world;" and antiquarians were not, perhaps,
very much surprised to learn, by the discoveries of
Mr. Layard, that the Assyrians knew and used both

kinds of arch in
their constructions.
Some interest, how-
ever, will probably
be felt to attach to
the two questions,
how they formed
their arches, and to
what uses they ap-
plied them.

All the Assyrian
arches hitherto dis-
covered are of brick.
The round arches
are both of the
crude and of the
kiln-dried material,
and are formed, in
each case, of bricks
made expressly for
vaulting, slightly
convex at top and slightly concave at bottom, with
one broader and one narrower end. The arches are

Arched Drain (North-West Palace, Nimrud).

* The earliest arches seem to be those of Egypt, which mount at least to the 15th century before our era. (Wilkinson, *Ancient Egyptians*, 1st series, iii. p. 317; Falkener, *Dædalus*, App. p. 288.) The Babylo- nian arches mentioned above (p. 104) cannot be much later than B.C. 1700. The earliest known Assyrian arches would belong to about the 9th cen- tury B.C.

of the simplest kind, being exactly semicircular, and
rising from plain perpendicular jambs. The greatest
width which any such arch has been hitherto found
to span is about fifteen feet.[*]

The only pointed arch actually discovered is of
burnt brick. The bricks are of the ordinary shape,

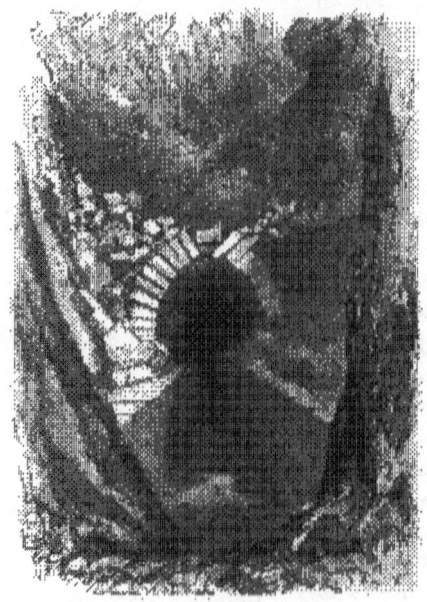

Arched drain (South-East Palace, Nimrud).

and not intended for vaulting. They are laid side
by side up to a certain point, being bent into a
slight arch by the interposition between them of
thin wedges of mortar. The two sides of the arch
having been in this way carried up to a point where

---

[*] Fergusson, *Handbook of Architecture*, vol. i. p. 173.

the lower extremities of the two innermost bricks
nearly touched, while a considerable space remained
between their upper extremities, instead of a key-
stone or key-brick fitting the aperture, ordinary
bricks were placed in it longitudinally, and so the
space was filled in.[1]

Another mode of constructing a pointed arch seems
to be intended in a bas-relief, whereof a representation
has been already given.[2]
The masonry of the arcade
in No. V. (p. 388) runs (it
will be seen) in horizontal
lines up to the very edge of
the arch, thus suggesting
a construction common in
many of the early Greek
arches, where the stones are
so cut away that an arched
opening is formed, though
the real constructive principle of the arch has no
place in such specimens.[3]

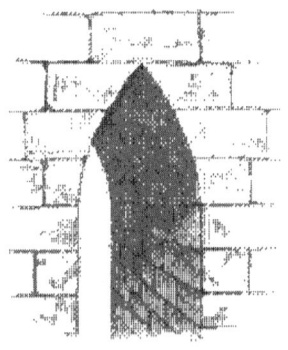

False arch (Greek.)

With regard to the uses whereto the Assyrians
applied the arch, it would certainly seem, from the
evidence which we possess, that they neither employed it as a great decorative feature, nor yet as
a main principle of construction. So far as appears,
their chief use of it was for doorways and gateways. Not only are the town gates of Khorsabad
found to have been arched over, but in the repre-

[1] Layard, Nineveh and Babylon,
p. 163.
[2] Supra, p. 388.
[3] See Smith's Dictionary of Greek
and Roman Antiquities, p. 125, 2nd
edition; and Mr. Falkener's Dædalus,
App. p. 288.

sentations of edifices, whether native or foreign, upon the bas-reliefs, the arch for doors is commoner than the square top. It is most probable that the great palace gateways were thus covered in, while it is certain that some of the interior doorways in palaces had rounded tops.[4] Besides this use of the arch for doors and gates, the Assyrians are known to have employed it for drains, aqueducts, and narrow chambers or galleries.

It has been suggested that the Assyrians applied the two kinds of arches to different purposes, " thereby showing more science and discrimination than we do in our architectural works;" that " they used the pointed arch for underground work, where they feared great superincumbent pressure on the apex, and the round arch above ground, where that was not to be dreaded."[5] But this ingenious theory is scarcely borne out by the facts. The round arch is employed under ground in two instances at Nimrud,[6] besides occurring in the basement story of the great tower,[7] where the superincumbent weight must have been enormous. And the pointed arch is used above ground for the aqueduct and hanging garden in the bas-relief, where the pressure, though considerable, would not have been very extraordinary. It would seem, therefore, to be doubtful whether the Assyrians were really guided by any constructive principle in their preference of one form of the arch over the other.

In describing generally the construction of the palaces and other chief buildings of the Assyrians,

4 Infra, p. 417.
5 Fergusson, *Handbook of Architecture,* p. 252.
6 Layard, *Nineveh and Babylon,* pp. 162 and 165.
7 Supra, p. 397.

it has been necessary occasionally to refer to their
ornamentation ; but the subject is far from exhausted,
and will now claim, for a short space, our special
attention.   Beyond a doubt the chief adornment,
both of palaces and temples, consisted of the colossal
bulls and lions guarding the great gateways, together with the sculptured slabs wherewith the
walls, both internal and external, were ordinarily
covered to the height of twelve or sometimes even
of fifteen feet.   These slabs and carved figures will
necessarily be considered in connexion with Assyrian
sculpture, of which they form the most important
part.   It will, therefore, only be noted at present
that the extent of wall covered with the slabs was,
in the Khorsabad palace, at least 4000 feet,* or
nearly four-fifths of a mile, while in each of the
Koyunjik palaces the sculptures extended to considerably more than that distance.

The ornamentation of the walls above the slabs,
both internally and externally, was by means of

Assyrian patterns (Nimrud).

bricks painted on the exposed side and covered
with an enamel.   The colours are for the most
part somewhat pale, but occasionally they possess

* Fergusson, *Palaces of Nineveh,* p. 265.

some brilliancy. Predominant among the tints are
a pale blue, an olive green, and a dull yellow. White
is also largely used; brown and black are not infrequent; red is comparatively rare.[*] The subjects
represented are either such scenes as occur upon

Assyrian Patterns (Nimrud).

---

[*] See Botta's *Monument de Ninive*, vol. ii. Plates 155 and 156; Layard's *Monuments of Nineveh*, 1st series, Plates 84, 86, and 87; 2nd series, Plates 53, 54, and 55.

the sculptured slabs, or else mere patterns, scrolls,
honeysuckles, chevrons, gradines, guilloches, &c.
In the scenes some attempt seems to be made at
representing objects in their natural colours. The
size of the figures is small; and it is difficult to
imagine that any great effect could have been
produced on the beholder by such minute drawings
placed at such a height from the ground. Probably
the most effective ornamentation of this kind was by
means of patterns, which are often graceful and
striking (see opposite page).

It has been observed that, so far as the evidence
at present goes, the use of the column in Assyrian
architecture would seem to have been very rare
indeed.[1] In palaces we have no grounds for thinking
that they were employed at all excepting in certain
of the interior doorways, which, being of unusual
breadth, seem to have been divided into three
distinct portals by means of two pillars placed towards
the sides of the opening.[2] The bases of these pillars
were of stone, and have been found *in situ*; their
shafts and capitals had disappeared, and can only be
supplied by conjecture. In the temples, as we have
seen, the use of the column was more frequent. Its
dimensions greatly varied. Ordinarily it was too
short and thick for beauty,[3] while occasionally it had
the opposite defect, being too tall and slender.[4] Its
base was sometimes quite plain, sometimes diversified

---

[1] Supra, p. 380, note [5]. Mr. Fox
Talbot supposes that he has found a
mention of columns in a description
given of one of his palaces by Sennacherib. (*Assyrian Texts Translated*,
p. 8.) But the technical terms in the
Assyrian architectural descriptions
are of such doubtful meaning that no
theory can at present be rested upon
them.

[2] Layard, *Nineveh and Babylon*,
p. 103; *Nineveh and its Remains*,
vol. i. Plan II. opp. p. 34, and p.
376. Columns may also have been
used to support a covered passage
across a court. (Supra, p. 389.)

[3] See above, p. 388, woodcut
No. V.

[4] Ibid., woodcut No. IV.

by a few mouldings, sometimes curiously and rather

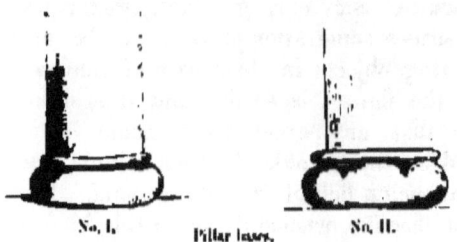

No. I.   Pillar bases.   No. II.

clumsily rounded (as in No. II. above). The shaft
was occasionally patterned.[*] The capital, in one

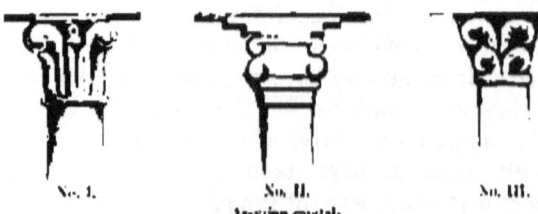

No. I.   No. II.   No. III.
Assyrian capitals.

No. IV.
Ibex capital.

instance (No. I.), approaches to the
Corinthian; in another (No. II.) it
reminds us of the Ionic; but the
volutes are double, and the upper
ones are surmounted by an awkward-
looking abacus. A third (No. III.)
is very peculiar, and to some extent
explains the origin of the second. It
consists of two pairs of ibex horns,
placed one over the other. With this
may be compared another (No. IV.),
the most remarkable of all, where we
have first a single pair of ibex horns,

---

[*] See above, p. 388, No. IV.

and then, at the summit, a complete figure of an
ibex, very graphically portrayed.

The beauty of Assyrian patterning has been
already noticed. Patterned work is found not only
on the enamelled bricks, but on stone pavement
slabs, and around arched doorways leading from one
chamber to another, where the patterns are carved
with great care and delicacy upon the alabaster.
The accompanying specimen of a doorway, which is
taken from an unpublished drawing by Mr. Boutcher,

Ornamental doorway (North Palace, Koyunjik).

is very rich and elegant, though it exhibits none
but the very commonest of the Assyrian patterns.
A carving of a more elaborate type, and one pre-

senting even greater delicacy of workmanship, has been given in an earlier portion of this chapter [*] as an example of a patterned pavement slab. Slabs of this kind have been found in many of the palaces, and well deserve the attention of modern designers.

When the architecture of the Assyrians is compared with that of other nations possessing about the same degree of civilisation, the impression that it leaves is perhaps somewhat disappointing. Vast labour and skill, exquisite finish, the most extraordinary elaboration, were bestowed on edifices so essentially fragile and perishable that no care could have preserved them for many centuries. Sun-dried brick, a material but little superior to the natural clay of which it was composed, constituted everywhere the actual fabric, which was then covered thinly and just screened from view by a facing, seldom more than a few inches in depth, of a more enduring and handsomer substance. The tendency of the platform mounds, as soon as formed, must have been to settle down, to bulge at the sides and become uneven at the top, to burst their stone or brick facings and precipitate them into the ditch below, at the same time disarranging and breaking up the brick pavements which covered their surface. The weight of the buildings raised upon the mounds must have tended to hasten these catastrophes, while the unsteadiness of their foundations and the character of their composition must have soon had the effect of throwing the buildings themselves into disorder, of loosening the slabs from the

---

[*] Page 350.

walls, causing the enamelled bricks to start from
their places, the colossal bulls and lions to lean over,
and the roofs to become shattered and fall in.   The
fact that the earlier palaces were to a great extent
dismantled by the later kings is perhaps to be attributed, not so much to a barbarous resolve that they
would destroy the memorials of a former and a
hostile dynasty, as to the circumstance that the more
ancient buildings had fallen into decay and ceased
to be habitable.   The rapid succession of palaces,
the fact that, at any rate from Sargon downwards,
each monarch raises a residence, or residences, for
himself, is yet more indicative of the rapid dete-
rioration and dilapidation (so to speak) of the great
edifices.   Probably a palace began to show unmistakable symptoms of decay and to become an
unpleasant residence at the end of some twenty-five
or thirty years from the date of its completion;
effective repairs were, by the very nature of the
case, almost impossible; and it was at once easier and
more to the credit of the monarch that he should
raise a fresh platform and build himself a fresh
dwelling than that he should devote his efforts to
keeping in a comfortable condition the crumbling
habitation of his predecessor.

It is surprising that, under these circumstances,
a new style of architecture did not arise.   The
Assyrians were not, like the Babylonians, compelled
by the nature of the country in which they lived
to use brick as their chief building material.   M.
Botta expresses his astonishment at the preference
of brick to stone exhibited by the builders of Khorsabad, when the neighbourhood abounds in rocky
hills capable of furnishing an inexhaustible supply

of the better material.[1] The limestone range of the
Jebel Maklub is but a few miles distant, and
many outlying rocky elevations might have been
worked with still greater facility. Even at Nineveh
itself, and at Calah or Nimrud, though the hills
were further removed, stone was, in reality, plentiful. The cliffs a little above Koyunjik are composed of a "hard sandstone,"[2] and a part of the
moat of the town is carried through "compact
silicious conglomerate."[3] The town is, in fact,
situated on "a spur of rock" thrown off from the
Jebel Maklub,[4] which terminates at the edge of
the ravine whereby Nineveh was protected on the
south. Calah, too, was built on a number of "rocky
undulations,"[5] and its western wall skirts the edge
of "conglomerate" cliffs, which have been scarped
by the hand of man.[6] A very tolerable stone was
thus procurable on the actual sites of these ancient
cities ; and if a better material had been wanted, it
might have been obtained in any quantity, and of
whatever quality was desired, from the Zagros range
and its outlying rocky barriers. Transport could
scarcely have caused much difficulty, as the blocks

---

[1] *Monument de Ninive*, vol. v. p.
64 : " La manière de bâtir les édi-
fices est d'autant plus singulière,
qu'à Ninive (Khorsabad) au moins
la pierre était très-abondante et de
bonne qualité, et que rien ne forçait
les habitans à se servir de briques."
And again, p. 65 : " L'abondance des
roches, soit calcaires, soit gypseuses,
pouvait leur fournir d'excellents ma-
tériaux aussi solides que faciles à
travailler."

[2] *Journal of Asiatic Society*, vol.
xv. p. 317.

[3] Ibid. p. 311. See above, p. 324.

[4] Ibid. pp. 317 and 323.

[5] Ibid. p. 347.

[6] Ibid. p. 346. It is very remarkable that Mr. Layard should so entirely have ignored these features of
the geology of Assyria in his account of the Assyrian architecture.
(*Nineveh and its Remains*, vol. ii.
ch. ii. pp. 250-275.) It would be
concluded from his account by a
reader not otherwise informed on the
subject, that no stone but the delicate
alabaster used for the bas-reliefs was
accessible to the Assyrian architects.

might have been brought from the quarries where they were hewn to the sites selected for the cities by water-carriage,—a mode of transport well known to the Assyrians, as is made evident to us by the bas-reliefs.

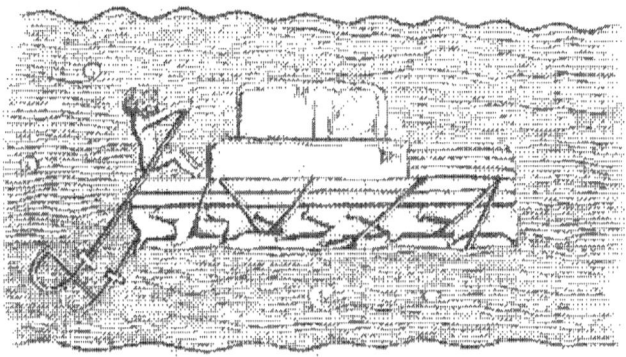

Water-transport of stone for building (Koyunjik).

If the best possible building material was thus plentiful in Assyria, and its conveyance thus easy to manage, to what are we to ascribe the decided preference shown for so inferior a substance as brick?   No considerable difficulty can have been experienced in quarrying the stone of the country, which is seldom very hard, and which was, in fact, cut by the Assyrians, whenever they had any sufficient motive for removing or making use of it.[1] One answer only can be reasonably given to the

---

[1] At Nimrud the western cliff is "artificially scarped" to make it a secure defence. (*Journal of As. Soc.* vol. xv. p. 346.) At Neboub the rock is tunnelled for some distance, and for a longer space "chiselled through a hard sandstone and surface-conglomerate to a depth perhaps of forty feet." (Ibid. p. 311.) At Nineveh the moat is carried "for upwards of two miles, with a breadth of 200 feet, through a peculiarly hard and compact silicious conglomerate." (Ibid. p. 320.) A very hard basalt was used in the palace temple at Khorsabad. (Supra, p. 371.)

question. The Assyrians had learnt a certain style
of architecture in the alluvial Babylonia, and having
brought it with them into a country far less fitted
for it, maintained it from habit, notwithstanding
its unsuitableness.[1] In some few respects, indeed,
they made a slight change. The abundance of stone
in the country induced them to substitute it in several
places where in Babylonia it was necessary to use
burnt brick, as in the facings of platforms and of
temples, in dams across streams, in pavements sometimes, and universally in the ornamentation of the
lower portions of palace and temple walls. But
otherwise they remained faithful to their architectural traditions, and raised in the comparatively
hilly Assyria the exact type of building which
nature and necessity had led them to invent and
use in the flat and stoneless alluvium where they
had had their primitive abode. As platforms were
required both for security and for comfort in the
lower region, they retained them, instead of choosing
natural elevations, in the upper one. As clay was
the only possible material in one place, clay was still
employed, notwithstanding the abundance of stone,
in the other. Being devoid of any great inventive
genius, the Assyrians found it easier to maintain and
slightly modify a system with which they had been
familiar in their original country than to devise a new
one more adapted to the land of their adoption.

Next to the architecture of the Assyrians, their
mimetic art seems to deserve attention. Though the
representations in the works of Layard and Botta,

---

[1] M. Botta winds up his remarks
on the strangeness of the Assyrian
architecture occurring where it does,
by suggesting "que les monuments
de Ninive sont postérieurs à ceux de
Babylone, et que c'est dans ce dernier
pays qu'il faut chercher l'origine de
l'art Assyrien." (p. 66.)

combined with the presence of so many specimens in
the great National Museums of London and Paris, have
produced a general familiarity with the subject, still,
as a connected view of it in its several stages and
branches is up to the present time a desideratum in
our literature,[1] it may not be superfluous here to
attempt a brief account of the different classes into
which their productions in this kind of art fall, and
the different eras and styles under which they naturally range themselves.

Assyrian mimetic art consists of statues, bas-reliefs,
metal-castings, carvings in ivory, statuettes in clay,
enamellings on brick, and intaglios on stones and gems.

Assyrian statues are comparatively rare, and, when
they occur, are among the
least satisfactory of this
people's productions. They
are coarse, clumsy, purely
formal in their design, and
generally characterised by
an undue flatness, or want
of breadth in the side view,
as if they were only in-
tended to be seen directly
in front. Sometimes, how-
ever, this defect is not apparent. A sitting statue
in black basalt, of the size
of life, representing an
early king, which Mr. Layard discovered at Kileh-

Assyrian statue (Kileh-Sherghat).

---

[1] Mr. Fergusson, who has treated
of the architecture of the Assyrians
with so much knowledge and ingenuity, says but little on the subject of their sculpture. Mr. Layard's
review of the subject in his first work
(Book II. ch. ii.) is the best, which at
present exists; but it is of necessity
incomplete, owing to the early period
in the history of Assyrian discovery
at which it was composed. Its views
are also occasionally open to dispute.

Sherghat,[1] and which is now in the British Museum, may be instanced as quite free from this disproportion. It is very observable, however, in another of

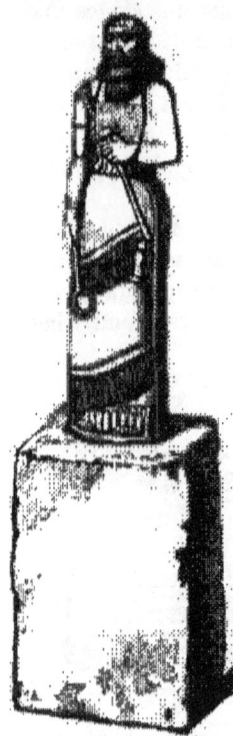

Statue of Sardanapalus I.
(from Nimrud).

the royal statues recently recovered,[2] as it is also in the monolith bulls and lions universally. Otherwise, the proportions of the figures are commonly correct. They bear a resemblance to the archaic Greek, especially to that form of it which we find in the sculptures from Branchidæ. They have just the same rudeness, heaviness, and stiff formality. It is difficult to judge of their execution, as they have mostly suffered great injury from the hand of man, or from the weather; but the royal statue here represented, which is in better preservation than any other Assyrian work "in the round" that has come down to us, exhibits a rather high finish. It is smaller than life, being about three and a half feet high: the features are majestic, and well marked; the hair and beard are elaborately curled; the arms and hands are well shaped, and finished with care. The dress is fringed elaborately, and descends to the ground, concealing all the lower

[1] See Layard, Nineveh and its Remains, vol. ii. pp. 51, 52.
[2] Layard, Nineveh and Babylon, p. 361. This statue is also in the British Museum.

part of the figure. The only statues recovered besides these are two of the god Nebo, brought from Nimrud,[4] a mutilated one of Ishtar, or Astarte, found at Koyunjik, and a tolerably perfect one of Sargon, which was discovered at Idalium, in the island of Cyprus.[5]

The clay statuettes of the Assyrians possess even less artistic merit than their statues. They are chiefly images of gods or genii, and have most commonly something grotesque in their appearance. Among the most usual are figures which represent either Mylitta (Beltis), or Ishtar.[6] They are made in a fine terra cotta, which has turned of a pale red in baking, and are coloured with a cretaceous coating, so as greatly to resemble Greek pottery.[7] Another type is that of an old man, bearded, and with hands

Clay statuettes of the god Nebo (?).

clasped, which we may perhaps identify with Nebo, the Assyrian Mercury, since his statues in the British

---

[4] One of these is figured above, p. 170. The actual statues are both in the British Museum.

[5] This statue is in the Berlin Museum.

[6] See above, p. 176.

[7] Birch, *Ancient Pottery*, vol. I. p. 124.

Museum have a somewhat similar character. Other forms are the fish-god Nin, or Nin-ip ; and the deities, not yet identified, which were found by M. Botta under the pavement-bricks at Khorsabad.

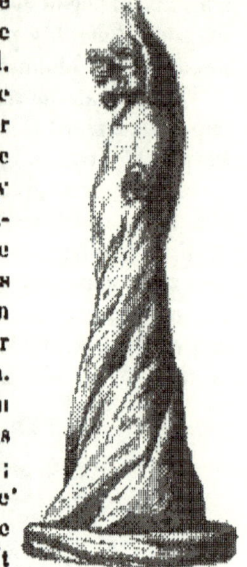

These specimens have the formal character of the statues, and are even more rudely shaped. Other examples which carry the grotesque to an excess appear to have been designed with greater spirit and freedom. Animal and human forms are sometimes intermixed in them ; and while it cannot be denied that they are rude and coarse, it must be allowed on the other hand, that

Clay statuette of the Fish-god.

Clay statuette from Khorsabad (after Botta).

they possess plenty of vigour. M. Botta has engraved several specimens,[1] including two which have the hind legs and tail of a bull, with a human neck and arms, the head bearing the usual horned cap.

Small figures of animals in terra cotta have also been found. They consist chiefly of dogs and ducks. A representation of each has been given in the chapter on the productions of Assyria.[2] The dogs discovered are made of a coarse clay, and seem to have been

----

[1] *Monument de Ninive*, vol. ii. plates 152 to 155.
[2] *Supra*, p. 293 (No. 1.) and p. 294.

originally painted.[*] They are not wanting in spirit; but it detracts from their merit that the limbs are merely in relief, the whole space below the belly of the animal being filled up with a mass of clay for the sake of greater strength. The ducks are of a fine yellow material, and represent the bird asleep, with its head lying along its back.

Of all the Assyrian works of art which have come down to us by far the most important are the bas-reliefs. It is here especially, if not solely, that we can trace progress in style; and it is here alone that we see the real artistic genius of the people. What sculpture in its full form, or in the slightly modified form of very high relief, was to the Greeks, what painting has been to modern European nations since the time of Cimabue, that low relief was to the Assyrians—the practical mode in which artistic power found vent among them. They used it for almost every purpose to which mimetic art is applicable; to express their religious feelings and ideas, to glorify their kings, to hand down to posterity the nation's history and its deeds of prowess, to depict home scenes and domestic occupations, to represent landscape and architecture, to imitate animal and vegetable forms, even to illustrate the mechanical methods which they employed in the construction of those vast architectural works, of which the reliefs were the principal ornamentation. It is not too much to say that we know the Assyrians, not merely artistically, but historically and ethnologically, *chiefly* through their bas-reliefs, which seem to represent to us almost the entire life of the people.

---

[*] According to Mr. Birch, the colours used were "blue, red, and black," and they were "laid on in a paste" (*Ancient Pottery*, vol. I. p. 125). At present the traces of colour on the dogs are very faint.

The reliefs may be divided under five principal heads :—1. War scenes, including battles, sieges, devastations of an enemy's country, naval expeditions, and triumphant returns from foreign war, with the trophies and fruits of victory ; 2. Religious scenes, either mythical or real; 3. Processions, generally of tribute-bearers, bringing the produce of their several countries to the Great King ; 4. Hunting and sporting scenes, including the chase of savage animals, and of animals sought for food, the spreading of nets, the shooting of birds, and the like ; and 5. Scenes of ordinary life, as those representing the transport and erection of colossal bulls, landscapes, temples, interiors, gardens, &c.

The earliest art is that of the most ancient palaces at Nimrud. It belongs to the latter part of the tenth century before our era ; the time of Asa in Judæa, of Omri and Ahab in Samaria, and of the Sheshonks in Egypt. It is characterised by much spirit and variety in the design, by strength and firmness, combined with a good deal of heaviness, in the execution, by an entire contempt for perspective, and by the rigid preservation in almost every case, both human and animal, of the exact profile both of figure and face.[1] Of the illustrations already given in the present volume a considerable number belong to this period. The heads on page 297, and the figures on page 303, represent the ordinary appearance of the men,[2] while animal forms of the time will be found in the lion on page 278, the ibex on page 279, the gazelle on page 282, the horse on

<hr/>

[1] The only exceptions are believed to be a few instances of lions' heads, and one human head on the ornamentation of dresses at Nimrud. (See Layard's *Monuments*, 1st Series,

Plates 9 and 50, fig. 7.)

[2] The woodcut on page 303 is also a good specimen of the defective perspective of the Assyrian artists.

page 291, and the horse and wild bull on page 284.
It will be seen upon reference that the animal are
very much superior to the human forms, a characteristic which is not, however, peculiar to the style of
this period, but belongs to all Assyrian art, from its
earliest to its latest stage. A favourable specimen of
the style will be found in the lion hunt which Mr.
Layard has engraved in his 'Monuments,'³ and of

Lion-hunt, from Nimrud.

which he himself observes, that it is "one of the finest
specimens hitherto discovered of Assyrian sculpture."⁴
The composition is at once simple and effective. The
king forms the principal object nearly in the centre of
the picture, and by the superior height of his conical
head-dress, and the position of the two arrows which
he holds in the hand that draws the bowstring, domi-
nates over the entire composition. As he turns round
to shoot down at the lion which assails him from behind, his body is naturally and gracefully bent, while
his charioteer, being engaged in urging his horses forward, leans naturally in the opposite direction, thus
contrasting with the main figure and balancing it.

---

³ *Monuments of Nineveh*, 1st Series, Pl. 10.   ⁴ Ibid. p. 3.

The lion immediately behind the chariot is outlined
with great spirit and freedom; his head is masterly;
the fillings up of the body, however, have too much
conventionality.   As he rises to attack the monarch,
he conducts the eye up to the main figure, while at
the same time by this attitude his principal lines form
a pleasing contrast to the predominant, perpendicular,
and horizontal lines of the general composition.   The
dead lion in front of the chariot balances the living
one behind it, and, with its crouching attitude, and
drooping head and tail, contrasts admirably with the
upreared form of its fellow.   Two attendants, armed
with sword and shield, following behind the living
lion, serve to balance the horses drawing the chariot,
without rendering the composition too symmetrical.
The horses themselves are the weakest part of the
picture; the fore-legs are stiff and too slight, and the
heads possess little spirit.

It is seldom that designs of this early period can
boast nearly so much merit.   The religious and processional pieces are stiff in the extreme;[1] the battle scenes
are overcrowded and confused;[2] the hunting scenes
are superior to these,[3] but in general they too fall far
below the level of the above-described composition.

The best drawing of this period is found in the
figures forming the patterns or embroidery of
dresses.   The gazelle, of which a representation has
been given (page 282), the ibex (page 279), the horse

<hr/>

[1] See Layard's *Monuments*, 1st
Series, Plates 12, 23, 24, &c.
[2] See particularly, in the same
work, Plates 13, 14, 19, 28, and 20.
[3] The hunt of the wild bull (Plate
11), a pendant to the hunt of the
lion above described, resembles it in

many respects, but on the whole is
decidedly inferior. Several hunting
scenes, possessing considerable merit,
are represented on the embroidery of
dresses. (See Pl. 44, fig. 6; Pl. 48,
figs. 4 and 6; Pl. 49, figs. 3 and 4;
and Pl. 50, fig. 1.)

(page 291), and the horseman hunting the wild-bull
(page 284), are from ornamental work of this kind.
They are favourable specimens perhaps; but, still,

Assyrian seizing a wild bull (Nimrud).

they are representatives of a considerable class. Some
examples even exceed these in the freedom of their
outline, and the vigorous action which they depict,

Hawk-headed figure and sphinx (Nimrud).

as, for instance, the man seizing a wild bull by the horn and fore-leg, which is figured page 431. In general, however, there is a tendency in these early drawings to the grotesque. 'Lions and bulls appear in absurd attitudes; hawk-headed figures in petticoats threaten human-headed lions with a mace or a strap, sometimes holding them by a paw, sometimes grasping them round the middle of the tail; priests hold up ibexes at arm's length by one of their hind-legs, so that their heads trail upon the ground; griffins claw after antelopes, or antelopes toy with winged lions; even in the hunting scenes, which are less simply ludicrous, there seems to be an occasional striving after strange and laughable attitudes, as when a stricken bull tumbles upon his head, with his tail tossed straight in the air, or when a lion receives his death-wound with arms outspread, and mouth widely agape.

Death of a wild bull (Nimrud).

King killing a lion (Nimrud).

The second period of Assyrian mimetic art extends from the latter part of the eighth to nearly the middle of the seventh century before our era; or, more exactly, from about B.C. 721, to B.C. 667.   It belongs to the reigns of the three consecutive kings—Sargon, Sennacherib, and Esar-haddon, who were contemporary with Hezekiah and Manasseh in Judæa, and with the Sabacos (Shebeks) and Tirhakah (Tehrak) in Egypt.   The sources which chiefly illustrate this period are the magnificent series of engravings published by MM. Flandin and Botta,[1] together with the originals of a certain portion of them in the Louvre; the engravings in Mr. Layard's first folio work, from pl. 68 to pl. 83; those in his second folio work from pl. 7 to pl. 56; the originals of many of these in the British Museum[2]; several monuments procured for the British Museum by Mr. Loftus; and a series of unpublished drawings by Mr. Boutcher in the same great national collection.[2]

The most obvious characteristic of this period, when

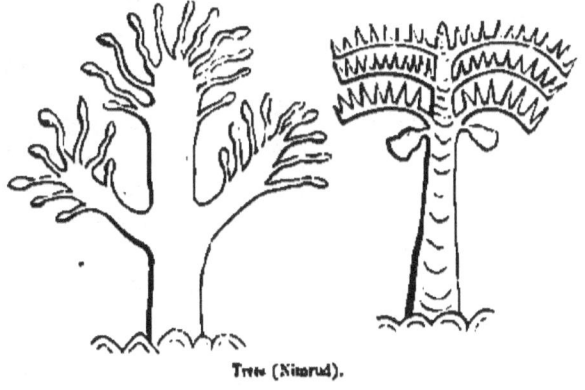

Tree (Nimrud).

---

[1] *Monument de Ninive*, Paris, 1849. The descriptive letter-press is by M. Botta.   The drawings were executed by M. Flandin, and engraved by MM.   Bellier, Péronard, Oury, and others.

[2] These drawings have been kindly placed at my disposal by Mr. Vaux, of the Antiquities' Department.

we compare it with the preceding one, is the advance
which the artists have made in their vegetable
forms, and the pre-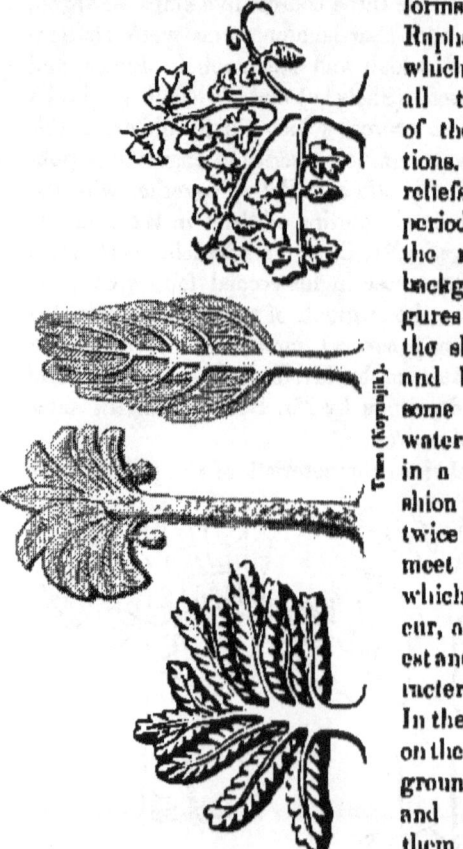
Raphaelite accuracy
which they affect in
all the accessories
of their representa-
tions. In the bas-
reliefs of the first
period we have, for
the most part, no
backgrounds.   Fi-
gures alone occupy
the slabs, or figures
and buildings.   In
some few instances
water is represented
in a very rude fa-
shion;[3] and once or
twice only do we
meet   with   trees,[4]
which, when they oc-
cur, are of the poor-
est and strangest cha-
racter (see page 433).
In the second period,
on the contrary, back-
grounds are the rule,
and slabs without
them form the ex-
ception. The vegetable forms are abundant and varied,
though still somewhat too conventional.   Date-palms,

---

[3] See Mr. Layard's *Monuments*, 1st Series, Plates 15, 16, 53, and 39, n.
[4] Ibid. Plates 13, 14, and 53.

firs, and vines are delineated with skill and spirit; other varieties are more difficult to recognise. The character of the countries through which armies march is almost always given [5]—their streams, lakes, and rivers, their hills and mountains, their trees, and, in the case of marshy districts, their tall reeds. At the same time, animals in the wild state are freely introduced without their having any bearing on the general subject of the picture. The water teems with fish, and, where the sea is represented, with crabs, turtle, star-fish, sea serpents, and other monsters.[6] The woods are alive with birds; wild swine and stags people the marshes.[7] Nature is evidently more and more studied; and the artist takes a delight in adorning the scenes of violence, which he is forced to depict, with quiet touches of a gentle character—rustics fishing or irrigating their grounds, fish disporting themselves, birds flying from tree to tree, or watching the callow young which look up to them from the nest for protection.[8]

In regard to human forms, no great advance marks this period. A larger variety in their attitudes is indeed to be traced, and a greater energy and life appears in most of the figures; but there is still much the same heaviness of outline, the same over-muscularity, and the same general clumsiness and want of grace. Animal forms show a much more considerable improvement. Horses are excellently portrayed, the attitudes being varied, and the heads especially delineated with great spirit (see overleaf). Mules and

[5] This is particularly the case in the sculptures of Sennacherib. In those of Sargon, backgrounds are still rather the exception than the rule.

[6] Botta, Monument de Ninive, vol. i. Plates 32 to 34; Layard, Monu- ments of Nineveh, 1st Series, Pl. 71.

[7] See the representations on pages 50 and 283.

[8] Monuments of Nineveh, 2nd Series, Pl. 40.

Grooms and horses (Khorsabad).

camels are well expressed,[*] but have scarcely the vigour
of the horses.   Horned cattle, as oxen, both with and

Assyrian oxen (Koyunjik).

without humps, goats,
and sheep are very skil-
fully treated, being re-
presented with much
character, in natural
yet varied attitudes,
and often admirably
grouped.

   The composition
during this period is
more complicated and
more ambitious than
during the proceding one; but it may be questioned

<hr />

[*] See above, p. 202.

whether it is so effective.   No single scene of the time can compare for grandeur with the lion-hunt above

Assyrian oxen (Koyunjik).

described.[16]   The battles and sieges are spirited, but want unity; the hunting-scenes are comparatively tame;[17] the representations of the transport of colossal

Assyrian goat and sheep (Koyunjik).

bulls possess more interest than artistic merit.   On the other hand, the manipulation is decidedly superior; the relief is higher, the outline is more flowing, the

---

[16] Pages 429, 430.
[17] No lion-hunt nor bull-hunt has been found in the sculptures of this time.   The chase seems confined to hares, gazelles, and birds.

finish of the features more delicate. What is lost in grandeur of composition is, on the whole, more than made up by variety, naturalness, improved handling, and higher finish.

The highest perfection of Assyrian art is in the third period, which extends from B.C. 667 to about B.C. 640. It synchronises with the reign of *Asshur-bani-pal*, the son of Esar-haddon, who appears to have been contemporary with Gyges in Lydia,[1] and with Psammetichus in Egypt. The characteristics of the time are a less conventional type in the vegetable forms, a wonderful freedom, spirit, and variety in the forms of animals, extreme minuteness and finish in the human figures, and a delicacy in the handling considerably beyond that of even the second or middle period. The sources illustrative of this stage of the art consist of the noble series of slabs obtained by Mr. Loftus from the northern palace at Koyunjik, and of the drawings made from them[2] and from other slabs, which were in a more damaged condition, by Mr. Boutcher, who accompanied Mr. Loftus in the capacity of artist. Both the slabs and the drawings form part of our National Collection; but the former only are accessible to the public generally. By the kindness of the Museum authorities, free access to the drawings has been allowed for the purposes of the present work, which will thus have the advantage of being illustrated from both sources.

Vegetable forms are, on the whole, somewhat rare.

---

[1] See below, chapter ix. There is reason to believe that the Eusebian date for Gyges (B.C. 698 to B.C. 662) is more correct than the Herodotean —B.C. 724 to B.C. 686.

[2] These drawings, being taken when the slabs were freshly exhumed, often preserve features which have disappeared during the transport of the originals and their preparation for exhibition.

The artists have relinquished the design of representing scenes with perfect truthfulness, and have recurred as a general rule, to the plain backgrounds of the first period.   This is particularly the case in the hunting-scenes, which are seldom accompanied by any landscape.   In processional and military scenes landscape is introduced, but sparingly; the forms, for the most

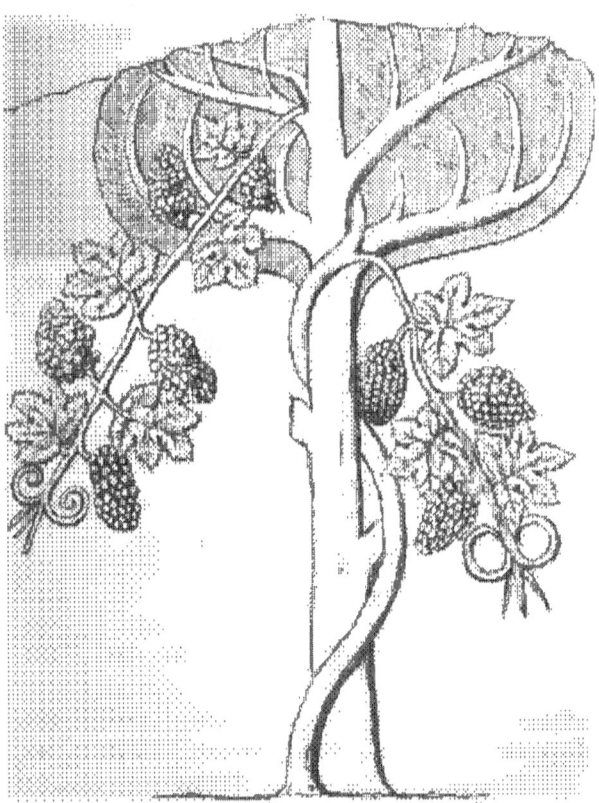

Vine trained on a fir (?), from the North Palace, Koyunjik.

part, resembling those of the second period.[1] Now and then, however, in such scenes the landscape has been made the object of special attention, becoming the prominent part, while the human figures are accessories. It is here that an advance in art is particularly discernible. In one set of slabs a garden seems to be represented. Vines are trained upon trees, which may be either firs or cypresses, winding

elegantly around their stems, and on either side letting fall their pendant branches laden with fruit. Leaves, branches, and tendrils are delineated with equal truth and finish, a most pleasing and graceful effect being thereby produced. Irregularly among the trees occur groups of lilies, some in bud, some in full blow, all natural, graceful, and spirited.

Lilies, from the North Palace, Koyunjik.

It is difficult to do justice to the animal delineation of this period, without reproducing before the eye of the reader the entire series of reliefs and drawings which belong to it. It is the infinite variety in the attitudes, even more than the truth and naturalness of any

---

[1] See the Illustration (No. V.) on page 388, which belongs to this time; and compare the trees with those represented, supra, p. 434.

particular specimens, that impresses us as we contemplate the series. Lions, wild asses, dogs, deer, wild goats, horses are represented in profusion; and we scarcely find a single form which is repeated. Some specimens have been already given, as the hunted stag and hind on page 282, and the startled wild ass on page 281. Others will occur among the illustrations of the next chapter. For the present it may suffice to draw attention to the spirit of the two falling asses in the subjoined woodcut (No. I.), and of the crouching lion in the woodcut (No. II., overleaf); to the life-like force of both ass and hounds in the representation (No. III., overleaf), and here particularly to the bold drawing of the one of the dog's heads in full, instead of in profile—a novelty now first occurring in the bas-reliefs.

No. I. Death of two wild-asses, from the North Palace, Kouyunjik.

As instances of still bolder attempts at unusual attitudes, and at the same time of a certain amount of fore-shortening, two further illustrations are appended. The sorely-wounded lion in the first (p. 443) turns his head piteously towards the cruel shaft, while he totters

No. II. Lion about to spring, from the North Palace, Koyunjik.

to his fall, his limbs failing him, and his eyes beginning to close. The more slightly-stricken king of beasts in the

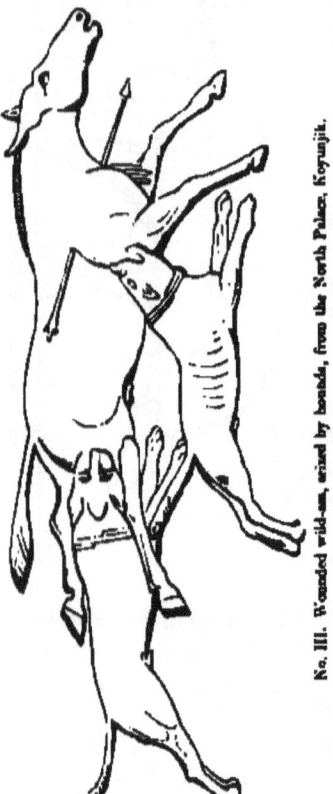

No. III. Wounded wild-ass, seized by hounds, from the North Palace, Koyunjik.

second (p. 444), urged to fury by the smart of his wound, rushes at the chariot whence the shaft was sped, and in his mad agony springs upon a wheel, clutches it with his two fore-paws, and frantically grinds it between his teeth. Assyrian art, so far as it is as yet known, has no finer specimen of animal drawing than this head, which may challenge comparison with anything of the kind that either classic or modern art has produced.

As a specimen at once of animal vigour and of the delicacy and finish of the workmanship in the human

forms of the time, a bas-relief of the king receiving
the spring of a lion, and shooting an arrow into his
mouth, while a second lion advances at a rapid pace a
little behind the first, may be adduced (see page 415).
The boldness of the composition, which represents the
first lion actually in mid-air, is remarkable; the drawing of the brute's fore-paws, expanded to seize his
intended prey, is life-like and very spirited, while the
head is massive and full of vigour. There is something

No. I. Wounded lion, about to fall, from the North Palace, Koyunjik.

noble in the calmness of the monarch contrasted with
the comparative eagerness of the attendant, who
stretches forward with shield and spear to protect his
master from destruction, if the arrow fails. The head of
the king is, unfortunately, injured; but the remainder
of the figure is perfect; and here, in the elaborate
ornamentation of the whole dress, we have an example
of the careful finish of the time—a finish which is so
light and delicate that it does not interfere with the
general effect, being scarcely visible at a few yards'
distance.

The faults which still remain in this best period of
Assyrian art are heaviness and stiffness of outline in

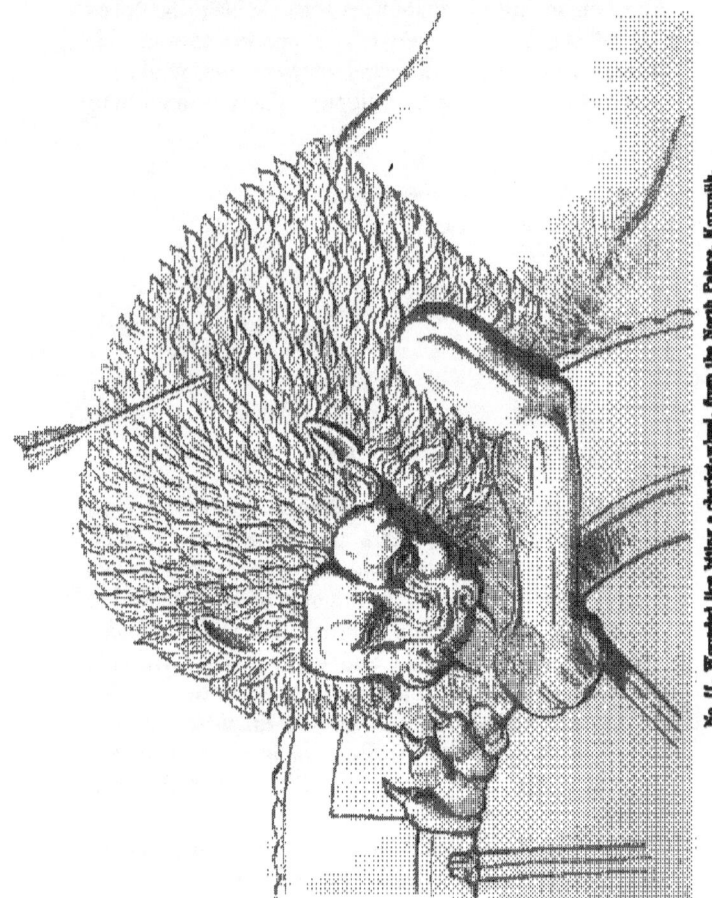

the human forms; a want of expression in the faces,
and of variety and animation in the attitudes; and an
almost complete disregard of perspective. If the
worst of these faults are anywhere overcome it would
seem to be in the land lion-hunt, from which the noble

No. II. Wounded lion killing a Chariot-wheel, from the North Palace, Koyunjik.

King shooting a lion on the spring, from the North Palace, Koyunjik.

head represented above is taken;[*] and in the river-
hunt of the same beast, found on a slab too much injured
to be removed, of which a representation is given on
the page opposite. From what appears to have
remained of the four figures towards the prow of
the boat, we may conclude that there was a good
deal of animation here. The drawing must certainly
have been less stiff than usual; and, if there is not
much variety in the attitudes of the three spearmen
in front, at any rate those attitudes contrast well, both
with the stillness of the unengaged attendants in the
rear, and with the animated but very different attitude
of the king.

Before the subject of Assyrian sculpture is dis-
missed, it is necessary to touch the question, whether
the Assyrians applied colour to statuary, and if so, in
what way and to what extent. Did they, like the
Egyptians,[ ] cover the whole surface of the stone with
a layer of stucco, and then paint the sculptured parts
with strong colours—red, blue, yellow, white, and
black? Or did they, like the Greeks,[ ] apply paint
to certain portions of their sculptures only, as the
hair, eyes, beard, and draperies? Or, finally, did
they simply leave the stone in its natural condition,
like the Italians and the modern sculptors generally?

The present appearance of the sculptures is most in

---

[*] See page 444. A representation
of the whole scene would have been
given, had this work been on a larger
scale; but it is impossible to do
justice to the highly-finished sculpture of this time within the limits
of an ordinary octavo. The scene
itself may be studied in the British
Museum. It occupies a portion of
the eastern wall in the underground

Assyrian apartment.
[ ] See Wilkinson's *Ancient Egyptians*, 1st Series, vol. iii. p. 300.
[ ] Ibid. p. 299. Wornum, in Smith's
*Dictionary of Greek and Roman An-
tiquities*, (ad voc. PICTURA), goes
somewhat further than Wilkinson;
but still maintains that the Greeks
did not colour the flesh of statues.

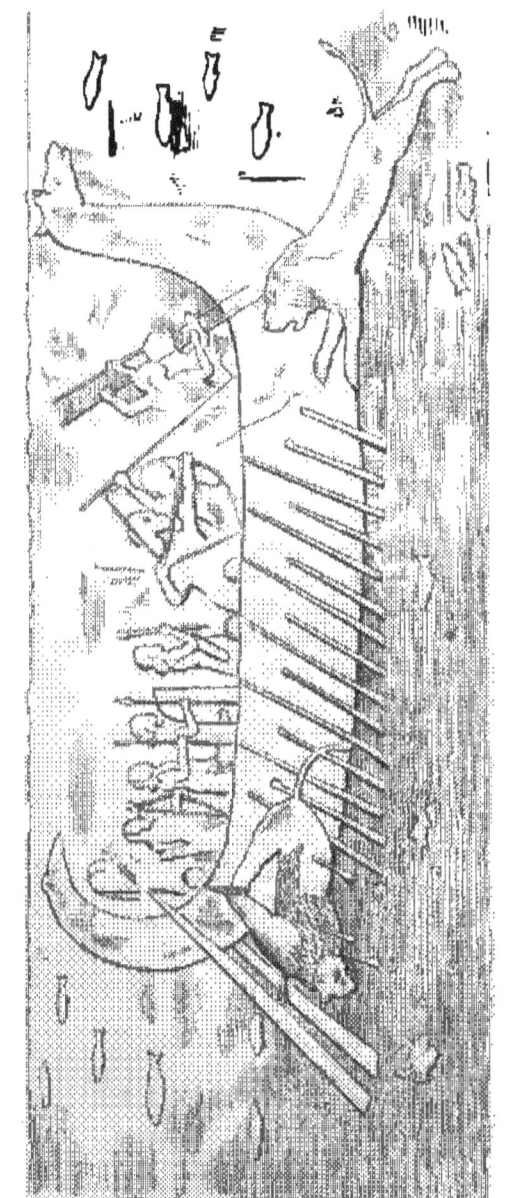

Lion-hunt in a river, from the North Palace, Koyunjik (ab. B. C. 660).

accordance with the last of these three theories, or at any rate with that theory very slightly modified by the second. The slabs now offer only the faintest and most occasional traces of colour. The evidence, however, of the original explorers is distinct, that *at the time of discovery* these traces were very much more abundant. Mr. Layard observed colour at Nimrud on the hair, beard, and eyes of the figures, on the sandals and the bows, on the tongues of the eagle-headed mythological emblems, on a garland round the head of a winged priest (?), and on the representation of fire in the bas-relief of a siege.[1] At Khorsabad, MM. Botta and Flandin found paint on the fringes of draperies, on fillets, on the mitre of the king, on the flowers carried by the winged figures, on bows and spear-shafts, on the harness of the horses, on the chariots, on the sandals, on the birds, and sometimes on the trees.[2] The torches used to fire cities, and the flames of the cities themselves, were invariably coloured red. M. Flandin also believed that he could detect, in some instances, a faint trace of yellow ochre on the flesh and on the background of bas-reliefs, whence he concluded that this tint was spread over every part not otherwise coloured.[3]

It is evident, therefore, that the theory of an absence of colour, or of a very rare use of it, must be set aside. Indeed, as it is certain that the upper portions of the palace-walls, both inside and outside, were patterned with coloured bricks, covering the whole space above the slabs, it must be allowed to be

---

[1] *Nineveh and its Remains*, vol. ii. p. 300.
[2] See M. Botta's *Monument de Ninive*, Plates 12, 14, 43, 53, 61, 62, 63, &c. Compare the general statement, vol. v. p. 178.
[3] See his *Voyage Archéologique à Ninive*, in the *Revue des Deux Mondes* for July, 1845, p. 106.

extremely improbable that at a particular line colour
would suddenly and totally cease. The laws of decorative harmony forbid such abrupt transitions; and
to these laws all nations with any taste instinctively
and unwittingly conform. The Assyrian reliefs were
therefore, we may be sure, to some extent coloured.
The real question is, to what extent—in the Egyptian
or in the classical style?

In Mr. Layard's "First Series of Monuments," a
preference was expressed for what may be called the
Egyptian theory. In the Frontispiece of that work,
and in the second Plate, containing the restoration of
a palace interior, the entire bas-reliefs were represented as strongly coloured. A jet-black was assigned
to the hair and beards of men and of all human-
headed figures, to the manes and tails of horses, to
vultures, eagle-heads, and the like; a coarse red-
brown to winged lions, to human flesh, to horses'
bodies, and to various ornaments; a deep yellow to
common lions, to chariot-wheels, quivers, fringes,
belts, sandals, and other portions of human apparel;
white to robes, helmets, shields, tunics, towns, trees,
&c.; and a dull blue to some of the feathers of winged
lions and genii, and to large portions of the ground
from which the sculptures stood out. This conception of Assyrian colouring, framed confessedly on
the assumption of a close analogy between the ornamentation of Assyria and that of Egypt,[*] was at
once accepted by the unlearned, and naturally enough
was adopted by most of those who sought to popu-
larise the new knowledge among their countrymen.
Hence the strange travesties of Assyrian art with

* *Monuments of Nineveh*, 1st Series, Description of the Plates, p. 1.

which we meet in so-called "Assyrian Courts," where
all the delicacy of the real sculpture has disappeared,
and the spectator is revolted by grim figures of bulls
and lions, from which a thick layer of coarse paint
has taken away all dignity, and by reliefs which, from
the same cause, have lost all spirit and refinement.

It is sufficient objection to the theory here treated
of, that it has no solid basis of fact to rest upon.
Colour has only been *found* on portions of the bas-
reliefs, as on the hair and beards of men, on head-
ornaments, to a small extent on draperies, on the
harness of horses, on sandals, weapons, birds, flowers,
and the like.   Neither the flesh of men, nor the bodies
of animals, nor the draperies generally, nor the backgrounds (except perhaps at Khorsabad[2]), present the
slightest appearance of having been touched by paint.
It is inconceivable that, if these portions of the sculptures were universally, or even ordinarily, coloured,
the colour should have so entirely disappeared in
every instance.   It is moreover inconceivable that
the sculptor, if he knew his work was about to be
concealed beneath a coating of paint, should have
cared to give it the delicate elaboration which is
found at any rate in the later examples.   All leads
to the conclusion that in Assyrian as in classical
sculpture, colour was sparingly applied, being confined to such parts as the hair, eyes, and beards of
men, to the fringes of dresses, to horse-trappings,
and other accessory parts of the representations.   In

---

[2] The opinion of M. Flandin, that
an ochre tint covered the flesh and
the backgrounds at Khorsabad, seems
to have been derived from a particular instance, where, according to
M. Botta, the colouring was accidental, and dated from a time subsequent to the ruin of the palace
(*Monument de Ninive*, vol. v. p.
179).

this way the lower part of the walls was made to harmonise sufficiently with the upper portion, which was wholly coloured, but chiefly with pale hues. At the same time a greater distinctness was given to the scenes represented upon the sculptured slabs, the colour being judiciously applied to disentangle human from animal figures, dress from flesh, or human figures from one another.

The colours actually found upon the bas-reliefs are four only—red, blue, black, and white.[1] The red is a good bright tint, far exceeding in brilliancy that of Egypt. On the sculptures of Khorsabad it approaches to vermilion, while on those of Nimrud it inclines to a crimson or lake tint.[2] It is found alternating with the natural stone on the royal parasol and mitre;[3] with blue on the crests of helmets,[4] the trappings of horses,[5] on flowers,[6] sandals,[7] and on fillets;[8] and besides, it occurs, unaccompanied by any other colour, on the stems and branches of trees,[9] on the claws of birds,[10] the shafts of spears and arrows,[11] on bows,[12] belts,[13] fillets,[14] quivers,[15] maces,[16] reins,[17]

---

[1] "On the sculptures I have only found black, white, red, and blue," says Mr. Layard (*Nineveh and its Remains*, vol. ii. p. 310); "and three colours alone were used in the painted ornaments of the upper chambers at Nimrud. At Khorsabad, green and yellow continually occurred on the bas-reliefs; at Koyunjik, there were no traces whatever of colour." But, in opposition to the statement in italics, M. Botta, the explorer of Khorsabad, observes, "Nous n'avons trouvé à Khorsabad sur les sculptures d'autres couleurs que le rouge, le bleu, et le noir." (*Monument*, vol. v. p. 178.) The green and yellow were confined to the enamelled bricks.

[2] Layard, *Nineveh and its Remains*, vol. ii. p. 311.

[3] Botta, *Monument de Ninive*, Plates 12, 63, and 113.

[4] Ibid. Plate 61.

[5] Ibid. Plates 53, 62, 63, &c.

[6] Ibid. Plates 43 and 113.

[7] Ibid. Plate 14.

[8] Ibid. Plate 43.

[9] Ibid. Plates 110, 113, and 114.

[10] Ibid. Plates 110 and 114.

[11] Ibid. Plates 61 and 65.

[12] Ibid. Plates 61 and 62.

[13] Ibid. Plates 62, 65, and 114.

[14] Ibid. Plates 12, 14, 62, and 65.

[15] Ibid. Plate 63.

[16] Ibid. Plate 114.

[17] Ibid. Plate 53.

sandals,[1] flowers,[2] and the fringe of dresses.[3] It is
uncertain whence the colouring matter was derived;
perhaps the substance used was the suboxide of
copper, with which the Assyrians are known to have
coloured their red glass.[4]

The blue of the Assyrian monuments is an oxide
of copper,[5] sometimes containing also a trace of
lead.[6] Besides occurring in combination with red in
the cases already mentioned, it was employed to colour
the foliage of trees,[7] the plumage of birds,[8] the heads
of arrows,[9] and sometimes quivers[10] and sandals.[11]

White occurs very rarely indeed upon the sculptures. At Khorsabad it was not found at all; at
Nimrud it was confined to the inner part of the eye
on either side of the pupil,[12] and in this position it
occurred only on the colossal lions and bulls, and a
very few other figures. On bricks and pottery it
was frequent, and there it is found to have been derived from tin;[13] but it is uncertain whether the
white of the sculptures was not derived from a commoner material.[14]

Black is applied in the sculptures chiefly to the
hair, beards, and eyebrows of men.[15] It was also

[1] Botta, *Monument de Ninive*,
Plate 81.
[2] Ibid. Plates 74 and 75.
[3] Ibid. Plate 63.
[4] See Dr. Percy's note in Mr. Layard's *Nineveh and Babylon*, p. 672.
[5] Layard, *Nineveh and its Remains*, vol. II. p. 310. Birch, *Ancient Pottery*, vol. i. p. 127.
[6] Birch, *Ancient Pottery*, vol. i. p.
149.
[7] Botta, *Monument*, Plates 110,
113, and 114.
[8] Ibid. Plates 110 and 114.
[9] Ibid. Plate 61.

[10] Ibid. Plate 62.
[11] Ibid. Plate 14.
[12] Layard, *Nineveh and its Remains*, vol. ii. p. 312, note.
[13] Birch, *Ancient Pottery*, vol. i.
p. 127.
[14] Mr. Layard conjectures that it
was obtained, as it is in the country
to this day, by burning the alabaster
or gypsum. (*Nineveh and its Remains*, vol. ii. p. 311.)
[15] Ibid. p. 312. For instances, see
Layard's *Monuments*, 1st Series,
Plate 82: Botta, *Monument*, Plates
12 and 43.

used to colour the eyeballs, not only of men, but also of the colossal lions and bulls.[1] Sometimes, when the eyeball was thus marked, a line of black was further carried round the inner edge of both the upper and the lower eyelid.[2] In one place black bars have been introduced to ornament an antelope's horns.[3] On the older sculptures black was also the common colour for sandals, which however were then edged with red.[4] The composition of the black is uncertain. Browns upon the enamelled bricks are found to have been derived from iron;[5] but Mr. Layard believes the black upon the sculptures to have been, like the Egyptian, a bone black mixed with a little gum.[6]

The ornamental metallurgy of the Assyrians deserves attention next to their sculpture. It is of three kinds, consisting, in the first place, of entire figures, or parts of figures, cast in a solid shape; secondly, of castings in a low relief; and thirdly, of embossed work wrought mainly with the hammer, but finished by a sparing use of the graving-tool.

The solid castings are comparatively rare, and represent none but animal forms. Lions, which seem to have been used as weights, occur most frequently.[7] None are of any great size; nor have we any evidence that the Assyrians could cast large masses of metal. They seem to have used castings, not (as the

---

[1] *Nineveh and its Remains*, vol. ii. p. 313.

[2] *Monuments of Nineveh*, 1st Series, Plate 92.

[3] Botta, *Monument*, Plate 43.

[4] *Nineveh and its Remains*, vol. ii. p. 312, note.

[5] Birch, l. s. c.

[6] *Nineveh and its Remains*, vol. ii. p. 311.

[7] Mr. Layard discovered sixteen of these lions in one place, (*Nineveh and its Remains*, vol. i. p. 128.) They had all rings affixed to their backs, which seemed to show the purpose for which they were intended. The largest of these lions was about a foot in length.

Greeks and the moderns) for the greater works of
art, but only for the smaller. The forms of the few
casts which have come down to us are good, and are

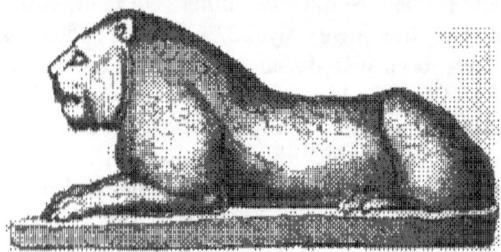

Bronze lion, from Nimrud.

free from the narrowness which characterises the representations in stone.[*]

Castings in a low relief formed the ornamentation of thrones, stools,[*] and sometimes probably of

Fragments of bronze ornaments of the throne, from Nimrud.

[*] Supra, p. 423.
[*] See Layard's *Nineveh and its* | *Nineveh*, vol. II. p. 301; Botta,
Monument, Plate 19.

chariots.[1]   They consisted of animal and human figures, winged deities, griffins, and the like.   The castings were chiefly in open work, and were attached to the furniture which they ornamented by means of small nails.   They have no peculiar merit, being merely repetitions of the forms with which we are familiar from their occurrence on embroidered dresses and on the cylinders.

Bronze casting, from the throne, Nimrud.

The embossed work of the Assyrians is the most curious and the most artistic portion of their metallurgy. Sometimes it consisted of mere heads and feet of animals, hammered into shape upon a model composed of clay mixed with bitumen.   Sometimes it extended to entire figures, as (probably) in the case of the lions

[1] Botta, Plate 17. It is uncertain whether the ornaments in this case, and in those referred to in the last note, were cast or embossed, since we have only the representations, not the originals themselves. The throne ornaments, however, were actually found (Layard, *Nin. and Bab.* pp. 198-200). They were castings in bronze.

clasping each other, so common at the ends of sword-
sheaths (see next page), the human figures which orna-

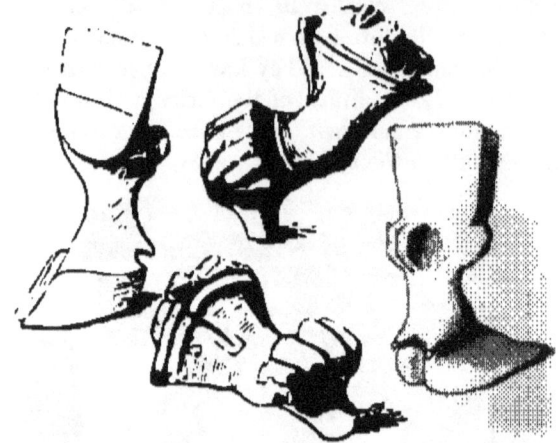

Feet of tripods in bronze and iron.

ment the sides of chairs or stools, and the like.[1] Occasionally it was of a less solid, but at the same time of

Bronze bull's head from throne.

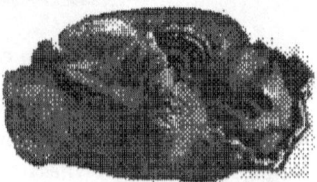

Bronze head, part of throne, showing bitumen
inside.

a more elaborate character.   In a palace inhabited by
Sargon at Nimrud, and in close juxtaposition with a mo-

---

[1] Here again we cannot be certain
whether the sculptures represent embossed work or castings. In delicate fabrics, like sword-sheaths, the
former seems more probable.

nument certainly of his time,[3] were discovered by Mr. Layard a number of dishes, plates, and bowls, embossed

End of a sword-sheath.
(N.-W. Palace, Nimrud.)

Stool or chair (Khorsabad).

with great taste and skill, which are among the most elegant specimens of Assyrian art discovered during the recent researches. Upon these were represented sometimes hunting-scenes, sometimes combats between griffins and lions, or between men and lions, sometimes landscapes with trees and figures of animals, sometimes mere rows of animals following one another. One or two representations from these bowls have been already given.[4] They usually contain a star or scarab in the centre, beyond which is a series of bands or borders, patterned, most commonly with figures. It is impossible to

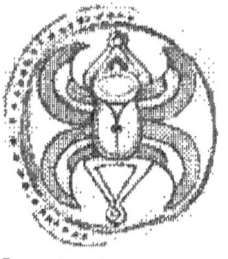

Engraved scarab in centre of cup.
(N.-W. Palace, Nimrud.)

---

[3] Layard, *Nin. and Bab.* p. 196.   Supra, pp. 281 and 283.

give an adequate idea of the delicacy and spirit of
the drawings, or of the variety and elegance of the
other patterns, in a work of moderate dimensions like
the present. Mr. Layard, in his Second Series of
'Monuments,' has done justice to the subject by pictorial representation,[*] while in his 'Nineveh and
Babylon' he has described the more important of the
vessels separately.[*] The curious student will do well
to consult these two works, after which he may examine with advantage the originals in the British
Museum.

One of the most remarkable features observable in
this whole series of monuments, is its semi-Egyptian
character. The occurrence of the scarab has been
just noticed. It appears on the bowls frequently,
as do sphinxes of an Egyptian type; while sometimes
heads and head-dresses purely Egyptian are found,

as the subjoined,[*] which
are well-known forms, and
have nothing Assyrian
about them; and in one or
two instances we even meet
with hieroglyphics,[*] the
onk (or symbol of life),
the ibis, &c. These facts

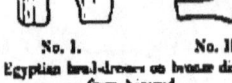

No. I.   No. II.
Egyptian head-dresses on bronze dishes,
from Nimrud.

may seem at first sight to raise a great question—
namely, whether, after all, the art of the Assyrians was

---

[*] Plates 57 to 67. The drawings
by Mr. Prentice, now in the British
Museum, are still more beautiful
than these plates, since they show the
wonderful colouring of the bronzes
at the time of their arrival.

[*] Pages 185-190.

[*] Mr. Layard calls No. I. a head
of Athor (*Nin. and Bab.* p. 187);
but there are no sufficient grounds
for the identification. The head re-

sembles the ordinary mummy type.
The head-dress (No. II.) is the well-
known double crown, worn both by
kings and gods, representing the
sovereignty over both the Upper and
the Lower country. (Wilkinson,
Ancient Egyptians, vol. iii. p. 354.)

[*] Layard, *Monuments*, 2nd Series,
Plate 61, B; *Nin. and Bab.* p. 187.
On the *ank* or *onk*, see Wilkinson,
vol. v. p. 283.

really of home growth, or was not rather imported from the Egyptians, either directly or by way of Phœnicia. Such a view has been sometimes taken ; but the most cursory study of the Assyrian remains, *in chronological order*, is sufficient to disprove the theory, since it will at once show that the earliest specimens of Assyrian art are the most un-Egyptian in character.   No doubt there are certain analogies even here, as the preference for the profile, the stiffness and formality, the ignorance or disregard of perspective, and the like ; but the analogies are exactly such as would be tolerably sure to occur in the early efforts of any two races not very dissimilar to one another, while the *little* resemblances, which alone prove connexion, are entirely wanting.   These do not appear until we come to monuments which belong to the time of Sargon, when direct connexion between Egypt and Assyria seems to have begun, and Egyptian captives are known to have been transported into Mesopotamia in large numbers.[*]   It has been suggested that the entire series of Nimrud vessels is Phœnician, and that they were either carried off as spoil from Tyre and other Phœnician towns, or else were the workmanship of Phœnician captives removed into Assyria from their own country.   The Sidonians and their kindred were, it is remarked, the most renowned workers in metal of the ancient world, and their intermediate position between Egypt and Assyria, may, it is suggested, have been the cause of the existence among them of a mixed art, half Assyrian, half Egyptian.[1]   The theory is plausible ; but upon the whole it seems more consonant with all the

---

[*] Isaiah xx. 4.   [1] Layard, *Nineveh and Babylon*, p. 192.

facts[a] to regard the series in question as in reality Assyrian, modified from the ordinary style by an influence derived from Egypt. Either Egyptian artificers—captives probably—may have wrought the bowls after Assyrian models, and have accidentally varied the common forms, more or less, in the direction which was natural to them from old habits; or Assyrian artificers, acquainted with the art of Egypt, and anxious to improve their own from it, may have consciously adopted certain details from the rival country. The workmanship, subjects, and mode of treatment, are all, it is granted, " more Assyrian than Egyptian,"[b] the Assyrian character being decidedly more marked than in the case of the ivories which will be presently considered ; yet even in that case the legitimate conclusion seems to be that the specimens are to be regarded as native Assyrian, but as produced abnormally, under a strong foreign influence.

The usual material of the Assyrian ornamental metallurgy is bronze, composed of one part of tin to ten of copper,[c] which are exactly the proportions considered to be best by the Greeks and Romans, and still in ordinary use at the present day. In some instances, where more than common strength was required, as in the legs of tripods and tables, the bronze was ingeniously cast over an inner structure

---

[a] It is urged that Phœnician characters appear on one of the plates (Layard, p. 188), that the scarab which occurs on so many of them (supra, woodcut on p. 457) is "more of a Phœnician than an Egyptian form" (ib. p. 186), and that some silver bowls of the same character, found in Cyprus, are almost certainly Phœnician (ib. p. 192, note). But these last may well be Assyrian, since some Assyrian remains have certainly been brought from the island ; and the other points are too doubtful and too minute to set against the strong Assyrian character of the great bulk of the ornaments and figures.

[b] *Nineveh and Babylon*, p. 192.

[c] Ibid. p. 101.

of iron.[4] This practice was unknown
to modern metallurgists until the discovery of the Assyrian specimens, from
which it has been successfully imitated.[5]

We may presume that, besides bronze,
the Assyrians used, to a certain extent,
silver and gold as materials for ornamental metal-work. The ear-rings, bracelets, and armlets worn by the kings and
the great officers of state were probably
of the more valuable metal, while the
similar ornaments worn by those of minor
rank may have been of silver. One solitary specimen only of either class has been
found;[6] but Mr. Layard discovered several
moulds, with tasteful designs for ear-rings,
both at Nimrud and at Koyunjik;[7] and
the sculptures show that both in these and
the other personal ornaments a good deal
of artistic excellence was exhibited. The
ear-rings are frequent in the form of
a cross, and are sometimes delicately
chased. The armlets and bracelets generally terminate in the heads of rams or
bulls, which seem to have been rendered
with spirit and delicacy.

By one or two instances it appears that
the Assyrians knew how to inlay one
metal with another. The specimens discovered are scarcely of an artistic character, being merely winged scarabæi out-

Ear-ring.
(N.-W. Palace,
Nimrud.)

Assyrian ear-rings
(Khorsabad).

---

[4] *Nineveh and Babylon*, p. 178.
[5] Ibid. 191, note.
[7] Mr. Layard found a gold ear-
ring adorned with pearls, together
with a number of purely Assyrian
relics, at Koyunjik (ib. p. 595). He
has figured it, p. 597.
[6] Ibid. pp. 595, 596.

Bronze cubes inlaid with gold. (Original size.)

lined in gold on a bronze ground.* The work, however, is delicate, and the form very much more true
to nature than that which prevailed in Egypt.

Egyptian scarab (from Wilkinson).

The ivories of the Assyrians are inferior both to
their metal castings and to their bas-reliefs. They
consist almost entirely of a single series, discovered
by Mr. Layard in a chamber of the North-West
Palace at Nimrud, in the near vicinity of slabs on
which was engraved the name of Sargon.[10] The
most remarkable point connected with them is the
thoroughly Egyptian character of the greater number, which, at first sight, have almost the appearance
of being importations from the valley of the Nile.
Egyptian profiles, head-dresses, fashions of dressing the
hair, ornaments, attitudes, meet us at every turn; while

* *Nineveh and Babylon*, p. 196.
" *Nineveh and its Remains*, vol.
ii. pp. 8-10 and p. 205. For other

discoveries of ivory objects, see
Nineveh and Babylon, pp. 179, 195,
and 362.

sometimes we find the representations of Egyptian
gods, and in two cases hieroglyphics within car-
touches (see overleaf). A few specimens only are of a
distinctly Assyrian type,
as the subjoined frag-
ment, figured by Mr.
Layard,[1] and one or
two others, in which
the guilloche border ap-
pears.[2] These carvings

Fragment of ivory panel, from Nimrud.

are usually mere low reliefs, occupying small panels
or tablets, which were mortised or glued to the wood-
work of furniture. They were sometimes inlaid in
parts with blue glass, or with blue and green pastes let
into the ivory, and at the same time decorated with
gilding. Now and then the relief is tolerably high,
and presents fragments of forms which seem to have

Fragment of a lion in ivory (Nimrud).

[1] *Monuments*, 1st Series, Plate 88, fig. 8.	[2] Ibid. Plate 90, figs. 17 and 22.

Figure and cartouche with hieroglyphics, on an ivory panel (North-West Palace, Nimrud).

had some artistic merit. The best of these is the fore
part of a lion walking among reeds (p. 463), which
presents analogies with the early art of Asia Minor.
One or two stags' heads have likewise
been found, designed and wrought with
much spirit and delicacy. It is remarked that several of the specimens
show not only a considerable acquaintance with art, but also an intimate
knowledge of the method of working
in ivory.[*] One head of a lion was
" of singular beauty," but unfortunately it fell to pieces at the very
moment of discovery.

Fragment of a stag in
ivory (Nimrud).

It is possible that some of the objects
here described may be actual specimens of Egyptian
art, sent to Sargon as tribute or presents, or else
carried off as plunder in his Egyptian expedition.
The appearance, however, which even the most Egyptian of them present, on a close examination, is rather
that of Assyrian works imitated from Egyptian models
than of genuine Egyptian productions. For instance,
in the tablet figured on the page opposite, where we
see hieroglyphics within a cartouche, the *onk* or symbol
of life,[*] the solar disk, the double ostrich-plume, the
long hair-dress called *namms*, and the *tam* or *kukupha*
sceptre[*]—all unmistakeable Egyptian features—we
observe a style of drapery which is quite unknown
in Egypt, while in several respects it is Assyrian, or
at least Mesopotamian. It is scanty, like that of all
Assyrian robed figures; striped, like the draperies of

* *Nineveh and its Remains*, vol.
ii. p. 10.
* See above, p. 458. The symbol
occurs at the foot of the chairs.

* See Mr. Birch's description in
Mr. Layard's *Nineveh and its Remains*, vol. ii. p. 11, note.

the Chaldæans and Babylonians; fringed with a broad fringe elaborately coloured, as Assyrian fringes are known to have been;[*] and it has large hanging sleeves also fringed, a fashion which appears once or twice upon the Koyunjik sculptures.[†] But if this

Royal attendant (Koyunjik).

specimen, notwithstanding its numerous and striking Egyptian features, is rightly regarded as Mesopotamian, it would seem to follow that the rest of the series must still more decidedly be assigned to native genius.

The Assyrian enamelled bricks are among the most interesting remains of their art. It is from them alone that we are able to judge at all fully of their knowledge and ideas with respect to colour; and it is

---

[*] See above, p. 452.
[†] Layard, *Monuments of Nineveh*, 1st Series, Plate 62. The hanging sleeve is, however, worn only on one arm.

from them also chiefly that an analysis has been made
of the colouring materials employed by the Assyrian
artists.   The bricks may be divided into two classes
—those which are merely patterned, and those which
contain designs representing men and animals.   The
patterned bricks have nothing about them which is
very remarkable.   They present the usual guilloches,
rosettes, bands, scrolls, &c., such as are found in the
painted chambers and in the ornaments on dresses,
varied with geometrical figures, as circles, hexagons,
octagons, and the like; and sometimes with a sort of
arcade-work, which is curious, if not very beautiful.[*]

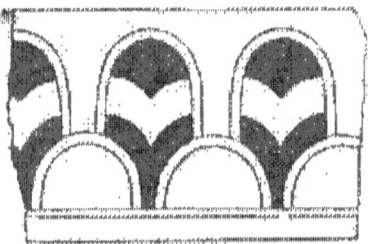

Arcade work, on enamelled brick (Nimrud).

The colours chiefly used in the patterns are pale
green, pale yellow, dark brown, and white.   Now
and then an intense blue and a bright red occur,
generally together;[*] but these positive hues are rare,
and the taste of the Assyrians seems to have led
them to prefer, for their patterned walls, pale and
dull hues.   The same preference appears, even more
strikingly, in the bricks on which designs are represented.   There the tints almost exclusively used are

[*] See Mr. Layard's *Monuments*, 1st Series, Plates 84, 86, and 87.
[*] Ibid. Plate 84, figs. 9 and 12.

pale yellow, pale greenish blue, olive-green, white, and a brownish black. It is suggested that the colours have faded,[1] but of this there is no evidence. The Assyrians, when they used the primitive hues, seem, except in the case of red, to have employed subdued tints of them, and red they appear to have introduced very sparingly.[2] Olive-green they affected for grounds, and they occasionally used other half tints. A pale orange and a delicate lilac or pale purple are found at Khorsabad,[3] while brown (as already observed) is far more common on the bricks than black. Thus the general tone of their colouring is quiet, not to say sombre. There is no striving after brilliant effects. The Assyrian artist seeks to please by the elegance of his forms and the harmony of his hues, not to startle by a display of bright and strongly-contrasted colours.

The tints used in a single composition vary from three to five, which latter number they seem never to exceed. The following are the combinations of five hues which occur:—Brown, green, blue, dark yellow, and pale yellow;[4] orange, lilac, white, yellow, and olive-green.[5] Combinations of four hues are much more common: e.g., red, white, yellow, and black;[6] deep yellow, brown black, white, and pale yellow;[7]

---

[1] Layard, *Nineveh and Babylon*, p. 106.

[2] There is a curious contrast between the bricks and the sculptures in this respect. In the sculptures there is no yellow, but abundance of red. It is a reasonable conjecture of Mr. Layard's, that in these "some of the red tints which remain were originally laid on to receive gilding." (*Nineveh and its Remains*, vol. ii. p. 313, note.)

[3] *Monument de Ninive*, Plate 155, figs. 3, 5, and 9. Mr. Layard says he found purple and violet on some of the Nimrud bricks (*Nineveh and its Remains*, vol. ii. p. 310), but he does not represent these colours.

[4] Layard, *Monuments*, 1st Series, Plate 84, fig. 2.

[5] Botta, *Monument de Ninive*, Plate 155, fig. 3.

[6] Ibid. fig. 2.

[7] Layard, *Monuments*, 2nd Series, Plate 55, fig. 6.

lilac, yellow, white, and green ;[1] yellow, blue, white, and brown ;[2] and yellow, blue, white, and olive-green.[10] Sometimes the tints are as few as three, the ground in these cases being generally of a hue used also in the figures. Thus we have yellow, blue, and white on a blue ground,[1] and again the same colours on a yellow ground.[2] We have also the simple combinations of white and yellow on a blue ground,[3] and of white and yellow on an olive-green ground.[4]

In every case there is a great harmony in the colouring. We find no harsh contrasts. Either the tones are all subdued, or if any are intense and positive, then all (or almost all) are so. Intense red occurs in two fragments of patterned bricks found by Mr. Layard.[5] It is balanced by intense blue, and accompanied in each case by a full brown and a clear white, while in one case[6] it is further accompanied by a pale green, which has a very good effect. A similar red appears on a design figured by M. Botta.[7] Its accompaniments are white, black, and a full yellow. Where lilac occurs, it is balanced by its complementary colour, yellow,[8] or by yellow and orange,[9] and further accompanied by white. It is noticeable also that bright hues are not placed one against the other, but are separated by narrow bands of white, or brown and white. This use of white

[1] Botta, *Monument de Ninive*, Plate 155, figs. 5 and 9.
[2] Layard, *Monuments*, 2nd Series, Plate 53, fig. 0.
[10] Ibid. Plate 53, figs. 3 and 4 ; Plate 54, figs. 12, 13, and 14.
[1] Layard, *Monuments*, 2nd Series, Plate 53, figs. 2 and 5 ; and Plate 54, fig. 9.
[2] Ibid. Plate 53, fig. 1.

[4] Ibid. Plate 54, fig. 7.
[4] Ibid. Plate 54, fig. 9.
[5] *Monuments*, 1st Series, Plate 84, figs. 9 and 12.
[6] Fig. 9.
[7] *Monument de Ninive*, vol. ii. Plate 155, fig. 2.
[8] Ibid. figs. 5 and 9.
[9] Ibid. fig. 3.

gives a great delicacy and refinement to the colouring, which is saved by it, even where the lines are
the strongest, from being coarse or vulgar.

The drawing of the designs resembles that of the
sculptures, except that the figures are generally
slimmer and less muscular. The chief peculiarity is
the strength of the outline, which is almost always
coloured differently from the object drawn, either
white, black, yellow, or brown. Generally it is of an
uniform thickness (as in No. I.); sometimes, though
rarely, it has that variety which characterises good

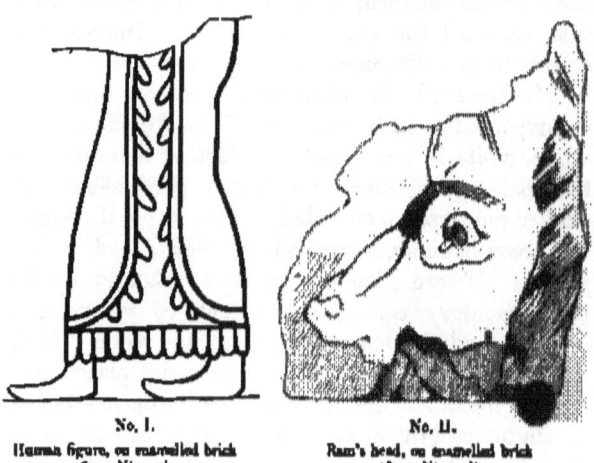

No. I.   No. II.
Human figure, on enamelled brick   Ram's head, on enamelled brick
(from Nimrud).   (from Nimrud).

drawing (as in No. II.). Occasionally there is a curious
combination of the two styles, as in the specimen opposite—the most interesting yet discovered—where the
dresses of the two main figures are coarsely outlined
in yellow, while the remainder of the design is very
lightly sketched in a brownish black.

King and attendants, on enamelled brick (from Nimrud).

The size of the designs varies considerably. Ordinarily the figures are small, each brick containing several; but sometimes a scale has been adopted of such a size that portions of the same figure must have been on different bricks. A foot and leg, brought by Mr. Layard from Nimrud, must have belonged to a man a foot high;[1] while part of a human face discovered in the same locality, is said to indicate, for the form to which it belonged, a height of three feet.[2] Such a size as this is, however, very unusual.

[1] Birch, *Ancient Pottery*, vol. i. p. 127. The fragment is figured in Mr. Layard's *Monuments*, 1st Series, Plate 84, fig. 2.   [2] Birch, p. 120.

It is scarcely necessary to state that the designs on the bricks are entirely destitute of *chiaroscuro*. The browns and blacks, like the blues, yellows, and reds, are simply used to express local colour. They are employed for hair, eyes, eyebrows, and sometimes for bows and sandals. The other colours are applied as follows:—Yellow is used for flesh, for shafts of weapons, for horse-trappings, sometimes for horses, for chariots, cups, ear-rings, bracelets, fringes, for wing-feathers, occasionally for helmets, and almost always for the hoofs of horses; blue is used for shields, for horses, for some parts of horse-trappings, armour, and dresses, for fish, and for feathers; white is employed for the inner part of the eye, for the linen shirt worn by men, for the markings on fish and feathers, for horses, for buildings,[3] for patterns on dresses, for rams' heads, and for portions of the tiara of the king. Olive-green seems to occur only as a ground; red only in some parts of the royal tiara; orange and lilac only in the wings of winged monsters.[4] It is doubtful how far we may trust the colours on the bricks as accurately or approximately resembling the real local hues. In some cases the intention evidently is to be true to nature, as in the eyes and hair of men, in the representations of flesh, fish, shields, bows, buildings, &c. The yellow of horses may represent cream-colour, and the blue may stand for grey, as distinct from white,

---

[3] Buildings are white, but the battlements and some courses in the stone are touched with yellow. A door in one is coloured blue. (Layard, *Monuments*, 2nd Series, Plate 53, fig. 5.)

[4] The authorities for these statements are Layard's *Monuments*, 1st Series, Plates 84 and 87; 2nd Series, Plates 53, 54, and 55; and Botta's *Monument de Ninive*, Plate 155.

which seems to have been correctly rendered.[*] The
scarlet and white of the king's tiara is likely to be
true. When, however, we find eyeballs and eyebrows white, while the inner part of the eye is
yellow,[*] the blade of swords yellow,[*] and horses'
hoofs blue,[*] we seem to have proof that, sometimes
at any rate, local colour was intentionally neglected;
the artist limiting himself to certain hues, and being
therefore obliged to render some objects untruly.
Thus we must not conclude from the colours of
dresses and horse-trappings on the bricks—which are
three only, yellow, blue, and white—that the Assyrians used no other hues than these, even for the
robes of their kings.[*] It is far more probable that
they employed a variety of tints in their apparel, but
did not attempt to render that variety on the ordinary painted bricks.[*]

The pigments used by the Assyrians seem to have
derived their tints entirely from minerals. The
opaque white is found to be oxide of tin; the yellow
is the antimoniate of lead, or Naples yellow, with a
slight admixture of tin; the blue is oxide of copper,
without any cobalt; the green is also from copper;
the brown is from iron; and the red is a suboxide
of copper.[*] The bricks were slightly baked before
being painted; they were then taken from the kiln,

---

[*] See the two fore legs of a horse
in a fragment figured by Mr. Layard,
Monuments, 2nd Series, Plate 54,
fig. 14.

[*] Ibid. fig. 7.

[*] Ibid. fig. 12.

[*] Ibid. fig. 14.

[*] Yellow, white, and a pale blue
or green, are the only colours on the
dress of the king figured above, p.

471.

[*] M. Botta's fragment (figured
Plate 155, fig. 2) is a unique specimen. Had it contained the robes of
the king as well as his head-dress,
we should probably have learnt the
real hues of the royal garments.

[*] Birch, *Ancient Pottery*, vol. 1, p.
128; Layard, *Nineveh and Babylon*,
p. 166, note.

painted and enamelled on one side only, the flux and
glazes used being composed of silicate of soda aided
by oxide of lead;[3] thus prepared, they were again
submitted to the action of fire, care being taken to
place the painted side upwards,[4] and having been
thoroughly baked were then ready for use.

The Assyrian intaglios on stones and gems are
commonly of a rude description; but occasionally
they exhibit a good deal of delicacy, and sometimes
even of grace.   They are cut upon serpentine, jasper,
chalcedony, cornelian, agate, sienite, quartz, load-
stone, amazon-stone, and lapis-lazuli.[5]   The usual
form of the stone is cylindrical; the sides, however,

Impression of ancient Assyrian cylinder, in serpentine.

being either slightly convex or slightly concave, most
frequently the latter.   The cylinder is always perforated in the direction of its axis.   Besides this
ordinary form, a few gems shaped like the Greek,

---

[3] Birch, l. s. c.; Layard, *Nineveh
and Babylon*, p. 672.
[4] This is evidenced by the bricks
themselves, where we can often see
that the melted enamel has run over

and trickled down the sides. (See
Birch, *Ancient Pottery*, vol. i. 128.)
[5] King's *Ancient Gems*, pp. 127-
129; Layard's *Nineveh and Babylon*,
pp. 602-604.

that is, either round or oval, have been found; and
numerous impressions from such gems on sealing-clay
shew that they must have been tolerably common.[*]
The subjects which
occur are mostly the
same as those on the
sculptures—warriors
pursuing their foes,
hunters in full chase,
the king slaying a
lion, winged bulls
before the sacred
tree, acts of worship
and other religious or
mythological scenes.

Assyrian seals.

There appears to
have been a gradual
improvement in the
workmanship from
the earliest period to
the time of Senna-
cherib, when the art
culminates. A cy-
linder found in the
ruins of Senna-

Assyrian cylinder, with the Fish-God.

cherib's palace at Ko-
yunjik, which is be-
lieved with reason

Royal cylinder of Sennacherib.

to have been his signet,['] is scarcely surpassed in
delicacy of execution by any intaglio of the Greeks.

[*] See Mr. Layard's *Monuments of Nineveh*, 2nd Series, Plate 69, Nos. 1 to 32.

['] Layard, *Nineveh and Babylon*, p. 160; King, *Antient Gems*, p. 120.

The design has a good deal of the usual stiffness, though even here something may be said for the ibex or wild-goat, which stands upon the lotus flower to the left; but the special excellence of the gem is in the fineness and minuteness of its execution. The intaglio is not very deep; but all the details are beautifully sharp and distinct, while they are on so small a scale that it requires a magnifying glass to distinguish them. The material of the cylinder is translucent green felspar, or amazon-stone, one of the hardest substances known to the lapidary.[1]

The fictile art of the Assyrians in its higher branches, as employed for directly artistic purposes, has been already considered; but a few pages may be now devoted to the humbler divisions of the subject, where the useful preponderates over the ornamental. The pottery of Assyria bears a general resemblance in shape, form, and use, to that of Egypt; but still it has certain specific differences. According to Mr. Birch, it is, generally speaking, "finer in its paste, brighter in its colour, employed in thinner masses, and for purposes not known in Egypt."[2]   Abundant and excellent clay is furnished by the valley of the Tigris, more especially by those parts of it which are subject to the annual inundation. The chief employment of this material by the Assyrians was for bricks, which were either simply dried in the sun, or exposed to the action of fire in a kiln. In this latter case they seem to have been uniformly slack-baked; they are light for their size, and are of a pale-red colour.[3]   The clay of which the

[1] King, Introduction, p. xxxvi.   [2] Ancient Pottery, vol. I. p. 106.
[3] Ibid. p. 108.

bricks were composed was mixed with stubble or
vegetable fibre, for the purpose of holding it together
—a practice common to the Assyrians with the
Egyptians[1] and the Babylonians.[2] This fibre still
appears in the sun-dried bricks, but has been destroyed
by the heat of the kiln in the case of the baked bricks,
leaving behind it, however, in the clay traces of the
stalks or stems. The size and shape of the bricks
vary. They are most commonly square, or nearly
so; but occasionally the shape more resembles that
of the ancient Egyptian and modern English brick,[4]
the width being about half the length, and the thickness half or two-thirds of the width. The greatest
size to which the square bricks attain is a length and
width of about two feet.[5] From this maximum they
descend by manifold gradations to a minimum of
one foot. The oblong bricks are smaller; they
seldom much exceed a foot in length,[6] and in width
vary from six to seven and a half inches. Whatever
the shape and size of the bricks, their thickness is
nearly uniform, the thinnest being as much as three
inches in thickness, and the thickest not more than
four inches or four and a half. Each brick was made
in a wooden frame or mould.[7] Most of the baked
bricks were inscribed, not however like the Chaldæan,[8]
the Egyptian,[9] and the Babylonian,[1] with an inscription in a small square or oval depression near the

---

[1] Wilkinson, in the author's *Herodotus*, vol. ii. p. 215; Birch, *Ancient
Pottery*, vol. i. pp. 12, 13. Hence
the complaints of the Israelites when
they received "no straw for their
bricks." (Ex. v. 7-18).

[3] Birch, p. 132.

[4] Ibid. p. 13, and p. 100.

[5] Twenty-two inches, according to
Mr. Birch (p. 100).

[6] The longest are 14½ inches. (See
Ancient Pottery, vol. i. p. 108.)

[7] Ibid. p. 107.

[8] Supra, p. 90.

[9] Birch, *Ancient Pottery*, vol. i.
pp. 15-18; Wilkinson, *Ancient Egyptians*, 1st Series, vol. ii. p. 97.

[1] Birch, p. 134; Layard, *Nineveh
and its Remains*, vol. ii. p. 187.

centre of one of the broad faces, but with one which either covered the whole of one such face, or else ran along the edge. It is uncertain whether the inscription was stamped upon the bricks by a single impression, or whether it was inscribed by the potter with a triangular style. Mr. Birch thinks the former was the means used, " as the trouble of writing upon each brick would have been endless." [2] Mr. Layard, however, is of a different opinion. [3]

In speaking of the Assyrian writing, some mention has been made of the terra-cotta cylinders and tablets, which in Assyria replaced the parchment and papyrus of other nations, being the most ordinary writing material in use through the country. [4] The purity and fineness of the material thus employed is very remarkable, as well as its strength, of which advantage was taken to make the cylinders hollow, and thus at once to render them cheaper and more portable. The terra-cotta of the cylinders and tablets is sometimes unglazed ; sometimes the natural surface has been covered with a " vitreous silicious glaze or white coating." [5] The colour varies, being sometimes a bright polished brown, sometimes a pale yellow, sometimes pink, and sometimes a very dark tint, nearly black. [6] The most usual colour however for cylinders is pale yellow, and for tablets light red or pink. There is no doubt that in both these cases the characters were impressed separately by the hand, a small metal style or rod being used for the purpose.

Terra-cotta vessels, glazed and unglazed, were in common use among the Assyrians, for drinking and

---

[2] Birch, p. 100.
[3] Layard, l. s. c.
[4] Supra, p. 320–321.
[5] Birch, *Ancient Pottery*, vol. i. p. 113.
[6] Ibid. p. 115.

Assyrian vases, amphoræ, &c. (after Birch).

other domestic purposes. They comprised vases,
lamps, jugs, amphoræ, saucers, jars, &c. The material
of the vessels is fine, though gene-
rally rather yellow in tone.[f] The
shapes present no great novelty,
being for the most part such as
are found both in the old Chaldæan tombs,[g] and in ordinary
Roman sepulchres.[h] Among the
most elegant are the funereal (?)
urns discovered by M. Botta at
Khorsabad, which are egg-shaped,
with a small opening at top, a
short and very scanty pedestal,
and two raised rings, one rather
delicately chased, by way of ornament. Another graceful form is
that of the large jars uncovered
at Nimrud (see next page), of which Mr. Layard

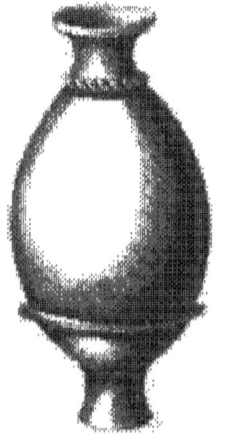

Funereal urn, from Khorsabad.

---

[f] Birch, *Ancient Pottery*, vol. i. p. 120.
[g] Supra, pp. 115, 116.   [h] Birch, p. 121.

Nestorian and Arab workmen, with jar discovered at Nimrud.

gives a representation.[1]   Still more tasteful are some
of the examples which occur upon the
bas-reliefs, and seemingly represent
earthen vases.   Among these may be
particularised a lustral ewer resting in
a stand supported by bulls' feet, which
appears in front of a temple at Khorsabad,[2] and a wine vase (see page opposite) of ample dimensions, which is
found in a banquet scene at the same place.[3]   Some

Lustral ewer, from a bas-relief, Khorsabad.

[1] *Nineveh and Babylon*, p. 574.
[2] See Botta's *Monument de Ninive*, vol. ii. Plates 141 and 162.
[3] Ibid. Plate 76; and see vol. v. p. 130.

of the lamps are also graceful enough, and seem to be the prototypes out of which were developed the more elaborate productions of the Greeks.   Others

Wine vase, from a bas-relief, Khorsabad.

are more simple, being without ornament of any kind, and nearly resembling a modern teapot (see No. IV.). The glazed pottery is, for the most part, tastefully coloured. An amphora, with twisted arms, found at Nimrud (see overleaf), is of two colours, a warm yellow, and a cold bluish green. The green predominates in the upper, the yellow in the under portion; but there is a certain amount of blending or mottling in the mid region, which has a very pleasant effect.   A similarly mottled character

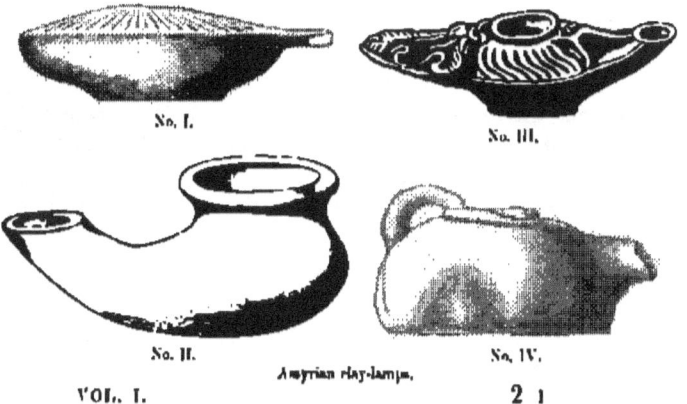

No. I.

No. III.

No. II.

No. IV.

Assyrian clay-lamps.

is presented by two other amphoræ from the same place, where the general hue is a yellow which varies in intensity, and the mottling is with a violet blue.

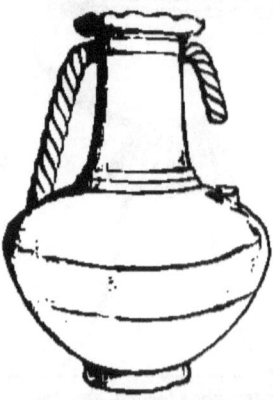

In some cases the colours are not blended, but sharply defined by lines, as in a curious spouted cup figured by Mr. Layard, and in several fragmentary specimens.[1] Painted patterns are not uncommon upon the glazed pottery, though upon the unglazed they are scarcely ever found. The most usual colours are blue, yellow, and white; brown, purple, and lilac have been met with occasionally. These colours

Amphora, with twisted arms (Nimrud).

are thought to be derived chiefly from metallic oxides, over which was laid as a glazing a vitreous silicated substance.[2] On the whole porcelain of this fine kind is rare in the Assyrian remains, and must be regarded as a material that was precious and used by few.

Assyrian glass is among the most beautiful of the objects which have been exhumed. M. Botta compared it to certain fabrics of Venice and Bohemia,[3] into which a number of different colours are artificially introduced. But a careful analysis has shewn that the lovely prismatic hues which delight us in the Assyrian specimens, varying under different lights

[1] See Layard's *Monuments*, 1st Series, Plate 85.
[2] Birch, *Ancient Pottery*, vol. i. p. 130.
[3] *Monument de Ninive*, vol. v. p. 173.

with all the delicacy and brilliancy of the opal, are due,
not to art, but to the wonder-working hand of time,
which as it destroys the fabric, compassionately invests

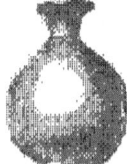  

Assyrian glass bottles and bowl.

it with additional grace and beauty.   Assyrian glass
was either transparent, or stained with a single uniform
colour.[1]   It was composed in the
usual way, by a mixture of sand
or silex with alkalis, and, like the
Egyptian,[2] appears to have been
first rudely fashioned into shape
by the blow-pipe.   It was then
more carefully shaped, and where
necessary hollowed out by a turning machine, the marks of which
are sometimes still visible.[3]   The
principal specimens which have
been discovered are small bottles
and bowls, the former not more

Glass vase, bearing the name of
Sargon, from Nimrud.

than three or four inches high, the latter from four to
five inches in diameter.   The vessels are occasionally
inscribed with the name of a king, as is the case in the

[1] An elaborate account of the process whereby the Assyrian glass has
become partially decomposed, and of
the effects produced by the decomposition, will be found in Mr. Layard's
Nineveh and Babylon, Appendix,

pp. 674–676, contributed to that work
by Sir David Brewster.
[2] Wilkinson, *Ancient Egyptians*,
1st Series, vol. iii. pp. 88, 89.
[3] Layard, *Nineveh and Babylon*,
p. 197.

famous vase of Sargon found by Mr. Layard at Nimrud
(see last page). This is the earliest known specimen
of *transparent* glass, which is not found in Egypt until
the time of the Psammetichi. The Assyrians used also
opaque glass, which they coloured, sometimes red, with

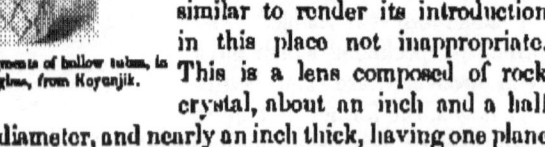

the suboxide of copper, sometimes
white, sometimes of other hues.
They seem not to have been able
to form masses of glass of any considerable size; and thus the employment of the material must
have been limited to a few ornamental, rather than useful, purposes. A curious specimen is that
of a pipe or tube, honeycombed
externally, which Mr. Layard exhumed at Koyunjik, and of which
the accompanying is a rough representation.

An object found at Nimrud in
close connection with several glass
vessels[1] is of a character sufficiently
similar to render its introduction
in this place not inappropriate.
This is a lens composed of rock
crystal, about an inch and a half

Fragments of hollow tubes, in
glass, from Koyunjik.

in diameter, and nearly an inch thick, having one plane
and one convex surface, and somewhat rudely shaped
and polished, which, however, gives a tolerably distinct
focus at the distance of $4\frac{1}{2}$ inches from the plane side,
and which may have been used either as a magnifying
glass or to concentrate the rays of the sun. The form
is slightly oval, the longest diameter being $1\frac{7}{10}$ inch,

---

[1] Layard, *Nineveh and Babylon*, p. 197.

the shortest $1\frac{7}{10}$ inch.   The thickness is not uniform,
but greater on one side than on the other.   The plane
surface is ill-polished and scratched, the convex one,
not polished on a concave spherical disk, but fashioned
on a lapidary's wheel, or by some method equally
rude.[1]   As a burning glass the lens has no great
power; but it magnifies fairly, and may have been
of great use to those who inscribed, or to those who
sought to decipher, the royal memoirs.[2]   It is the
only object of the kind that has been found among
the remains of antiquity, though it cannot be doubted
that lenses were known and were used as burning-
glasses by the Greeks.[3]

Some examples have been already given illustrating
the tasteful ornamentation of Assyrian furniture.   It
consisted, so far as we know, of tables, chairs, couches,
high stools, footstools, and stands with shelves to hold

No. I.   No. II.   No. III.

Ordinary Assyrian tables, from the bas-reliefs.

the articles needed for domestic purposes.   As the
objects themselves have in all cases ceased to exist,
leaving behind them only a few fragments, it is
necessary to have recourse to the bas-reliefs for such

[1] See the description furnished to
Mr. Layard by Sir David Brewster.
(*Nineveh and Babylon*, p. 197, note.)
[2] Vide supra, p. 830.
[3] This is evident from Aristophanes
(*Nub.* 746-749), where Strepsiades
proposes to obliterate his debts from

the waxen tablets on which they
are inscribed by means of "that
transparent stone wherewith fires are
lighted." (τὴν λίθον τὴν διαφανῆ, ἀφ'
ἧς τὸ πῦρ ἅπτουσι.)   Compare also
Theophrast, *De Igne*, 73.

notices as may be thence derived of their construction and character. In these representations the most

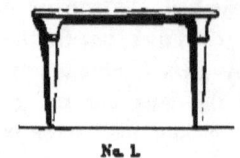

No. I.

ordinary form of table is one in which the principle of our camp-stools seems to be adopted, the legs crossing each other as in the woodcuts on the last page. Only two legs are represented, but we must undoubtedly regard these two as concealing two others of the same kind at the op-

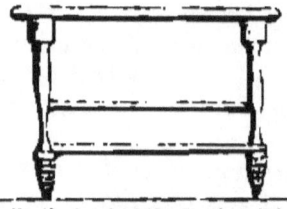

No. II. Assyrian tables, from bas-reliefs (Koyunjik).

posite end of the table. The legs ordinarily terminate in the feet of animals, sometimes of bulls, but more commonly of horses. Sometimes between the two legs we see a species of central

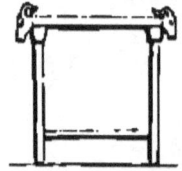

No. III. Table, ornamented with rams' heads (Koyunjik.)

pillar, which, however, is not traceable below the point where the legs cross one another. The pillar itself is either twisted or plain (see No. III. on last page).

No. IV. Ornamented table (Khorsabad).

Another form of table, less often met with, but simpler, closely resembles the common table of the moderns. It has merely the necessary flat top, with perpendicular legs at the corners. The skill of

the cabinet-makers enabled them to dispense in most
instances with cross-bars (see No. I.), which are
however sometimes seen (see No.
II., No. III., and No. IV.), uniting the legs of this kind of tables.
The corners are often ornamented
with lions' or rams' heads, and the
feet are frequently in imitation of
some animal form (see No. III. and
No. IV.). Occasionally we find a

Three-legged table (Koyunjik).

representation of a three-legged table, as the above
specimen, which is from a relief at Koyunjik. The
height of tables appears to
have been greater than with
ourselves; the lowest reach
nearly to a man's middle;
the highest are level with
the upper part of the chest.

Assyrian thrones and
chairs were very elaborate.
The throne of Sennacherib
exhibited on its sides and
arms three rows of carved
figures, one above another,
supporting the bars with
their hands. The bars, the
arms, and the back were
patterned. The legs ended
in a pine-shaped ornament,
very common in Assyrian
furniture. Over the back
was thrown an embroidered
cloth, fringed at the end,

Sennacherib on his throne (Koyunjik).

which hung down nearly to the floor. A throne of
Sargon's was adorned on its sides with three human

figures, apparently representations of the king, below

Arm-chair or throne (Khorsabad).

which was the war-horse of the monarch, caparisoned as for battle.[5] Another throne of the same monarch's had two large and four small figures of men at the side, while the back was supported on either side by a human figure of superior dimensions.[6] The use of chairs with high backs, like these, was apparently confined to the monarchs. Persons of less exalted rank were content to sit on seats which were either stools, or chairs, with a low back level with the arms.[7]

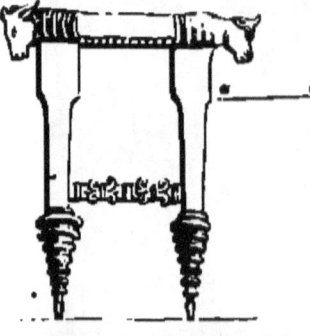

Assyrian ornamented seat (Khorsabad).

Seats of this kind, whether thrones or chairs, were no doubt constructed mainly of wood. The ornamental work may, however, have been of bronze, either cast into the necessary shape, or wrought into it by the hammer. The animal heads at

---

[5] Botta, *Monument de Ninive*, vol. i. Plate 17.
[6] Ibid. Plate 18.
[7] In the series from which this representation is taken the figures appear seated in such a way as would imply that the actual seat was level with the dotted line *ab*.

the ends of arms seem to have fallen under the latter description.[a] In some cases, ivory was among the materials used: it has been found in the legs of a throne at Koyunjik,[b] and may not improbably have entered into the ornamentation of the best furniture very much more generally.

The couches which we find represented upon the sculptures are of a simple character. The body is flat, not curved; the legs are commonly plain, and fastened to each other by a crossbar, sometimes terminating in the favorite pine-shaped ornament. One end only is raised, and this usually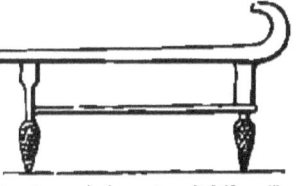

Assyrian couch, from a bas-relief, Koyunjik.

curves inward nearly in a semicircle. The couches are decidedly lower than the Egyptian;[c] and do not, like them, require a stool or steps in order to ascend them.

Stools, however, are used with the chairs or thrones of which mention was made above—lofty seats, where such a support for the sitter's feet was imperatively

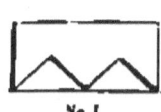

No. I.

No. III.

Assyrian footstools (Koyunjik).

required. They are sometimes plain at the sides, and merely cut *en chevron* at the base; sometimes highly ornamented, terminating in lions' feet supported on cones, in the same[d] (or in volutes) supported on balls,

[a] Layard, *Nineveh and Babylon*, p. 199.
[b] Ibid. p. 198.
[c] Wilkinson, *Ancient Egyptians*, 1st Series, vol. ii. p. 201.
[d] See the Woodcut on p. 487.

and otherwise adorned with volutes, lion-castings, and the like. The most elaborate specimen is the stool hitherto inedited (No. III.), which supports the feet of Asshur-bani-pal's queen on a relief brought from the North Palace at Koyunjik, and now in the National Collection. Here the upper corners exhibit the favourite gradines, guarding and keeping in place an embroidered cushion; the legs are ornamented with rosettes and with horizontal mouldings; they are connected together by two bars, the lower one adorned with a number of double volutes, and the upper one with two lions standing back to back; the stool stands on balls, surmounted first by a double moulding, and then by volutes.

Stands with shelves often terminate, like other

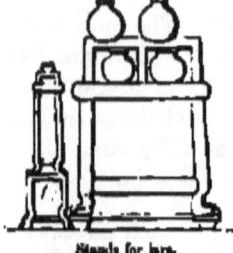

Stands for jars.

articles of furniture, in animals' feet, most commonly lions', as in the accompanying specimens.

Of the embroidered robes and draperies of the Assyrians, as of their furniture, we can judge only by the representations made of them upon the bas-reliefs. The delicate texture of such fabrics has prevented them from descending to our day even in the most tattered condition; and the ancient testimonies on the subject are for the most part too remote from the times of the Assyrians to be of much value.[2] Ezekiel's

notice[3] is the only one which comes within such a
period of Assyria's fall as to make it an important
testimony, and even from this we cannot gather much
that goes beyond the evidence of the sculptures.
The sculptures show us that robes and draperies of
all kinds were almost always more or less patterned;
and this patterning, which is generally of an extremely elaborate kind, it is reasonable to conclude
was the work of the needle. Sometimes the ornamentation is confined to certain portions of garments,
as to the ends of sleeves and the bottoms of robes or
tunics; at others it is extended over the whole dress.
This is more particularly the case with the garments
of the kings, which are of a magnificence difficult to
describe, or to represent within a narrow compass.
One or two specimens, however, may be given almost
at random, indicating different styles of ornamentation
usual in the royal apparel. Other examples will be
seen in the many illustrations throughout this volume
where the king is represented.[4] It is remarkable that
the earliest representations exhibit the most elaborate
types of all, after which a reaction seems to set in—
simplicity is affected—which however is gradually
trenched upon, until at last a magnificence is reached

---

ments as embroidered. It remained
for the later Roman poets to determine that the colour of the robes was
purple, and that their ornamentation
was the work of the needle.

³ *Perfusæ ostro vestes
Assyriæ signatur acu.*"
            Claudian. xliv. 96, 67.

These rare Assyrian garments were
said to have been adopted by the
Medes, and afterwards by the Persians. (Diod. Sic. ii. 6, § 6.) They
were probably of silk, which was
produced largely in Assyria (Plin.

II. N. xi. 22), whence it was carried
to Rome and worn both by men and
women (Ib. xi. 23).

³ Ezek. xxvii. 23, 24: "Haran
and Canneh and Eden, the merchants
of Sheba, Asshur, and Chilmad, were
thy merchants. These were thy
merchants in all sorts of things, in
blue clothes and broidered work
(רִקְמָה), and in chests of rich apparel,
bound with cords and made of cedar,
among thy merchandise."

⁴ As on pp. 364, 368, 487, &c., of
this volume.

little short of that which prevailed in the age of the
first monuments. The draperies of Asshur-idanni-pal
(Sardanapalus) I., in the north-west palace at Nimrud,

Royal embroidered dress (Nimrud).

are at once more minutely laboured and more tasteful
than those of any later time. Besides elegant but
unmeaning patterns, they exhibit human and animal
forms, sacred trees, sphinxes, griffins, winged horses,

Embroidery on a royal dress (Nimrud).

and occasionally bull-hunts and lion-hunts. The
upper part of this king's dress is in one instance
almost covered with figures, which range themselves
round a circular breast ornament, whereof the following is a representation. Elsewhere his apparel is
less superb, and indeed it presents almost every

Circular breast ornament on a royal robe (Nimrod).

degree of richness, from the wonderful embroidery of the robe just mentioned to absolute plainness, in the celebrated picture of the lion-hunt.[4] With Sargon, the next king who has left many monuments, the case is remarkably different. Sargon is represented always in the same dress—a long fringed robe, embroidered simply with rosettes, which are spread somewhat scantily over its whole surface. Sennacherib's apparel is nearly of the same kind, or, if anything, richer, though sometimes the rosettes are omitted.[5] His grandson, Asshur-bani-pal, also affects the rosette ornament, but reverts alike to the taste and the elaboration of the early kings. He wears a breast-ornament containing human figures, around which are ranged a number of minute and elaborate patterns.

To this account of the arts, mimetic and other, in which the Assyrians appear to have excelled, it might be expected that there should be added a sketch of their scientific knowledge. On this subject, however, so little is at present known, while so much may possibly become known within a short time, that it seems best to omit it, or to touch it only in the lightest and most cursory manner. When the numerous tablets now in the British Museum shall have been deciphered, studied, and translated, it will probably be found that they contain a tolerably full indication of what Assyrian science really was; and it will then be seen how far it was real and valuable, in what respects mistaken and illusory. At present this mine is almost unworked, nothing more having been ascertained than that the subjects whereof the tablets treat

[4] Supra, p. 429.
[5] See Layard, Monuments, 1st Series, Plate 77; 2nd Series, Plate

42. The omission may be from mere carelessness in the artist.

are various, and their apparent value very different. Comparative philology seems to have been largely studied, and the works upon it exhibit great care and diligence. Chronology is evidently much valued, and very exact records are kept whereby the lapse of time can even now be accurately measured. Geography and history have each an important place in Assyrian learning; while astronomy and mythology occupy at least as great a share of attention. The astronomical observations recorded are thought to be frequently inaccurate, as might be expected when there were no instruments, or none of any great value. Mythology is a very favourite subject, and appears to be treated most fully; but hitherto cuneiform scholars have scarcely penetrated below the surface of the mythological tablets, baffled by the obscurity of the subject and the difficulty of the dialect in which they are written.[1]

On one point alone, belonging to the domain of science, do the Assyrian representations of their life enable us to comprehend, at least to some extent, their attainments. The degree of knowledge which this people possessed on the subject of practical mechanics is illustrated with tolerable fulness in the bas-reliefs, more especially in the important series discovered at Koyunjik, where the transport of the colossal bulls from the quarry to the palace gateways is represented in the most elaborate detail.[2] The very fact that they were able to transport masses of stone

---

[1] The mythological tablets are always in the *Hurbar* or old Chaldean language, and in very few instances are furnished even with a gloss or explanation in Assyrian. (See Sir H. Rawlinson's Essay "On the Religion of the Babylonians and Assyrians" in the author's *Herodotus*, vol. i. p. 685; note.)

[2] This series is excellently represented in Mr. Layard's *Monuments*, 2nd Series, Plates 10 to 17.

many tons in weight, over a considerable space of ground, and to place them on the summit of artificial platforms from thirty to eighty (or ninety) feet high, would alone indicate considerable mechanical knowledge. The further fact, now made clear from the bas-reliefs, that they wrought all the elaborate carving of the colossi before they proceeded to raise them or put them in place,[*] is an additional argument of their skill, since it shows that they had no fear of any accident happening in the transport. It appears from the representations that they placed their colossus in a standing posture, not on a truck or waggon of any kind, but on a huge wooden sledge, shaped nearly like a boat, casing it with an openwork of spars or beams, which crossed each other at right angles, and were made perfectly tight by means of wedges.[1] To avert the great danger of the mass toppling over sideways, ropes were attached to the top of the casing, at the point where the beams crossed one another, and were held taut by two parties of labourers, one on either side of the statue. Besides these, wooden forks or props were applied on either side to the second horizontal cross-beams, held also by men, whose business it would be to resist the least inclination of the huge stone to lean to one side more than to the other. The front of the sledge on which the colossus stood was curved gently upwards, to facilitate its sliding along the ground, and to enable it to

---

[*] Mr. Layard at first imagined that the contrary was the case (*Nineveh and its Remains*, vol. ii. p. 318); but his Koyunjik discoveries convinced him of his error (*Nineveh and Babylon*, pp. 105, 106).

[1] The nineteenth century could make no improvement upon this. Mr. Layard tells us that "*precisely the same* framework was used for moving the great sculptures now in the British Museum." (*Nineveh and Babylon*, p. 112, note.)

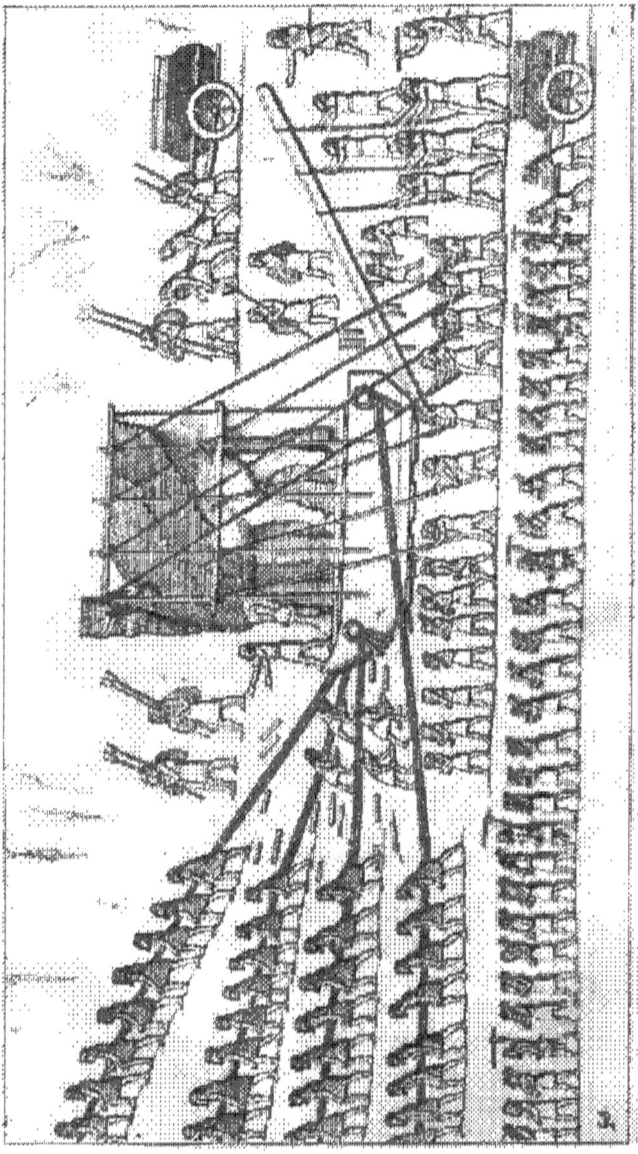

Assyrians moving a human-headed bull (partly restored from a bas-relief at Koyunjik).

rise with readiness upon the rollers, which were continually placed before it by labourers just in front, while others following behind gathered them up when the bulky mass had passed over them. The

motive power was applied in front by four gangs of men who held on to four large cables, at which they pulled by means of small ropes or straps fastened to them, and passed under one shoulder and over the other, an arrangement which enabled them to pull by weight as much as by muscular strength, as the

Labourer employed in drawing a colossal bull (Kouyunjik).

annexed figure will plainly show. The cables appear to have been of great strength, and are fastened carefully to four strong projecting pins: two near the front, two at the back part of the sledge, by a knot

so tied that it would be sure not to slip. Finally, as in spite of the rollers, whose use in diminishing friction, and so facilitating progress, was evidently well understood, and in spite of the amount of force applied in front, it would have been

Attachment of rope to sledge, on which the bull was placed for transport (Kouyunjik).

difficult to give the first impetus to so great a mass, a lever was skilfully applied behind to raise the hind part of the sledge slightly, and so propel it forward, while to secure a sound and firm fulcrum, wedges of wood were inserted between the lever and the ground. The greater power of a lever at a distance from the fulcrum being known, ropes were attached to its upper end, which could not otherwise have been reached, and the lever was worked by means of them.

We have thus unimpeachable evidence as to the mode whereby the conveyance of huge blocks of stone along level ground was effected. But it may be further asked, how were the blocks raised up to the elevation at which we find them placed? Upon this point there is no direct evidence; but the probability is that they were drawn up inclined ways, sloping gently from the natural ground to the top of the platforms. The Assyrians were familiar with inclined ways,[1] which they used almost always in their attacks on walled places, and which in many cases

Part of a bas-relief, showing a pulley and a warrior cutting a bucket from the rope.

they constructed either of brick or stone.[2] The Egyptians certainly employed them for the elevation of large blocks;[3] and probably in the earlier times, most nations

---

[1] The "banks" of Scripture (2 Kings, xix. 32; Is. xxvii. 33).

[2] See Mr. Layard's *Monuments*, 2nd Series, Plates 18 and 21.

[3] The great stones of which the pyramids were built were certainly raised from the alluvial plain to the rocky platform on which they stand in this way. (Herod. ii. 124; compare Wilkinson in the author's *Herodotus*, vol. ii. p. 200, note.) Diodorus declares that the pyramids themselves were built by the help of mounds (i. 62, §6). This, however, is improbable.

who affected massive architecture had recourse to the
same simple but uneconomical plan.* The crane and
pulley were applied to this purpose later. In the
Assyrian sculptures we find no application of either
to building, and no instance at all of the two in combination. Still each appears on the bas-reliefs separately—the crane employed for drawing water from
the rivers and spreading it over the lands,* the pulley
for lowering and raising the bucket in wells.

We must conclude from these facts that the Assyrians had made considerable advances in mechanical
knowledge, and were in fact acquainted, more or less,
with most of the contrivances whereby heavy weights
have commonly been moved and raised among the
civilized nations of Europe. We have also evidence
of their skill in the mechanical processes of shaping
pottery and glass, of casting and embossing metals,
and of cutting intaglios upon hard stones.* Thus it
was not merely in the ruder and coarser, but likewise in the more delicate processes that they excelled.
The secrets of metallurgy, of dyeing, enamelling, in-
laying, glass-blowing, as well as most of the ordinary
manufacturing processes, were known to them. In
all the common arts and appliances of life, they must
be pronounced at least on a par with the Egyptians,
while in taste they greatly exceeded, not that nation
only, but all the Orientals. Their " high art " is no
doubt much inferior to that of Greece ; but it has real

---

* It is the most reasonable supposition that the cross-stones at Stone-
henge, and the cromlech stones so
common in Ireland, were placed in
the positions where we now find them
by means of inclined planes afterwards cleared away.

* See the representation, p. 271.

' It must be remembered that the
Assyrians cut not merely the softer
materials, as serpentine and alabaster,
but the gems known technically as
" hard stones "—agate, jasper, quartz,
sienite, amazon stone, and the like.
(See King's *Ancient Gems*, p. 127.)

merit, and is most remarkable, considering the time
when it was produced. It has grandeur, dignity,
boldness, strength, and sometimes even freedom and
delicacy; it is honest and painstaking, unsparing of
labour, and always anxious for truth. Above all, it
is not lifeless and stationary, like the art of the
Egyptians and the Chinese, but progressive and
aiming at improvement.[*] To judge by the advance
over previous works which we observe in the sculptures of the son of Esar-haddon, it would seem that if
Assyria had not been assailed by barbaric enemies
about his time, she might have anticipated by above
a century the finished excellence of the Greeks.

---

[*] See the summary on this subject in the author's *Herodotus*, vol. i.;
Essay vii. § 42.

END OF VOL. I.